# THE SWISS SETTLEMENT of SWITZERLAND COUNTY INDIANA

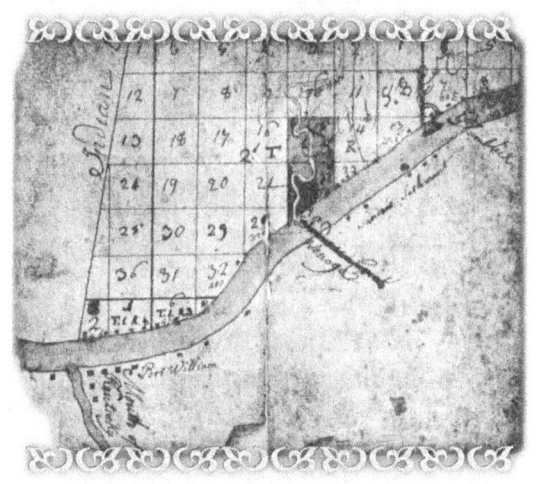

*Perret Dufour*

WITH AN INTRODUCTION BY
HARLOW LINDLEY

HERITAGE BOOKS
2011

# HERITAGE BOOKS
*AN IMPRINT OF HERITAGE BOOKS, INC.*

Books, CDs, and more—Worldwide

For our listing of thousands of titles see our website
at
www.HeritageBooks.com

A Facsimile Reprint
Published 2011 by
HERITAGE BOOKS, INC.
Publishing Division
100 Railroad Ave. #104
Westminster, Maryland 21157

Copyright © 1925 by the
Indiana Historical Commission

Originally published 1925:
Wm. B. Burford, Contractor for State Printing and Binding
Indianapolis

— Publisher's Notice —
In reprints such as this, it is often not possible to remove blemishes from the original. We feel the contents of this book warrant its reissue despite these blemishes and hope you will agree and read it with pleasure.

International Standard Book Numbers
Paperbound: 978-1-55613-092-2
Clothbound: 978-0-7884-8653-1

# Preface

Perret Dufour was born August 21, 1807, in Jessamine County, Kentucky, where his family was engaged, with others, in developing what they called the "First Vineyard." In March, 1809, he went with the family to the "Second Vineyard," where Vevay, Indiana is now located. Here he lived until his death on January 5, 1884.

From an early age he was active in public affairs, and occupied many positions of importance in the growing community: he was postmaster of Vevay for eight years; justice of the peace for over twenty years; and in 1842 was elected a member of the state legislature. He was also a ruling elder in the Presbyterian Church. During most of his life he was engaged in merchandising.

He was a son of John Francis Dufour, who was connected with the Swiss vineyards in America from their beginning, and a nephew of John James Dufour, who more than any other person is to be regarded as their founder. His wife, who survived him, was Eliza M. Clarkson, daughter of Abner Clarkson, who also figured in the early history of Vevay. These associations, together with an extraordinarily retentive and accurate memory, made him the repository of local traditions. He also preserved many family papers and used public records extensively. He was well qualified, therefore, to be chronicler of the Dufour family and of early Vevay.

In 1869, Perret Dufour contributed to the *Vevay Democrat* a series of articles on pioneer days in the community, and in 1876, historical material written by him appeared in the *Vevay Reveille*. This latter was used as the basis for the "History of Switzerland County" printed on pages 989-1138 of the *History of Dearborn, Ohio and Switzerland Counties, Indiana* (Chicago, 1885). In 1921, the *Vevay Enterprise* reprinted some of the earlier newspaper material. The articles from the *Vevay*

*Democrat* were reprinted in the four numbers of the *Indiana Magazine of History,* volume 20 (1924).

The most complete manuscript of Perret Dufour's historical narrative which has been preserved, and evidently the one in which he gathered together the sum of all his historical labors, was written in 1876, chiefly in the summer and early fall. Corrections and additions were embodied in this as late as the early fall of 1882, bringing to date references to individuals and lists of public officers. Thirty-four of the thirty-five installments of the manuscript written in 1869 for the *Vevay Democrat* have also been preserved. Both the 1876 and 1869 manuscripts, together with a number of other documents, the most important of which appear in the appendix of this volume, have been presented to the Indiana State Library by Mrs. Bettie Dufour Smith, of Vevay, granddaughter of Perret Dufour.

The 1876 manuscript, here printed complete for the first time, constitutes the text of this volume. It is printed as originally written, the revisions and additions incorporated in it being given in the notes. To make the history as complete as possible, supplementary material from the manuscript of 1869, so cited, is also printed in the notes. The punctuation and the paragraphing of the manuscript are not always clear, but have been followed as closely as possible. Very often dashes were used instead of periods. Professor Logan Esarey, of Indiana University, explains that this resulted from the use of a quill pen, with which it was difficult to make dots; consequently periods have been substituted for the dashes in such instances. The italics of the original have been omitted where they coincided exactly with quoted sections. Newspaper titles have been italicized.

Miss Nellie C. Armstrong and Mrs. Ruth Williams Spilver prepared the manuscript for publication and made most of the notes. Miss Mayme Snipes, head of the Switzerland County Public Library at Vevay, has been of very great help in securing material and in furnishing local data. Professor Gino A. Ratti, of Butler College and Professor Charles Mosemiller, of Indiana University, have assisted in the translation of some of the French documents in the appendix.

CHRISTOPHER B. COLEMAN,
*Director of the Indiana Historical Commission*

# Contents

| | PAGE |
|---|---|
| Introduction | xiii |
| The Swiss Settlement of Switzerland County | 1 |
| Appendix | 219 |

(1) Patent for Jean Jaques Dufour, Jr. (2) Recognition of Common Rights in Noville and Rennar. (3) Instructions for Mr. Jeanfrancois Dufour. (4) Account of the Possessions of the Dufour Family in America, Rendered to the Father. (5) Daybook of Jean Jaques Dufour . . . on his Travels.

| | |
|---|---|
| Notes | 351 |
| Index | 409 |

# Illustrations

| | PAGE |
|---|---|
| Deed of Vineyard Lands to Swiss Colonists | *Frontispiece* |
| Beginnings of New Switzerland | 16 |
| Old Vineyard Terraces | 38 |
| Site of John Francis Dufour's Home | 38 |
| Plan of Vevay, 1838 | 61 |
| Vevay Currency | 78 |
| Home of John David Dufour | 100 |
| Home of John Francis Dufour—the Ferry House | 100 |
| Jean Daniel Morerod Home | 154 |
| Later Picture of Morerod Home | 154 |
| Wine Casks in Morerod Home | 204 |
| Trunk which Contained Dufour Papers | 204 |
| Commission of John James Dufour to his Eldest Son | 219 |

# Introduction

The little Swiss colony which settled along the Ohio River at Vevay, in what is now known as Switzerland County, Indiana, was composed of French Swiss citizens of the commune of Chatelard, district of Vevay, Canton de Vaud, Switzerland.

John James Dufour was the first person of this colony to arrive in America. He made his first trip in March, 1796, visiting Berne, Lausanne, Rouen, and Paris before embarking on the brig *Sally*, destined for Philadelphia. He went as far west as St. Louis. During the trip, he carefully viewed the land along the Ohio and Mississippi rivers. In 1798, he made a trip on horseback from Pittsburgh to Lexington, Kentucky, arriving at Lexington on August 28, where a vineyard association was organized. He made an extensive search for a suitable place for a vineyard and after making a report to the association, they decided on October 2, 1798, to purchase a tract of 630 acres in the big bend of the Kentucky River, four miles above the mouth of Hickman's Creek. The work was begun by clearing the land and preparing it for grape culture and fruit growing, help being hired to clear it ready for the plow. The clearing was continued through the fall, winter, and spring, so that in the spring of 1799 some six acres were planted in vines.

John James Dufour, in his *Vine-Dresser's Guide*, says that the Kentucky association was formed under the same principles as the one at Philadelphia, "though not knowing, however, which of those societies had been first; but the Kentucky Vineyard Society, may be with great propriety considered as the beginner, the true introducer of the cultivation of grape vines into the United States."[1]

---

[1] John James Dufour, *The American Vine-Dresser's Guide*, 8 (Cincinnati, 1826).

On January 29, 1799, John James Dufour left the "First Vineyard" for New York and Philadelphia to purchase grapevines and fruit trees for the commencement of the vineyard and orchards. Ten thousand vines were purchased, representing thirty-five varieties of the best grapes. The greater part was obtained from the gardens of a Mr. Legaux, Spring Mill, near Philadelphia. Others were secured in a garden at New York, and a small part bought from a German nurseryman at Baltimore. More vines were later brought directly from his own vineyards in Switzerland, when his brothers and sisters came to America. On March 6, 1799, he returned to the "First Vineyard." The vines and trees were planted during the month of April, 1799, and grew so well that in the spring of 1800, John James Dufour wrote to his father, brothers and sisters, giving them an account of the splendid growth of the vines and advising them to make preparations to come and join him the next spring.

There were seventeen members of the little band that on the first day of January, 1801, gathered together at Lausanne, Switzerland, to bid farewell to home and friends before embarking for the new home they were seeking in the wilderness of America. There were young men and maidens, matrons and infants, men of mature years, and youths of tender age. The silent resourceful heroism of that little band of French Swiss commands the admiration of the world today.

As the last farewell was spoken, the last look given to mountains and lake, the aged father Dufour bade them kneel while he asked God's blessing upon them and His guidance and protection during their long journey over land and sea. Father Dufour besought them to keep the Sabbath holy and, until a church could be built, to assemble every Sunday in one of their homes for religious services. To this end he sent them books of sermons in the French language and sermons of his own writing, some of which found their way to New York,

## HISTORY OF SWITZERLAND COUNTY     xv

where they were translated and circulated as tracts. Nearly all these French Swiss were Presbyterians, and they kept the faith, following the teachings of their forefathers during many trials of spirit and body. Father Dufour concluded the parting ceremonies by reading the Ninetieth Psalm, recommending it to the prospective voyagers for their future guidance and instruction, asking particularly that it be read at the funeral service of each one of these Swiss emigrants and their descendants, a wish which has been carefully complied with, even to the present generation.

In May, 1801, the following seventeen persons arrived at Norfolk, Virginia, after a boisterous voyage of one hundred days: Daniel Dufour and Frances E. Dufour, his wife; Jeane Marie Dufour; Antoinette Dufour; John Francis Dufour; Susanne Margarette Dufour; John David Dufour; Peter Borallay, his wife, his son Peter, and daughter; Philip Bettens, his wife and daughter; Jean Daniel Morerod; Francis Louis Siebenthal and his son, John Francis Siebenthal.

These people crossed the Allegheny Mountains in wagons to Pittsburgh. The women and children and those that could not walk were weighed and brought as freight by the hundred pounds. Arriving at Pittsburgh, they proceeded down the Ohio River and were met by John James Dufour at Marietta, Ohio, on June 18. They went the remainder of the way to Lexington, Kentucky, by land, arriving on July 3, and were present at a barbecue and celebration on the Fourth. On July 6, this colony arrived at the "First Vineyard." John James entered into an arrangement with his brothers and sisters to work the vineyard from that time as common property.

The Swiss colony stopped for some months in Kentucky before proceeding down the Kentucky River to the Ohio in order to reach the Indiana lands which had been purchased for them by John James Dufour. The beauty of hilltop and river appealed to these weary wanderers far from home, and inspired them with new hope and courage. The Ohio River with its picturesque banks and musical ripple of waters, the song of the wild birds, the many-hued flowers of the woods offered a warm welcome to these tired home-seeking people. The solitude of centuries untold was broken. Those were happy days in the wilds of Indiana, clearing the land, building log cabins, making furniture and spinning-wheels, planting, harvesting and milling—while the sound of the clanging loom and the buzz of the spinning-wheel kept time with the rhythm of the axe in the woodlands beyond. The story of sacrifice and the adherence to principle was told in echoes that were wafted from all these industries.

But it was not all work, for these homes of long ago were merry many a night with music and the dance. The Swiss were warm-hearted and hospitable and enjoyed entertaining their friends, especially the Kentuckians from across the river. Dancing was a favorite amusement, and the old-time fiddler was an important character in the community. His tunes were often lacking in time and melody, but as they served the dancers, criticism was never heard.

With reference to the Kentucky, or "First Vineyard," John James Dufour says in the *Vine-Dresser's Guide:* "Three years we were in full expectation, and worked with great courage—a great many species of vines showed fruit the third year; one vine of the sweet water was full of eminently good grapes . . . . [but] a sickness . . . took hold of all our vines except the few stocks of Cape and Madeira grapes, from each of which we made the fourth year some wine. . . .

"The failure of the first plantation caused a relaxation among the shareholders, and not only a great difficulty was experienced in collecting the subscribed money, but the subscription of all the shares was never performed, so that all our stock was made use of, for paying the hiring of negroes and other hands, and we

# HISTORY OF SWITZERLAND COUNTY xvii

were never able to purchase a single share or even to pay for the land."[1]

The vineyard association dissolved and the full burden of the "First Vineyard" rested on the colony of Swiss. John James Dufour says that they kept good courage and began anew, with the Cape and Madeira grapes of which they had had so few at first. John James was obliged to return to Europe in 1806 and remained there during and after the War of 1812, until 1816. John Francis and Daniel Dufour tried to keep the vineyard going but did not succeed. One spring the entire crop was taken by the early frosts. They abandoned the place in 1809, crossed the Ohio River and joined others of the colony who had started the second vineyard at Vevay in 1802, and who were having success.

In 1802, John James Dufour petitioned Congress to pass an act authorizing him and his associates to enter lands in Indiana on an extended credit, with a view of giving them an opportunity of introducing the culture of the grape into the United States. On the first of May, 1802, an act was passed by Congress giving them the privilege of selecting land on a credit of twelve years. The payment fell due in 1814. Since John James Dufour was in Europe, and because it was considered unsafe to cross the Atlantic Ocean during the war, he sent a memorial to Congress stating the fact, and Congress passed an act extending the term of payment five years. John James Dufour returned in 1816, and the final payment for the lands at two dollars per acre at 6 per cent per annum, was completed the next year.

Under this act, about 2,500 acres had been selected, and approximately 1,200 acres more adjoining were entered and paid for in the usual way. This land extended down the Ohio River from Hunt's Creek to Indian Creek, and after the colonists began to settle there, they gave it the name of New Switzerland.

The first few years were spent by the colonists in

---

[1] Dufour, *Vine-Dresser's Guide*, 9-10.

clearing the land, fencing it and preparing it for the plow, and in building their homes, which were of substantial brick construction. The lands were covered with heavy forests of beech, poplar, oak and elm, and a thick undergrowth overrun with wild vines.

The first wine was made in 1806 and 1807. The quantity was limited, but it was very good in quality. The vineyards were enlarged each year; in 1808 the vintage yielded 800 gallons and in 1809, about 1,200 gallons. In 1817, Samuel R. Brown wrote: "As early as 1810, they [the Swiss] had eight acres of vineyard, from which they made 2,400 gallons of wine, which, in its crude state, was thought by good judges, to be superior to the claret of Bordeaux. . . . The principal proprietors of the vineyards, are the Messrs. Dufours, Bettens, Morerod, Siebenthal . . . . they also cultivate corn, wheat, potatoes, hemp, flax, etc."[1] Edwin Dana, in 1819 says: "In 1815, about 100 hogsheads of wine were produced."[2] Five thousand gallons of wine were reported in 1828. Timothy Flint spoke of having "seen vineyards in Kentucky on a small scale. But this experiment on such a noble scale, so novel in America, was to me a most interesting spectacle."[3]

The history of this Swiss colony was written by Perret Dufour, son of John Francis Dufour, one of the founders. In May, 1924, the writer visited Vevay and secured from Mrs. Bettie Dufour Smith the complete history together with the series of articles prepared for the newspapers, original family manuscripts, and early manuscripts concerning Switzerland County.[4]  HARLOW LINDLEY,
August 1, 1924                                          Earlham College

---

[1] Samuel R. Brown, *The Western Gazetteer; or Emigrant's Directory*, 60 (Auburn, N. Y., 1817).

[2] Edmund Dana, *Geographical Sketches on the Western Country: designed for Emigrants and Settlers*, 118 (Cincinnati, 1819).

[3] Timothy Flint, *Recollections of the Last Ten Years, passed in occasional Residences and Journeyings in the Valley of the Mississippi*, 59 (Boston, 1826).

[4] These records were carefully preserved in an old trunk, a picture of which appears opposite page 204.

# The Swiss Settlement
*of*
## Switzerland County

"Up to 1765 Southeastern Indiana of which Switzer-
"land County was a part, was used by the "Six Nations"
"confederacy composed of the Delawares, Ningos,
"Shawness Wyandottes, Twightees, and Tuscaroras
"tribes of Indians[1] and by the Chippewas, Cognewagas,
"Miamis and Senecas, as a common hunting ground; and
"by a Special treaty among themselves it was declared
"that no settlements should be made in the Territory
"bounded by the Scioto Ohio, and Ouabach (Wabash
"rivers—but that tract should always remain undis-
"turbed as a hunting ground for all. It was doubtless
"during those days, and for some length of time after,
"the scene of many daring deeds, of Cunning artifice,
"of deadly struggles, of wise statesmanship, of selfish
"intrigues of wrong to the weak, of cringing to the
"strong, of ardent patriotism, and of base fraud and
"treachery. Human nature is and always has been the
"same; and in the absence of any record we may not
"presume too much in claiming for our portion of In-
"diana a fair proportion of the ordinary incidents of
"human life without the restraints of modern civiliza-
"tion. At this tim[e] 1765 Indiana was an unknown
"and unexplored wilderness region to the English,—its
"history, resources, and productions were unknown. No
"white man had ever traversed it except a few French
"traders and missionaries whose accounts were vague
"and unfavorable. It was reported to be a wilderness
"in which ferocious beasts of prey roamed, and the most
bloodthirsty and formidable Indians were the only human beings inhabiting that vast unexplored region."

"The Indians themselves, gave vague and uncertain
accounts of it, which all tended by their unfavorable

prospects to deter the English from either exploring or forming settlements within its borders."

"The only certain massacre of whites by the Indians within the bounds of Switzerland County, that any mention has been made, that the writer recollects of a man whose name was said to be "Jones" was murdered and scalped by Indians near the mouth of Grants Creek. The creek it is said was named in memory of one Colonel "Grant" who with a small force from Kentucky was out on a scouting expedition after Indians who had committed depredations on the Kentucky side of the Ohio river many years since.

"One other person it is said was murdered and scalped by Indians near the mouth of Briants [Bryant's] Creek but whose name is not now recollected.

There was a terrible battle, and subsequent massacre of officers and men in the Service of the United States, while on their way down the Ohio river to join the forces under General George Rogers Clark, near about the mouth of Laughery creek where [there was] a party under the command of an officer named Laughery the Creek of that name below Aurora Indiana being named in memory of the *Colonel* Laughery.[1]

The account of this massacre is thus described in the private journal of Lieutenant Isaac Anderson who was one of the captives taken by the Indians who after his release, went to Philadelphia and afterwards came west and settled in Cincinnati in 1788, and remained there till 1813 when he removed to Butler County Ohio on the west side of the Miami River above the mouth of Indian Creek, where he died December 18th 1839 aged 81 years and nine months[2]

"In the spring of 1781, General George Rogers Clark, was making arrangements for an excursion against the Indians of the northwest—and made a requisition on Colonel Archabald Laughery, who was county Lieutenant of Westmoreland County to raise 100 or more volunteers to assist him   Colonel Laughery immediately raised a party of men for the purpose and Captain Robert Orr, an Irishman by birth who was second in Command, Captain Shannon, Lieutenant Isaac Anderson, and ensign Patrick Hunter, all Irishmen, were the other officers of this party.

On the 24th of July they rendezvoused at a Blockhouse Eleven miles west of Hannastown; the whole party when assembled numbered 107 mounted men—the next day they set out for fort McHenry (now Wheeling) where they were to meet and form a Junction with General Clarks forces, but on their arrival there Clark had marched to a point 12 miles below, leaving provisions a boat and orders to follow him—they were detained some days, preparing boats for the transportation of themselves and horses—on arriving at the place appointed [they found] Clark had left the day before. He had left Major Cracraft with a guard of six men, and a boat, for the transportation of the men and horses, but without provisions, and a scant supply of ammunition—promising to await their arrival at the mouth of Kenhawah [Kanawha] river. Arrivin there they found a letter fastened to a pole, stating that Clark was obliged to go on, without making the promised halt, to prevent the desertion of his forces, and ordered them to follow him to the falls of the Ohio where Louisville now stands—"

"The little band were now in a deplorable condition, in a strange and unexplored wilderness, their supplies nearly exhausted, and no source from which to draw more, Clark having them all. The river [being] low and they unacquainted with the channel, it was impossible for them to overtake him. Colonel Laughery at once ordered Captain Shannon, with seven men, to take a boat, try to overtake Clark, and procure the needed supplies. Captain Shannon had gone but a few miles when he was captured by the Indians, together with the letter to Clark telling him of their situation. The same day Colonel Laughery, arrested nineteen deserters from Clarks army, but with great lack of judgment, released them and most of them immediately joined the Indians.

"The Indians had been apprised of the expedition, but supposed that Clark and Laughery had consolidated their forces, and had been afraid to attack them on account of the cannon which Clark carried.

"They learned from their captives, and the deserters, the true condition of Colonel Laughery and his men and collected a large force Just below the mouth of the Great Miami river. They then posted the prisoners in a conspicuous place on the right bank of the Ohio, opposite the head of an Island, eleven miles below the Miami, and three miles below a smaller creek, and promised to spare their lives if they would decoy Laughery and his men to land as they passed down.

"In the evening of August 24th Laughery saw smoke just above the mouth of the Great Miami, and smouldering fires which, he thought to be those of Colonel Clarks camp of the previous night. Laughery proceeded down the river as fast as possible, although the men were completely exhausted by their slow progress and starving condition. Despairing at length of overtaking Clark they landed at ten oclock in the morning of the 25th of August, at a convenient spot in the mouth of a creek on the right bank of the Ohio river, Eight miles below the mouth of the Great Miami in what is now southeastern Indiana. This creek and the Island a short distance below it, have since been called Laughery Creek and island, in memory of the gallant commander of this party.

"The Indians who were waiting a short distance below to intercept them, were soon informed by runners of their position. Some of the men had removed the horses from the boats and had turned them loose to feed, while others were cutting grass to keep them from starving till they reached the Falls 112 miles distant. One of the party killed a buffalo and all who were not cutting grass or guarding horses, were gathered around a fire that had been kindled, busy preparing a meal, when suddenly

DEED OF VINEYARD LANDS TO SWISS COLONISTS

they were assailed by a volley of rifle bullets from the nearest woods, and the Indians appeared in great force, yelling like fiends incarnate. The men though surprised, seized their arms and defended themselves as long as their ammunition lasted, and then attempted to escape by means of their boats; but the boats were unwieldy, the river low, and the force too much reduced to be made available. At last they launched the boats and attempted to cross the river, but they were intercepted by another party in canoes, who fired into them with murderous effect."

"Thus unable either to escape or defend themselves they were compelled to surrender, and the whole detachment was either killed or taken captive.

"Colonel Laughery and a number of his party were murdered after they Surrendered, but the Indians were restrained from further bloodshed by the arrival of a chief who commanded—the celebrated Brant—who, apologized for the massacre. He did not approve of their conduct and said it was impossible to control the Indians; that the murder of Colonel Laughery and his men was to revenge the massacre of some Indian prisoners by Colonel Broadhead on the Muskingum a few months before.

"The Indians engaged in this battle numbered over 300 and were composed of various tribes; among these and the prisoners and plunder were divided, according to the number of warriors engaged. Next day the[y] set out to return to the Delaware Towns, and met Colonel Caldwell with a force of British and Indians on their way to the Falls of the Ohio to attack General Clark. They remained with them two days, and Brant and many of the warriors returned to the Ohio with Caldwell. The prisoners were taken to Detroit arriving there October 11th and were placed in the hands of the British, who removed them to Montreal, where they remained in captivity until the close of the war, the next year when the[y] were exchanged."

In 1783 the State of Virginia Ceded to the United States all her title to the Territory northwest of the Ohio River, which comprised the now states of Ohio, Illinois, Wisconsin and Michigan. In 1800, that territory was divided and, the present limits of Ohio was made one territory with Chil[l]icothe as the seat of government—and the balance of the territory to the Mississippi river was made one territory named Indiana Territory with Saint Vincennes (Vincennes) as the seat of Government. In 1809, this Indiana Territory was divided into two territories by a line drawn from the mouth of the Wabash river and Post Vincennes due north the eastern Territory being named Indiana and the western Illinois.

In 1801 Dearborn County was organized in Indiana Territory and embraced within its limits, Switzerland County as to the present extent of its territory including that portion stricken off to Ripley County many years since and known as "Ross Township", and remained so untill 1809 when all below Grants Creek was organized into Jefferson County.[1]

Such then was the situation and condition of the territory of South Eastern Indiana of which Switzerland County forms a part, at the several dates given in the foregoing narrative, say for Seventy to one hundred years ago. Now in every direction throughout South eastern Indiana, and Switzerland County, may be seen, well improved and cultivated farms, fine buildings, prosperous cities towns and villages, fine orchards, loaded with fruit, magnificent fields of grass and grain, and last though not least School houses, colleges, and churches, with all the signs of modern civilization and improvements, a contented, happy and prosperous people—just imagine, that all these changes have been brought about by the energy and industry of our forefathers, within the last one hundred years.

Dearborn County continued to embrace Switzerland and Jefferson, or part of Jefferson until some time in 1810 when the present Territory of Dearborn and Ohio counties constituted Dearborn County, and Switzerland County was part of Jefferson County untill 1814 when Switzerland County was organized as a separate and distinct county.[1]

The first settlers, of the county, or rather of the territory embraced in the limits of the county, were the Cottons, Dickason, Picketts, Drakes, Maguire, Rayl David and Stewart, who severally settled within a few miles of the present location of Vevay. William Cotton, and Griffith Dickason settled on Indian Creek sometime in 1798 or 1799, Heathcoat Picket above the mouth of Hunts Creek about 1796 or 97 David at the mouth of Hunts Creek about the year —— Robert and Benjamin Drake two brothers about 1799 or 1800. Maguire whose Christian name is not known about 1800, John Rayl about 1801, and James Stewart about the year 1799 or 1800, and then a part [of] the Swiss colony became their neighbors in the spring of 1803 which colony of Swiss continued increasing in numbers from that time untill 1809— and as that Swiss colony has contributed much to the settlement and improvement of the County it will be appropriate to give the reader a history of the conception and formation of that colony and of those composing it.[2]

### History of the Dufour Family.

John James Dufour the father of the Dufours who came to America in 1801 was a citizen of the Commune of Chatelard District of Vevay Canton de Leman, which name was changed to "De Vaud" in Helvetia.[3]

His sons John, James [John James], and Daniel were the issue of a first marriage, the children by a second marriage were Jeane Marie, born May 4th 1779. Antoinette, born March 8th 1771 [1781?]—John Francis born May 15th 1783, Susanne Margaritte born October 5, 1785, John David born 3rd November 1788 and Amie born February 28th 1791.

The father of these children wishing them to follow

the occupation in life which he and his father and grandfather before him had followed, they being "vinedressers" and not having means sufficient to establish them all in that business, concluded to make arrangements for their emigration to America, where with the means he could give them they could each secure a good tract of land on which to commence their business of cultivating the vine. Accordingly in the month of March 1796 John James Dufour the eldest son, who, was deprived of the right hand and arm up to near the elbow, left his native village on his voyage to America. Visiting Berne, Lausanne, Rouen and Paris [he] came to Havre where he engaged passage on the Brig Sally destined for Philadelphia, for which passage he paid Fifty dollars also the freight of his trunks and to be fed at the second table during the passage.

The vessel sailed on the 10th of June and landed at Philadelphia on the 12th of August—leaving Philadelphia he proceeded towards the great west passing through Wilmington Del. and Baltimore crossed the Allegany mountains to Pittsburgh, then to Marietta Ohio where he stayed a day or two, when he started down the river to visit Illinois—during that trip he went to Kaskaskia, Saint Louis and other points on the Mississippi river and purchased a large quantity of lead, which he sent up the river in a barge he had hired to Pittsburg. The barge sunk and he had a great deal of trouble, and a great risk of loosing the whole cargo—for it was in February that he started for Illinois—and the Mississippi and Ohio rivers were very high while making the voyage up the Ohio with the barge.

The lead was disposed of at Pittsburg, some left with merchants on commission and some of it was not disposed of untill work was commenced at the "First Vineyard" when he exchanged some for iron nails and other articles needed in the cultivation of the land.

During his trip down the river from Marietta he viewed the land along the Ohio river, and also along the

## HISTORY OF SWITZERLAND COUNTY 9

Mississippi from the mouth of the Ohio up as far as Saint Louis—he then went to Lexington Kentucky, having traveled on horseback from Pittsbu[r]gh, through Wheeling, Va. Washington Ky arriving at Lexington on the 28th of August 1798—he then went to Frankfort, and in company with Mr. Brown, Senator in Congress (I suppose, as he in his notes calls him the Senator)[1] made an extensive search for a suitable place for a vineyard. He then started to coast along the Kentucky river —arrived next day at Steels. The next day [he] arrived at Anderson near General Scotts—next day arrived near Cords ferry—next day arrived at David Walkers near the Hickman road but found no place that pleased him except one near Frankfort but the price was too high—next day he arrived at Lexington left his horse, and went on foot to Cleaveling (perhaps Cleaveland) landing there he procured a canoe and he descended the river to the mouth of Hickman Creek. On the 2d of October 1798 he arrived at Lexington once more.

On his arrival he reported to the Vineyard Society[2] that he had seen 3 or 4 places, which pleased him on which to establish a vineyard—and it was decided to purchase in the Big bend of the Kentucky river four miles above the mouth of Hickman creek a tract of 630 acres of one James Haselrig.

On the 13th of October he contracted for the agent of the Society for the purchase of the land for the vineyard, of James Haselrig and prepared to commence work on the land. The work was commenced by clearing the land and preparing it fit to set out vines—persons being hired to clear it ready for the plow at a stipulated price per acre. The clearing was continued through the balance of the fall and the winter and spring so that in the spring of 1799 there was some 6 or 7 acres planted out in vines.

On the 29th of January 1799 John James Dufour, left the First Vineyard (as he termed it) for New York and

Philadelphia via Crab Orchard The Wilderness, Powells Valley, Clinch river, Russell courthouse, Rock Gapp, Wolf Creek, Walkers Creek Botetout, Lexington, Charlottesville, Monticello, Richmond, Fredericksburg, Alexandria, Washington City and Baltimore to procure grape vines to set out, for the commencement of the vineyard. 10,000 vines were purchased at Philadelphia of one Legau[x] at from four to Eight Dollars per hundred comprising thirtyfive different varieties for which $338.00 was paid—a small lot of vines were purchased at Baltimore for which $15.33 [was paid]. Thirty-six fruit trees were purchased to plant on the vineyard farm for which Twelve dollars was paid. A lot of different kinds of seed were also purchased for which Two Dollars and fifty cents was paid.

Having finished his purchases of vines and fruit trees on the 6th of March 1799 John James Dufour commenced his return Journey to the First Vineyard. The cost of transporting the vines and trees to Pittsburg was Ninetyfour dollars.

The vines and fruit trees thus purchased were planted out during the month of April 1799 and grew rapidly in the rich virgin soil of the river bottom and grew so well that in the spring of 1800 John James Dufour wrote to his father brothers and sisters, giving an account of the rapid growth of the vine and advising them to be making preparations to come and join him the next Spring. In the meantime he caused the vineyard to be cultivated and attended in a proper manner. On the 14th of November 1799 he had a settlement of accounts with the Vineyard Company for moneys received by him and paid out on account of the company and it was found that there was a balance due him of Four hundred and thirty one Dollars and Eleven cents—as certified on the Book of account kept by him with the Company by C. Banks acct.

The vineyard was worked and dressed by laborers white and Black under the superinte[n]dance and direc-

# HISTORY OF SWITZERLAND COUNTY    11

tion of John James Dufour until the arrival of his brothers and sisters in 1801.

Let us now turn our attention for a while to the other side of the Atlantic, to the home of the Dufour family and see them and their friends meeting

To bid farewell to their native land.

On the first of January 1801 Daniel Dufour, Francis [Frances] E. Dufour his wife, Jeane Marie Dufour, Antoinnette Dufour, John Francis Dufour Susanne Margarette Dufour John David Dufour, Peter Borallay, his wife his son Peter and a Daughter, Philip Bettens, his wife and Daughter Jean Daniel Morerod, Francis Louis Siebenthal, his son John Francis Siebenthal in all seventeen Souls met at the appointed place in their native village for the purpose of taking a last, long farewell, of home, friends, native country and all the comforts and Luxuries of a country that had been settled for centuries to cross the Broad Atlantic, to find a home in an almost unknown and howling wilderness, where instead of the voice of kind friends and the ringing of the church bells their ears would be saluted by the whoop of the wild Indian and the howl of the wolf.

It must have been an affecting scene to behold these young men and women, some in their teens and two or three infants and youth[s] of tender years Standing there receiving the kind farewell of friends and relatives, and bidding farewell to friends, relatives and home perhaps never to see each other again this side of Eternity to settle in such a wilderness as this part of Indiana then was—and to see the aged father Dufour with his snow white head standing in their midst praying to God to give them a prosperous voyage, to protect them in their wanderings in the wilderness and asking that they might all so live as to please Him that they might all meet in that Heavenly Home prepared for all who love and serve Him in this life.  These Seventeen persons proceeded to Havre where they took passage for America.

After a boisterous voyage of One hundred days they

arrived at Norfolk Virginia in May 1801—from thence they crossed the Allegany mountains in wagons to Pittsburg.—The women, small children and those that could not walk were weighed and brought as freight by the hundred pounds—Arriving at Pittsburg they proceeded down the Ohio river—and were met by John James Dufour (who had heard that they were on the way down the river) at Marietta Ohio on the 18th of June, arriving at Maysville which was then called Limestone, they went by land to Lexington where they arrived on the 3rd day of July and were present at a barbacue and celebration of the 4th day of July 1801.

On the 6th of July The Dufour Brothers and Sisters and their companions in the voyage arrived at the first Vineyard. John James Dufour entered into an arrangement with his brothers and sisters to work the vineyard from that time as common property.

From that agreement it is proper to suppose that in the Settlement made in November 1799 that the company had been dissolved.

They continued to work the vineyard under that arrangement except as one or other of the Sisters married until 1804. In 1802 Jean Daniel Morerod Married Antoinette Dufour, and they and Philip Bettens his wife and daughter came down the Kentucky river to the mouth and up the Ohio to their land. John James Dufour accompanied them, when they landed John James Dufour took an axe and stepping on shore said "I will cut the first tree on our lands," ascended the steep bank and felled a sapling near, where the house now stands in which Charles Norrisez now [1869] resides.

The reasons given by John James Dufour, which induced him to come to America are thus, given by himself, and also the manner in which the "First Vineyard" association was organized, he says—

"When I took the resolution to come to America, to "try the cultivation of the grape I was but fourteen; and "I came to this determination by reading the newspapers

"which were full of the American Revolutionary War,
"and contained many letters from officers of the French
"army aiding the Republicans, which complained of the
"Scarcity of wine among them, in the midst of the great-
"est abundance of every thing else; and by inspection of
"maps I saw that America was in the parrallel of the
"best wine countries in the world—like Spain, South of
"France, Italy and Greece: I then made the culture of
"the grape, of its natural history, and of all that was
"connected with it my most serious study, to be the better
"able to succeed here. It is that resolution which made
"me a vine dresser, although some may think I am not
"fit for it, being maimed in my left arm. It was it,
"which made me lose several chances of getting rich, in
"my journeying through America, because it had so com-
"pletely absorbed all my other thoughts; and it was also
"that resolution, which made me accept a proposal of an
"association for the cultivation of the grape in Ken-
"tucky, under the same principles of [as] the one es-
"tablished at Philadelphia, though not knowing, how-
"ever which of those societies had been the first; but
"the Kentucky Vineyard Society, may be with great
"propriety, considered as the beginner, the true intro-
"ducer of the cultivation of grapevines into the United
"States; although it proved to be a ruinous affair, both
"to the share holders and their vine dresser—neverthe-
"less, millions will accrue to the country at large, from
"the school made here. Some of my readers, who may,
"like me, have been loosers in that undertaking, will see
"here with satisfaction, the reason why it failed, and
"how by a different management, it may now be a more
"profitable establishment even than the United States
"Bank. When I first came to Lexington I was requested
"and encouraged to make a trial on the culture of the
"grape; but I was left with little courage by what I
"had seen done. They offered to help, and the following
"scheme of an association was agreed to—To subscribe
"200 shares, at $50 each—40 of the shares were to be

"mine as my salary to conduct the business, until it
"would become productive; after that, I was to have
"1000 per year out of the pr[o]duce, and nothing if
"there should be none, so that the subscribers put their
"money and I my time at stake. The produce of the
"160 shares was to be appropriated as follows:

| | |
|---|---|
| For 633 acres of land | $ 633 |
| For 5 families of Negroes | 5000 |
| For tools, vi[c]tuals, and other support until the place would be productive | 1000 |
| Expenses of getting vine scions | 800 |
| Incidental expenses | 567 |
| | $8000 |

"The plan was well laid, if we had perfected it, but
"in 1799 too anxious to begin, we went into business be-
"fore all the 160 shares were subscribed for, and while
"there was but very little money collected—five acres
"were planted with 35 different species of the best
"grapes, a great part was obtained by purchase from Mr.
"Legau[x], at Spring Mill near Philadelphia, and others
"gathered in the gardens of New York   a small part
"bought of a German nursery man at Baltimore, and
"another small part brought directly from my own vine-
"yards in Swisserland when my brothers came over to
"join me; three years we were in full expectation and
"worked with great courage—a great many species of
"Vines showed fruit, the third year; one vine of the
"sweet water was full of eminently good grapes, fully
"ripened by the first of September. A few bunches that
"I carried to Lexington were admired beyond any thing.
"But alas! it was the first and last year that, that vine
"ever bore fruit, a sickness took hold of all our vines,
"except the few stocks of Cape and Madeira grapes, from
"each of which we made the fourth year some wine which
"was drank by the Shareholders in Lexington in the next
"March. The failure of the first plantation caused a

"relaxation among the shareholders, and not only a
"great difficulty was experienced in collecting the sub-
"scribed money, but the subscription of all the shares
"was never performed, so that all our stock was made
"use of, for paying the hiring of negroes and other
"hands, and we were never able to purchase a single
"share or even pay for the land; then the whole burthen
"of the establishment rested on our family, who kept
"good courage, for we had begun anew with the Cape
"and Madiera grapes, of which we had so few at first
"that it required several years to have enough of them;
"thus we went on until 1806 when I was obliged to go
"back to Europe, and our family parted. My two young
"brothers (John Francis and John David) who tried to
"keep the place, found themselves too weak to support
"it; and one frosty spring having took all their crop; and
"knowing that those of the colony who had begun in
"1802 on the Ohio were successful and had suffered
"nothing by frost, they abandoned the place to an Ameri-
"can tenant, who supposed we had a bad title to the
"land, obtained a new warrant, and became owner by a
"patent, and let all the vines go to destruction. At my
"return from Europe in 1816, on account of the war
"between the United States, and England, which pre-
"vented my coming sooner, I found the vineyard grown
"up with briars, and I had to have recourse to law to
"have the intruder ejected."[1]

From the foregoing it appears that there must have been great anxiety on the part of John James Dufour and his two young brothers as he terms them for a fair and vigorous effort made by them, to test the feasibility of a successful introduction of the cultivation of the grape vine in the United States, as Congress had sold to John James Dufour and his associates, a tract of land on the borders of the Ohio river, on a portion of which the City of Vevay was laid out and lying between Indian and Plum Creeks, that John Francis Dufour continued to attend to the First Vineyard until 1809 when he removed to New Switzerland.

## The Lands taken up by the Colony

In 1802 John James Dufour petitioned congress to pass an act authorizing him and his associates to enter lands on an extended credit, with a view of giving them an opportunity of introducing the culture of the grape in the United States.

On the first of May 1802 an act was passed by congress and became a law giving them the privilege of selecting four Sections of land on a credit of Twelve years.[1] Under that act about 2,500 acres were selected. About 1,200 acres more adjoining was entered and paid for, as other purchasers of the public land entered land —and after they commenced settling on these lands, the Colonists give to it the name of New Switzerland. There were but few settlers near these lands when the settlement by the Swiss families was commenced.

The lands thus selected were fractional Sections Seven and Eighteen in Town 1 of Range two, sections Twelve and fifteen, and fractional Section Thirteen Fourteen, Twenty Two, Twenty Three, and Twenty Seven in Town Two of Range three west extending along the Ohio river from Hunts Creek down to the lands of Francis E. Mennet, whose father Samuel Mennet, Frederick L. Raymond, Frederick Deserens, Louis Gex and Luke Oboussier had joined the Swiss Colony and purchased some of the lands.

The lands thus selected by John James Dufour and his associates were divided and sold in the following manner.

The lands of Samuel Mennet were first set off. Next above 319 acres to Louis Gex and Luke Oboussier, who had 50 acres just below the tract on which the widow Norrisez now resides    150 acres just below the Gex tract to Frederick Louis Raymond and Frederick

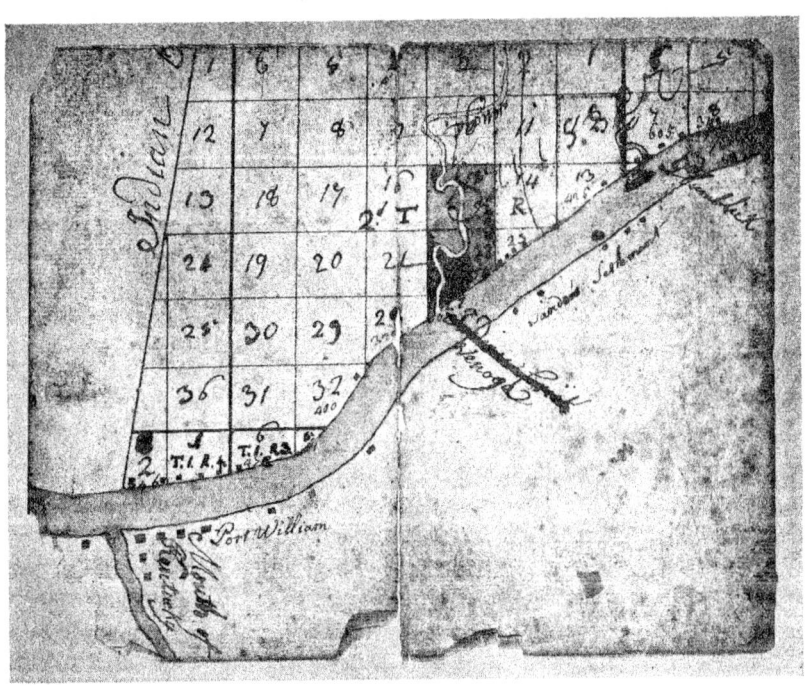

BEGINNINGS OF NEW SWITZERLAND

[Fractional sections 7 and 18 in township 1, range 2 west, sections 12 and 15, and fractional sections 13, 14, 22, 23, and 27 in township 2, range 3 west, were first selected by John James Dufour and his associates. The significance of the shading of section 15, and fractional sections 22 and 27 is not known. Port William is now known as Carrollton, Plumblick as Plum Creek, and Venoge Creek, which divides the present townships of Craig and Jefferson, as Indian Creek. The city of Vevay lies in fractional sections 13, 14, and 23. *The Atlas of Switzerland and Ohio Counties, Indiana*, published by J. D. Lake and Company (Philadelphia, 1883), contains large scale maps of the district.]

# HISTORY OF SWITZERLAND COUNTY 17

Deserens, 160 back from the river in Section fifteen to James Stewart.

The next tract commencing on the river was set off for John Francis Siebenthal and contained about 192 acres being the tract owned by the heirs of William Norrisez. The next was a tract of 192 acres set off to David Golay—now owned by Danglade. The next tract of 192 acres was set off for Philip Bettens. The next tract of 192 acres above the Bettens tract was set off for Jean Daniel Morerod. The next tract above was set off for Daniel Dufour, and contained 192 acres,—next above that [the] tract to John Francis Dufour was laid off to contain 214 acres as it was run so as to include the in lots of the original plat of Vevay—next above one Share of 192 acres for John James Dufour—and one above that of 192 acres to Daniel Vincent Dufour son of John James Dufour—one above the last of 192 acres for John David Dufour—one above that for Antoinette Dufour then Morerod—one above that of 192 acres for Susanna Margarette Dufour—and one above that of 192 acres for Jeane Marie Dufour—these lands have since been divided and subdivided and much of it is now owned by other persons than the descendants of the first settlers. Besides these lands John James Dufour purchased at a public sale of public lands at Cincinnati 795 acres of land on the Ohio river above the mouth [of] Log Lick Creek and below Florence.

Sometime in 1806 Jeane Marie Dufour was married to John Francis Siebenthal and Susanne Margaritte Dufour was married to Elisha Golay and they left the first Vineyard and came to New Switzerland.

In 1804 John Francis Dufour having attained his majority not wishing to work the vineyard in common, each of the Brothers and sisters were allowed wages for their work.

Samuel Mennet it appears was in the United States at the time the Dufour family left their native country

—he married in the neighborhood of the First Vineyard a Miss Hogan.

In 1804 Louis Gex and his brother in Law Luke Oboussier, David Golay and his family, Frederick Louis Raymond, and Frederick Deserens came to New Switzerland.

In 1806 John James Dufour left the First Vineyard to return to his native country to settle up his affairs in that country, sell some property and make such arrangements as were necessary to be made in order that he might be prepared to pay for the land bought of the United States. On the 9th of April 1806 he took passage at New York on board the brig Young Edward, Captain Patterson Morris, in the Steerage, the passage charged being Fifty Dollars.[1] On the 15[th] May he arrived at Plymo[u]th, England remained in England until the 27th June, went to Rotterdam, Breda, Antwerp, Bonne, Hall & Pond in Holland Paris and Dijon in France, arriving at Montreux a suburb of Vevay on the 20th of August 1806.

Here he employed himself in arranging his business affairs and selling some pieces of property he had, to raise the money to pay on the land bought of the Government—however he did not get his affairs arranged so as to return, before the war of 1812 between Great Britain and the United States commenced—the payment for the lands falling due in 1814[2] and it not being considered safe to make the voyage across the Atlantic during the war, he sent a memorial to congress, stating the facts, and congress passed an act extending the time of payment five years longer.[3] He returned in 1816, and the final payment for the lands at Two Dollars per acre and Six per cent per annum interest was completed in 1817. Those of the colony here and who had commenced improvements were fearful the land would be forfeited for non payment, as there was no prospect of making the amount from the sale of the products of the farms.

The products of the First Vineyard in the year 1803

## HISTORY OF SWITZERLAND COUNTY 19

was considerable—the friends of the project resolved to send a Specimen of the wine to the City of Washington. For this purpose two kegs containing about Five gallons each, which were so arranged that they might be thrown across a pack saddle on a horse. John Francis Dufour Started for Washington City on horseback, leading a horse with the kegs of wine, and arrived in that city safely—the wine was presented to a committee of Congress by President Thomas Jefferson for the Vineyard association.

The lands selected by the colony of Swiss was divided according to the following covenant.

"A COVENANT OF ASSOCIATION FOR THE SETTLEMENT OF THE LANDS OF SWITZERLAND ON THE OHIO RIVER."

"The congress of the united States of America, in "order to encourage the cultivation of the vine, having "granted to John James Dufour and his associates the "power of buying four sections or tracts of land by an "act entitled "An act to authorize J. J. Dufour and asso- "ciates to buy a certain parcel of land issued on the 1st "of May 1802." The subscribers, vine dressers by trade "or sons of Vine dressers, forming exclusively this asso- "ciation mentioned by the law in order to promote the "views of Congress, and to fulfill the engagements re- "quired by said law and those to which they have vol- "untarily submitted in their petition presented to "congress on this subject have agreed to submit to the "following conditions:"

"1st. To plant the vine and make their principal busi- "ness their cultivation.

"2nd. Not to be able either to sell or dispose of his "share in whatever manner unless the receipts and cer- "tificates attesting the payment of the whole of said "share."

"3rd. The choice of the lands being made by a majority "of the associates upon the tracts or sections No. 12 and "14 and fractions 13 and 23, 2d Township 3d range con- "taining in the whole 1,879 70/100 acres registered on "the 11th of June 1802 having still one tract or section "to choose—but fractions 13 and 23 are not together a "whole section, it follows that the total purchase amounts "to but 2,519 70/100 acres which are divided into thir- "teen shares containing each 193 80/100 acres and num- "bered from west to east to wit: one for each of the "following—John James Dufour, Daniel Dufour John "Francis Dufour David Dufour Aime Dufour, Daniel "Vincent Dufour, Jane Maria Dufour, Antoinette Dufour "Susannah Margarita Dufour, Francis Louis de Sieben- "thal John Francis de Siebenthal Jean Daniel Morerod "Philip Bettens."

"4th. The said lands being on the Ohio river, and "being surveyed diagonally with the river, it is agreed "that each lot shall meet the river, and its breadth upon "said river shall be as follows: The most Western or "No. 1, 67 poles; No. 2, 65 poles No. 3, 63 poles, and "so on; and in order to run at right angles the lines "of length of each lot, said Dufour engages himself to "do every thing in his power to obtain the fraction and "section adjoining the Western side; and in that case "every lot shall be drawn in length for quantity, at right "angles with the course of the river upon the above "breadth."

"But if in the course of six years, the said straighten- "ing cannot be made the lots shall remain parallel to "the lines north and south run by the survey. Agreed "moreover that Francis Louis de Siebenthal shall have "lot No. 1, Philip Bettens No. 2, John Daniel Morerod "No. 3, John Francis de Siebenthal No. 4, and the family "Dufour the other nine lots. Being reserved here that "if the family Dufour furnishes John Francis de Sieben- "thal to the west end adjoining lot No. 1, as much "ground measured in the same manner as lot No. "4, Siebenthal shall be bound to receive the said ground "in lieu of No. 4, which shall belong to the Dufour fam- "ily; provided the said exchange takes place before the "end of the year 1808."

"5th. In order to establish order, from the beginning "it is agreed to leave a road 100 feet in breadth along "a line run on the Second bank, which shall be planted "with four rows of trees at 33 feet distance, and front-"ing said road shall the buildings be placed."

"6th. In order to indemnify the family of the Dufours "of the costs and trouble, they have been at, (at least "John James Dufour) by travelling in the united States "to choose a convenient place of settlement, and pre-"senting a petition to congress, it shall be given him "or family the sum of $100 for each lot to be paid before "the 1st of January 1812 diminishing six per cent unto "the day of payment, upon the sum that shall have been "paid before that time— As security of the "said covenant each of us engages the whole of his prop-"erty present and hereafter and in witness puts his "name and seal this 20th of January 1803 at first vine-"yard:"

"JOHN JAMES DUFOUR"
"DL DUFOUR BLANC"[1]
"JOHN F. DUFOUR"
"F. L. DE SIEBENTHAL"
"J. F. DE SIEBENTHAL"
"JEAN DL MOREROD"
"J. PHILIP BETTENS"

SEAL

"Attest"
"W. MENTELLE"
"LEWIS HOGAN"

"I certify this to be as exact a translation as can pos-"sibly be made of the French Original, as to the sub-"stance of it, and nearly the same words."

"CHAS. MENTELLE."

As to the road 100 feet wide provided to be laid out the writer remembers well, to have travelled along the road and seen the trees along in front from the lane at the lower side of the Norrisez farm, which was the tract of F. Louis De Siebenthal up to where main cross street in Vevay now runs—and when the town was laid out

Main Street was made 99 feet wide and continued that Width on up to plum Creek in accordance with the provisions in the Covenant above mentioned.

As a matter of history, here is a receipt given by the Sheriff of Dearborn County for taxes in 1810.

"Received of John F. Dufour his tax in full for the year 1810..........$1.00.

J. HAMILTON *Shff*.

The signer of this receipt was sheriff of Dearborn county for several years.

The improvements that were being made by the Colonists were the building of houses, clearing and fencing the land and preparing it for the plow. As these lands were covered by the heaviest of forest trees, walnut, poplar and oak trees of enormous size—with thick undergrowth of smaller trees and grape vines it was with difficulty that a person could travel through the river bottoms. These almost impenetrable forests were more congenial for the abode of the Indian, bear, wolf, catamount and wild can [cat], than for civilized men who had inhabited a land that had been cleared and cultivated for centuries. Suffice it to say that these Swiss families had "come to stay" or in other words to find a home and with their vigorous arms and determined energies and courage to clear up the land and cultivate it as a means of procuring a sustenance for themselves and families.[1]

Samuel Mennet commenced his improvement on the land now owned by Francis E. Mennet his son. Raymond & Deserens commenced improvements just above the mouth of Indian Creek. Mr. Gex and his brother in law Oboussier commenced improvements on their lands—in fact all those who had come to their land were busily engaged in clearing up land. John Francis Dufour who was still at the first vineyard, had hired some person to clear some of his land between where Liberty and Vineyard Streets run to the river—and had quite a large

## HISTORY OF SWITZERLAND COUNTY    23

field cleared and planted in corn, and a few vines set out before he came to New Switzerland with his family.

The first of the colony had as neighbors when they came to New Switzerland, a family named Maguire who lived in a cabin near where William Halls house stands, John Rayl who lived in the bottom opposite the foot of Vevay Island, Heathcoat Picket the grandfather of Benjamin Picket living near where the Brick house stands on the farm above the mouth of Hunts Creek now owned by Julius McMakin—Griffith Dickason and William Cotton who lived on Indian Creek near to where John Bakes resides—

Any one who has assisted in opening a new settlement know[s] very well what an undertaking it must have been for persons who had been born and reared in a country that dated its settlement back to the time of the Ceasars, and who knew nothing about the use of the axe as our "Yankees" do.

These persons had been accustomed to all the necessaries and many of the luxuries that could be had in an old settled and well cultivated country, and they were now in a wilderness far from any market in which to purchase coffee, chocolate and other articles of food, and also of clothing—Cincinnati at that time being the nearest and most convenient place at which to obtain these articles.

It is related of the Bettens and Morerod families which were small at that time they as yet having no cow—their neighbor Maguire furnished them milk every other day—that on the day they got milk they used coffee and on the day they got no milk they took the cloth in which the coffee was pounded (having no mill to grind it) and smelt of it to get the flavor of the coffee.

During the year 1804 and 1805 the lands began to be cleared up more rapidly, so that in 1805 a considerable crop of wheat was raised—the Straw being saved in a very neat manner to be made into Straw hats. The Dufour Sisters made a great many of these hats. On one of the trips made to Cincinnati by some of the colonists, Mr. Morerod took up with him two or three dozen of these hats—while going up the street with these hats on his shoulder, a crowd ran after him to see what he had—when they saw what he had they bought freely and he sold nearly all of them along the street at from two dollars and fifty cents to three dollars each.

Mr. Morerod used to relate many incidents in relation to his farming, raising a crop and then the protecting of it from the ravages of the wild animals and fowls which visited his fields. I recollect to have heard him relate that one fall in particular wild turkeys were so numerous that he had to watch his hogs when he fed them corn, to keep the turkeys off for they eat corn as fast as the hogs. If a turkey was wanted for the table he had only to select one that he thought was fat and knock it over with a club or stick which he said could be done almost every time he fed his hogs. Bear, Deer and turkeys were so plentiful that there was no danger of starving for want of flesh to eat.[1]

About this time the Indians on the Wabash had been troublesome, and about Vincennes, and the settlers began to take precautions against surprize but they were not molested and matters were going on pro[s]perously for the new settlement. Vineyards were being set out as fast as it was possible to prepare the land for that purpose.

But still the settlement was almost shut out from the world around them. If they wished to get letters or papers from their friends, or to send any they were obliged to go to Port William (now Carrollton [Ky.]) that being the nearest post office and that supplied with a mail once in two weeks or at most once a week.

These were privations to which we at the present day, who have a daily mail which brings us our letters and papers from every point of the compass and Six land mails a week are complaining because the authorities at Washington City have told us in plain language "You

## HISTORY OF SWITZERLAND COUNTY 25

shall not have a daily mail from Cincinnati and one from Louisville," for we can get news direct from London, Paris, from the Pacific coast and from the "rest of Mankind" in a few hours What would some of our "Young America" say if they had to go to and settle in such a country, and undergo the privations the settlers in this part of Switzerland County had to endure.

Nothing occurred to retard the clearing up of the land. The settlement was not molested by the Indians, and all enjoyed remarkably good health. They began to gather about them cattle horses and hogs, but the hogs had to be carefully cared for to prevent the bear and wolf from killing them which was of frequent occurrence. Their fields vineyards and orchards began to make quite a contrast with the surrounding forests.

The first wine made was in 1806 or 1807 the quantity was quite limited but of a very good quality—but still the vineyards were enlarged every spring so that the bearing vines became more numerous from year to year, and the quantity of wine also increased every year until the vintage of 1808 yielded 800 gallons and that of 1809 about 1200 gallons of wine.

Orchards were planted so soon as land could be prepared for planting the trees, and in a few years quite large orchards were in a thrifty condition, and comme[n]cing to bear fruit.

This will bring us to a point where some of the incidents transpiring in the early part of 1809 will be related—and still the settlers were obliged to go in canoes, skiffs and perogues to Cincinnati for their salt, iron, nails groceries and dry goods not yet privileged to enjoy the convenience and luxury of a Steamboat ride to the "Queen City."

In March 1809 John Francis Dufour left the First Vineyard and came down the Kentucky river in some kind of a boat to the mouth and the Ohio being high some of his friends in New Switzerland came down to help him up with the boat which contained all his moveable goods, his wife Polly Dufour (who is still living at the advanced age of 87 years) and his son (Perret Dufour) a child of 18 months old. On reaching the mouth of Indian creek there arose a storm and fearing the boat might sink his wife and child were put on shore and some of the heavy articles among which was a hand mill were thrown overboard.[1]

He built a cabin about 20 feet long by about 14 wide, one story and a half high, with round logs which were afterwards "scutched" down on the inside—the logs were cut in the immediate vicinity of the spot where the cabin was raised so that when the "raising" took place the logs were near enough to be carried. That cabin stood on the lot at the corner of Market and Main Cross Streets, on the spot where William Archers kitchen stands. Into this cabin he moved with his wife and son, and turned his attention to clearing more land, planting more vineyard and raising a crop.

During the year 1809 the colonists enjoyed excellent health and it was surprising that they enjoyed such health considering the hardships and privations they had to undergo. They had cleared a good quantity of land planted Several acres of vines which began to bear a very good crop, and numbers of fruit trees, some of which bore fruit during this year.   But yet one great difficulty and source of inconvenience had to be overcome as all their letters and papers going through the mail had to go to the Post office at Port William.

John Francis Dufour drew up a memorial to the Post Master General which was signed by all the citizens of the colony and the neighborhood and sent to the Honorable B. Thurston who was a senator or representative in Congress[2]—upon the receipt of the memorial Mr. Thurston laid it before the Deputy Post Master General, which he communicated to Mr. Dufour by letter of which the following is a copy,

## HISTORY OF SWITZERLAND COUNTY 27

"Washington Feb. 9, 1810"

"Sir"

"I received your letter with the memorial enclosed to "the Post Master General, and shortly after waited on "the Deputy Post Master General (Mr. Granger being "confined with sickness) and laid before him your said "memorial and am happy to inform you, that your de-"sires will be complied with, both in regard to the estab-"lishment of a Post office at Vevay, and your appointment "as Post Master. You may shortly expect to hear from "the Deputy Post Master General on this subject, who "promised to enclose you your commission. I am re-"joiced to hear of your success in the cultivation of the "vine and wish you all manner of success in the future. "I feel no claim to the compliments you have been pleased "to bestow on me in regard to my zeal for encouraging "the improvements of the western country &c., but should "be happy to deserve such if it shall ever be in my power "to render you service.

"With a sincere desire that yourself and your com-"patriots may reap a good harvest from your labors, "which must essentially redound to the public good,

"I am

"Your humble servant"

"B. Thurston."

This letter was directed to John Francis Dufour, Port William Kentucky.

The commission, appointing John Francis Dufour of New Switzerland, Dearborn County, Indiana Territory, Deputy Postmaster at New Switzerland aforesaid at Vevay, and bears date the 23rd day of March 1810 and is signed by Gideon Granger, Postmaster General. Mr. Dufour continued to serve as postmaster at Vevay under that commission until the first of October 1835 he having on the 20th of September 1835 tendered his resignation to the Post Master General to take effect on the 1st of October. Although the Post Office was named Vevay the town was not laid out untill October 1813, three years after the establishing of the Post Office.

In the fall of 1810 the Swiss settlement extended from about where Liberty Street of Vevay now is to where Francis E. Mennet lives, and had augmented from the three first families numbering Seven persons, to thirteen families numbering Sixty Six persons. As they owned the land about the mouth of Indian creek, they changed the name on account of the great number of creeks in the United States called "Indian"—the name given it by them was Venoge" after a small river in the Canton de Vaud—which empties into the beautiful lake of Geneva, on the banks of which most of these Swiss were born and raised. A description of the settlement cannot be better given, than by inserting here an account of it written by John F. Dufour in the fall of 1810 which is as follows—

"New Switzerland is situated on the right bank of the "Ohio river in Jefferson County, Indiana Territory, about "seven miles above the mouth of the Kentucky river. "This Settlement was begun in the Spring of 1803, by "some Swiss of the Canton de Vaud formerly a part of "the Canton of Berne. Their principal object is the in- "troduction of the culture of the grape vines in this coun- "try.           This settlement, or the place called "New Switzerland, extends from about three quarters of "a mile above Plum Creek, down the river to the mouth "of Venoge Creek, known by the name of Indian creek "a distance of about four and a half miles fronting the "river and extending back for the quantity of 3,700 acres "of land—2500 acres of which they purchased under a "law of Congress in favor of John James Dufour and his "associates allowing them twelve years to pay for it from "1802 the time of the purchase: the balance they have "bought as other purchasers and paid for it. The lower "end about two miles along the river, is occupied by thir- "teen Swiss families, composed of Sixty Six persons of "every age. Ten of these families have successively

## HISTORY OF SWITZERLAND COUNTY    29

"come to join the three first who had begun the settle-
"ment."

"Had it not been for the difficulties in crossing the
"Ocean it is believed the whole distance of four and one
"half miles would be filled up with as many more of these
"industrious people.    The improvements of
"the Swiss are considerable considering the time when
"they began, the few hands employed and their inexpe-
"rience in the way of improving land in this country.
"They have now about One hundred and forty acres of
"land under cultivation, about Eight of which are plant-
"ed in grape vines, and now bearing, which offer to the
"eye of an observer the handsomest and the most inter-
"esting agricultural prospects which has perhaps ever
"existed in the United States of America."

"There are about Eight or nine acres more planted in
"grape vines, which are not yet bearing, and they keep
"planting more every spring. The crop of wine of this
"year (1810) has exceeded the quantity of 2,400 gallons
"the quality of which is thought by judges of wine to be
"superior to that of the Claret of Bordeau. The black
"grapes with which it is made are originally from the
"Cape of Good Hope. Out of the 2400 gallons, about
"120 was white or yellow wine, made with the Maderia
"grapes. These two kinds of wine are the only ones
"which have hitherto succeeded, but others are going to
"be tried and it is very probable some of them will also
"produce good wines. When the vines shall be older,
"and the vinedressers be able to let their wines acquire
"age before they sell it, its quality will be much superior
"to what it is now, and there is no doubt but in the
"course of a certain number of years the United States
"will be able to do without importing wine. That
"precious culture will be tried in different parts of the
"union and will undoubtedly multiply rapidly. The Swiss
"will encourage it with all their power. They give slips
"gratis to whoever will plant them, with directions and
"instructions as to their cultivation."

"The Swiss also cultivate Indian corn, wheat, potatoes "hemp, flax, and other articles necessary to farmers al- "though in Small quantities. Some of their women "manufacture a certain quantity of Straw hats, which "they sell in Cincinnati, and on the river to trading boats "which usually stop there to buy them to carry them "to the Mississippi country, where they are very ready "sale. They are made in a fashion quite different from "other straw hats. They are made by tying the straws "together, instead of plaiting and sewing the plaits. It "is one of Mr. Dufours sisters who has first brought the "art to this western country and perhaps into the United "States."

"New Switzerland has the advantage of two roads "One is a fork from the road leading from Lawrence- "burg to Port William, taking off to the left about one "mile and a half before arriving at Venoge or Indian "Creek, and leads to Dufours ferry, opposite which is "a road leading to Frankfort and Lexington Kentucky— "the other road is one leading from the upper end of Jef- "ferson County down to Madison all along the river. "There is also a post office by the name of Vevay, which "is the name of a town intended to be shortly laid off "in the center of New Switzerland for the accommoda- "tion of mechanics."

Such then was the condition of the new settlement in 1810. As to mills nearly every family had a hand mill. The nearest mill was on the other side [of] the river four miles from the river called "Scotts mill" and a horse mill at that.[1]

### As to Schools

They were almost unknown, in 1812 & 1813 Lucien Gex taught School in a log house about where Samuel E. Pleasants resides—he taught french only. Nathan Peak who lived on a 20 acre piece of land in Section 12 which 20 acres of land is now owned by William Protsman taught school at his house. Samuel Butler is perhaps

## HISTORY OF SWITZERLAND COUNTY 31

the only Scholar who attended his school now living. After the town was laid out the lot on which Joseph Peelman resides and the two next to them belonged to the "Vevay Seminary". A school house of hewed logs was built on the spot where Peelmans house stands and scholl was regularly taught there. James Rous father of Zadig and Percy Rous taught in that school house. At an early day after the town of Vevay was laid out a School was taught in a Small log house on Ferry Street, below where the Russell house stands. One Sylvanus Waldo a brother of Otis S. Waldos father taught School for some time. The writer recollects of being a pupil in each of these schools.[1]

The first child born in the Colony was a daughter of Mr. Bettens in 1803. She was the wife of Henry Brachman, Esqr. of Cincin[n]ati and died a few years since. The next was a daughter of Mr. Morerods born in 1804, she is still living in Vevay.[2] That daughter was Mrs. Harriet Tandy.[3]

The next was a daughter of Daniel Dufour born in 1804. She is still living, was the wife of John M. King who was the first Auditor of Switzerland County after the Creation of that office in 1841.[4]

During the winter of 1810-11 and Spring and Summer of 1811 frequent depredations were committed by the Indians on settlements west and northwest of New Switzerland—the news of which caused the Colonists to be on the alert and all meet at one house to pass the night and have centries posted. this was kept up for some time, the men working through the day in the fields and clearings. This state of things continued untill sometime during the spring of 1812.[5] Elisha Golay who was a captain of the militia received orders to enlist men in his company by voluntary enlistment.

This order and similar orders to captains of other companies were promptly obeyed and a company raised and placed under the command of Captain Golay who received orders to proceed to the frontier and range east and west along the north line of Jefferson county as far as the settlements extended. On his arrival at the frontier he was ordered to proceed without delay to build a block house of such size and form as would most securely and conveniently accommodate a detachment of from forty to fifty men including officers.[1] The Block house was built within the limits of Jefferson county and was for many years familiarly known as "Buchannons Station". The names of that Company were Captain Elisha Golay, Lieutenant William Blankenship, 1st Sergeant Luke Oboussier, 2nd Sergeant Beverly Vawter, 3rd Sergeant Peter Storm, 4th Sergeant Thomas Whitson, 1st Corporal John Hall, 2d Corporal Abraham Cline; Privates, Lewis Golay, John Tague, James Picket, Peter Mosbyer, James Edwards, Samuel Lattimore, James Hicks, Achillis Vawter Joshua Tull, William Chambers, Lewis Blankenship, Squire Hall, Daniel Demaree, William Laughridge, Stephen Rutherford William Fidds, Osborn Monroe, Williamson Dunn, Thomas Taylor and Booth Thomas.[2]

In 1811 severe shocks of earthquake were frequent— the same shocks no doubt which were so violent along the Mississippi river and Caused the opening and the sinking of the earth at and about New Madrid. On one night while the mail carrier was staying at the house of John Franics Dufour, his horse was tied to the end of the cabin. In the night the shocks were so severe that the inmates of the cabin were awakened, not knowing what caused it. At first they thought Indians had surrounded the house and were trying to get into it—but hearing no noise, they thought it might possibly be the horse rubbing against the cabin. In the morning feeling the house shake looking out of the window to the south west the trees were seen to be swaying to and fro, as though the wind was blowing but it was quite still— then it was ascertained that it was an earthquake. The shocks were felt at intervals for two or three days.

## HISTORY OF SWITZERLAND COUNTY 33

During the years 1812-13 & 14 all business relating to the business of Jefferson County, of which what is now Switzerland County formed a part, was transacted at Madison.[1] The population of this part of the County had increased so that the assessor for 1812 was appointed from among the citizens of this part of the county. In February 1812 John Francis Dufour was appointed by the court assessor for and within the county of Jefferson. In October of that year he was appointed County Surveyor of Jefferson County by Thomas Posey then Governor of the Territory.

After the war with Great Britain had commenced the Indians in the northern and western parts of the Territory became quite hostile to their white neighbors and it was ordered that a company of Rangers to guard the frontier should be formed. A company was formed, by enlistments from the several compani[e]s of militia. Those from the company about New Switzerland and vicinity were John Stepleton, William Keith, Samuel Peak, Lewis Golay David Golay, Peter Nighswonger, Thomas Rayl, Peter Lock James Picket, Jessee Warden James A. Stewart, one White William Miller his father Abraham Miller, Edward Violet. These rangers went into the interior, up Laughery Creek near to where Versailles now stands and rang[ed] west a considerable distance—at one time they went to Fort Harrison.[2]

During the years 1812, 1813 and 1814 the population of this part of the State was considerably increased. In 1812 the population within the present limits of Switzerland County was about 900, in 1813 at the time Vevay was laid out it was about 1,000 and was mostly confined to the immediate vicinity of the river and creek bottoms —in 1815 the population was ascertained to be 1,800.[3]

The vineyards began to produce, and still more was being planted—the vintage of 1812 produced 800 gallons more than that of 1810. The production continued to increase from year to year, until in 1818 there were Seven thousand gallons of wine made. At the time of the greatest prosperity of the grape culture the number of acres in vines was Forty five or Fifty, and the quantity of wine made exceeded Twelve Thousand gallons.[1]

The vineyards were places of resort for those who visited Vevay, some perhaps from curiosity and to have a wine party. On such occasions during court weeks Lawyers and Judges were in the habit of spending an evening or an afternoon in quaffing some of "Father Morerods" wine.

It happened on such occasions sometimes that some one of the company would indulge rather freely of the wine, making it necessary for one of his companions, and often two or three to assist him in getting to his lodgings at the hotel up Town. On some of these occasions the Governors of Indiana, Senators and Representatives in Congress have been know[n] to participate in these social gatherings and thus the fame of "Vevay Wine" was spread abroad.

In the spring of 1813 it having been decided by John Francis Dufour to lay off the town of Vevay[2]—the lots in the origanal part of Vevay were laid out partly in the Woods, and partly in a "dead[e]ning" & some cleared land. The town plat was made out and recorded in the Recorders office of Jefferson County at Madison. Notice of the sale of the lots, was given through the papers published at Cincinnati, Louisville, Lexington and Frankfort—the sale took place in November 1813. The sale was cried by John M. Johnson, Elisha Golay acting as clerk of the sale. At that sale persons from abroad purchased lots; Jeremiah Smock of Fayette County Ky. purchased lot No. 135 Jacob Mikesell purchased lot No. 133 Wm McIlvain lot No. 124, Peter Mikesell No. 134, John Patterson 129, John Hill of Scott County Ky No. 125, Joab Madison No. 152 Jessee Lamme Nos. 165, 166, 167, and 168, Abner K. Starr No. 123, John Scott Nos. 85, and 87, Joseph Noble Nos. 58 and 91. These are the per-

# HISTORY OF SWITZERLAND COUNTY 35

sons from abroad who purchased lots at the sale. The price of lots varied considerably the lowest price being $22 for lot No. 26—the hig[h]est price being $92 for lot No. 66. Other lots were sold during the fall and winter at private sale.

During the Spring and Summer of 1814 buildings were being put up rapidly in different parts of the town. The first house put up was a log house by Samuel Butler and his father, on the lot where the Thiebaud house in which the Bank is now kept stands. The same spring Joshua Jones who came down the river from about Grants Creek had a set of house logs hewed at Grants Creek ready to put up a house there—but he rafted them in the river, floated them down to Vevay, and built a house with them on the lot now owned by James F. Bristow—on Main Cross Street—and there commenced making split bottomed chairs.

John Scott the fatherinlaw of James Cole, build a hewed log house on the lot where the New Baptist church now stands, and carried on his trade of Tailor. During the spring of 1814 John Dumont came to Vevay and built a house on the spot where the present building owned by Amie Morerod stands. As the town had during the spring shown some permanent signs of improvement— and the population of the territory which was that year organized into a County had augment[e]d to 1600 and was constantly augmenting, it was proposed to have a county organized off the upper end of Jefferson county to suit the convenience of the Citizens who were compelled to go from above where Patriot now stands to Madison, to transact their ordinary county business— accordingly a petition signed by the citizens was presented to the Territorial Legislature praying for the organization of such county. John Francis Dufour and Elisha Golay [who] were the most active and influencial friends of the measure attended the session of that Legislature as lobby members and had the satisfaction of having their efforts crowned with Success.[1]

It may not be generally known, that there is a part of this County east of the first principal meridian line which runs north and south from the mouth of the Great Miami river—the lands in this county were surveyed in 1797, 1798, 1800 and 1801. The lands entered at the land office at Cincinnati extended down to a line drawn from opposite the mouth of [the] Kentucky river running in such a direction as to strike Fort Recovery—and that line is called the Old Indian Boundary as that was a line established by Waynes treaty by which the Indians ceded to the United States their title to the lands to that line. Below that line the lands were in the Jeffersonville Land district. There is I believe only one entire Congressional Township of land in this county all the others being only parts of Townships in the northern side of the county and along the river and the Indian boundary there are many fractional townships—I will now give the date of

Entry of some of the lands

in Town. 1. Range 1 E. Frac. Sec. 31, entered July 2, 1801 by John Hopkins containing 322 acres—Sec. 6, and fract. Sec. 5, 7 and 8. Decr 2 1806 containing 1507 acres by Oliver Orm[s]by—Frac. Sec 18 July 24, 1809 by John Andrews, containing 360 acres. In town 2 Range 1 E. Sec 31, Frac. Sec. 29, 30 and 32 entered April 26, 1804 by Patric[k] Donahoe containing 1412 acres. In town 1 Range 1 W. Frac. Sec 5 and 6 entered sept 10, 1804 by John Buchannon and William Philips containing 208 acres. In Town 2 R. 1 west Sec. 6, entered Sep 4, 1804 by Patrick Donahoe and containing 647 acres N. E. qr. of Sec 27 entered July 15th, 1805 by Lewis Jones containing 160 acres. Frac. Sec. 34, entered Sept 18, 1804 by Martin Baum containing 376 acres—Frac Sec 35 entered Sept 4, 1804 by Patrick Donahoe containing 505 acres—Frac. Sec. 36 entered July 2, 1801, by Thomas Hopkins, containing 626 acres—There was no other lands entered in this Township until in 1812.

In Town. 1 Range 2w Frac. Sec. 1 and 2 entered by

## HISTORY OF SWITZERLAND COUNTY 37

John James Dufour April 10, 1801 containing 797 acres —Frac. Sec 3, entered by Thomas Hopkins July 14, 1801 containi[n]g 303 acres. Frac Sec. 7 and 18 entered by John James Dufour and his associates Sept 14, 1804. No other lands entered in this Township untill 1813

In Town. 2, R. 2w S. E. qr Sec 25 entered by William White December 25, 1809 contain[in]g 160 acres—N. E. qr. sec 36 entered Dec 14, 1809 by John Fenton containing 160 acres S. W. qr Sec 35 entered March 16, 1810 by John Gullion containing 160 acres—No other land entered in this township until 1812. In Town. 3. R. 2w no land entered in this Township until 1812.

In Town 2 Range 3w N.W. qr Sec 2 and S. W qr Sec. 2 entered Oct 9, 1804 by Griffith Dickason and Stilwell Heady contai[nin]g 325 acres—Sec 12 and 15 and Frac Secs 13, 14, 22, 23, 27 entered June 11, 1802 by John James Dufour and his associates containing 2,357 acres —Frac. Sec 32 and 33. Dec 12, 1809 by George Craig containing 432 acres—No other lands entered in this Township until 1811.

In Town 3 R. 3w S. E. qr Sec. 34 entered by William Cotton June 10, 1805 containing 164½ acres

No other lands entered in this township until 1811

In Town 4, R. 3w. none entered until 1817.

In Town 1 R. 4 Frac Sec 1. entered Jany 11, 1810 by James McKay. Frac. Sec. 2, entered Sept. 22, 1804 by Thomas Thompson. In T. 2 R. 4w, the first entry was made in 1815 the last 1835 In T. 3 R. 4w, the first entry was made in 1814 last in 1816

This comprises all the Townships and fractional Townships in Switzerland County in the Cincinnati land district.

In the Jeffersonville District no entries of land in Switzerland County were made until 1812 and the last in 1839.[1]

It will be seen that the early entries of the lands in the county were made in the bottoms along the Ohio river and near thereto.

In the fall of 1813 Robert Bakes established a carding machine on the lot Corner of Main and Vineyard Streets now owned by George W. Hathorn.[1] In the Spring of 1814 from representations made to him by Robert Bakes, James Rous the father of Zadig and Percy Rous came to Vevay and settled on a lot on the western side of Vineyard Street and there Lucien Rous a son of James Rous was born he being the first male child born in Vevay.

In 1814 John Francis Dufour built a two story hewed log house on the Corner of Market and Main Cross streets on the lot now owned by William Archer. In that House courts were held for some time, and for many years the Post office and office of the Clerk of the county were kept in that house.[2]

The Territorial Legislature having organized a county, they gave to John Francis Dufour the privilege of giving the name to the county, when he signified his preference for its being named "Switzerland" which name was inserted in the act organizing the county. The Governor of the Territory having the power to appoint all the necessary officers, in the exercise of that power appointed the following persons    For associate Judges of the circuit Court William Cotton and James McClure—Sheriff John Francis Siebenthal Coroner Ralph Cotton—Clerk John Francis Dufour    Recorder John Francis Dufour —County Surveyor Elisha Golay. The Commissions were all dated the 15th of September 1814 except that of Recorder which was dated 11 October 1814 signed by Thomas Posey Governor and John Gibson Secretary. Here is a copy of one of those commissions

"INDIANA TERRITORY S.S."

"THOMAS POSEY, Governor and Commander-in chief of Indiana Territory

"To all to whom these presents shall come Greet[in]g

"Know you, that I have constituted and appointed, and

OLD VINEYARD TERRACE

SITE OF JOHN FRANCIS DUFOUR'S HOME

"by these presents do constitute and appoint Ralph Cot-
"ton, of the County of Switzerland gentleman to be Coro-
"ner of our said County of Switzerland during our
"pleasure; and do hereby authorize and empower him to
"do and perform all and whatsoever to the office and duty
"of Coroner in our said County of Switzerland doth any-
"way belong or appertain. In testimony whereof I have
"hereto set my hand, and caused the seal of the Territory
"to be affixed at Jeffersonville in said Territory, the fif-
"teenth day of September, in the year of our Lord one
"Thousand Eight hundred and fourteen and of the Inde-
"pendence of the United States the thirtyninth.
"By the Governor."                              "TH. POSEY"
"JN. GIBSON, *Secretary.*"

The commissions of the other officers were in the same words as the one given above with the exception of the name of the person, and the office to which he was appointed.

It now became necessary that these officers should be sworn into office, and it would appear that there was no person authorized by law to administer oaths in the county—the Governor made the following appointments and commissioned the persons, to administer the oath [of] office to those appointed to the Various offices.

"THOMAS POSEY Governor and Commander-in chief of the Indiana Territory."

"To WILLIAM COTTON sends Greeting"

"Know ye that I have by these presents authorized you
"to administer the Oath of office as prescribed by law to
"John Francis Dufour clerk of the circuit Court for the
"county of Switzerland. Given under my hand and the
"seal of the Territory of Indiana at Jeffersonville the
"Sixteenth day of September Eighteen hundred and four-
"teen and of the Independence of the United States the
"thirtyninth.
"By the Governor"                               "TH. POSEY"
"JN. GIBSON *Secretary.*"

The oath was administered and entered on the back of the commission in the following words

"INDIANA TERRITORY SWITZERLAND COUNTY SS"

"The within named John Francis Dufour personally "appeared before me and took the oath prescribed by law "more effectually to prevent duelling, and the oath to sup- "port the constitution of the United States, together with "the oath of Clerk of the Circuit court of the aforesaid "County. Given under my hand this 4th day of October "1814."

"WM. COTTON"

It appears that there was still no person authorized by law to administer the oath of office to the other officers of the County, Judges and military officers as [so] the Governor issued his commission to John Francis Dufour as follows—

"THOMAS POSEY Governor and Commander in chief of the Indiana Territory"

"To JOHN FRANCIS DUFOUR sends Greeting."

"Know ye that I have by these presents, authorized and "empowered you to administer the Oath or oaths of office "as prescribed by law to all officers civil and military "who are or may hereafter be appointed for the county of "Switzerland."

"Given under my hand and the seal of said Territory "at Jeffersonville the fifteenth day of September "Eighteen hundred and fourteen, and of the Independ- "ence of the United States the Thirtyninth

"By the Governor"

"TH. POSEY"

"JN. GIBSON *Secretary.*"

The oath of office having been administered to all the County officers—the necessary machinery for the transaction of all the business of the county was ready for business. Yet there was no permanent place named for holding the Courts. The naming of the place of holding the courts was the duty of the County Court. Provisions

## HISTORY OF SWITZERLAND COUNTY 41

for that purpose were made by a law of the Territory passed in 1813 prescribing the manner of establishing seats of Justice in newly organized counties.[1] The associate Judges, constituted the County Courts. They had the same duties in relation to County business to perform that our Boards of County Commissioners now perform.

In The act organizing the County of Switzerland Jesse L. Holman, the father of Hon. Wm. S. Holman representative in Congress—Joseph Short and Alexander A. Meek a lawyer residing in Madison were appointed commissioners to locate the seat of Justice of Switzerland County.[2]

The Commissioners above named met in Vevay on the 17th day of October 1814 for the purpose of selecting the most eligible place for the seat of Justice of the county and to receive any proposals and donations which might be made by the citizens of different localities, for the benefit of the County.

The propositions of the proprietors of the town of Vevay were the following

"The subscriber proposes to the commissioners, ap-"pointed for the fixing of the Seat of Justice of Switzer-"land County to give to said County, the square in the "town of Vevay known in the Original plat of said town "by the name of public Square, containing two acres of "land for the purpose of erecting the public buildings, "thereon provided the seat of Justice of said County be "fixed on said Square. He also offers a Subscription in "the name of the subscribers thereto to the amount of "upwards of Two thousand four hundred dollars, and lot "No. 92 in said town, which he respectfully submits to "their consideration"   "JOHN FRANCIS DUFOUR."

"VEVAY Oct 17, 1814."
"I further promise to use my best endeavors to pro-"cure more subscribers to the aforesaid subscription "paper, which I expect to obtain to a considerable "amount."   "JOHN FRANCIS DUFOUR."

"In addition to the within proposals we Jointly agree "and obligate ourselves to have conveyed to the agent of "this county to be appointed by the court of said county "of Switzerland, the in lots numbered Thirtythree and "Sixty.

"DL DUFOUR BLANC"
"JOHN FRANCIS DUFOUR."[1]

Benjamin Drake who owned the land where the town of Florence now stands, made a proposition to the Commissioners to have the seat of Justice fixed on Fractional Section 6 T 2 R 1. west.

Propositions were also made by parties living in what is now known as "Egypt Bottom" for the location of the seat of Justice on Frac. Sec 35. T 2 R 1 which is about Two miles above the mouth of Bryants Creek

A proposition was also made, and submitted to the commissioners to locate the seat of Justice on Frac Sec No. 3 T. 2 R. 2 west.

The first meeting of the County court was held on the 28th October 1814,[2] and the first record Book in which the proceedings of that court were recorded consists of about half a quire of common fools cap paper sti[t]ched together and unruled at that. The first entry is as follows—

"At a Special County Court, began and held at the "house of Robert M. Trotter in the town of Vevay in and "for Switzerland County on Friday the 28th day of Oc- "tober 1814    Present the Honorables William Cotton "and James McClure associate Judges of the Circuit "Court for said county and authorized to transact county "business.

"Jesse L. Holman presented to the court the following "report to wit:"
"To the Honorable Judges of the Circuit Court of Swit- "zerland County."
"We the undersigned three of the commissioners ap- "pointed by the Legislature of Indiana Territory for the

# HISTORY OF SWITZERLAND COUNTY 43

"purpose of fixing the seat of Justice in and for the
"county of Switzerland met agreeably to the law estab-
"lishing the county of Switzerland, in the town of Vevay
"in said County on the 17th day of October 1814 and
"being first duly sworn proceeded to examine the most
"elegible place for the seat of Justice in said County
"and to receive any proposals and donations which might
"be made for the benefit of said County, when the pro-
"posed donations marked A, Aa and Aaa were made by
"the Citizens of Vevay provided the seat of Justice
"should be established in said town—and the proposed
"donation marked B. was made by Benjamin Drake pro-
"vided the seat of Justice was established on fraction 6
"Town 2 Range 1 west; and it being inconvenient to pur-
"sue the object of our meeting further at present we
"postponed a further, examination, until Wednesday the
"26th instant and appointed the house of Benjamin
"Drake, as the place of our meeting on the last named
"day.

"Wednesday, October 26th 1814,"

"Agreeably to our former determination we met on
"this day at the house of Benjamin Drake in said county
"when and where, we received the proposed donation
"marked C. provided the seat of Justice was fixed on
"Fraction 35. Town 2 Range 1 west; and marked D. and
"E. provided said seat of justice was fixed on fraction
"3 town 2 Range 2 west and the additional proposed
"donations marked F provided said seat of Justice was
"fixed on fraction 6, Town 2 range 1 aforesaid.

"Whereupon on Thursday the 27th October 1814, we
"proceeded to examine the places above proposed (ex-
"cept) the fraction 35 aforesaid which from its extreme
"southea[s]twardly situation we considered as entirely
"ineligible and also to examine, the boundaries, the land
"and the central parts of said County, and take into con-
"sideration the extent of the county the quality of the
"land and the prospect of the future, as well as the
"weight of the present population, together with the

"probability of future divisions, we have fixed upon the "public Square in the Town of Vevay in fraction 23 and "14 in Town 2 Range 3 west, as the most eligible place "for the permanent seat of Justice of said county and "do hereby declare, that it is our opinion Judgment and "determination that the seat of Justice for said County "be fixed and remain permanently at the place aforesaid, "Given under our hands and seals at Vevay this 28th "day of October 1814 Commissioners fees to wit. "J. Short six days J. L. Holman Seven days. A. A. Meek "seven days."

"JACOB SHORT."
"JESSE L. HOLMAN"
"ALEX. A. MEEK."

On the next day the Court divided the county into two Townships, and named the lower one on the river extending back to the north boundary of the County, Jefferson and the upper one Posey[1] and appointed the place of holding elections in Posey Township at the house of Lewis Jones Williams Peirson being appointed Inspector. The court also appointed the place of Holding elections in Jefferson Township at the house of Robert M. Trotter, John Dumont being appointed inspector.

Robert Cotton, a brother of William Cotton, Charles F. Krutz, father of Wm G. Krutz of Florence and Joseph Noble father of Charles, Lewis and Oliver Noble were appointed constables of Jefferson Township, and William Campbell the grandfather[2] of Wm. & Charles Protsman and Caleb Mounts, were recommended to the governor as proper persons for the office of Justice of the peace for Posey Township, and George Craig father of Mrs. Tabitha O. Kyle for Justice of the peace for Jefferson Township.

Elisha Golay who had been appointed Surveyor declined to accept and John Gilliland was recommended by the Court to the Governor as a suitable person to be appointed Surveyor.

## HISTORY OF SWITZERLAND COUNTY 45

On the 25[th] of November 1814 the court[1] appointed Elisha Golay agent of the county and instructed the agent "to cause a Jail house to be built on the Corner of lot number 60 in the town of Vevay" The Jail was built and on the 30th March 1815 the Court directed the agent "to pay Hiram Ogle the sum of Money which he as agent of the County was bound to pay him for building a Jail house in the town of Vevay in and for said county." That Jail was of hewed logs about 1 foot square, one story high. It appears that there had been no necessity for using the Jail up to 3rd May 1815 as the court on that day directed the agent of the county to "procure a strong lock for the Jail, also a strong padlock and cause them to be put on the doors of said Jail also a doublebolt padlock for the gable end door."[2]

Some years after a prisoner made his escape from said Jail by sawing off one of the logs, and pushing it so as to make an opening large enough to get through—sometime afterwards a prisoner named Thomas Coen, set fire to the Jail made his escape and set on the top of the hill back of town and saw it burn down.

On the 30th of March 1814 the court directed Elisha Golay agent for the county to "cause to be advertized in the *Kentucky Reporter, Liberty Hall,* and *Western Eagle* that on Tuesday the Second day of May 1814 there would be let to the lowest bidder, the building of a brick court house on the public square.[3]

On the Second day of May 1814 the court directed that the Court house should be 36 by 32 feet. The county agent let the building of the same to John Tandy of Gallatin County Ky at the sum of Seventeen hundred and five dollars—the agent also let the clearing off of the public square to Samuel Davis for $26.75.

The court house was not completed so as to be used for some time[4] and Stephen C. Stevens was appointed to have the Bar in the Court room properly arranged.

John Dumont was a Justice of the peace in 1814.

George Craig was the first lister of property for tax-tion—Ralph Cotton the next—Allen Wiley was the third. He performed the duties of the office and, filled his various appointments for preaching throughout the county. He was the first Methodist preacher who preached regularly in this county. At one time he was recommended to the Governor as a suitable person to be appointed Justice of the peace.   Ralph Cotton who was first appointed coroner declined and John Dumont was appointed in his stead.

In 1814 the out lots were laid out, two of five acres each were reserved for a scite for a tan yard   they were purchased by F. S. Lindley who established a tannery on them and continued the business for many years —part of one of these out lots was reserv[ed] for a burying ground—which is the one now used for that purpose. The first person buried in that lot was Mrs. Nighswonger the grandmother of Mrs. Elizabeth Dalmazzo widow of Joseph Dalmazzo[1]—the second was Mrs. Butler mother of Samuel Butler.[2] The first burial at which religious services were observed was the burial of Mrs. Cole the mother of Daniel and Thomas T. Cole. The services were performed by Allen Wiley of the Methodist Church.

The citizens of Vevay early organized a library association known by the name of "Vevay literary Society"[3]

They had accumulated many books by donation and purchase—John Francis Dufour being authorized by the society to procure donations of book[s]—when visiting Lexington Ky on business he received a donation of many volumes. That Library was well patronized until about 1829 or 1830 when James Rous, removed from his farm to Vevay, when he became librarian—the books still remained in his possession. Where they finally went to I am not able to say.

John Dumont was President of the Literary Society, George Coggshell, Robert M. Trotter and Daniel Dufour

Blanc Directors. Eight lots were reserved for the Society and the Legislature in 1816 passed an act incorporating the "Literary Society of Vevay."[1]

During the Summer of 1814 Vevay and the surrounding country improved considerably. There were several stores two or three taverns, two or three blacksmith shops one or two tailors, a chair factory, a manufactury of "Big" and little wheels and reels [and] a hatters shop.[2]

Wolves were very numerous and did great damage to hogs and even calves. The Legislature of the territory passed an act allowing a bounty of One doller for each wolf scalp, which the person claiming the Bounty should prove to the Satisfaction of the county court, he or she had killed—under that law an allowance was made by the County Court as follows.

"Elizabeth Jones is allowed one dollar for the Scalp of a wolf killed by her in 1814."

Heathcoat Picket and his brother James were out hunting on the ridge just west of Jacksonville near where there was a "bear wallow" Heathcoat went on one side of the ridge and James on the other, thinking to chase a deer around to the other, while thus separated James was surrounded by a pack of wolves which commenced howling, with their heads raised as if looking at something in the tree tops. Heathcoat hearing the wolves, went over to where the noise was when he saw the wolves around James and James looking up into the trees to see what the wolves were barking or howling at. Heathcoat asked James what does this mean—James replied "these dogs have treed something, see how they are barking at it" James had taken the wolves to be dogs.

Among the early settlers in the upper end of the county were James McC[l]ure who was Judge of the courts, Ezekiel and Joshua Petty, Peter Lostutter, Lewis Jones, George and Elisha Wade Caleb Mounts, Williams Pierson, Benjamin and Robert Drake, the Vandoren family

John Kilgore William Campbell, Robert Gullion, Amos A. Brown, John Neal, Charles Campbell, Job and James Treusdel, William Johnson, William White, the Wallicks, McCrearys, [and] McCorcles.[1]

The first taverns kept in Vevay were kept by Thomas Armstrong, Philo Averil[2] William Cooper Samuel Fallis, Jonas Baldwin David McCormick William T. Huff and others not necessary to mention.[3] Thomas Armstrong and William T. Huff in fact kept the only taverns in the town with the view of accommodating travellers—

By the law then in force none but tavern keepers were permitted to retail liquors by the small or as was then the common expression "by the half pint" and persons applying for tavern license[4] were required to prove to the satisfaction of the county Court that they had a certain number of extra beds and extra Stable room for a certain number of horses. In some instances this law was evaded. At one time a person wishing to obtain license to retail the ardent by the "half pint" and not having the requisite number of spare beds and stable room, rented of a neighbor for a week or ten days the Stable room required and borrowed the requisite number of extra beds and fitted them up in his house—he called someone to come and see that he had the beds and stable room went before the county court, proved by his witness that he had the required number of extra beds and extra Stable room, license was granted him—that day or the next the borrowed beds were returned, and the man went on with his tavern in the usual way of such Taverns.

Thomas Armstrong at first kept his tavern in a two story hewed log house[5] on the lot where John F. Doans residence stands. Afterwards he built the house in which John L. Thiebaud resides and kept tavern there for many years.

William T. Huff built a brick house at the corner of Ferry and Main Street where the LeClerc house stands and kept his tavern there for many years.[6]

The taxes for 1816 levied in the county were as follows.

# HISTORY OF SWITZERLAND COUNTY 49

On every horse, mule, and ass above 3 years old 25 cents

On first rate land 37½ cents per 100 acres

On Second rate land 25 cents per 100 acres

On third rate land 12½ cents per 100 acres

On Stallions at the rate at which they stand by the Season

On town lots and houses 50 cents per 100$ of their value

On George Ash's ferry $2.50

On Edward McIntires ferry $2.50

On John Francis Dufours ferry at Vevay $5.00

On George Craigs ferry $1.00

On F. Louis Raymonds ferry on Indian creek 50 cents

And the following taxes were levied as road tax:

On Daniel Dufours Store $3.00

On Lucien Gex Store $3.00

On Isaac Stanleys store $3.00

On David McCormicks Store 50 cents—On Joseph Bentleys store 75 cents,

On Jonathan Reeders store 75 cents—

On James Dalmazzo store 25 cents

In 1812[1] Amie Dufour the youngest of the Dufour Brothers who had been left behind to complete his education came to the colony of New Switzerland. During the Voyage across the Atlantic the vessel on which he embarked was captured by a British cruiser, and in consequence was detained many months before reaching the United States. He was finally landed at Boston and not having funds sufficient to defray his travelling expences, by stage he set out from Boston on his Journey to the West, on foot travelling from Boston to Pittsburg on foot often at night sleeping in a Barn. Arriving at his sisters Morerod, he remained there for some years. He assisted in making and laying up the Brick of the dwelling house still standing on the Morerod farm near Vevay.[2]

Sometime in 1814 Bazilla Clark came to Vevay and established a nail factory on the lot at the west Corner of Main and Walnut Streets—the nails were cut by horse power[1]—the nails sold for 25 cents per pound.

The first Brick building put up in Vevay was the Courthouse. The walls were put up in the summer of 1815, and completed so that the October term 1816 of the Circuit Court was held in it. In the fall of 1815 Lucien Gex built a small brick house one story high on Main Street opposite Mrs. Ormsbys, which is still to be seen.

Richard Dumont the father of John J. Dumont of Indianapolis and C. T. Dumont of Cincinnati Ohio was to be married to Matilda Philips and was speaking about going to Madison for his license. John Francis Dufour told him if he would wait a week or ten days he could get [a] License at Vevay as he expected his commission as clerk within that time. Mr. Dumont told him he would see his intended and if she would consent to postpone their marriage until that time and if she would he would be very glad to do so. Their marriage was postponed, and on the 6th day of October 1814 the Licence was granted, being the first marriage license granted after the organization of the County—and they were married on the same day by William Cotton associate Judge.

There appears on the Marriage Record of that early day the following certificate of a marriage

"This is to certify that the marriage of Hugh Mc-
"Creary and Rebecca White being advertised according
"to law, was solemnized by me one of the Justices of the
"peace of Switzerland County on the 3rd November
"1814, Witness my hand and seal the 8th Novr 1814"
"ROBT. M. TROTTER J. P. (Seal.)"

The first deed recorded in the Recorders office of the County was dated 16th January 1815 executed by Isaac Bledsoe and Elizabeth Bledsoe his wife of Gallatin County Kentucky to Robert McKay for 155 acres of land

# HISTORY OF SWITZERLAND COUNTY     51

being part of Frac sec. No. 5, Town 1, Range 3: the consideration being $612.00.

Among the early traders down the river were George Turner who lived on the opposite side of the river, the father of Robert and John Turner, who made yearly trips down the river.[1] One fall Mr. Turner bought many wild turkeys—cut the breast out put them in Barrells and made a brine to keep them[2]

The officers of the county first commissioned by the Governor whose names have been heretofore given[3] continued in office untill the admission of the State into the Union.

The attorneys admitted to practice in the court of the county from the organization of the county until the organization of the State Government are as follows
Amos Lane, William Hendricks John Test, James Noble John Lawrence, Pinkney James, Stephen C. Stevens Alexander Holton, Joseph F. Farley, Reuben Kidder, Hezekiah B. Hull, Edward Nichols, D. T. Maddox and Jeremiah Sullivan. Two of these James Noble and William Hendricks were senators from the state in the United States Senate. Three Amos Lane William Hendricks and John Test were Representatives in Congress from the district of which Switzerland county formed part, and Two Jeremiah Sullivan and Stephen C. Stevens were Judges of the supreme court of Indiana.

All of these have ceased from their earthly labors.

Judge Sparks was on the bench only at the October term 1814 and March term 1815. Judge Noble held but one term of the Court—June term 1815.

The October term 1815 of the court was held by William Cotton and James McClure the associate Judges. At the March Term 1816 Jessee L. Holman presided and was the Judge of the Circuit until the organization of the State Government, when we find him on the Supreme Court bench.

During one of the early terms of the court an amusing scene occurred in the Court room just before the opening of the Court—the two associate Judges were sitting on the bench conversing when a wag who was present seated himself to the right of the two associates and called the attention of the bystanders exclaiming "I'll bet ten "dollars there's one hundred Judges on the bench" some- "one turned to him and said "How do you make that" "Just look" said the wag "and I'll show you" then pointing to himself he said "a figure one" then pointing to the two associates "and two cyphers make 100" when he left the bench amid a roar of laughter from the bystanders.

James Noble, John Test and William Hendricks were the prosecuting attorney[s] from the organization of the County, until the organization of the State; and received for their Services $16. and 25$ the former being the lowest and the latter the highest allowance made to be paid out of the county Treasury.

Among the first indictments found by the Grand Jury was one against David Beebee for selling unwholesome flesh, tried at the second term of the Court by a Jury composed of Robert McKay Robert Bakes, Ralph Cotton Jr. Robert Cotton John M. Johnson, William Campbell, Rawleigh Day, Thomas Paxton, Adam Cline, Walter Clark John T. Demming and Luke Oboussier, and acquitted.[1]

The first business in relation to Decedents affairs was an application of Job Trusdell to have a deed made to him for 257 acres of land he had purchased of Charles Campbell, for which he held said Campbells bond, who had departed this life after the execution of said Bond. The court ordered that the bond be filed with the clerk. The administrators of Campbells estate moved the court to appoint three commissioners to make said deed to said Trusdell according to the tenor of the bond and the act of assembly approved Sept 17, 1807.[2] This order was made by the Court May 3rd 1815.

## HISTORY OF SWITZERLAND COUNTY 53

Amos Brown was appointed by the court at a special session on the 28th Octr 1815, a trustee to lease the School Sections within the Township of Posey and John Francis Dufour a trustee to lease the School Sections within the Township of Jefferson.[1]

According to the Territorial law a person who was unable to pay his debts might be imprisoned in the County Jail and confined to the prison bounds which then extended to the limits of the Town.[2]

There appears but two cases of record during the Territorial Government, within this county.

The court house and Jail having been completed and paid for out of monies subscribed except about Sixty Dollars, the balance was paid to the county agent who gave a receipt therefor as follows.

"Received of John Francis Dufour and Daniel Du-
"four by the hands of John Francis Dufour the sum of
"$63 being the amount uncollected of the Subscribers to
"the subscription for public buildings in Vevay which
"said John Francis Dufour and Daniel Dufour were Se-
"curity for as appears by the annexed obligation and
"which $63 is in full discharge of said obligation."

"ELISHA GOLAY *agent for S. C.*"

Among the early settlers in the lower end of the county were George Craig, Stuman Craig, Joshua Cain Robert McKay, James McKay Abisha McKay and George Ash.

In 1805 or 1806 the residents in that part of the county built a block house in which to shelter the women and children, on an alarm being given of the approach of Indians. George Craig himself resided on the opposite side of the river but had occasion to come to this side, and had frequently sheltered in this block house—he finally purchased a large tract of land on which he located cleared the land and planted a large orchard. He was asked why he planted such a large orchard, his reply was "That my grand children may have plenty of apples to eat."[3]

Charles Muret the father of Julius Muret, Mrs. Mary McCormick widow of John McCormick, John L. Muret (Decd) Benjamin Muret, was the only physician in the colony for many years before 1813.[1] Although he was the only physician he had not much practice, for there was little sickness, and the citizens did not send for a physician for every little illness, cholic or such diseases as those of the present day are in the habit of doing. Doctor Muret went on a flat boat to New Orleans and there he became fireman in a steam mill to raise means to pay his passage to Europe—he sailed for Europe landed at Havre where he had an uncle who was a banker. After landing he made his way to the office of his uncle, having reached the office he enquired of a "domestique" if Mr. ———— his uncle was in the office. The "domestique" eyed the Doctor from head to foot asked in a haughty manner what he wanted    the Doctor replied "I wish to see and speak to him"    the "domestique" inquired what business he had with the Banker. The Doctors only reply was "I wish to see him.  I must and will see him" and instantly forcing his way into the office although the domestique used every effort to prevent his entering—entering the private room of the Banker with his clothing and appearance not in the best condition—he made himself known to his uncle who gave the Doctor an order on a clothier for a suit of clothes, after he was decently dressed with cane in hand he returned to his uncles office, where meeting the "domestique" he addressed him "You Scoundrel and puppy why did you insult me this morning"    The "domestique" asked his pardon and appeared sorry.  The doctor said to him in a haughty and angry tone "You Scoundrel and puppy I will learn you how to insult gentlemen hereafter.  Do you know who you treated so shamefully this morning, I will let you know that I have been "fireman" in America" whereupon the "domestique" bowed, Scraped, and asked a thousand pardons, supposing that he had insulted an American officer of a high rank.

# HISTORY OF SWITZERLAND COUNTY 55

In 1810 or 1811 during the canvass for the election of a Delegate to Congress from Indiana Territory the slavery question was agitated to some extent, Jonathan Jennings being the anti-Slavery candidate and was opposed by John Lawrence. Jennings was elected and became a very prominent opponent to the admission of slavery in Indiana when it should become a state. At one time John Francis Dufour being at Lexington Ky. called on Henry Clay[1] during his conversation with Mr. Clay he enquired of him what he thought of the young delegate from Indiana Territory. Mr. Clay replied that he was a promising young man but thought he was wrong in his opposition to admitting slavery into the State which was to [be] formed of Indiana Territory.

Mr. Jennings continued ste[a]dfast in his opposition to making Indiana a Slave State, and lived to be the president of the convention which framed the first constitution of Indiana, was elected the first governor of the State and was several times elected to congress.[2]

In the fall of 1815 William C. Keen came to Vevay he was a practical printer—had a printing press and materials at Hamilton Ohio, which were all boxed up ready to be shipped but some one had a mortgage on it for something near $200 which he was unable to pay—he called on John Francis Dufour and represented how matters about his press, stood. Mr. Dufour went to Hamilton paid off the mortgage on the press and materials, brought it to Vevay and sometime early in 1816 a paper called the *Indiana Register* was commenced and carried until about Decr 1817[3] by John Francis Dufour William C. Keen and Robert Burchfield under the firm name of Dufour Keen and Co. at which time the partnership was dissolved by mutual consent. On the dissolution of that partnership John Francis Dufour became sole proprietor and editor and Robert Burchfield whose services Mr. Dufour Secured was the printer. The publication of the *Indiana Register* was continued by Mr.

Dufour and Burchfield until sometime in 1819 or 1820 when John Douglass came to Vevay took charge of the office and published the paper for a year or two—when Mr. Douglass removed to Corydon Ind. and thence to Indianapolis where he established the *Indiana State Journal.*

William C. Keen again commenced the publication of the *Register*,[1] and continued its publication until 1826 when Thomas Berryman and John Allen came to Vevay and took charge of the office and published the paper, for two years or more. John Allen left (leaving Berryman still at Vevay) located in Salem in 1831 or 1832[2] where he published the *Annotator* until his death by cholera in 1833.[3] Berryman continued in Vevay untill about 1831 or 1832 during this interval Keen removed to Printers retreat[4] taking the printing establishment with him and there publishing in partnership with one Child the *Weekly Messenger* which was continued until about 1836, when Child removed to Warsaw Ky[5] with the press and material. In 1832 Richard Randall commenced the publication of the *Monitor* which was continued for three or four years[6]—when Randall took his press and materials to Madison or Vernon.

Switzerland County could not now boast of having a paper published within her limits.

Soon after the presidential election of 1836 Isaac Stevens[7] came to Vevay and commenced the publication of the *Village Times*[8] which he continued to publish until about the time of the Canvass of 1840 being opened. Edward Patton sold the printing press and types to W[ilson] H. Gray with the understanding that he was to publish a Democratic paper, but he changed his politics and became a Whig and was about changing the paper to a Whig paper. Patton however interfered and took the press from Gray and the paper was conducted by the Democratic Central Committee during the summer and fall of 1840.[9] The Whigs procured a new press and type and Gray published the *Indiana Statesman*

## HISTORY OF SWITZERLAND COUNTY 57

during the campaign and until sometime in 1842 when the publication of the *Statesman* was entirely suspended and the press and type disposed of. In 1841 James G. Fanning came to Vevay and published the *Spirit of the Times* which was continued until 1843. Isaac Stevens then took charge of the press he had brought here and in connection with Benjamin L. Sinimons [Simmons] published the *Indiana Palladium* for two or three years—when they disposed of the establishment to Chas. S. Horton, brother in law of J. C. and Walter H. Wells, who published the *Ohio Valley Gazette* for two years or more—when Horton sold out to Otis S. and Frederick J. Waldo who continued the publication of a Democratic paper a short time—then the paper became neutral in politics and finally in 1853 or 1854 it became a Know-nothing organ.

In the fall of 1855 Charles Scott came to Vevay and commenced the publication of the *News*[1]   he sold out to P. H. Hale a young Vermont Lawyer who soon failed and the press and material went into the possession of B. F. Schenck who in connection with Merrit W. Tague continued the publication of the *News* for a year or two when the establishment was disposed of by B. F. Schenck to F. J. Waldo of the *Revielle* and the two were united and under the control of F. J. Waldo—which is in part the present establishment of the *Revielle* office of the present day and now conducted by Wm. J. Baird.

In 1869 Thomas T. [D] Wright came to Vevay with printing press and material and commenced the publication of the *Vevay Democrat* until the fall of 1874 when he disposed of the office to Irvin Armstrong, who has just commenced the second year of his control of the *Democrat* office.[2] This gives as full a history of the printing business in Switzerland County as can be brought to my mind at present.

In 1824 the list of lands and town lots returned delinquent for non payment of Taxes in Dearborn County was published in the *Indiana Register* published in Vevay a copy of which is now in the possession of Perret Dufour in Vevay.

On the second Monday in May 1816 delegates from the several Counties of the Territory were elected to meet in convention to form a Constitution for the state—the candidates in this County were William Cotton and John Dumont. William Cotton was elected. The convention met at Corydon on the second Monday in June and on the 29th day of June the convention having completed their labors the Constitution was signed by the delegates—that constitution was adopted by the people, and was in force until the adoption of the present constitution in 1851.

The first election under the Constitution for the election of officers of State, and County officers was held on the 3rd day of February 1817. A Governor and Lieutenant Governor were elected at that election—the county officer[s] of Switzerland County elected at that election were for Clerk John Francis Dufour— for associate Judges William Cotton & James McClure Sheriff John Francis Siebenthal—Coronor Frederick Waldo—County Commissioners James Rous, Caleb Mounts and Isaac Stanley.

On the 17[th] March 1817 the first term of the Circuit Court was held in the County, John Test the presiding Judge and William Cotton and James McClure associate Judges on the Bench.[1] At this term of the court—James Dill, Hezekiah B. Hull, Miles C. Eggleston, John Lawrence, Samuel Merrell, Reuben Kidder, Stephen C. Stevens, Alexander A. Meek, Amos Lane, Joseph F. Farley were admitted ex gratia to practice law at this court.[2]

Stephen C. Stevens was appointed prosecuting attorney during the term of the Court.

On the fourth day of the term the following order was made by the Court "The court now continues the appointment of Stephen C. Stevens Esqr. as prosecuting

# HISTORY OF SWITZERLAND COUNTY 59

attorney for the county of Switzerland for and during good behavior.

The prosecuting attorney was allowed $40 for his services during the term—the associate Judges $10 each and the Bailiffs George Wade, Newton H. Tapp and Frederick Waldo $5 each.

The county Commissioners held their first meeting on the 10th day of February 1817 at the Courthouse in Vevay the day fixed by law for their first meeting in the several counties of the State.[1]

The business transacted at that Session of the Board of Commissioners was the dividing [of] the county into five Township[s]—Posey, Cotton, Ross, Craig and Jefferson,[2] ordering that an election be held in the several Township[s] of the County on Saturday the 22nd day of February 1817 for the purpose of electing Justices of the peace. Posey to elect two, Cotton one, Ross one, Craig two, Jefferson Two. The Board ordered that on Saturday the first day of March 1817 an election be held at the Court house in Vevay to elect two additional Justices of the peace who should reside at the County Seat.

The Board appointed the place of holding elections in the Several Townships in Posey at the house of Elizabeth Searcy—in Cotton at the house of Lot Hammond in Allensville—in Ross, at the house of William Ross—in Craig at the house of Daniel Bray—in Jefferson at the Court house in Vevay. The Board also appointed inspectors of Elections, in Posey, Williams Pierson—in Cotton Joseph Pugh in Ross, James Wilson—in Craig George Craig—in Jefferson Lawrence Nihell.[3]

The Board of Commissioners met again on the 12th May 1817. They appointed constables for the several Townships for Posey Township George Wade and Martin Adkins—for Jefferson Township Newton H. Tapp, James Dugan and Frederick Waldo—for Ross Township Larkin Cook—for Craig Township Abram Vandusen.

They appointed Listers of taxable property, as follows for Posey, George Wade, For Jefferson Joseph Noble, for Cotton George Bennet, for Ross Larkin Cook and for Craig John Wright.[1]

The Second term of the circuit court was begun and held on the 16th June 1817.[2] The October term 1817 was held by the associate Judges alone no presiding Judge appearing. The April Term 1818 the Judge did not appear until the Second day.[3]

At the July term—1818 Stephen C. Stevens resigned his office of Prosecuting attorney and Hezekiah B. Hull was appointed in his stead.

At the March term 1819 John Watts the father of Col Johnson Watts was on the Bench as president Judge having been appointed by the governor to fill a vacancy occasioned by the resignation of the former Judge.[4]

At the February term 1820 no president Judge appeared and the two associates Abner Clarkson and Ralph Cotton held the court.[5]

At the May term 1820 Miles C. Eggleston first set on the bench as president Judge which position he held for so many years.

It is not certainly known what the population of the county was in 1820 for the reason that the person appointed to take the census of that year was taken sick and never completed the enumeration and what he had done was not done very accurately. The assessor of the county appointed to take an enumeration of the free white males above the age of 21 years returned 1,122 which multiplied by five, the average estimated proportion of the whole to the free white males of 21 years of age and upwards, amounts to 5,610, so it may be safely said that the population of the County amounted to that number.

Vevay in 1820 contained upwards of 100, log brick and frame dwelling houses (the log outnumbering both brick and frame nearly two to one) a brick Courthouse, a stone Jail, a brick market house, a printing office, post

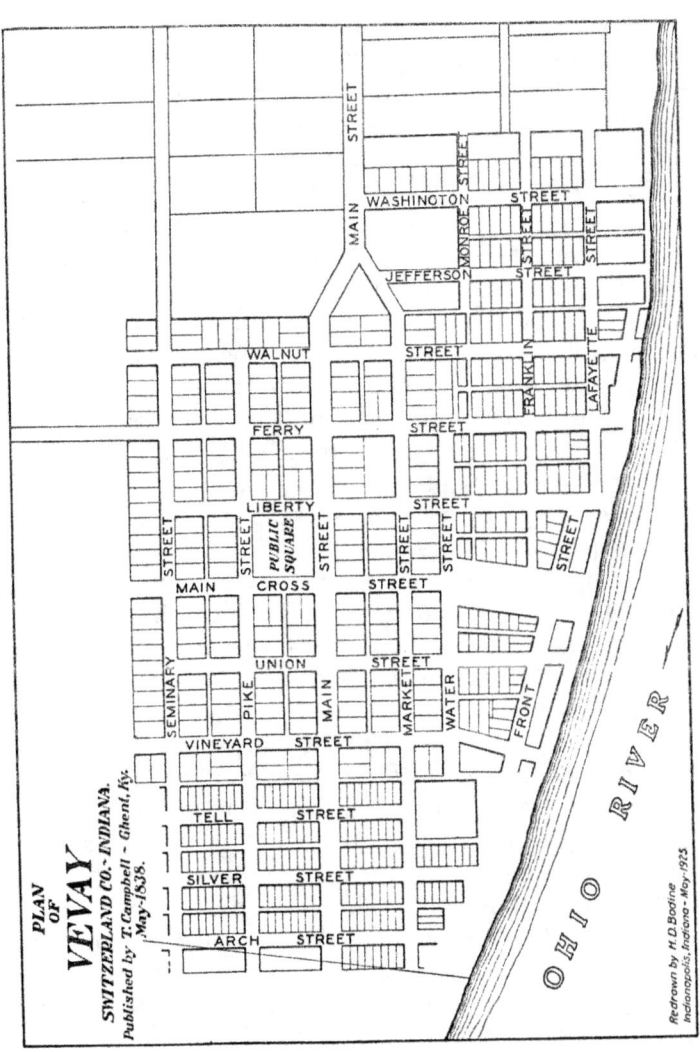

office an ox saw mill, two horse grist mills, Three taverns, or Hotels—a seminary of learning, a circulating Library, a branch of the State Bank of Indiana, Three black smith shops and two Free Mason Lodges, but no meeting house or church although there was much talk of the Methodists and the presbyterians building each a place for public worship. The population of Vevay was then about 600 and the influx of strangers was so great that many small houses contained two or three families—in the summer of that year it became very sickly and as a natural consequence owing to the crowded condition of the inhabitants, many died of the prevailing billious fever, which was of a very malignant form. Many corpses after laying for a few hours became very yellow which caused many persons to pronounce it "Yellow fever". More than one sixth of the population [died] during that summer and fall and Vevay for many years afterwards was considered abroad a very sickly place and was shunned by persons seeking a western town in which to locate. The sickness that prevailed in Vevay that Summer was not confined to Vevay alone for nearly the whole western country was visited by the prevailing fever. It was several years before the prejudice against the place for being a sickly place was removed from the minds of Strangers.

For several years¹ the products of the farm were very low as compared with prices of the present day for instance eggs which now sell readily for from 10 to 25 cents per dozen, sold for 1 to 1½ cents per dozen —butter which now sells for 25 cents per pound, sold for 6¼ cents per pound—Chickens which now command from two to three dollars per dozen, sold for from 37½ to 50 cents per dozen—Pork which now sells at from 7 to 8 dollars per hundred pounds, sold for from $1.25 to $2.00 per 100 pounds—corn then sold at from 12½ to 18¾ cents per bushel—Wheat 31¼ to 37½ cents per bushel    potatoes from 6¼ to 12½ cents per bushel, and remember that at these prices the merchant buying

# HISTORY OF SWITZERLAND COUNTY 63

paid for the articles of produce purchased in good[s] out of his store. In the spring good country cured bacon hams could be purchased at from 2 to 2½ cents per pound.

In 1818 a farmer living a few miles back from Vevay brought 1000 pounds of pork to town, being offered only $1.25 per hundred in good[s] refused to take that price took it to Louisville where he realized $1.75 per hundred and was three days and two nights in returning up the river against the current.

As early as the fall of 1817 a sabbath school was commenced in Vevay by Mrs. Clarkson wife of Abner Clarkson and Miss Hester Welsh, (daughter of Dr. & Rev. James Welsh a Presbyterian minister) in the court house and was continued during the summer for several years Samuel Merril some two years after it was commenced gave it his support and he became the superintendant.

From about 1814 till 1818 there was preaching frequently, by a Mr. Vawter, Mordecai Jackson, John Graham and others of the Baptist persuasion—and by Allen Wiley of the Methodist persuasion, and Occasionally a Presbyterian minister would be travelling, stop at Vevay and would preach a sermon or two. Daniel Dufour from the time of his first coming to the Colony in 1804 untill as late as 1817 was in the habit of reading a sermon to the colonists every Sunday. Perhaps, the Presbyterians were first [to] organize a church in Vevay—For from 1814 until about 1827 there was no organized church in Vevay or its immediate Vicinity on this side of the Ohio river—but as stated above there was frequently preaching by Baptist and Methodist ministers or local preachers up to about 1818 or 1819 when Dr. James Welsh a Presbyterian minister began preaching weekly on Sabbaths in the Court house and although there was no regularly organized Presbyterian church, he continued to preach until his suspension from the ministry by the Presbyt[e]ry of Cincinnati about the year 1825 (perhaps it was Oxford Presbyt[e]ry). In 1824 a Presbyt[e]ry was formed in Indiana comprizing seven ministers, thirty one organized churches, and a missionary society, and comprized the whole of the state west of a line drawn due north from the mouth of the Kentucky river.

On the 28th of January 1828 a meeting of those persons friendly to the Presbyterian Church was held in Vevay for the purpose of electing ruling elders of the church to be formed in this place. Rev. Ludwell G. Gaines acted as moderator by order of the Presbyt[e]ry of Cincinnati. Edward Patton was clerk of the meeting —Israel R. Whitehead and James G. French were chosen to receive and count the votes—William French, Morgan Patton, and David Walker formerly a ruling elder in the church at Log Lick were elected.

David Walker was the father of Judge Charles E. Walker of Madison Ind.

The church thus organized during the winter and spring of 1828 raised by voluntary subscription about $270, in sums of from $1 to $30, and had donated to them by Daniel Vincent Dufour only son of John James Dufour, the lot on which the present Presbyterian church now stands—and during the summer and fall of that year, had, erected a brick church edifice but so badly built that it became very much delapidated. In that building they worshiped until about 1837 or 1838 when the church having been reduced by the removal of members to other parts of the country became nearly extinct. The buil[d]ing became so delapidated that it was not considered safe to occupy it, but it was given over to a flock of sheep that ran about the commons—these sheep going in it during the heat of the day for shelter.

During this period of time the Church enjoyed the ministerial services of Revd L[udwell] G. Gaines, Joshua L Wilson R[obert] B. Dobbins J. Thompson ———
Thomas, Peter Munfort John Morral, William Lewis

## HISTORY OF SWITZERLAND COUNTY

Henry Little, William J Montieth, James Hummer and George B. Bishop.

In 1842 Revd L. R. Booth of Allensville came and preached one third of his time under favorable circumstances in the Baptist Church in Vevay.

In May 1842 with the assistance of J[ohn] M. Dicky of New Washington a Presbyterian church was reorganized. Horatio Waldo Ann Waldo William Norrisez Mary Norrisez and Alexander Edger being received on certificate—Martha B. Mendenhall, Amity McMillen, Nancy Gilbert and Elizabeth Hamilton being received on evidence of their regular standing as church members, Lewis Munson, Rebecca Munson, Mehetabel Waldo, Hannah Davis and Mary Ann Gray being received on examination, were at their own request constituted a Church of Christ.

At a meeting of the members of the church held on the 20th day of August 1842 at that meeting it was resolved "that the meeting house and lot belonging to the Presbyterian church at Vevay shall hereafter belong exclusively to that Branch of the Presbyterian church known by the name of the New School."

At that meeting three Trustees were elected, and they were directed to have the Meeting house repaired so soon as means could be procured. Rev L. R. Booth continued to preach for the church until in 1844 when the old church had been taken down and rebuilt, when the Rev. Hiram Wason who had been laboring with the people as Minister was in January 1845 ordained and continued to supply the pulpit of that church untill 1857 when [he] removed to Lake County Indiana. Since Mr. Wason left the church has been supplied with the labors of Revd A. C. Hovey, A. S. Ried, E. C. Haskell, Henry P. Higby, L. R. Booth, M. D. A. Stein, and Thomas Whalon who is still supplying the pulpit of the church.[1]

The foregoing in relation to the Presbyterian church of Vevay is in the main correct for they are statements made after examining the records of the church. In the

66    INDIANA HISTORICAL COLLECTIONS

"Religious Intelligence" column of the *Cincinnati Gazette* of the 3rd July 1869 is the following—

"The Rev. R. Hammond was the first Methodist minister who preached in the State of Indiana. This was in the year 1819 under a walnut tree near where the state house now stands."[1]

This statement although it may be true does not therefore show that Mr. Hammond was the first Methodist minister who preached in Indiana—for the Revd Allen Wiley preached in Switzerland County as early as 1814 and it is certain that he preached a funeral sermon in Vevay in 1816 and Abner Clarkson who was residing in Madison Ind from 1813 to 1816 heard Mr. Wiley preach in Madison during that time. There was no regularly organized Methodist church in Vevay until about 1823 or 1825. In 1837[2] The Methodists built a Brick church on the lot on which the present "Ruter Chapel" stands previous to which time their meetings were held in the Court house, the School houses, and the Old Presbyterian church. The Revds. Mr. [John] Strange, Allen Wiley, [Joseph] Tarkington, [Martin] Ruter—Enoch G. Wood James Jones and H. J. Durbin are among the preachers who were on Vevay Circuit and as presiding Elders whom the writer can now recollect.

The Baptists held their meetings for many years in the school houses of the town, but more frequently in a log house which stood near where Ulysses P. Schencks ice house now stands—in that house the writer frequently heard Rev. John Graham preach. Mordecai Jackson father of Ibzan Jackson of Posey Township Henry D. Banta frequently preached in that house and occasionally Mr. Clark the father of Lewis A. Clark preached in that house. Mr. Clark was blind and had been from his youth—after being introduced to a person and conversing with him a short time—he would recollect that person and call him by name so soon as he heard his voice a long while, yes two or three years after his first conversation with him—he had a son (Orange Clark) living in Mississippi whom he visited occasionally, travelling all the way by land having a small boy to accompany him as guide. Once in Vevay the writer enquired of him "Where are you going" He replied "to see my son in Mississippi".

At a meeting of the Baptist Church of Christ held in Vevay Switzerland Co Ind on the 29th day of December 1832 the following persons united themselves for the purpose of forming an arm of the Regular Baptist Church. John R. Cotton, Benoit Courvoissier, Thomas Morris Augustine Courvoisier, Frederick L. Thiebaud, Henriette Thiebaud, Caroline E. Thiebaud, Lucy Dalmazzo, Lydia Kirtley, William Price and Mordecai McKenzie—at which meeting Rev. John Wilson, was called to the chair and Rev. John R. Cotton appointed Secretary. It was resolved that the first Saturday and Sunday in February 1833 be the time for organizing this church and the sister Churches of Indian Creek, Mount Pleasant, Jefferson Bethel and Long Run be solicited to aid and assist in organizing this Church. It was also resolved, that this church be called the "Switzerland Baptist Church. After the church was organized and were soliciting subscriptions to aid in the building of the house of Worship, the Committee called on John Francis Dufour, who subscribed and gave a bond for a deed for the South East half of lot No. 71 on the original plat of the in lots of Vevay, which bond was executed to Henry D. Banta, William Price and Mordecai McKenzie, Trustees of the "Swi[t]zerland Baptist Church" provided a Brick meeting house was built on the same within 18 months, not less than 30 feet wide by 40 feet long and 13 feet high between the floor and ceiling. The house was built and completed and was the one occupied by the Baptists untill their new church edifice was finished and they removed to it. Some two or three years after the completion of the building it was represented to John Francis Dufour by the trustees that the bond was lost, but wished him to make the deed which he did, but as the trustees were "Anti Missionary" they insisted on having the deed made to the "Regular Anti Missionary Church". The Church thus organized and in the Church edifice thus erected the Baptist congregation of Vevay continued to Worship until perhaps in 1873, when they removed to and occupied their imposing edifice on the South corner of Main Cross and Pike streets. They have had as ministers who statedly preached in the Church in Vevay Revd. John Wilson, John R. Cotton, Henry D. Banta, Mr. [F. S.] Riley, Mr. [F. D.] Bland, Mr. Brand and others whose names the writer does not now recollect and for the last three or four years, the Revd T. Warren Beagle.

Among the early revivals of religion in this neighborhood may be named one which Commenced in Craig Township under the preaching of Revd Henry D. Banta and John Graham. They had preaching in several neighborhoods in that Township, frequently at the house of Mr. Thiebaud being on the same farm where Justin Thiebaud now resides—and these person[s] who were to receive the ordinance of Baptism, were to meet at Mr. Thiebauds on the bank of the Ohio river there to be baptized "as there was much water there." An incident may be very appropriately related here, to show the depravity of the human heart, when not under the influence of that Gospel which proclaims "On earth peace good will to man". At a time when several persons were to receive baptism, and the minister was wading out to ascertain the depth of water, and condition of the bottom, a person standing by siezed a good sized dog by the neck and threw it into the water near the minister exclaiming "There is one of your congregation baptized."

Daniel Dufour frequently had his Swiss neighbors, brothers Sisters, brothers in law and those who understood the French language to meet on Sunday when Psalms were sung, and he would read a prayer—and then read a sermon.[1] This was continued for many

## HISTORY OF SWITZERLAND COUNTY 69

years. One Sabbath he had read a very impressive and affecting sermon which caused nearly all his hearers and himself to shed tears. He was relating the circumstance to several among whom was Joseph Malin. Malin said to him did you cry—He replied "Yes the sermon was so affecting I be damn[ed] if you had heard it you would have cry[ed] too."

There have been some very extensive revivals of religion in the County more particularly among the Methodist[s] during their Camp Meetings and in 1840 at the Methodist church in this place when upward of 150 were received into the Church on probation during a meeting which lasted for about two weeks.

In early days perhaps in 1826 the Universalists had preaching in Vevay very often. James Kirby (the grandfather of Samuel E and James K. Pleasants) had been attending a meeting that was in progress and prevailed on Abner Clarkson to attend one evening. On their way home after the Sermon Mr. Kirby remarked to Mr. Clarkson "That's the right doctrine". A few days after Mr. Kirby and Mr. Clarkson were together talking & during their conversation Kirby remarked "Well Clark-"son the doctrine we heard preached the other night will "do very well to live by, but on ref[l]ecting about it I "don't believe it will do to die by."  This Mr. Kirby about 1817 was the owner of a Steam Boat called "Vesta." It is said that on one dark night when a[s]cending the river, near to or above the mouth of Big Bone creek, Mr. Kirby who was captain saw something ahead which he took to be a boat and called out "Show your light". No light being shown or answer returned, the pilot was directed "to go ahead", when the "Vesta" struck a large rock which for many years was known and named "Kirby Rock". The "Vesta" sunk.

In 1811 or 1812 a person by the name of J. F. Buchetee came into New Switzerland and taught School for awhile

He was a scholar and proficient in the Languages. He composed an ode in Latin entitled the "Empire of Bacchus" which was translated by Wm. Priestly. The translation is as follows.

"Empire of Bacchus"

Translated from the Latin of J. F. B.
By W. P.

"Columbia rejoice! smiling Bacchus has heard
    Your prayers of so fervent a tone
And crown'd with the grape, has kindly appear'd
    In your land to establish his throne.
This God from Lemand to dull care a foe
    Will clothe each rich hill with the vine
And charm'd with the prospect, each bosom shall glow
When warm'd with the heart cheering wine.

Let others extol as they quaff from the bowl
    Of the Juices Pomana has sent;
Be they brandy or rum which unnerve the soul
    Or whiskey, the bane of content.
Let us worn with hardships, the vinedressing Swiss
    Who toil the rich cluster to rear,
Reap the fruit of past labor, and riot in bliss,
While we drown in sweet wine every care.

Let those who beheld us with aspect malign,
    And denied their assistance of yore
Be debarr'd e'en a drop of the care soothing wine
    And drink water[1] evermore.
But you who have so nobly tender'd your aid
    To us, to your country a friend,
Approach the gay board—the full bowl is displayed
Drain the Goblet—each sorrow unbend.

Wine, precious cordial, dispels gloomy cares;
    Itself is an ocean of wealth.
The Vigor of body and mind it repairs,
    And pale sickness it changes to health.
O, Friends! Let us drown former cares in the cup
    As the mirth making nectar we drain;
Let us toast ruddy Bacchus at each cheering sup;
A carol with joy the sweet strain.

Blest God, who the soul with fresh Spirit inspires,
   And the mind from dull sorrow sets free,
Who fans in the bosom Loves ec[s]tatic fires,
   Full casks we would offer to thee.
Great King of the Goblet! Let each fertile hill.
   Delight you, with rich vintage crown'd
O! Cherish the vine and the nectar distill
Till each cellar with nectar abound

Subdue for the vine the chill breezes that blow,
   And screen it from Sol's parching power
And shield the ripe clusters that temptingly glow
   From Autumn's moist ruinous show'r.
Should the frost and the heat and chill rains be remote,
   The vine its red bunches will rear;
And each happy soul in the blest Juice may float
And quaff nectar'd sweets all the year.

Hail, Bettens and Morerod! Blest be each name!
   Sons of Bacchus your names shall endure
And Siebenthal shall flourish immortal in fame
   And you too vine-rearing Dufour.
Columbia will give to true merit its meed
   Future ages will laud you on high,
And Libra and Scapio[1] will gladly recede
To yield you a seat in the sky.

Redouble your plaudits, blest friends of the glass
   For a treasure more precious than gold.
We present in the wines which in flavor surpass
   The Falernian so boasted of old,
Columbia majestic, in War's garb array'd
   Pray the Gods still to prosper the vine
Give thanks to the Swiss, and O! lend them your aid
Who have toil'd to present you with wine.

It is believed that this is perhaps only the second time the above poem has been made public. If any of the votaries of Bacchus shall read it, the mission its author designed for it will have been performed.[2]

In 1818[3] the Legislature of Indiana passed an act chartering the "Jeffersonville Ohio Canal Company" which had for its object the construction of a Canal around the falls of the Ohio river on the Indiana side. The Company was organized, a Board of Directors elected and James Scott selected as President. This company was authorized by an act passed by the legislature to raise funds to construct the canal by means of a lottery. Agents were appointed to receive subscriptions of stock. John Francis Dufour was appointed agent of the Company at Vevay[1] and William Cotton and John Gilliland assistants.

On the 12th of Decr 1818 Mr. Dufour received the following letter of instructions

"SIR. The Board of directors of J. O. C Co. have made "the following regulation for the purpose of facilitating "the sale of Lottery tickets: Ordered that any agent for "selling tickets may sell to any person, who may purchase "ten tickets or more, on a credit taking a negotiable note "payable in some good Bank provided said Bank will re-"ceive said note and pass the amount to the credit of the "Jeffersonville Ohio Canal Company, with assurance that "the money will not be drawn from said bank until the "drawing of the lottery shall be completed."

"J. BIGELOW *President pro. Tem.*"[2]

Signed

"H WEBSTER *Secty.*"

This regulation, succeeded to the entire satisfaction of the Directors.[3]

On the 10th of April 1818 the president by letter informed Mr. Dufour that the drawing of the Lottery had commenced. A Statement of the drawing on the 15th of April 1818 showed that ticket No. 5,816 drew a prize [of] $500    No. 1,638 $100; No. 10,118 $50 and 32 other tickets drew each a prize of $5, and 65 other tickets drew each a Blank.

In transmitting this statement Mr. Bigelow wrote Mr. Dufour the following

# HISTORY OF SWITZERLAND COUNTY

"DEAR SIR,
"I enclose you $15 to purchase some Vevay wine, that "which is unmixed, by any kind of preparation would be "preferred. . . . On the first Monday of next month, "we commence the canal and I would be glad to have a "little wine of domestic manufactury to drink on the "occasion."

On the first Monday of May 1818 the canal was commenced, on which occasion, there was no doubt much eating drinking and speaking done, but to little effect so far as the making of the canal was concerned. A few rods were dug a few feet deep and the enterprize came to a dead stop.

On the 30th of January 1818 the Literary Society of Vevay held a meeting at the office of Samuel Merrill when the following Question was proposed and discussed
"Would it be policy in our Government to form an alliance with the Patriots of Mexico and South America"

About the year 1817 the settlement in Pleasant Township known as the "Dutch" settlement began to be formed. Cornelius A Voris, the Carnines, Demarees, Vandevers and Harmons, and others of those old settlers came from Kentucky principally, and in a few years that part of the County commenced increasing in population quite rapidly. It was but a few years after until the farmers from that locality began to supply the citizens of Vevay with, butter, eggs and chickens during the summer and pork venison, oats wheat, flax & in the fall, and winter. They soon organized a church, and built a log meeting house near the Cross roads near David Henrys, which has since been replaced with a neat and comfortable frame building. It is of the Presbyterian Church.

On the west side of Pleasant Township and in the South west corner of the Township, a number of Scotch families settled as early as 1817 1818 and 1820 and their numbers were increased from time to time by accessions until quite a large settlement of these industrious and worthy people was made and extends over into Jefferson county. Among the number now recollected were the four Brothers, William, James, John and Samuel Culbertson the Mortons, Glenns, Makensies, Scotts and many others whose names are not recollected.[1]

About the same period a number of Scotch families commenced a settlement on Long Run, among whom were Niel McCallum, Duncan McCallum, John McCallum, Donald Cowan, the Malcomsons John Anderson and perhaps one or two other families not now recollected. They were what are known as "Seven[th] day Baptists". It was rather novel to the citizens, to travel up "Long Run" on a Saturday and see none of those people stirring about—and passing on Sunday to see every one able to do any work out in the clearing chopping piling and burning brush and rolling logs.

Philip and John Romeril[2] settled on Long Run above these Scotch families. During the absence of the family, except a sister, some demon in human shape passing by, with deadly aim shot the sister dead. When the other members of the family returned they found her lying cold, in death. Suspicion was fixed on a person named Long but no proof of his guilt could be brought against him and he was set at Liberty.

The Detraz family came to Vevay in 1816 or 1817. They had not been here long, until the old gentleman while bathing in the river was drowned. His body was found at Madison, an inquest was held by Abner Clarkson (now of Vevay) who being Justice of the peace acted as coroner. The remains were inter[r]ed at Madison. The family left consisted of his widow (second wife) three sons by a former marriage, John, Benjamin and Francis and two sons by the last marriage Abraham and Louis, the latter now residing on the land that had been entered as a home for the father and his wife and two younger sons. About this period[3] Fred-

## HISTORY OF SWITZERLAND COUNTY    75

erick L. Grisard (father of the Frederick L. Grisard of our day), and his brotherinlaw Belrichard came to Vevay settled below Indian Creek—on the land owned by Leclerc and part by William Tilly where Mr. Grisard carried on his occupation of Black smith for some years[1] when he sold his land and came to Vevay and bought lots where R. F. Grisard now resides. Mr. Belrichard was a shoe maker, carried on the business for a few years when he removed to Louisville, died and left a son and daughter.

About this period a Swiss named James Bolens came to Vevay bringing with him George Tandy and two or three other young men who were not able to pay their passage, Bolens paying their passage—which they repaid with interest in a year or two.[2] The Pernet family came about the same time and settled at Mount Sterling where they remained some time. The old gentleman became deranged and hanged himself. His son John sold out and went to Covington.[3] David Emanuel his other son remained in Mount Sterling many years[4] kept a house of entertainment where Ralph Cotton resides—removed to Bethlehem in Clark County where he died.

The Thiebaud family came to the county about the year 1817, and settled on the farm on which Justin Thiebaud now resides. If ever a family could be said to be industrious the Thiebauds as a family could be so called. The old lady was an extraordinary woman in many respects, she was a loving wife, kind an[d] indulgent mother, a good neighbor, a valued citizen and a pious Christian—and one whose example if followed by all would lead to prosperity and happiness. There were two sons Charles Thiebaud who lived in Vevay many years and died about 1872—and Justin who lives below Indian Creek—on the farm on which the parents lived and died. There were five daughter[s]. One married Mr. Bachman of Madison Ind. One married David E. Pernet—one married Benoit Courvoissier and was the mother of Frederick L. Courvoissier late a county treasurer of this county One married Thomas A. Haskell and now lives in Craig Township—one married Ulysses P. Schenck the successful merchant and Produce dealer of Vevay. About this period John James Philip Schenck his wife and son Ulysses P. then a lad of about 10 years old came to the country and settled on a farm on the hill back of the Thiebaud farm. He was a tinner, and as there was no tinner in Vevay Mr. Schenck did all the mending of tin ware and making new, at his home coming to town once or twice each week a[nd] taking home with him all the tin ware needing to be mended that he had collected together in Town, and returning it repaired when he next came to town. This he continued to do for some time when he removed to Shippingport, Ky and continued in business there during the constructing of the canal, at which he made a good sum of money[1] with which he purchased the farm on which he resided for many years. His son Ulysses P. commenced business at Louisville and there carried on business untill about 1837 when he purchased the lot on which his present business house stands, and has continued in business ever since. His successful career as a merchant and produce dealer is known to most of the farmers of Switzerland County.[2]

Frederick L. Grisard one of our successful mechanics came to the United States with his father and mother in 1818 when about 10 years of age. In 1824 he placed himself under the instruction of a Mr. Osserlee of Cincinnati to learn the profession of Blacksmith. In 1827 he commenced business in Vevay with success, and gained the reputation of being the best workman of the kind for many miles round about Vevay.[3]

Joseph Malin came to Vevay in 1816[4] and commenced the saddling business which he continued to carry on until about 1833 or 1834. When he first came to Vevay he opened his shop in one room of the building now occupied by Robert A Knox.[5]

Abner Clarkson came to Vevay in the fall of 1817 opened a store and commenced selling goods in one room

# HISTORY OF SWITZERLAND COUNTY 77

of the house in which Joseph Malin had his saddlers shop.

In 1816 or thereabout a man by the name of Smith came to the county—settled near the place now known as Quercus Grove, where he commenced taking the Oak bark grinding it, and packing it into hogsheads or casks. The bark thus prepared he shipped on flatboats to New Orleans and thence to England, for coloring cloths and yarns. He succeeded in getting a quantity sufficient to load one or two flatboats which he sent to New Orleans in charge of Edward Patton, as super cargo. Whether Patton went with these cargoes to England or not is not known to the writer. This man Smith had the cognomen of "Rarified Smith" applied to him, on account perhaps of some theory advanced by him of using rarified air for the purpose of propelling machinery instead of steam. It is thought Smith left the "Bark Works" about 1821 or 1822 for he had left before Martin R. Green came there in 1823.

In the early days of the settlement about Vevay and perhaps untill 1825 or 1826 it was customary for families to have the Shoes and Clothing for the family made up at the house. In order to have this done the Cloth needed, the calf skins, kip skins and upper and sole leather was procured—the Shoemaker hired at from 8 to 10 dollars per week to come to the house and cut and make two or three pairs of shoes for each member of the family. The tailor was in like manner hired at from 8 to 10 dollars per week to cut and make such coats vests and pants as were needed by the male members of the family. In this manner well does the writer remember when in the fall of the year his father would bring home the leather and cloth and inform his wife that the tailor and shoemaker would come next week.

About the close of the war of 1812 small change was very scarce, and it was difficult to make change in the transaction of business. To obviate this difficulty in a measure resort was had to cutting the silver coins in halves quarters and Eighths. Often to make the most of the silver, one dollar was cut so as to make nine instead of Eight pieces, a half dollar often cut in two halves, or four quarters. In handling much of this cut money persons were liable to have their pockets worn out in a short time consequently sometimes an odd "nine pence" would be lost. The writer well recollects when his father was postmaster that a notice "no cut money taken for postage" was to be seen in a conspicuous place in the Post office. Some of the business men of the town issued tickets of 6¼-12½-18¾-25 and 50 cents, which were received by all in business in change. These tickets were redeemed when, three or five dollars were presented, in current bank notes. Lucien Gex, Rawleigh Day, John Francis Dufour and two or three others and the Corporation of Vevay issued such tickets which passed currently.[1]

At the time the Stone Jail was built the county commissioners at the request of the Contractors, with a view of having Small change issued County orders for 6¼-12½-25 and 50 cents in part pay to the contractors, for building the Jail. The Contractors were Samuel Merril and Channing Madison.

In 1814 the Bank of Vincennes was chartered by the Territorial Legislature which bank was in existence at the Commencement of the State Government. In January 1817 the Legislature of the state passed an act adopting the Bank of Vincennes as the State Bank of Indiana until the 1st of October 1835 and no longer.[2] The stock was increased by an additional $1,000,000, divided into ten thousand shares of $100 each. Three Thousand Seven hundred and fifty shares $375,000 were reserved to the State to be subscribed for from time to time, as it should be found convenient, having due regard to the funds out of which such shares should be payable. The remaining Six thousand two hundred and fifty

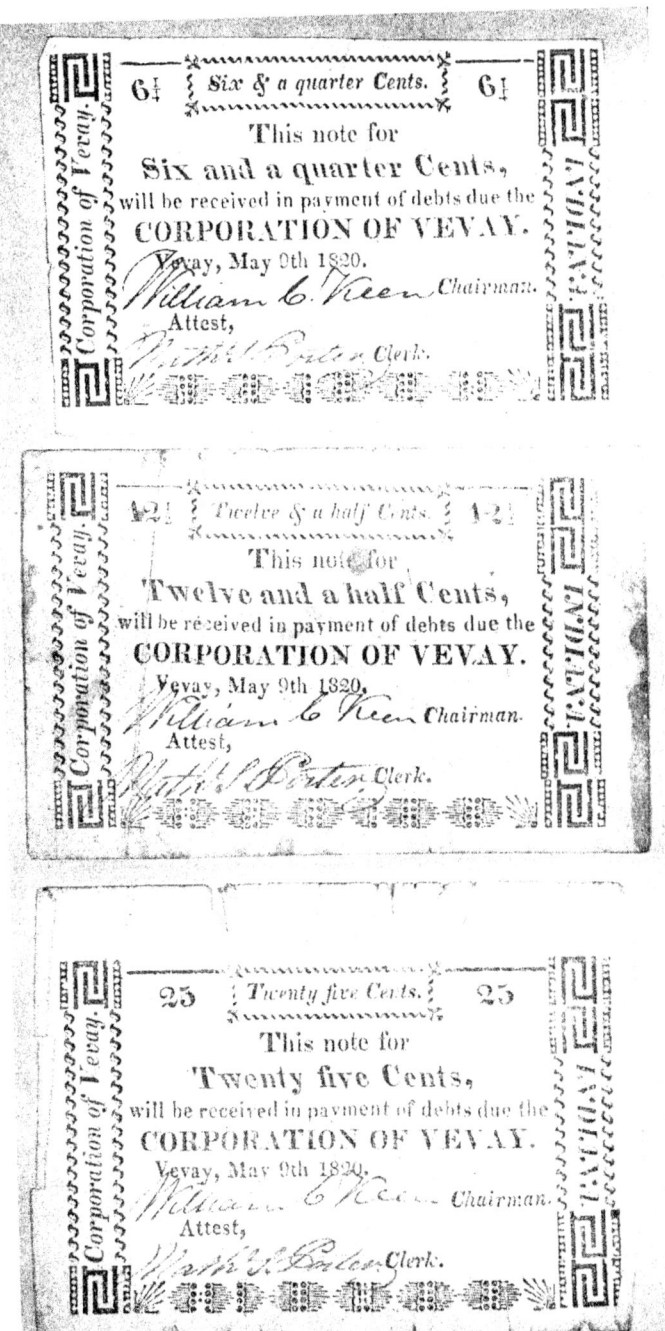

VEVAY CURRENCY

## HISTORY OF SWITZERLAND COUNTY 79

shares should be subscribed by individuals or others as specified in said act. By the 3rd Section of the act subscriptions for three thousand shares were to be made on the first day of April 1817. In Switzerland County Subscription Books were to be Opened at Vevay in said County under the direction of John Gilliland, Lawrence Nihell and Daniel Dufour for two hundred shares.

The stock for the Branch at Vevay was subscribed and the bank went into active operation in the Summer or fall of 1817 and continued in operation until February 1820 when it together with the parent institution at Vincennes and all other branches thereof failed and went into Liquidation.

In 1819 the directors of the Vevay branch authorized the issuing of a certain amount of one, three and five dollar notes and sent to the printers at Cincinnati Reynolds & Co. to have them printed. The notes thus printed were put in circulation and passed currently. Unfortunately for the Bank, by some mistake or other five hundred $5 notes more than were authorized were printed, and signed by some person other than the president, and many of them thus counterfeited were found in circulation.

This fraud upon the bank was discovered by John F. Dufour the president, while in Cincinnati on business for the Bank.[1] Calling on Hugh and James Glenn to receive of them $2,500, which they had collected of Elijah Pierson for the Bank, one of the Glenns placed on the table several bundles of the notes of the Branch Bank receivable in payment of debts due the Bank saying to Mr. Dufour "Here are $2,500 in Vevay receivables. I "counted the most of them myself last night, and some "are in the same bundles as they came out of the Bank." Mr. Dufour was about taking the Bundles without counting, but on looking at one of the Bundles he saw that ones, threes, and fives, were mixed together. He then concluded to count it. While counting he perceived some of the fives had a forged signature, which he threw out and told Glenn he would not receive them, as they were counterfeit—Glenn insisting that they were genuine. After considerable conversation about the matter they concluded to search the other bundles and found a number of the fives with forged signatures. The plate appeared to be genuine. The number of these bills in Mr. Glenns possession were between 150 and 200. Immediately on this discovery Mr. Dufours suspicions were aroused.

On leaving Glenn's Mr. Dufour went to the printers who had printed these bills, [and] upon enquiry found they had printed five hundred $5. bills, more than the Bank had authorized and they were returned to the bank by the person entrusted with having them printed.

Mr. Dufour made a statement of these facts for the "Royal Arch Masons" at the time and they were afterwards published in the *Vevay Times* and *Switzerland County News* of the 29th December 1838.

On the 7th of February 1820 a statement of the condition of the Bank was made, and certified as correct by John F. Dufour John Gilliland and Thomas Armstrong a committee appointed for the special purpose, and all the property, books, and papers of said Branch Bank were delivered by the cashier to John F. Dufour except two bills of exchange which were in the Bank of Cincinnati for collection.[1]

On the 19th of February 1820 John F. Dufour delivered the same to Isaac Blackford Agent and received from the agent a receipt as follows "19th February 1820, "received the Branch Bank in the situation as certified "by the committee within named and the book[s] papers "and furniture thereto belonging from the said John F. Dufour, President."       "ISAAC BLACKFORD, *Ag't*

Thus ended the Branch Bank at Vevay.[2]

The physicians who practiced in the early settlements of this part of the County were Charles Muret, a Dr

## HISTORY OF SWITZERLAND COUNTY 81

Norton who came here in 1813 or 1814, Dr. John Mendenhall Dr. Wm. Stephenson Dr. James Welsh, Dr. Hotchkiss; Dr. Stall Dr. Forbes, Dr. [Samuel W.] Clarkson, Dr. [Joseph] McCutchen were the physicians who practiced prior to 1840.[1]

In the earlier days of the state until perhaps 1824 or 1825 whipping on the bare back was a punishment inflicted on persons convicted of Larceny. Under that law but two persons received that punishment in this county. At the November term 1818 one John J. Jones was tried and found guilty of stealing a gun—and the verdict of the Jury was,[2] "We the Jury find the defendant guilty "as charged in the indictment, that the gun had not been "returned, that it was worth $18, we do assess and "say the defendant shall pay a fine of $18, and shall be "whipped on his naked back Ten Stripes." A motion for a new trial was made and overruled; a motion in arrest of Judgment was made and likewise overruled. The defendant was sentenced by the court "that the defendant be taken to some convenient place on the 14th "day of Novr 1818 at 3 Oclock P. M. then and there to "be whipped on his naked back ten Stripes." This sentence was executed by John F. Siebenthal the then sheriff, by applying ten stripes well laid on with a cowhide, in the presence of a great throng of bystanders.

The other was the case of Abraham Levi who was at the September term 1821 of the Circuit Court found guilty of Larceny (horse Stealing) sentenced to pay a fine of $70, imprisoned one day and receive forty stripes on his bare back. This sentence as to the forty stripes was executed by Israel R. Whitehead the then sheriff by taking the said Levi to the corner of the estray pen, and tying him to the corner post—then calling on James Rous the father of Zadig and Percy Rous, to count the stripes as he applied them—he laid on the forty stripes with a new cowhide, which so lacerated the back of Levi that it was with difficulty, room could be found for the last 10 or 15 without striking in one of the stripes before inflicted. This was the last punishment of the kind inflicted in the county, and was witnessed by many spectators. The writer witnessed both and Zadig Rous, witnessed the last. If there are any other persons living who witnessed, the infliction of these punishments besides the writer and Zadig Rous, it may be Abner Clarkson.

The time of the appearance of the Steam Boats on the Ohio river is not exactly known, but it must have been after the spring of 1809 as John F. Dufour had removed to New Switzerland. It was rumored in the settlement that a steam boat would pass down, some time during the day. John F. Dufour, Daniel Dufour, Jean Daniel Morerod, started up the river and went above the head of the island, and awaited the arrival of the Steam boat, which came along. They paddled the Canoe in which they had gone up the river, to the steam boat, got on board and came down as far as the mouth of Indian Creek where the boat stopped to let them get into the Canoe. This must have been about 1811 or 1812.

The first steamboats, of any considerable size that were navigating the Ohio river were built about the year 1819 to 1821. The Velocipede, General Green, Ploughboy, Highland Laddie, and Eliza are the Steamers of the early days now recollected by the writer. The Velocipede was caught in a storm near Vevay, and her upper deck was considerably damaged. The General Green struck a snag and sunk damaging the cargo, which was principally Coffee. The Ploughboy in 1822 or 1823 was running up the Wabash River. A notice of this is taken from an old Vincennes paper of April 3d 1822 "On Tuesday morning last the citizens of this place were "gratified by the appearance of the Steam Boat, Plough "Boy. Captain Beacon, bound for Terre Haute, being "the second boat that has ascended the Wabash."

In those days Steam boat traveling was very slow com-

## HISTORY OF SWITZERLAND COUNTY 83

pared with the present day. In 1823 the writer was two days and two nights on the trip from Vevay to Cincinnati on the Highland Laddie a small boat owned by Duncan McCallum, one of the early Scotch settlers on Long run.

About the years 1813, 14, 15, Barges and keel boats were used in transporting produce, Iron, and salt along the Ohio & Mississippi rivers. Joseph Bosseau who came to this place in 1813, together with his brother John were regularly engaged in keel boating.[1] Joseph Bosseau is still living 2½ miles from Vevay, and is in his 84th or 85th year[2]— he Bosseau made one or two trips to New-Orleans and back, Several trips to Saint Louis and back

on one of the trips from Saint Louis, he came across on foot by land being Six or seven days on the way. He made one trip up the Mississippi river to Prairie du Chein [Chien] with provisions for the garrison stationed there. He also made trips up the Cumberland river to Nashville and up the Tennessee river to the Muscle Shoals—and the Kentucky river to Subletts ferry, to which latter point iron and groceries were taken, and from which tobacco whiskey and bacon were brought on the return trip.

He also put his shoulder to the pole and assisted in pushing the keel boat up the Monongahala river as far as Brownsville, which was in those days called Redstone[3] also up the Mu[s]kingum river to Zanesville, several times to Pittsburgh, and many times to the Kenhawha [Kanawha] salines taking up whiskey, bacon coffee, sugar and other groceries and return[ing] loaded with salt.[4] The last trip made to Kenhawha was for Jacob R. Evertson taking up whiskey bacon and groceries and a few dry goods. Fearing that Evertson would not allow him a ration of whiskey he had provided for himself a gimblet, when removing a hoop he could bore a hole, and draw a coffee pot full of whiskey and replace the hoop.

In the keelboat and Barge business James Kirby was

engaged for some years with one or two barges, one of which he afterward converted into a Steam boat.

On the visit of General Lafayette to Cincinnati in 1825[1] an artillery company[2] composed of a number of the Swiss, went to Cincinnati taking with them the cannon they used at a later date named "Old Betts", to participate in the reception of the General. Some of the members of the company who declined going up, predicted that, those who went would not be noticed by any one, among the thousands who would be present to welcome the nations guest.

On their arrival, they were met at the landing by members of the Committee of arrangements, and by members of the artillery Company of Cincinnati. As the Swiss boys were about hawling their gun up the bank by hand one of the officers of the day informed them that in a short time a span of horses would arrive to take the gun up to enter into the procession to be formed. In a short time a span of fine blacks was hitched to the gun and the Swiss boys, marching along in martial order, soon became the observed of all observers. The exercise of firing was very good and the two companies vied with each other which should excel. The Vevay company by the rapidity with which they fired their gun, so far outdid the Cincinnati Company, that they received the praise of every person, and even General Lafayette, who was introduced to the Captain and his men by John James Dufour the father of the Captain of the Company, gave them the praise of being the most accurate in artillery tactics of any company he had met with on his present visit to the United States. Lafayette enquired of the Captain and his men where they had received instruction in artillery tactics, and had quite a lengthy conversation with them. On being informed that they had come about 70 miles up the river, he replied "My friends you have put yourselves to a great inconvenience to come so far to see me, who am only a man."

## HISTORY OF SWITZERLAND COUNTY 85

In 1812 Hiram Ogle, the father of Achillis & Hiram Ogle came to the neighborhood of Vevay and settled on Indian Creek immediately below Griffith Dickason. He contracted with John David Dufour to clear some land in the Ohio river bottom opposite the Island above Vevay. He cleared for him under that contract ten or twelve acres and a two story hewed loghouse was built on that land. The house stood somewhere near where the barn of Mrs. Jagers now stands. Mr. Ogle and his neighbor Dickason, became rivals in raising corn; for one, two or perhaps three years Mr. Dickason raised more corn than Mr. Ogle. Ogle then took an oath that he would not shave until he raised more corn than Dickason and he kept that oath, for the writer recollects to have been at Ogle's at a corn husking the year that Ogle raised more corn than Dickason. At that corn husking, which was during the day time, there was much fun and frolic among all present, for the girls of the neighborhood had met for a quilting and a dance was in expectancy in the evening. A few days after the husking and quilting, Ogle happening in town was asked which raised the most corn, he or Dickason, when he replied "by G—d I did, dont you see I have shaved."

Some time about these times Ogle was at Robert McKay's at a corn husking, and some persons from the neighborhood of Port William, Ky., were also there. A quarrel was commenced between some of the Kentuckians and McKay and a neighbor during which each party said what they could do, as was usual in quarrels. The Kentuckians bantered the Indianians to meet them on the other side of the river and they would fight it out. The banter was accepted. McKay called on Ogle (who was a very large and stout man) to go over with them to have the fight. Ogle said he would go. McKay said they would get Noah Pritchet to go over too (Pritchet was a very large and stout man), for, said McKay, "he is a big fellow, and that will scare the Kentuckians, although Pritchet is a d—d coward." These three, McKay,

Ogle, Pritchet, with several others, went over at the appointed time, and it was said that there was no fight, for the Kentuckians were afraid to fight such powerful men as McKay, Ogle, and Pritchet. Mr. Ogle was the contractor for building the first Jail in the County, in 1814.

Johnson Brown came to this part of the state about the time William Cotton came, but returned to Kentucky. He came back again in a few years, married one of William Cotton's sisters; took the fever and ague; recovering he returned to Kentucky again—returned again in 1814, lived for some time in the house owned by the Pleasant heirs, at the corner of Walnut and Pike Streets which then belonged to David McCormick—he moved to Long Run and lived for many years on a part of the School Section near Siebenthals mill, where he manufactured powder—for many years the only powder used by the hunters of his neighborhood for many miles around. At his house, the hunters, when on a squirrel hunt would meet to get the powder to be used and to count the scalps. He was justice of the peace in Craig Township for many years. For some years previous to his death he resided in Jefferson County west of Moorefield. At the age of 103 or 104 he could with his rifle shoot a squirrel in the tallest tree; in that respect he was a remarkable man. He died some four or five years since in the 106th or 108th year of his age. He was the father of Samuel Brown of Jefferson County, Joseph and Ralph Brown of this county, and Several daughters.

In 1815 George G. Knox the father of Robert A. George P. and James Knox, came to reside in Vevay, he having sometime in 1814 purchased the lot at the S. E. corner of Pike and Vineyard streets, and contracted for the building of a log residence, which is still standing on the spot where built. He came from Frankfort Ky where he had been carrying on the Cabinet making business—which he continued after coming to Vevay for many years. He was a good workman and no doubt there are in families in this county pieces of furniture of his make. He served as Treasurer of the county for several years. At one time while he had his shop in a log house that stood about where the frame house now owned by Abner Clarkson on Market street stands, he together with two or three other mechanics and Doctor John Mendenhall were working on a perpetual motion [machine] which they were constructing and which was kept a secret. The project failed.

Solomon Stow the father of U. H. and Shilometh Stow, came to the county about the year 1820 and resided in Vevay for some time. There were several brothers. Mr. Stow went out into the neighborhood of Printers Retreat, where he remained some years, during which he had established the reputation of a first class barn builder—he having put up the second hay barn built in the county, Cyrus Hatch having put up the first and in a few years there were many good frame barns through that part of the County. Having entered or bought the lands where U. H. and Shilometh Stow now reside, he built on it and commenced improving the lands, and putting up substantial barns. After his death, his sons Uzial H. and Shilometh, continued cultivating and improving the lands, which are now the best cultivated and arranged farms in the county. They have turned their attention to fruit culture, and from their orchards for the last three or four years the citizens of Vevay and the Country round about have been supplied with choice peaches. The Brothers Stow are among our most valued and enterprising farmers, and engage in every enterprize that has in view the furnishing of luxuries and necessaries, to suit the tastes and fancies of the good liver, or the epicure.

This winter of 1875-76 has been so mild, that but few persons having ice houses have been so fortunate as to have the ice to fill them. Yet Mr. U. H. Stow (although ice froze only two or three inches thick) has by his ingenuity, filled his ice house with ice Eight inches thick from a pond on his farm.

In 1818 or 1819 Robert Bonner[1] and Francis Bonner,[2] the latter the grandfather of the Francis Bonner, now living in Vevay, and in the grocery business with ─────── Cain, built an ox saw mill in the river bottom on what are now lots No. 238 and 239 in J. F. Dufour's addition to Vevay on Ferry Streets. The propelling power of the mill was a large tread wheel upon which from 6 to 8 oxen were placed, to cause it to run with sufficient force to do any execution. The mill never did much in sawing—but was financially the cause of the owners failure.

About the same time or perhaps a year later, Judge James Lee, the father of Mrs. Jane Stevens of Madison Indiana the widow of Stephen C. Stevens, built an ox grist mill on the lot now[3] owned by Dr. Jacob W. Thompson—this mill was designed to manufacture all the wheat raised in this part of the county but proved a failure in every respect. The wheel was an enormous tread wheel, to be propelled by placing on it six or Eight heavy oxen —it never did anything in the manufacture of flour, but proved an unprofitable investment for the proprietor and an utter failure to the realization of the expectations of Judge Lee.

Some years after Joshua Smithson who was carrying on the Cabinet making business erected a carding machine on the lots where John Gills grist mill now stands and continued Carding for some time by horse power— and finally he erected a Cotton Gin on a small scale and on which for some years he ginned all the cotton raised about in the different neighborhoods in this county and from the opposite side of the Ohio river, which amounted to several hundred pounds yearly. The writer has seen cotton growing on the farm of Jean Daniel Morerod just below Vevay and in fact nearly all the farms in "Switzerland" as the settlement below Vevay was termed. No doubt the counterpane made of cotton grown in this coun-

# HISTORY OF SWITZERLAND COUNTY 89

ty "in early times" and in the possession of Mrs. Constant Golay, who is a daughter of Jean Daniel Morerod, mentioned in the *Revielle* of the 25th of March 1876, was made of Cotton raised on the farm of her father and ginned at Joshua Smithsons Gin. Mr. Smithson afterwards had an engine attached to his mill and run it for some years with but one accident occurring—the head of the boiler was one day blown out causing great consternation in the neighborhood for a time but fortunately no one was injured although many were much frightened. Mr. Smithson eventually sold out to William C. Keen.[1]

The engine which Mr. Smithson put into this mill was built by Frederick L. Grisard, who was carrying on the blacksmith business and Lewis Golay, who had served an apprenticeship at engine building with a person in Cincinnati Ohio by the name of Tift. All the wrought iron work about it was worked by F. L. Grisard and the polishing and finishing by Lewis Golay and the engine put up and put in running order by Lewis Golay—this was the first Steam engine set up in Vevay, if not in Switzerland County.

In the early settlement of this part of Indiana it was very common for Deer hunters from the opposite side of the Ohio river to come over among the hills back from the river, and between Indian and Plum Creeks, with a pack of hounds, and start up deer, when the deer would make for the river pursued by the hounds. The deer being closely pursued by the hounds, would plunge into the river and swim to the opposite shore, where persons watching for them could kill them as they neared the shore—in this manner many deer were captured by the hunters.

This was not followed by these persons merely for the flesh and hides, but for the amusement of the chase. Among the Kentucky neighbors who delighted and indulged in the excitement of the Chase were the Sanders', Craigs Tandys, Lindsays and others whose names are not now recollected. Samuel Sanders, the proprietor of Ghent (Uncle Sam as he was familiarly called) was one who seemed to delight in this sport more than any of the others; as late as 1817 to 1818 he used frequently to come over to this side of the river with his pack of hounds numbering near a dozen, and go back into the hills, and during the day the ears of the citizens of Vevay would be saluted with the cry of the pack of hounds, coming towards town in chase of a fine buck, who, apparently to elude the hounds would plung[e] into the river—and swim to the opposite shore, there to meet his death from the deadly rifle of some unerring marksman lying in wait for his approach.

In the early days of Vevay there were men, who wished to make money without work, and without giving an equivalent for the goods and wares received by them. One John B. Menola built the fram[e] house at the N. E. corner of Main and Walnut streets now owned by Mrs. Julia LeClerc, finished the lower story for a bar room in one end and a billiard table in the other; the second story was divided into rooms which were used for games of different kinds, a roulette table in one room, and the others for those wishing to play at cards. In this house some of the our [sic] business men of that day spent their evening in drinking and gaming, some at billiards, some at roulette, and some at cards. Two or three of the merchants then in business here were so infatuated about gaming, that one of them, become bankrupt and two others become so seriously involved by the losses they sustained, that they were compelled to suspend business for a time. Prosecutions were instituted against the proprietor of the establishment, and to escape being arrested and brought to trial, [he] absented himself from the county, and while thus absent, his creditors came to Vevay took possession of his effects, out of which to make their claims, and thus broke up this gaming house. One Citizen of Vevay who died a few years since, used to declare that he could win his hat full of money any night he went there from the merchants of Vevay.

In 1816 Dr. Joshua Haines, of Rising Sun; Dr. Martin, of New Liberty, Ky; and Samuel Merrill, of Vevay; then of Corydon, and lastly of Indianapolis, three young men seeking a home in the west, left their New England home and journeyed westward. The latter of these, Samuel Merrill, located at Vevay. In 1817 Mr. Merrill was admitted to practice law in the Courts of Switzerland County. When he came to the County he had not an over supply of this worlds goods, but he applied himself to his profession, taught school, and was soon appointed lister of the taxable property of Switzerland County, and he is known to have said he had no horse, and needed all the money he would receive for his services. He actually undertook and completed taking the list of taxable property of the county, travelling over the whole county, which then included Ross Township (or the horn as it was termed) which extended up to or near Olean, now in Ripley county, on foot. He was afterwards successfull in the practice of the law and was elected to represent the County in the Legislature of the State, while the seat of government was at Corydon. As a candidate for representative at one time Daniel Haycock a revolutionary soldier was his opponent,[1] and by some means, in Ross Township, a man by the name of Laycock was voted for instead of Haycock, which was the cause of Merrills election. As the votes of La[y]cock added to Haycocks would out number the votes cast for Mr. Merrill,—it was found out afterwards that those who voted for La[y]cock in Ross township thought he was a candidate voted for all over the county.

At another election for Representative Mr. Merril was a candidate and he appeared to be very acceptable to a majority of the voters, and it was thought he would have no opposition. However some persons for sport a few days before the election prevailed upon one Abraham Miller to become a candidate and about 10 days before the election he was thus announced as a candidate

"To the voters of Switzerland County"

"Having, at the solicitations of my friends and neighbors consented to become a candidate for Representative in the legislature of Indiana, I pledge myself, if elected, to use to the utmost of my abilities, to support such measures only as will be beneficial to the County I represent, and the State at large. Respectfully

his<br>ABRAHAM     MILLER.<br>mark

Mr. Miller was an honest old farmer and as was the case with many who were raised in the western wilds, was an uneducated man; and in thus consenting to become a candidate no doubt, was like his friends and neighbors anticipating some rare sport during the remainder of the Canvass, and on election day.

The day of election came, and as Mr. Miller was a voter of Jefferson Township, he came to Vevay on the morning of election day full of fun and frolic, electioneering to secure votes, which he did with a great deal of success at the polls of Jefferson Township. During the day his friends and he himself appeared to be confident of his election, for he went to some of the prominent men about Vevay and assured them he did not wish to be elected; that he and some of his neighbors, seeing there was no opposition to Sam. Merrill, had determined to have a candidate and some sport out of his candidacy.

He appeared fearful he might be elected, and stated to some of his friends, that if he was elected he did not know what in the devil he would do, for he was not able to fill the place as he ought to fill it, and such other expressions. He received a very fair proportion of the votes cast, but was defeated by about fifty or seventy five

## HISTORY OF SWITZERLAND COUNTY 93

votes. Mr. Merrill was about the close of the session of the legislature elected Treasurer of State, which he continued to hold for some time—[1]

In those days days "Whiskey" might be said to be "King" for with the aid of whiskey men rolled logs, conducted wood choppings, husked corn, raised houses, and with whiskey as an aid men of bad habits were elected to fill offices, the duties of which they were incapable of performing, while those who were deserving, of good habits and capable were left to take "back seats." It was the rule that when a man became a candidate for an office he was under obligations to treat his friends and all who drank whiskey, at every time he happened to meet [them] at a grocery or tavern where it was sold.

On election day every candidate had one or more bottles of liquor set out upon the counter of every grocery near the polls with his name printed in Capitals and pasted on to the bottle—of this bottle his friends were expected to partake as often as they desired on election day, but by degrees that rule began to be set aside.[2]

In 1832 the writer became a candidate for Justice of the peace, and was obliged to submit to the rule of treating and on the day of election was "honored" with having his name on one or more bottles in every place where the "ardent" was sold—and the cost of that one days treating in this manner cost him $9.87½c.

In 1837 he again became a candidate for the same office, but this time his opponent and his friends were too much on the alert, and they succeeded in chartering every bar in Vevay, thus depriving him of the means (as was supposed by his opponents) of securing his election. His friends got possession of the room [on the] S. E. corner of Main and Ferry Streets Vevay—procured two buckets full of whiskey and a bucket of sugar and on the morning of the election opened a free house calling all who wished to drink whither friend or opponent, and those friends had the satisfaction of electing the writer by a large majority. Since that year the practice of treating on election days began to get into disrepute, and may be said to be now entirely out of practice in Switzerland County.

John Dumont once made the assertion, that "The re-"tailers of Spirituous liquors control[l]ed the legisla-"ture  That is that whoever they supported for representative was sure of an election.

Yet even in those days Indiana can boast of some of her most honest legislators—men who had the best interest of the state at heart—men who were not always trying to initiate some scheme or new measure, whereby they might fill their own pockets at the expense of the honest farmers and tax payers of the State. It is true some had very crude notions of the best manner to develope the resources of the State.

As an example, a worthy Senator representing Ripl[e]y and Switzerland Counties in the Senate of Indiana, conceived the idea of having a prison erected in such a manner that it could be placed upon wheels, and moved along the state roads, that were then being opened and worked, and made so secure that convicts could be locked up at night, and employed through the day in working on the roads. In that manner it was contended the labor of the convicts could be made available in Opening and working the roads throughout the State, that were established by legislative enactment. He advocated, this measure with much zeal, but failed in having it become a law. That Senator was George Craig, and, no matter what may be said of that measure, would it not be a profitable undertaking at the present time.

When railroads were first spoken of in Indiana a worthy representative from one of the Counties on the Wabash river, and in whose representative district it was necessary to make what is usually termed "Corderoy roads," which were made by laying rails or poles twelve or fourteen feet long across the road so as to make the road passable in the Spring and winter season, in reply to a Speech made in the House of Representatives by a member favorable to railroads, is said to have said "In my county we have as good rail roads, as in any county in the State of Indiana or in the world, for they are made of oak rails that can not be surpassed by those in any part of the country for durability."

It is said of another representative from a Wabash river county—that when it was in contemplation of building a canal along the Wabash river, and when speaking of the cost of its construction, he declared it as his firm belief that "the cost of the construction of a canal from Fort Wayne to Vincennes could be entirely paid in coon skins taken along the route of the proposed canal."[1]

Oliver H. Smith, when he first came to the State, came to Vevay, with all his earthly goods tied in a handkerchief. He remained but a short time—he was employed to conduct a case before a Justice of the peace, and with the amount he received as his fee, paid off his Board bill, and went to Brookville or Connorsville, where he opened a small grocery and commenced the practice of the law. These facts Mr. Smith related to the writer in 1842. His subsequent career in the affairs of Indiana are familiar to almost every Indianian.[2]

Benjamin Drake who was proprietor of New York now Florence[3] had a Brother Robert Drake, who married a sister of Heathcoat Picket—lived in Plum Creek for some time removed to Arnolds Creek and came to Pleasant Township and purchased part of Section 16, or the School Section—while living on Plum Creek in the year 1800 he had a daughter born who is now living and is 76 years of age. She is no doubt the oldest person now living in the County born within its bounds. She is the mother of Asa Newton.

While speaking of the Picket family—it may not be

amiss to state here that Heathcoat Picket perhaps made more trips to New Orleans as pilot of flat boats and returned by land through the Indian Country on foot than any other person of his or any other period—he is said to have made over twenty trips—he also built the first flat boat, known as "Orleans boat" ever built in the County of Switzerland.

Many flat boats for taking produce to New Orleans have been built in the County—a large poplar tree was felled a cut, from 50 to 70 feet long sawed off, two sides hewn down—then rolled in some manner up on some kind of trussels to be far enough from the ground that a whip saw could be used, then the Gunwales were sawed—when a board or two 2½ inches thick would be sawed off the whole length of the gunwales—these boats were made about 16 or 17 feet wide.

As is now well known that this county does not abound in minerals it may, be of interest to state that many years ago salt was made at a salt spring some where on Grants Creek. Laurence Nihell many years since attempted to get salt by sinking a well near Jacksonville. Mr. Nihell had sunck his well to the depth of 125 or 150 feet, and, as he expected with a fair prospect of having his enterprize crowned with success, some evil disposed person brought all his anticipations to an unexpected stand still. This was done with the intent no doubt of injuring Mr. Nihell—and it was accomplished by dropping as was supposed the handle of a skillet into the well so that when the auger was let down no impression could be made; and after many fruitless attempts to sink the well deeper the enterprize was abandoned by Mr. Nihell after he had expended nearly Six hundred dollars in the undertaking.

At one time a man came about Vevay and informed John Francis Dufour, that he knew where a lead mine could be found on the land of Elisha Golay (now belonging to Charles O. Hastings) and exhibited specimens of the ore he said he had found the man would show the place for 20 dollars or he would work it on the shares. On inspecting the place where the lead mine was said to be located Mr. Dufour found some pieces of lead ore —but being satisfied, that the man wished to get money out of him for his pretended discovery, did nothing more than enter into a written agreement for working the mine and dividing the profits. The written agreement was signed, and the man left as he said to go after his apparatus to work the mine and return in a short time—but has never been heard from since.

It required an affidavit to be made that persons applying for marriage license were of the required age, the man 21 and the woman 18 years of age. It was very common for persons from Kentucky to come over to Vevay to be married—there was a man on the Kentucky side of the river who almost invariable came over with such, and he was always ready to make the affidavit no matter whether the parties were of the proper ages or not. The plan adopted was this—the figures 21 were written on two pieces of paper and one put in each of the mans shoes—the figures 18 were written on two pieces of paper and in like manner placed in the ladies shoes—so when the shoes were put on each was over their required ages—and this affidavit maker was in this manner prepared to perjure himself and as he supposed to evade prosecution for his perjury.

At the March term 1817 of the Circuit Court a case of murder was tried and the accused acquitted. The murder was committed under the following circumstances. The sheriff had a warrant for the arrest of a man named Caldwell who resided in a building on the lot where Rodolph F. Grisards house stands, and Caldwell, resisting the sheriff in the execution of the warrant, stood with his rifle in hand swearing he would shoot the first man who came on the poarch to arrest him—several attempts were made to get on the poarch when Caldwell raised his rifle as though he was going to shoot. There happened to pass about this time Jessee Murphy who had a rifle with him loaded—when the sheriff summoned him and several others to assist him in making the arrest— an advance towards the house of Caldwell was made when Caldwell leveled his gun to fire on the foremost— at which the sheriff ordered Murphy to fire on Caldwell, that he must be taken dead or alive—upon hearing which Caldwell opened the bosom of his shirt and dared Murphy to shoot. At this time another advance was made, when Caldwell again leveled his rifle to shoot. The Sheriff again directed Murphy to shoot Caldwell which he did placing the bullet in Caldwells breast killing him instantly. Murphy was indicted for murder, and upon being arraigned before the Court he plead "not guilty". A jury was empannelled to try the case composed of the following named persons—Thomas Evans, Joseph Noble, Henry Hanas Robert Cotton, Lawrence Nihell, Richard Woods, William Searcy, David Penwell, John Dumont, Bazilla Clark Ralph Cotton and John Mendenhall, who after hearing the evidence introduced retired to consult of their verdict—and afterwards returned a verdict of "not guilty". This case was tried at the first term of the Circuit Court under the state Government.

In 1815 John Brown father of James Brown Esqr came to the County and settled on the land where James Brown now resides. His dwelling was a two story hewed log house on the opposite side of the road nearly opposite to the brick dwelling now occupied by his son James. He was soon after he came to the County elected a Justice of the peace and served one or two terms of five years each. His son James Brown has served as Justice of the peace in Jefferson Township twenty one years. James Brown has grown up with the county and has seen the forests that stood on the lands in his neighborhood, cleared up and the fields to yield their rich

## HISTORY OF SWITZERLAND COUNTY 99

harvests of hay grain and other products which constitute the true wealth of the county. About the same time Peter Harper settled on the farm now owned by Jonathan McMakin, and in a small one story log house on the opposite side of the road from McMakins present residence lived and died and raised his family having cleared up the lands and made them suitable for tilling. His brother William Harper settled on the quarter section immediately north, the same now owned by Huldah Sullivan, and was purchased of William Harper, by Nathan Walden, and deeded by Walden and his wife to Mrs. Sullivan who is a daughter of Nathan Walden. Nathan Walden was one of the early mail carriers in this part of the country. In his youth he was mail carrier and contractor between Lawrenceburgh and Salisbury Indiana. The route was discontinued, but neither Walden, or the Postmasters at the ends of the route being notified of its discontinuance, Walden continued carrying the mail on that route for about two years without receiving any pay from the Government. He informed James Noble, then Senator in Congress from Indiana who resided in Brookville of the affair. Senator Noble assured him he would call at the department for an explanation, which he did and ascertained that the route had been discontinued over two years. The department being made to know to the satisfaction of the P. M. General that neither Walden or the Postmasters at the ends of the route had been notified of its discontinuance, orders were issued for the payment to Walden for the services rendered, which amounted to a considerable amount. With this he secured the quarter Section of land now owned by his son Henry. About 1814 to 1816 he was carrying the mail from Cincinnati O. to Jeffersonville Indiana, during which time the lands were being entered at the land office at Jeffersonville—and many persons sent by him the number of the Section and the Quarter of land they wished to enter and the money to pay into the Land office. For this service he was paid perhaps a couple of dollars by each person for whom he performed such service, which no doubt amounted to many dollars. In later years Mr. Walden was a contractor for carrying the mails on many important routes passing through the county—by which with perseverance energy and economy he amassed a good fortune, which he has distributed to his Sons and Daughters—three sons and three daughters.

Hiram Ogle was a contractor for carrying the mails for many years from Vevay to Georgetown Ky and other routes not now recollected.

James Dugan and James Ringo were also among the early contractors for carrying the mails which supplied the Post office at Vevay.

From the establishment of the Post office at Vevay to the present time the Post Masters were John Francis Dufour from 1810 to 1835, John M. King from 1835 to 1837—Perret Dufour from 1837 to 1841—W. H. Gray from 1841 to 1843—Abner Clarkson from 1843 to 1845, Perret Dufour from 1845 to 1849, James Harwood from 1849 to 1853, R. J. Lanham from 1853 to 1857, George C. Patton from 1857 to 1861, F. L. Courvoisier from 1861 to 1862, Frederick J. Waldo from 1862 to 1865,[1] James Harwood from 1865 to the inauguration of Andrew Johnston—George C. Patton from the inauguration of Andrew Johnston to 1869 J. C. Long from 1869 to the present time and will be no doubt until 1877.[2]

There are now living in Vevay and its vicinity persons who were born in the Swiss colony and its vicinity who recollect the fears, entertained by the settlers, of Indian depredations. The writer well remembers, of his father having gone back to the "first Vineyard" and Lexington on business—that his mother (who died on the 4th of March 1876) taking her three children Perret, Marcellina, and Hevila over the river and staying at Samuel Sanders during, her husbands absence, for fear the In-

HOME OF JOHN DAVID DUFOUR

HOME OF JOHN FRANCIS DUFOUR—THE FERRY HOUSE

## HISTORY OF SWITZERLAND COUNTY 101

dians might make an attack on the family. The writer well recollects meeting Indians, and that, they offered the "pipe of Peace" and he took the pipe and put it to his mouth as if to smoke, which was taken by the Indian as a sign of friendship.

Mrs. Lucy Detraz can relate the appearance of some Indians who came to her fathers (Jean Daniel Morerods) house—she was near the fence on the side of the house next to where the town of Vevay is laid out—when the Indians came to the fence from the direction of Vevay got over and went to the house set their rifles by the door, and began muttering to John David Dufour (her uncle) who was then living with them. Lucy was so frightened that she ran up into the loft and got into a barrell to hide from the Indians.

It is true[1] that within the last fifty years Vevay & the whole of the great west have been scourged with sickness, disease and death.

In the year 1820 there was a great emigration from the western part of New York and Pennsylvania bordering on the Allegany river down the Ohio river, and the population of Vevay was almost doubled during that year. In the latter part of Summer every house and cabin in Vevay that was tenantable was filled to overflowing with these emigrants. The summer proved to be very sickly, the prevailing disease being *Billious fever* and the new settlers of Vevay not being acclimated fell victims to the prevailing fever, and the small houses being very much crowded two and three families of from 3 to 5 persons each occup[y]ing a house with two rooms 15 or 16 feet square, there were great numbers died—in some houses there was not one able to help take care of the sick and no doubt many died for want of proper attention. The population of Vevay at that time was between five and Six hundred—one Sixth of whom fell a prey to the prevailing fever in many cases the corpses turned as yellow as those who died of yellow fever.[2]

It was for many years after this that Vevay was accounted a sickly place, and persons wishing to settle in a town on the Ohio river would shun the town as though pestilence and death would be their portion if they settled in Vevay.

In 1827 Vevay and the river bottom from Plum Creek down to Indian Creek a distance of four miles was visited with a similar fever and along the river bottom between these two creek[s] nearly one hundred deaths occurred.

In 1833 some parts of Switzerland County was visited with *Cholera,* below Indian Creek several deaths occurred. George Craig fell a victim to the disease and in a family of Lusters, there were several deaths and others not now recollected.

In the same year the disease made its appearance in Pleasant Township, and many deaths occurred. Dr. Hotchkiss & perhaps his wife (the father and mother of George A. and Luther Hotchkiss) one Banta a tanner who lived on and & [sic] owned the farm and built the brick house that John S. Olmstead owned at one time and many others whose names are not now recollected fell victims to that scourge, and yet there was not a case originated in Vevay, untill within the last few years.

It can be ascerted without successful contradiction that a tract of country on both sides of the Ohio river embracing Switzerland County on the Indiana side and the same length along the river on the Kentucky side and extending back ten or twelve miles is as healthy and desirable a location for persons wishing to make a permanent settlement for life for the purpose of farming as can be found anywhere on or along the Ohio river—the lands yield a rich return to the farmer for his labor, and lying between the two great cities of Cincinnati and Louisville the farmer has as good market for the products of the farm as can be found any where unless it be a person of a restless and roving disposition.

As one proof of the location being healthy, the reader is refered to the number of aged person[s], about Vevay

# HISTORY OF SWITZERLAND COUNTY 103

and throughout Switzerland County several being over 90 and hundreds over 70 who have lived here over 50 years.

In Feb 1814 Henry Hannas Came to the County, with his family consisting of his wife, son William and three daughters. He rented of John Francis Dufour the farm on Indian Creek where George Tandy lived so long. There was about 12 acres cleared in the Creek bottom, which was planted in corn and cultivated entirely by William Hannas—a good crop of corn was raised by him although in June of that year there was a rise of the Ohio the backwater running up the Creek, inundating the Creek bottoms—which killed all the corn on the bottoms below—but Hannas' corn was not hurt much by the water which was attributed to the fact that the land was not broken up, only "listed" and planted. William Hannas was born in Garrard County Kentucky on the 18th of September 1797 and died near Moorefield and was able to ride to Vevay and transact his business until his death 1881. Mr. Hannas relates that on the night of the 4th day of April 1814 there fell a snow 12 inches deep which was measured by Hiram Ogle on a plank at the saw mill that stood on Indian Creek on the land now owned by John Bakes.

In the fall of 1814 Mr. Hannas removed to the land on which John F. Cotton now resides, and in 1820 built a horse mill which did a good deal of grinding for the surrounding country.

One night shortly after they had removed, a bear came in among the hogs, caught one which caused it to squeal, when William Hannas took his gun and although it was dark he fired in the direction of the squealing hog and drew blood from the bear but did not kill it. About that time a bear could be seen every day one went out into the woods. One would say it was a wild country if they should see a bear every day in the woods. William

Hannas says he would often see bears, when he had no gun with him they would be scratching up yellow Jacket or Bumble bees nests—which they devoured with avidity. There came to the county with the Hannas Family one Thomas Evans, who settled the farm once owned by Walter Scott, which Mr. Scott bought of the Evans heirs.

After the farmers began to raise wheat some of the horse mill owners procured bolts, and flour began to be used more than ever before. Of the horse mills of early days, the writer recollects one opposite Carrollton owned by Edward McIntire the grand father of Joseph H. Netherland, one on what is now the pauper farm, then owned by James Rous, one in Vevay on the lot on which the Russell house now stands owned by one McFall, one on the farm which Samuel Protsman owned, which was built by John Protsman the father of Samuel and William Protsman; one in the edge of Cotton Township in Sec. 7, T 2, R. 2, near to Andrew Houze's present residence— and owned by James Dugan, and the one built by Henry Hannas already mentioned. Griffith Dickason and William Cotton built water mills on Indian Creek on their respective lands which were great conveniences to the surrounding farmers. At quite an early day of the settlement at Vevay they went to mill at Hartford. To get there they put their sacks of wheat or corn in a canoe went up the river to the mouth of Laughery Creek, thence up the creek as far as they could go with the canoe, there they hired some one to furnish horses to take their grists to the mill perhaps four or five miles, and when ground to bring it back to the Canoe. If we were compelled to go through the same process at this day to get our bread we would be sure to think and that truly that we had to "earn our bread by the sweat of the brow."

Some years the wheat crop was of such a nature that the bread made from the wheat flour caused persons to vomit freely after eating of it, which was the reason of the

## HISTORY OF SWITZERLAND COUNTY 105

wheat being termed "Sick wheat". The writer recollects of some three or four such crops, but has no recollection of more than two in succession—this occur[r]ing at different times.

Robert Bakes the father of John Bakes built in early days a mill on Long Run on the Scite of Ben. F. Siebenthals mill which had a very large wheel and the water was led along the side of the hill to where the wheel received the water. This mill did a good business for many years while there was water sufficient to run it. During the summer months very frequently there was very little if any water in the Creek. If clouds should rise in the west and show signs of rain, and the Clouds passed, and no rain fall so as to raise the creek, it is said that Bakes charged Rous (who had the horsemill on the hill) with having a long pole with some charm attached to the end of it that he raised in such a manner as to divide the clouds, and turn the rain in such a direction that it would not supply Bakes' mill with water so that he (Rous) would get the grinding to do for his horse mill.

The forests in the Ohio river bottoms were very dense, and there were many very large Poplar, Walnut, Oak, an[d] Beech trees. One very large poplar stood for some years near the house John F. Dufour first built, which was on the land which is now the lot in Vevay owned by William Archer—that poplar was full 5½ or 6 feet in diameter across the stump and was Sixty or Seventy feet high to the first limb. At one time while Mr. Dufour was absent from home, on business at the first Vineyard in Kentucky—there was a very severe wind Storm which broke off one of the limbs in the top and carrying it over the house to the opposite side Mrs. Dufour was very much frightened by the occurrence, and the same afternoon Peter Vanbriggle who had chopped and cleared land for Mr. Dufour chanced to come to the house inquiring for letters, was asked by Mrs. Dufour if he would chop that tree down. He said he would, but said he "What will Mr. Dufour say when he comes home and finds that tree chopped down." Mrs. Dufour said she did not care what he said, she would not be so frightened again for a dozen such trees—and that the next storm might blow it down on the house and kill her and the children. The tree was cut down that and the next day.

There stood a very large and a very tall walnut tree on the lot about where Julius Blach's present residence stands, and it stood there untill several years after a frame and brick building was erected on the corner lot where John Melchers residence stands. The persons living in that building began to entertain fears that a storm might blow it down on to the building and Mr. Dufour who still owned the lots on which the tree stood, was requested to have it felled. He consented to do so as soon as the nuts on the tree were ripe. Accordingly in the fall the tree was chopped down, made up into rails, and the writer and his brother gathered six or Eight cart loads of walnuts and hawled them home, to the Corner of Main Cross Streets and Market Street where William Archer resides.

There was left standing solitary and alone on the land about where Mr. Demans and Duhlmires residences stand an enormous Burr Oak tree which was fully Six feet in diameter at the butt. That tree was cut down about the year 1825 or 1826, the body made into flat rails, and the top and other parts made into cord wood for John F. Dufour by Benjamin Hilderbrand. There was 8 railcuts 10 feet in length which made several hundreds if not thousands of excellent rails and some 8 or 10 cords of wood.

The timber that has been destroyed, by dead[e]ning or girdling the trees, and they standing until becoming doated would fall to the ground, there lay and rot or rolled into heaps and burned, on the bottom lands be-

## HISTORY OF SWITZERLAND COUNTY 107

tween Indian and Plum Creeks if standing on the lands at this day, would bring more money than the land could now be sold for at this present time. But at that time the timber was valueless after the land was fenced and buildings erected. Just let the reader imagine how many feet of lumber, a poplar, oak or walnut tree from 3 to 5 feet in diameter and sixty or Seventy feet from the butt to the first limbs, would make and the price such lumber as they would make now sells for and he can form some idea of what the value of such a forest of trees would now be.

A little incident about the plan adopted by Dr. James Welsh in 1819 to have an unsightly Poplar stump, which Stood about the Centre of Main Cross Street and on the hill side about where the lower line of Market Street would cross. The stump was some ten or twelve feet high and was cut so high on account of its being a double tree and too large, knotty and cross grained to be chopped nearer the ground  consequently a scaffold was made for the chopper to chop one fork at a time. Dr. Welsh had the boys of the neighborhood to meet on Saturday afternoon's and dig and throw out the dirt. At length he arrived at the conclusion, that it was rather hard work for the boys—so he procured a long solid Stick about 5 feet long, had it sharpened to a point, tapering gradually —this stick was driven in[to] the ground about 3 feet, then drawn out, leaving a hole, which he caused to be filled full of corn, so that hogs passing, could get a taste, when they would continue rooting until they got to the bottom of the hole, several of these holes being made and filled at the same time. After the hogs had rooted so as to get to the bottom of the holes, loosening the earth, the boys were set to work throwing the dirt from the roots and stump. This was repeated, so that during the fall of that year the earth was removed sufficiently to enable a chopper to get at the roots, chop them off and then the stump was rolled out of its bed. Reader, whether man, or boy, have you ever assisted in removing stumps in that manner, as the writer in his boyhood has assisted.

An incident that occur[r]ed at Cincinnati in 1825, on the reception of General Lafayette, was omitted in relating the affair, [and] will be given here. While the General was on the stand surrounded by the elite of the day, there was perceived in the crowd as though attempting to approach the noble "guest" an old and feeble woman, leaning on her staff. She made her way through the crowd into the presence of the General, extending her trembling hand. The General siezed it, and the woman looking up into his face remarked, "you do not remember me". He replied, "I do not." She said, "You recollect of a woman bringing you milk when you was imprisoned in the batile?" "Yes", replied the General. "I am the person" said the woman, and the tears rolled down the cheeks of the General, who had stood before the cannon of the British at Yorktown, with out his cheeks blanc[h]ing or fearing danger. Another incident: While the Vevay artilleiists were firing their cannon Andrew Bornard, perceived a coal of fire that by some means had fallen among the powder and cartri[d]ges. With coolness and firmness he snatched the live coal from the cartri[d]ge and prevented an explosion that, it is said, by those who were present, would have caused the death or maiming or perhaps both of a number of persons.

Many amusing incidents could be related of the militia and militia training or musters. About the year 1817 and 1818, the military companies of Jefferson, Craig Pleasant & and part of Cotton Township, composed the 14th regiment Indiana militia—and the companies of that regiment were comman[d]ed by Captains, Francis S. Lindley George G. Knox, Charles Henderson, Henry Peters, John Stepleton James Downey William C. Mitchel and John Fox, the latter being captain of a cavalry Company—one battallion paraded in Vevay every year, and the other occasionally at Jacksonville, and other points in the vicinity—in the fall of 1816 or spring of 1817 an election was held for the purpose of electing the officers of the regiment—The contest was quite Spirited between Raleigh Day and Paxton W. Todd for the office of Colonel—Day however was made Colonel and Todd Lieutenant Colonel. The regiment generally performed military duty at Vevay and were drilled in the bottom between the Town and the river—on the occasion of these military parades the town was filled to overflowing, not only by the military but by boys and rosy cheeked lasses old men and women who came to see the wonderful military exploits, of their sons, brothers, husbands and sweethearts. On these occasions the Colonel who was in the habit of imbibing too freely of the "ardent" often became patriotic, when he would exclaim, "I can fight a funeral and die the death of a pilgrims progress, for my father was a dutchess and my mother was a duke" and "I am Rawleigh Day, Colonel of the bloody 14th regiment of Indiana militia", to the great amusement and merryment of those who heard him[1]—the men who composed the companies formed into this regiment, were required to meet armed and equip[p]ed as the law directed. The most of them came with "Corn stalk guns" and the other equipments to correspond, for the purpose of being taught the art of war so that they would be of service in defending their country in time of war.

At the time of the Blackhawk war, or some other Indian war on the western border—the first battallion was ordered to meet on the market square in Vevay on a certain day for the purpose of drafting a certain number of men, to march to the west to put an end to Indian depredations. It was a wonderful affair, for in nearly every company a great proportion of their men were taken sick a few days before the time appointed to meet, and one or two men, cut the forefinger of the right hand off so as to be disqualified to serve and thus escape the draft. The live and healthy men met; about 30 were drafted but were never required to go to the front.

In the fall of 1815 William C. Keen a practical printer, came to Vevay,[1] representing to John Francis Dufour, that he had a printing establishment and materials, boxed up and ready for shipping, at Hamilton, Ohio, but was detained by parties who held it by a mortgage for about $200, which he was unable to pay, and wished Mr. Defour to see if he could get the press and materials, and bring them to Vevay, to commence the publication of a newspaper. Mr. Dufour went to Hamilton and made the necessary arrangements and purchased the mortgage on the press &c. and placed them in the custody of John Wilson, with a request that he would have them sent to Vevay, Mr. Wilson himself coming to Vevay with the press & and afterwards moved to Vevay built a mill now owned by John Bakes and distillery, became one of the associate Judges of Switzerland County.

Early in the Spring of 1816, John Francis Dufour, William C. Keen and Robert Burchfield, under the firm name of Dufour Keen and Co commenced the publication of a weekly paper the *Indiana Register* which was continued until December 1817—when the partnership was dissolved. On the dissolution of the partnership, John Francis Dufour became sole proprietor and publisher and Robert Burchfield printer. The publication of the paper was continued by Dufour and Burchfield until some time in 1819 or 1820—during part of that time the name was changed to *Indiana Register and Vevay and Ghent Advertizer* when John Douglass came to Vevay took charge of the office, published the paper a year or two, and then removed to Corydon Indiana, then the seat of Government of Indiana, and thence to Indianapolis where he established the *Indiana State Journal*.

Keen, after Douglass left, resumed the publication of the *Register* and continued its publication until 1826, when Thomas Berryman and John Allen came to Vevay, took charge of the office and continued the publication of the paper for two years or more. Allen left Vevay removed to Salem and commenced the publication of a paper named the *Annotator* continued its publication until his death from Cholera in 1833. Berryman remained in Vevay became contractor for carrying the mails—and was county surveyor for some time.

During this interval Keen removed to Printers Retreat (now the Jackson farm between Vevay and Jacksonville) taking the press and printing material with him where he in partnership with one Child published the *Weekly Messenger* until 1836 when Child removed to Warsaw Ky. taking with him the press and material.

In 1832 there being no paper published in Vevay Richard Randall came here with a printing establishment and commenced the publication of the *Monitor* which he continued for three or four years—when he left Vevay taking his printing establishment with him to Madison or Vernon. There was then no paper published in Vevay; soon after the Presidential election in 1836 Isaac Stevens came to Vevay bringing with him a printing press and materials, and commenced the publication of the *Village Times* which was conducted as a neutral paper, in politics untill 1838 or 1839 when it was changed from a neutral to a Democratic paper and was conducted as a Democratic paper until the commencement of the canvass in 1840. Edward Patton sold the establishment to Wilson H. Gray, with the understanding that Gray was to continue the paper as a Democratic paper—but just before the Whigs held their county Convention Gray changed to be a Whig, and was about to commence the publication of the paper as a Whig paper. Patton however interposed, took possession of the office, and the paper was conducted by the Democratic Central Committee during the Canvass assisted by Elwood Fisher, and untill the fall of 1840.

The Whig candidate for State Senator Joseph C.

Eggleston purchased a new press and materials, put it under the control of Gray who commenced the publication of the *Indiana Statesman* and continued its publication during the Canvass for the State and Presidential elections in 1840 and untill 1842 when the publication of the *Statesman* was suspended and the material disposed of.

In 1841 James G. Fanning came to Vevay, took charge of the Democratic printing establishment, commenced the publication of the *Spirit of the Times*, which was continued until 1843. Isaac Stevens again took charge of that paper and establishment, and in connection with Benjamin L. Simmons published the *Indiana Palladium* for two or three years—when they disposed of the establishment to Charles S. Horton, a Brother-in-law of Jacob C and Walter H. Wells, who changed the name of the paper to *The Ohio Valley Gazette* and continued its publication for about two years when he disposed of the same to Otis S. and Frederick J. Waldo, who changed the name to *Indiana Revielle*. They continued its publication as a Democratic paper for a short time; then as a neutral paper until 1853 or 1854, when it became a *Know nothing organ*. In 1855 Charles C Scott came to Vevay commenced the publication of of the *Weekly News* which he continued for about a year when he sold to Peter H Hale a young Vermont Lawyer who soon failed, and the office went into the possession of Ben. F. Schenck, who in connection with Merit W. Tague Esqr. continued the publication of the *News* for a year or two.

In Decr. 1860 Wm. J. Baird became proprietor of the *News* office and on the 1st of January 1861 he formed a partnership with Frederick J. Waldo, when the *News* was consolidated with the *Revielle* the paper being called the *Revielle and News* In April 1861 Baird sold his interest in the office to Waldo and left Vevay. In December 1863 Waldo sold the *Revielle* office to William J. Baird and Isaac W. Bristow. Bristow retired from the

## HISTORY OF SWITZERLAND COUNTY 113

office during the following May. Since then the paper has been published by William J. Baird.

In 1869 Thomas D. Wright came to Vevay with a printing office, commenced the publication of the *Vevay Democrat* and continued untill 1873 or 1874, when his son John H. Wright became proprietor, and published the *Democrat* for about one year when he disposed of the office to Irvin Armstrong (a son of Lieutenant William Armstrong who lost his life in the battle before the City of Mexico in Mexico in 1847)—who is the present editor and proprietor.[1]

Keen who was the pioneer newspaper man in Switzerland County, served as Justice of the peace in Vevay, Judge of the Probate court—Post Master at Printers Retreat, was convic[t]ed in the U. S. District Court of Indiana of robbing letters while Postmaster; Sent to the penitentiary at Jeffersonville, pardoned by President Van Buren, returned to the County, set up a small mill in Florence, finally went to Philadelphia where he died at Germantown one of the suburbs.

John Douglass left Vevay went to Corydon—thence to Indianapolis where he founded the *Indianapolis Journal* and conducted it for some years, perhaps until his death.

John Allen went to Salem Ind—founded the *Annotator* published it until his death. Thomas Berryman left Vevay but where he went to is not known.

Richard Randall went to Vernon and was at the last accounts of him by the writer working in a printing office.

James G. Fanning removed to Ohio.

Isaac Stevens, started a book store in Vevay—then went into the Drug business. He is now engaged in the grocery business He has been repeatedly elected to local offices. He is one of our most enterprizing and liberal citizens.

Wilson H. Gray went to California got rich and died. Charles S. Horton was appointed to a Government office by President Pierce—on account of being attacked by that fatal disease Consumption he was compelled to abandon his appointment, and shortly after died.

Peter H. Hale who created quite a sensation by his fiery editorials and challenging a prominent citizen of Vevay to fight a duel was appointed to office by President Buchannon—his cash account with the Government would not balance, so he went to Cuba.

Charles C. Scott went into the drug business in St. Joe Mo. made money, endorsed, and lost it. Is now publishing a daily paper and making money.

Merit W. Tague became a clerk and book keeper—was Chief Clerk in the Quarter Masters Department at Nashville Ten. during the war Is now Justice of the peace and engaged in the Real estate and I[n]surance agency business.[1]

Otis S. Waldo has been engaged in the Grocery business for many years—and has added to his stock, Dry goods Boots and shoes.

Ben. F. Schenck who edited the *News* is[2] in Florida on account of ill health—has been engaged in merchandizing in Vevay with U. P. Schenck his father—has become wealthy and built a residence near town which is the finest house for a residence in the County.[3]

Frederick J. Waldo was appointed Post Master during President Lincolns administration—was in the Grocery and Furniture business. For some years was United States assessor of Internal revenue for this county. At present he is residing in Rising Sun and is publisher of the *Rising Sun Recorder* one of the largest and best papers in South eastern Indiana.

Benjamin L. Simmons—was merchandizing at East Enterprize for many years—is at present engaged in business at Markland in this county.[4]

Thomas D. Wright left Vevay, went to Aurora and published a paper in the interest of the "Grangers" went to Madison, and finally to Leesburgh Va where he published a paper for a short time and on the 26th of April

1876 was in Vevay at the time of the Odd fellows celebration—[1]

John H. Wright was in Vevay two or three weeks since, but what business he is engaged in at present is not known.[2]

The foregoing in relation of printing offices and printers and publishers of newspapers in Switzerland County is thought to be as near correct as can be made out at this time from memory.

William D. M. Wickham who was apprenticed to Dufour Keen and Co. to learn the art of printing went into Rush county during the early days of that county set up a printing press on a large stump, and on that press and stump printed the first paper ever printed in Rush County—he was a nephew of John Dumont—a son of Mrs. Jane Murphy, whose first husband was named Wickham, her second Steele, and her third and last was Jessee Murphy who lived and died near Fairview in Cotton Township.

In 1815 or 1816 a family by the name of Vairin came to the neighborhood of Vevay, purchased a piece of land of Louis Gex Oboussier being now part of the farm owned by J. J. P. Schenck in his life time. The family consisted of the father and mother and three sons, Justus, Augustus and Julius. Justus was married to Miss Victoir Helvetia Gex on the 12[th] day of December 1817 by Elishea Golay Justice of the pea[c]e. They had one child a son named John Peter. Mr. Vairins wife died—and he was married again on the 9th October 1824 to Miss Sarah Wright by John Francis Dufour associate Judge. Mrs. Vairin died some years since leaving Two sons and four daughters—the last named sons and his sisters, are the inheritors of the large tract of land in Craig Township, which was purchased many years since in the name of Mary Wright, a sister of Mr. Vairins last wife; there being no other heirs but these children of Mr. Vairin by his wife Sarah.

The two sons of Mr. Vairin are in business in New Orleans the daughters are residing in Owensboro—Ky near which place they and the brothers & half brother own a farm which descends to them through the father.

Augustus Vairin was married to Miss Susan S. Pernet, on the 5[th] of October 1818 by Elisha Golay Justice of the peace went to New Orleans, died and shortly after his widow died leaving one Son Augustus who was in Vevay three or four years since, and was at that time with his cousin at Owensboro Kentucky.

Julius Vairin went to New Orleans many years ago got into business made a fortune, died leaving it to his brother Justus.

In the early settlement of this country many persons, who were disposed to profit by the ignorance of others in relation to the manner of obtaining lands from the government and make money off of the unsuspecting and ignorant foreigners and others on whom they could practice their projects, with success, formed many land associations for that purpose. One association or company was in that business named "Tombigbee land company" which offered some 200 acres of land on the Tombigbee river to all who became members of the Company, by paying in hand 5 or 10 dollars and subscribing the articles of association. For a short time they had two or three persons in the Swiss Colony of New Switzerland who were induced to pay their money, but they never realized any benefit from it.

In the year 1821 one Captain May who represented himself as an agent of Lord Selkirk made his appearance at Neville in the Canton Berne, Switzerland in Europe. His object was to organize a Swiss Colony to settle in "Selkirk Settlement" in British America. He gave a very favorable account of the country, of its products

## HISTORY OF SWITZERLAND COUNTY 117

and the advantages the colonists would enjoy in that fine country as depicted to them by this agent. It was represented that fruits of all kinds were produced in that Country even some of the tropical fruits.

Upon these representations of Captain May one John J. Simon a professor in the educational institutions of his native country was induced to accept the proposition[s] of Captain May, which were that Mr. Simon should have four hundred acres of land, and that each colonist should pay him ten days work on his land each year, to pay him for the tuition of their children—upon this representation of the Country and its fruits, many supposed that this settlement was on the "Red River" of Louisiana and not on the "Red River of the North." One young man though, a student contended, that it was in British America.

Accordingly in May 1821 Mr. John J. Simon, his wife and only child Zelia C. left Neville in the Canton of Berne on their Journey to America, descended the Rhine to a seaport in Holland, where they embarked on a vessel and after a voyage of three months or more, and being among Icebergs—at one time lying alongside of one for sometime, in company with four other vessels, the passengers visiting the several vessels over the ice—and had balls, or dancing parties on the ice they finally in the month of August arrived at Hudsons bay, where remaining a few days they procured three small boats, in which they ascended Nelsons river to lake Winnipeg—then along and across the lake to the mouth of the Red River of the North Thence up Red River a distance of Eighteen or Twenty miles to Fort Gary. The river closed with ice and navigation was suspended soon after their arrival at fort Gary and remained closed untill in May or June following, so they remained during the winter, during which time they spent nearly all their means. They paid Eigh[t] dollars per bushel for wheat, which was dried by the fire and ground on a coffee mill which is at present in the possession of the daughter now in Vevay—potatoes Eight dollars per bushel—maple sugar two dollars per pound, salt one dollar per quart—tobacco two dollars per pound, and as Mr. and Mrs. Simon both used Snuff, they bought plug tobacco dried it by the fire and rubbed it fine, for use. Finding that they could not live there, in June 1822 they left fort Gary, and proceeded up the river to Pembina. The river being low the Chippewa and Souix Indians being at war it was not deemed safe to continue their journey in the boat by the river—so they hired two horses and carts at three dollars per day, and men to hunt, to keep them supplied with provisions, they having provided themselves with sugar and coffee at Pembina as they were forced to travel among the Indians. One of the horses attached to one of the carts was killed by the Indians, so one of the carts had to be abandoned, the balance of the Journey with one horse and cart was accomplished, arriving at Lake Travers[e] where they remained some time, (they being the first white women who crossed the prairie). The several tribes of Indians were collected at the time at Lake Travers[e] to receive their annuities from the United States, which was being paid to them at that place, it was deemed unsafe for the party to continue their Journey until the Indians had separated and returned to their own settlements. After the dispersion of the Indians they proceeded on their journey, and arriving at the Saint Peters (now Minnisota) river, two canoes were built in which they and their goods were placed, and they descended the river to the mouth—along the Saint Peters river from where they took the canoes to the mouth there was but two trading posts, one occupyed by a person named Green, the other by a person named Preston. They left for Fort Snelling with letters of recommendation to the Indian agent, or commandant of the Fort. They arrived at the Fort and were introduced to Colonel Snelling. It being late in the fall Mr Simon was advised to remain during the winter, which he did. During the winter Mr.

Simon's daughter instructed the daughters of Colonel Snelling in the French language. During their stay at Fort Snelling the steam Boat Virginia, a Stern wheel boat, with supplies for the fort was expected to arrive. It had been known for three weeks that the boat was to arrive, so even the Indians became anxious to see the much talked of Steam Boat. On the arrival of the boat the landing was crow[d]ed with soldiers from the fort and Indians from the neighborhood. After the boat was moored to the shore, she commenced blowing off steam, which so frigh[t]ened the Indians, that they threw themselves to the ground as though their legs were cut off— then they decamped as though some foul fiend was pursuing them.

In due time after the opening of the navigation Mr Simon his wife and daughter shipped on a Keel boat for Saint Louis. In descending the Mississippi from Fort Snelling to Saint Louis it was observed that Scarcely any timber had been cut along the river bank and that but few houses were to be seen—from fort Snelling to Prairie du Cheine [Chien] no buil[d]ing were seen—one was standing where Dubuque is now located.

They arrived safely at Saint Louis where they remained a short time— shipped on a Keel boat at Saint Louis for Shippingport Ky, were in Saint Louis on the 4th of July—made the trip from Saint Louis to Shippingport (the cooking all being done during the trip on the keel boat) in a little over one month landing at Shippingport in August. At Louisville Mr. Simon his wife and daughter took passage on the steamer "Eliza" for Vevay, and landed at Mr. Morerods just at the lower end of Vevay in August 1823. Five weeks after their arrival at Vevay Mr. Simon being taken sick died leaving his wife and daughter with only 50 cents in money among Strangers in a strange land—but among those strangers they found tender hearted people and hospitable friends in the family of Mr. Morerod. Mrs. Simon and her daughter were left alone, the daughter being in her 16th year turned her attention to teaching French and sewing as a means of supporting herself and her mother. In the year 1828 that daughter was married to Frederick L. Grisard and are yet both living[1] and the parents of Rudolph F. Grisard Frederick L. Grisard Jr of Vevay James S. Grisard of Cincinnati O. and three daughters who are married. Mrs. Simon died on the 26th day of Decr 1856 in the 87th year of her age[2]

During the period between 1820 and 1826 the slavery question was agitated considerably in Kentucky, by those advocating colonizing the negroes and Sending them to Africa, and those advocating emancipation being in favor of ridding the state of the blight of slavery—and many of those holding slaves in opposition to both schemes,—the question was being warmly agitated in the County bordering on the Ohio river, immediately opposite Switzerland County—which caused some little defection among church members and ministers. The question became so warmly discussed in Gallatin County Ky that a Baptist minister who espoused the cause of emancipation, to avoid the turmoil occasioned by the difference of opinion, in 1823 removed from Fredericksburg, (now Warsaw) to Switzerland county, where he continued to preach for many years—when finally he removed to Decatur County Indiana where he died a few years since. That minister was the Revd. John Pavy the father of Samuel H. Pavy of Craig Township. One of Mr. Pavy's sons (Absolem) is at this time preaching out west—among the Indians as a missionary as the writer now recollects.

About the same time some question arose, among the Baptist brethren in the upper end of the County which caused the withdrawal of the Revd. Alexander Sebastian from the communion of that Church and quite a number of the members withdrew with him. Mr. Sebastian organized a Separate Church organization of the Baptists, who were disposed to subscribe to his views. One church

# HISTORY OF SWITZERLAND COUNTY 121

was organized in Cotton Township between East Enterprise and Quercus Grove, where he continued to preach for several years—in Ripley County in the neighborhood of Cross Plains a church was organized by him. They took the name of "Separate Baptists"; whether the organization is still continued since Mr. Sebastians death is not known to the writer.

As Mr. Sebastian was the founder of this church organization and had been deposed from the ministry by the regular Baptist organization—a question was raised as to his authority to solemnize marriages.

Some one who questioned his authority appeared before the Grand Jury of Switzerland County, and procured his Indictment against him for solemnizing a marriage without authority of law, he having been deposed from the ministry by the regular church of which he had been a member and minister.

The case was tried in the Circuit Court, Miles C. Eggleston being the president Judge at the time. Mr. Sebastian produced the records of his church organization, introduced the Clerk who kept the records of the Church, Joseph McHenry of Cotton Township, proved the record introduced to be the record of the Church.

By that record it appeared that he together with a number of others had organized themselves into a church, and that the church had called him to "minister unto them in Holy things" and had licensed him to preach.

The Judge in his charge to the Jury said there was no mode prescribed by our laws by which Churches were to be organized—that if the Jury believed from the evidence, there was actually a church organized by those persons named in the records and that the defendant was licensed to preach the Gospel they should acquit him. The Jury were but a few moments in making up their minds and returned a verdict of "not Guilty."

During the years 1823, 1824 and 1825, The farmers were annoyed with squirrels, which abounded in such numbers as to destroy a great proportion of the corn crops of the County.

It was customary during the spring Summer and fall for the farmers and others who wished to participate in the labor, and the sport of a squirrel hunt to meet at some appointed time and place and form parties or companies to compete with each other in the destruction of this destructive little animal.

On the 6th of March 1824 a party of twenty nine men met at Mount Sterling, formed two companies one under the direction of John Stepleton as captain, with sixteen men—the other under the direction of John F. Cotton with Twelve men. They hunted one day, and notwithstanding the weather was very unfavorable—considerable snow on the ground, and very windy, they destroyed 1007 of these destructive little animals. They met at Mount Sterling to count their game, or the scalps of their game, with the following result.

| Stepletons men | | Cottons men | |
|---|---|---|---|
| John Stepleton | 71 | John F. Cotton | 28 |
| James Picket | 48 | John Citti | 43 |
| Ira Everden | 33 | Barnabas Newkirk | 48 |
| Jonah Stow | 23 | William Brown | 56 |
| David Sheldon | 20 | William Keith | 46 |
| William Cotton Jr | 23 | Friend Thrall | 30 |
| Jacob Stickler | 45 | Elijah Dickason | 42 |
| Nathanial Mix | 65 | George W. Probasco | 18 |
| Zenas Sisson | 28 | Thomas Heady | 22 |
| Beal | 18 | Allen Burton | 30 |
| Bebus | 29 | James Cotton | 34 |
| Elson | 23 | James Brown | 52 |
| John H. Brown | 50 | Jacob Kern | 3 |
| Lester | 13 | | |
| Thomas McIntire | 28 | | |
| Peter Harper | 38 | | |
| | 555 | | 452 |

# HISTORY OF SWITZERLAND COUNTY

A squirrel hunt took place in Craig Township, on the 17th and 18th of March 1824, and on the 19th they met at Johnson Brown's on Long Run, to count their game with the following result—

| | | | |
|---|---|---|---|
| William Roberts | 125 | Jessee Warden | 48 |
| Redding Roberts | 112 | Samuel Brown | 167 |
| Peter Vanbriggle | 83 | Johnson Brown | 135 |
| Abisha McKay | 52 | James Brown | 115 |
| Joseph Brown Senr. | 169 | James A. Stewart | 85 |
| Moses Lutz | 70 | Isaac Richards | 66 |
| Daniel Bray | 114 | Nathaniel Gerard | 43 |
| Joseph Brown | 61 | Philip Ramseyer | 81 |
| William J. Stewart | 78 | Lewis C. Bakes | 36 |
| Hezekiah Roberts | 59 | Eugene Dutoit | 32 |
| Abraham Parkinson | 82 | Zadig Rous | 78 |
| Daniel Ramseyer | 44 | Lewis F. Golay | 39 |
| | 1049 | | 925 |

It was agreed to hunt one day more on the 15[th] of April and a Subscription was raised to procure powder and lead. It was thought if the people in that neighborhood and the other settlements would persevere the numerous race of squirrels would be very much diminished. It was the belief that one fourth of the corn crop, had been destroyed by squirrels the three preceeding years.

Up to the time of the hunt above noticed it was ascertained that the number killed was as follows
at the Mt. Sterling hunt
 by 29 men   one day   1007
at the Craig Township hunt
 by 14 men   two days   1974
at a hunt in Pleasant Township
 by 18 men   two days   1067
 Total by 61 men   4048

But the grand hunt of the season was one in the neighborhood of Mount Sterling on the 27th of March by thirty men one party of 14 men under John Stepleton as leader or captain and the other of 16 men under Henry Cotton as leader. The hunters met at Cottons still house and counted their game, with the following result—

| Stepletons party | | Cottons party | |
|---|---|---|---|
| John Stepleton | 205 | Henry Cotton | 413 |
| James Brown | 361 | John F. Cotton | 218 |
| Ira Everdon | 163 | Jonathan A. Gerard | 243 |
| William Cotton Jr. | 121 | Samuel Peak | 625 |
| James Picket | 85 | William Brown | 106 |
| Lewis W. Beal | 177 | John H. Brown | 247 |
| John Stickler | 212 | William Keith | 750 |
| Alexander Nelson | 192 | Jacob Kern Jr. | 236 |
| Peter Harper | 147 | Allen Burton | 159 |
| Nicholas Boyland | 74 | Benjamin Picket | 81 |
| James Dugan | 100 | John Citti | 103 |
| Andrew Bellons | 83 | Lyman Mix | 13 |
| Zenas Sisson | 60 | George W. Probasco | 115 |
| Nathaniel Mix | 120 | Miles Mendenhall | 50 |
| | | Friend Thrall | 129 |
| | | Bunn Green | 204 |
| | 2100 | | 3692 |

This is all the data the writer has from which to give the particulars of other squirrel hunts during the year 1824. There was one hunt on Tapps Ridge but the number of men and their names, who were engaged in that hunt are unknown to the writer. The number of scalps brought in by that party was 3166,—making in all 13,006 killed in the hunts here recorded. During the time that squirrels were so plentiful, great numbers swam the Ohio river from the Kentucky side to the Indiana side—when great numbers were captured and killed along the river, of which no account is given. In Vevay they could be killed any day off of the shade trees along the streets—and along the river bank above and below town.

Of the persons who participated in the two Mount Sterling hunts who are now living the writer can men-

## HISTORY OF SWITZERLAND COUNTY 125

tion William Cotton, Jr. John F. Cotton, Elijah Dickason, James Brown, Lewis W. Beal, Benjamin Picket and Miles Mendenhall— and of those who were engaged in the Craig Township hunt William Roberts Joseph Brown Samuel Brown, Daniel Ramseyer and Zadig Rous are the only ones that are still living as far as known by the writer.[1] Some of those who participated in these squirrel hunts were the best marksmen with a rifle in this part of the county and were always successful at the shooting matches, at which a beef was to be shot for—the beef being, killed, divided into quarters and the hide counted as one quarter thus making five quarters to be awarded as prizes to the persons making the best shots. Some of the best marksmen frequently came off with more than one quarter, sometimes with three prizes. Some of the persons named above as still living can no doubt recount many of the "Center" shots that were made by them or some one of their more successful competitors.

It was customary about Christmas and New Year to have a shooting match for turkeys. The person having a gang of turkeys, would give notice to the marksmen who wished to take a chance or chances in the shooting match that on a certain day he would have a lot of turkeys put up to be shot for at 12½ or 25 cents a shot. The marksmen would meet on the day at the appointed place—a turkey would be tied by the legs and set off one hundred yards, the men take their turns at sho[o]ting, the one who was so good a shot as to hit the Turkey became the owner of it.

In that manner the man who put up the turkey would realize a good price for them, and the successful shot get a turkey for a small price but very often a man would pay for shot after shot spend a good amount of money and get no turkey.

The fact that there were so many good marksmen in the earlier days of the settlements of this county is no doubt attributable in a great measure to the practice of those men for these shooting matches, where they were desirous of being called the best shot in the neighborhood.

Under the territorial legislature and for sometime under the State Government it was the law that if a debtor had no property subject to execution the officer was commanded by the writ to deliver the debtor to the Jailor to be detained in the County Jail until discharged by due course of law. The following is the copy of an execution issued by John Meek a Justice of the peace of Jefferson County.

"INDIANA TERRITORY Jefferson County"

The UNITED STATES to JOHN ROBERTS Constable of said County Greeting: Whereas Judgment hath been rendered before me one of the Justices assigned to keep the peace of the County aforesaid; in favor of John Reed plaintiff against Wilford Hagan defendant in an action of damages for five dollars and forty eight cents damages, also 90 cents costs you are therefore hereby commanded, within twenty days to levy the same on the goods and chattels of the said W. Hagan and make sale thereof according to law, and within the time specified by law, pay the said debt and cost to me, the said Justice or the person entitled to receive it; and if goods and chattels cannot be found or shewn by the said W. Hagan, sufficient to satisfy, the said debt and costs and 20 cents for this execution, together with constables commission, and serving this writ, whereon to levy, you are hereby commanded to take the body of the said W. Hagan if he is to be found within your bailiwick, and him convey and deliver to the jailor of the county aforesaid, within twenty days, who is hereby required to take the said W. Hagan into his custody and him safely keep until discharged by due course of law, herein fail not. Given under my hand and seal this 24th day of September in the year 1816." "JOHN MEEK J. P." (seal)"

# HISTORY OF SWITZERLAND COUNTY 127

[To show] That the law remained the same under the State Government a copy of an execution issued by Abner Clarkson justice of the peace of Jefferson County elected at the first election after the organization of the State Government is given below—

"STATE OF INDIANA Jefferson County S S

To PETER HEMPHILL Constable of Madison Township Greeting:

Whereas William Chittenden, assignee of James Wilson assignee of James B. Humphrey obtained judgment against Davis Wilkill and Colby Underwood before me a Justice of the peace of Madison Township for a debt of $2.60½ cts. and costs on the 11th day of July inst. you are therefore commanded to levy the said debt and costs that may accrue, of the goods, and chattels of the said Davis Wilkill by distress and sale thereof returning the overplus if any to the said Davis Wilkill, but for want of such property whereon to levy then take the said Davis Wilkill, to the jail of said County, there to be detained until said Debt and cost that may accrue shall be paid or he be otherwise legally discharged and of this make legal service and due return. Given under my hand and seal this 23rd day of July 1817."

ABNER CLARKSON J. P. (Seal)

Sometime in the year 1819 there was in the prison bounds of this county several persons against whom Judgments were obtained executions issued, and the officer not finding any property whereon to levy had delivered them over to the jailor—but the execution plaintiffs refusing to pay the Jailor for keeping them, confined in the Jail and feeding them, they gave bond and security, that they would not go out side the prison bound, which was within the limits of the town—and as most of them resided in town they could live with their families. Among the number were Charles Henderson, John Mendenhall James Dalmazzo—Edward Patton, and John F. Siebenthal. Siebenthal did not live in town, but on the farm where the widow Norrisez family now resided, but in a log house that stood fronting the river up near the line of the Danglade farm. The jailor gave notice to the execution plaintiff that he would not board Siebenthal without he paid the board. The execution plaintiff refused to do so. Siebenthal gave bond with John F. Dufour his security to keep the prison bounds. Siebenthal applied for board but no person would board him, and the execution plaintiff refusing to furnish him board, he left town and returned home.

Suit was brought on the Bond against Siebenthal and Dufour—which was decided in their favor the court holding that the execution plaintiff was bound to pay his board. All those persons above named as having been in custody of the Jailor or in the prison bounds, afterward paid up all their debts.

Henry Clay who was ever, the friend and advocate of every undertaking which had for its object, or was calculated to advance the settlement and improvement of the "Great West" was at quite an early day visiting the Swiss Colony of New Switzerland, and became the guest of John Francis Dufour, and Louis Gex Oboussier, when he drank some of Mr. Gex's best wine, which he thought was very fine, and was far better then the imported European wines brought out West. Mr. Gex presented him with one dozen bottles, which were properly packed and taken to Mr. Clays residence at Lexington Ky. Mr. Clay having some of his particular friends, at his residence, and [they] were drinking some of the European wines he had collected and Stowed away in his cellar Some one of the guests was loud in his praise of the good quality of the wine the company were then drinking. Mr. Clay remarked that [he] had a dozen bottles of native wine presented to him by one of his Swiss friends of New Switzerland, and which was made by him of grapes grown in his vineyard on the border of the Ohio river. Mr. McAfee who was once governor of Kentucky and a guest at that time remarked—"Mr. Clay should at any rate bring us a bottle, that we may taste and pass our opinions on its quality." Mr. Clay accordingly had a bottle of Mr. Gex's make of wine brought in. It was uncorked, smelled of and pronounced to be whiskey. Supposing a mistake had been made in getting the bottle, another and another was brought in, until the whole dozen had been, tested, and every bottle proved to be "Whiskey."

Mr. Clay was much chagrined at his not being able to have the good qualities of Mr. Gex's wine tested and praised by his near neighbors and friends who had met on that occasion to have a friendly meeting. he said "there is some mistake about this affair."

Sometime after the mistake was explained thus. His son James B. Clay, who no doubt, (and it is said to be the truth), preferred the taste of Mr. Gex's wine to that of the whiskey in his father's cellar; opened bottle after bottle of the wine occasionally drank of it, until the bottle was empty, then refilled it with whiskey sealed it and set it by (untill the last of the dozen bottles was served in like manner, thus leaving his father with a dozen bottles of whiskey instead of the Dozen bottles of Mr. Gexs manufacture of wine—this incident was related to the writer by Lucien Gex living on the bank of the Ohio river above Ghent, who is a grandson of Mr. Gex who presented the Dozen bottles of wine to Mr. Clay.

He derived his information in Mercer County Kentucky some years since, in a conversation he heard between some gentlemen, one of whom was a brother to Governor McAfee—when he heard the name of Gex mentioned, as the person who had made Mr. Clay the present of the wine, he remarked "that Mr. Gex was my grandfather."

As heretofore mentioned the first board of commissioners of the County was elected in Feb. 1817. James

130     INDIANA HISTORICAL COLLECTIONS

Rous to serve until the August election in 1818 Isaac Stanley to serve until the August election in 1819 Caleb Mounts to serve until the August election in 1820. At the August election in 1818 Thomas Gilliland was elected to succeed James Rous, and Isaac Stanley having resigned, the Circuit Court appointed George Craig to fill the vacancy. Craig was present as Commissioner at the November Session 1817, and served until the August Election 1818 when Dr. John Mendenhall was elected to fill the vacancy. At the August election 1819 William Campbell was elected. At the August election 1820 William Ross of Ross Township was elected. At the August election in 1821 Henry Banta was elected.

During the Session of the legislature of 1821-1822 part of Ross Township which was called the "Horn" was attached to Ripley county and as William Ross one of the County Commissioners resided in that part of the township that was detached from Switzerland and attached to Ripley county [he] became a resident of Ripley County thus creating a vacancy which would make it necessary to elect his successor at the next August election.

At the February session of the board of Commissioners, it was ordered that, that part of Ross Township which would remain in Switzerland County, after the taking effect of the act of the General assembly attaching a part of Switzerland County to Ripley county be attached to and made a part of Pleasant township.

At the August election 1822 Thomas Gilliland was re-elected Commissioner and Lucien Gex was elected to fill the vacancy occasioned by the disqualification of William Ross.

At the August election 1823 William Gard was elected Commissioner. At the August session Thomas Gilliland, and Henry Banta who was re-elected at the August election, were required to take and did take an oath in relation to County orders.

The law in relation to the transaction of County business having been altered by the legislature, abolishing the office of County Commissioners, and transferring that business to the Justices of the peace of the county— on the 1st Monday in September 1824 the Justices of the County were required to meet and organize the board by choosing one of their number President.[1] Accordingly on that day, John Smith, Samuel Jack, and Caleb Mounts of Posey Township, Joseph Pugh and Joseph McHenry of Cotton, Thomas Wiles and William C. Keen of Jefferson Township met and took the oath that was required to be taken by the County Commissioners. William C. Keen was appointed President of the Board. An order was passed by the board requiring the Clerk to report to the Prosecuting attorney the names of the Justices who failed to attend the meetings of the Board as required by law. At the Sept. Session 1825 Edward Patton was elected president. At the November 1825 Session of the board, in addition to those attending the first session, Johnson Brown, John Elam, Samuel Beal, Edward Patton and William J. Stewart Justices of the peace were in attendance.

The law makers of Indiana about this time in the history of the State appear to have been very unstable in their ideas of the manner in which County business should be transacted for during the month of January 1826 an act was passed requiring the Voters in the several townships of the counties to elect at their Spring Township election, one Justice of the peace of their respective townships to act as "Supervisor" for the township, who when elected were to meet (the first time) on the first Monday in the Month of May to transact the county business and were to be designated as "The Board of Supervisors."[2]

Accordingly in May 1826, Samuel Beal of Jefferson Amos A Brown of Posey, Joseph Pugh of Cotton, John Elam, of Pleasant and Johnson Brown of Craig Township met as the first Board of Supervisors of Switzerland County. This continued to be the manner of

## 132    INDIANA HISTORICAL COLLECTIONS

transacting County business until 1831 during which time, Samuel Jack John Gibbons, and Aribert Gazley Justices of the peace of Posey Pruit Harvey of Craig, George E. Pleasants of Jefferson and Joseph McHenry of Cotton Township served as supervisors from their respective townships.

At the November Session 1829 of the Board of Supervisors the petition of William Campbell and others praying the formation of a new township, of portions of Jefferson and Posey Townships was presented to the Board—no further action was taken on the petition during that Session but [it] was continued until the next Session.

At the May Session 1830 of the Board, the matter was taken up and the board passed an order laying off the new township by the name of Jackson Township, and it does not appear that any further action was taken in the matter by the board until the May Session 1831 of the board, when the matter was taken up, and the action of the board in making the order for the formation of the new township was reconsidered, and the order of the board in the matter with the exception of the name of the Township was Confirmed, and the Township was named "York" instead of "Jackson." The place of holding elections in said Township was fixed at the house of Charles F. Krutz in the town of New-York (now Florence)[1] and William White appointed inspector of elections in said Township. An election for one Justice of the peace was ordered to be held & notice thereof to be given by the sheriff.

On the 16th day of May 1831, Amos A. Brown filed his bond and took the oath of office as Justice of the peace for said "York" township, and was consequently the first Justice of the peace of York Township.

Some few years after the town of New York was incorporated by an act of the legislature,[2] and consequently an additional Justice of the peace was elected to reside within the corporation limits of the Town and

# HISTORY OF SWITZERLAND COUNTY 133

George Land who had removed into the town about that time was elected Justice of the peace.

The Legislature having at the Session of 1830-31 passed an act changing the mode of transacting the county besiness from the Board of Supervisors to a Board of County Commissioners—three to be elected at the August election 1831[1] The County was divided into 3 districts numbered respe[c]tively 1st 2nd and 3rd districts—the first district to be composed of Craig and Jefferson Townships, the second of York and Posey Townships, the third of Cotton and Pleasant Townships, one Commissioner to be chosen in each district—one for one year, one for two years and one for three years, and at each August election thereafter one to be elected. At the first election, on the 1st Monday in August 1831, Lyman W. Mix was elected for the 1st district to serve one year William Scudder in the second district for two years and Enos Littlefield in the third district for three years. At the August election 1832, Lyman W. Mix was re-elected in the first district for three years—in 1833 William Scudder re-elected in the second district for three years in 1834 Eden Edwards was elected in the third district for three years—in 1835 Philip Bettens Jr. was elected in the first district for three years—in 1836 Colin McNutt was elected in second district for three years—in 1837 Eden Edwards was re-elected in the third district for three years—in 1838 Philip Bettens Jr. was re-elected in the first district for three years—in 1839 Andrew Stewart was elected in the second for three years—in 1840 David Henry was elected in the third district for three years—in 1841 John James P. Schenck was elected in the 1st district for three years.

At a special meeting of the Board of County Commissioners on the 9th of August 1841, an act having been passed by the legislature at the session of 1840-1841 authorizing the board to appoint one of their number President, and transferring the duties of Clerk to the board from the Clerk of the Circuit Court to the County Auditor,[1] David Henry was unanimously chosen President, and John M. King the County Auditor elect entered upon the duties of clerk of the Board. In 1842 Andrew Stewart was re-elected in the second district for three years.

In June 1842 David Henry resigned his office as commissioner—and at the August election 1842 William Flynn was elected to fill the vacancy in the 3rd district—at the September Session 1842 John James P. Schenck was elected president of the board. In 1843 David Shull was elected in the 3rd district for three years. In 1844 Lewis W. Beal was elected in the 1st district for three years. In 1845 Arthur Humphrey was elected in the Second district for three years—in 1846 Harvey Littlefield was elected in the third district for three years. In 1847 Daniel Ramseyer was elected in the first district for three years. In 1848 William Howe was elected in the second district for three years. In 1849 Jacob Shull was elected for the third district for three years and re-elected in 1852 for three years. In 1850 John Weaver was elected in the 1st district for three years, re-elected in 1853 for three years. In 1851 James S. Furgeson was elected in the second district for three years and re-elected in 1854.

In 1854 Charles A. Gary was elected in the third district for three years.

Since then the first district has been represented on the Board by William Anderson who was on the board from 1859 up to September 1870 or 1871—and by William M. Patton for three years up to the commencement of the term of service of David Scott.

The Second district has been represented on the board since Furgeson was a member, by Bela Herrick, Jacob R. Harris, William H. Cunningham, and Philip Bettens, until the term of Service of Col. William Stewart commenced.

The third district has been represented on the board

since the termination of the term of service of Charles A. Gary—by Lemuel Wiley Luther M. Hotchkiss, Benjamin L. Simmons Augustus Welch, and Harvy Littlefield up to the commencement of the term of service of William J. Gibbs.

David Scott is at present commissioner for the 1st district   William Stewart is the present Commissioner for the 2d District   William J. Gibbs the commissioner for the 3d District at this time.

At the October election, 1876 commissioners are to be elected in the first and third district[s] as successors of David Scott and William J. Gibbs.

The foregoing is as correct a history of [those] who have transacted the business of the County since its formation and of the changes made at different times by the Legislature, in the manner of transacting that business as can be given.

For many years the business of the Township was transacted by three trustees and a Township Clerk. The Township Clerk was the Inspector and the Trustees the Judges of all elections held in their respective townships.

### Office of Sheriff

John F. Siebenthal was sheriff under the territorial government by appointment by Gov. Posey from the organization of the County in 1814 until the organization of the State Government in 1817. Was elected at the first election in Feby 1817 and served until August 1820. In August 1820 Israel R. Whitehead was elected for 2 years from 21st August 1820.

John F. Siebenthal was elected in August 1822 for two years and re-elected in 1824 for two years.

In August 1826 Ralph Cotton was elected for two years—died before his term of office expired and William Keith was appointed by the Governor to serve until his successor was elected.

At the August election 1829 Henry Banta was elected

for 2 years from 3rd August 1829—and in 1831 was re-elected for two years.

In August 1833 Ralph B. Cotton was elected for two years and re-elected in 1835 for two years. In August 1837 Henry McMakin was elected for two years—and re-elected in 1839 for two years from the 19th of August 1839.

In August 1841 William Price, was elected for two years, served but a short time when he gave up the office to Joseph Malin, who served as Deputy for Mr. Price.

In August 1843 Henry McMakin was again elected for two years, and was in August 1845 defeated for re-election by John R. Morerod who was elected for two years.

In August 1847 Percy Rous was elected for two years and was re-elected in August 1849 for two years. In 1851 August 1851 John W. Gray was elected for two years his term of service expiring in Sept. 1853.

The time of holding the annual election was changed from the 1st Monday in August to the 2nd Tuesday of October by the Constitution now in force—at the election in October 1852 being the first election, under the present constitution Samuel W. Howard was elected for two years from the 5th of September 1853, which term expired September 1855.

At the October election 1854 Harris Keeney was elected for two years, from the 5th September 1855, and was re-elected in October 1856 for two years from September 1857.

At the October election 1858 William Mead was elected for two years from September 1859. At the October election 1860 William Mead was re-elected for two years fro[m] September 1861.

In October 1862 Larkin Johnston was elected for two years from September 1863 and re-elected in October 1864 for two years from September 1865. In October 1866 Mathew Worstell was elected and served till 1st

## HISTORY OF SWITZERLAND COUNTY 137

November 1869, from September 1867—and was re-elected in October 1870 and served until October 25, 1872.

At the October election 1872 John Armstrong was elected and served until the 30th October 1874 was re-elected at the October election 1874 for two years which expires in October 1876—A success[or] is to be elected at the October election 1876. the candidates for nomination, before the convention of the Republican party which meets on the 10th of June, are now busily engaged in marshaling their friends for the contest before the convention which meets tomorrow—this paragraph being, written, on the 9th day of June, 1876. The convention of the Democrats to meet on the 17th of June.

### OFFICE OF CLERK OF THE CIRCUIT COURT

John Francis Dufour was appointed Clerk by Thomas Posey Gov. of Indiana Territory in 1814, at the organization of the County—and on the organization of the State Government he was elected by the voters of the County in February 1817—to serve Seven years—which expired in February 1824.

At the August election 1823 the time for electing a Successor—Israel R. Whitehead, John Gilliland and William C. Keen were the candidates before the people for their suffrages. The contest was quite spirited, the friend[s] of the candidates using every means in their power to secure the Success of their favorite. Whitehead was elected receiving 6 or 8 votes more than either of the other candidates. Keen being the next highest, served notice on Whitehead of his intention to contest his election—the contest was either abandoned or decided in Whiteheads favor, as he served his term of seven years—and at the August election 1830 was a candidate for re-election Edward Patton being the opposing Candidate. Patton was elected.

At the August election 1837 Patton was re-elected. At the August election 1844 Patton was again re-elected and continued to serve until April 1849 when he died thus creating a vacancy.

William Patton late County Auditor was appointed on the 23rd day of April 1849 to serve until a successor to Edward Patton could be elected and qualified.

On the first Monday in August 1849 Charles T. Jones was elected to serve the unexpired term of Edward Patton which expired February 24th 1852.

At the August election 1851 Ira N. Malin was elected to serve Seven years from the 24th February 1852, but as the present constitution had been adop[t]ed before his term of office commenced, he was commissioned for four years only that being the length of time clerks would serve under the new Constitution, thus causing his term of office to expire in November 1855.

The time of holding the annual election being changed by the present Constitution from the 1st Monday in August to the Second Tuesday in October—so that at The October election 1855 Oliver Ormsby was elected to serve four years—and at the October election 1859 he was re-elected for four years but served only until December 1852 [1862] he having become so dissipated as to be unfit for business at times—his securit[i]es requiring him to give additional bond which failing to do the office was declared vacant, he was deposed from office and William Rous on the 29th of December 1862 was appointed to serve until the October election 1863.

At the October election 1863 William Rous was elected for four years from 1st November 1863.

At the October election 1867 Charles Heath was elected for four years, which would expire the first of November 1871—but on account of his health being somewhat impaired, and the laws being modified or changed so that the salary and fees would not Justify him in discharging some duty imposed on clerks since his election, in February 1871. [He] Resigned the office, and Alfred Rous was appointed to serve for the unexpired term.

At the October election 1870 Alfred Rous was a can-

## HISTORY OF SWITZERLAND COUNTY 139

didate for clerk and was opposed by Joseph H. Netherland the latter being elected over Rous by 9 or 10 majority. At the October election 1874 Joseph H. Netherland was re-elected over Thomas Watts his opponent by a majority of 8 or 9 votes, for four years from 4th November 1875 and is at this time serving as clerk of the Circuit Court of the county.[1]

### OFFICE OF COUNTY TREASURER

Samuel Fallis was appointed County treasurer by the Board of Commissioners, at the February Session 1817, consequently he was the first Treasurer of the County—he was reappointed at the February Session in 1818 and in 1819 & in 1820. On the 3rd day of February 1819 the Board settled with Samuel Fallis as treasurer, when it was found that the County was indebted to him in the sum of $85.20.

At the February Session of the Board in 1821, Joseph Malin was appointed treasurer and in 1822 at the February Session he was reappointed. In settleing with the board Feby session 1822 it was found that the County was indebted to him as treasurer in the sum of $20.43 3/4. Malin was reappointed Treasurer in February 1823, & 1824 and in January 1825. In a settlement with the board February session 1824 there was found to be $17.38 in his hands.

In a settlement with the Board of Justices in November 1824 the county was found to be indebted to Malin the Treasurer $123.32 2/3. Malin as treasurer was required by the board of Justices to furnish the Board with a Statement of the condition of the County treasury from the year 1820 to Jany 1825 which he did, by that Statement it appeared that there was in the treasurers hands a balance of $56.27 1/4. At the September Session 1825, of the Board of Justices Joseph Malin tendered his resignation to the Board which was reluctantly accepted, and Ira Mendenhall appointed to fill the Vacancy. Malin settled his accounts as county treasurer, with the

Board of Justices and the County was indebted to him in the sum of $95.37.

Ira Mendenhall was reappointed year after year until May 1830, when George G. Knox was appointed on the 4th of May 1830 and was appointed year after year until August 1841. The legislature having at the Session of 1840-41 changed the law requiring the Treasurer to be elected by the voters at the annual election.

At the August election 1841 Frederick L. Grisard was elected Treasurer, being the first treasurer elected by the voters of the county. Mr. Grisard however resigned the office in June 1842 and James S. Carter was appointed to fill the vacancy but did not qualify and William Hall was appointed to serve the remainder of Grisards term of office which expired in 1843. William Hall was elected in August 1843 for two years 1845, for two years, in 1847 for two years and in 1849 for two years. At the August election 1851 John F Doan was elected and served two years. At the next election which was held the 2d Tuesday in October 1852 the time of holding the annual election being changed by our present constitution to that time George H. Kyle was elected and served two years, from the 1st Septr. 1853 to Septr 1855. At the October election 1856 John R. Morerod was elected for two years from the 1st Sept. 1855—and was reelected at the October election 1856 for two years from 1st Sept. 1857. At the October election 1858 Ira N. Malin was elected for two years from 1st Sept. 1859. At the October election 1860 John R. Morerod was elected for 2 years from 1st September 1861. In 1862 Eli T. Ogle was elected for 2 years from 1st Sept 1863, and reelected in 1864 for 2 years from 1st Sept 1865.

In 1866 Frederick L. Courvoissier was elected for two years from 1st Sept 1867, and reelected in 1868 for two years from 1st Sept. 1869.

In 1870 Joshua D. Griffith was elected for two years from 1st Sept 1871.

# HISTORY OF SWITZERLAND COUNTY 141

In 1872 Augustus Welch was elected for two years from the 1st Sept. 1873.

In 1874 Francis M. Griffith was elected for two years from the 1st Sept 1875.[1]

## RECORDERS OFFICE

John Francis Dufour was appointed by Thomas Posey Governor of Indiana Territory, Recorder of the county in October 1814 at the organization of the County and served as such after the organization of the State Government until February 1817.

At the first election under the State Government in February 1817 Thomas Armstrong was elected for seven years from February 1817 to February 1824. On the first Monday of August 1823 Abraham B. Dumont was elected for Seven years from Feb. 1824. On the first Monday of August 1830 Ira Mendenhall was elected for Seven years from Feby 1831, and re-elected on the first Monday of August 1837 for seven years from February 1838.

On the first Monday of August 1844 Ira N. Malin was elected for Seven years, from February 1845.

The next election for Recorder after Ira N. Malins term of service expired, was on the Second Tuesday of October 1852, at which election James H. Titus was elected and served until the 1st of November 1855.

At the October election 1855 William H. H. Kelso was elected for four years from 1st November 1855.

At the October election 1859 Horace B. Herrick was elected for four years from the first of November 1859.

At the October election 1863 Lewis F. Works was elected for four years from the first of November 1863.

At the October election 1867 John T. Schroeder was elected for four years from the first of November 1867.

At the October election 1870 John P. White was elected for four years from first November 1871, and was re-elected at the October election 1874 for four years from the 1st of November 1875, and is at present serving his last term as Recorder.

### OFFICE OF COUNTY AUDITOR

The law creating the office of County Auditor first came in force in 1841[1] and at the August elections of that year John M. King was elected the first Auditor of the County for four years, consequently his successor was elected on the 1st Monday in August 1845.

On the first Monday in August 1845 Aurelius W. Dumont was elected for four years,—but died before his term of service expired—and at the September session 1849 of the Board of County Commissioners Robert N. Lamb was appointed Auditor to serve as such until the August election 1850. Daniel Ramseyer William Howe and Jacob Shull were the commissioners at that session of the Board.

At the August election 1850 Robert N. Lamb was elected for four years and at the October election 1853, Lamb was reelected for four years from Sept or November 1854, which would expire in 1859. At the October election 1859 Lawrence W. Gordon was elected for four years from November 1859 and in 1863 was re-elected for four years which expired in November 1867.

At the October election 1867 Major William Patton was elected for four years from November 1867—and in 1871 he was re-elected for four years which expired in November 1875.

At the October election in 1874 John Gill was elected for four years from the 1st November 1875 at which time he entered upon the discharge of the duties of the office and is at present attending to the duties of the office.[2]

The number of acres of land in Switzerland County according to Government surveys, on file in the Auditors office at Vevay is as follows

| | | | | | | |
|---|---|---|---|---|---|---|
| In | Township 1 | of Range | 1 | East | | 1,961.31 |
| In | " 2 | of " | 1 | " | | 1,411.90 |
| In | " 1 | of " | 1 | West | | 208.47 |
| In | " 2 | of " | 1 | " | | 21,890.96 |
| In | " 3 | of " | 1 | " | | 7,252.25 |
| In | " 1 | of " | 2 | " | | 3,815.84 |
| In | " 2 | of " | 2 | " | | 23,453.17 |
| In | " 3 | of " | 2 | " | | 7,623.05 |
| In | " 1 | of " | 3 | " | | 202.92 |
| In | " 2 | of " | 3 | " | | 16,678.32 |
| In | " 3 | of " | 3 | " | | 21,889.78 |
| In | " 4 | of " | 3 | " | | 6,802.65 |
| In | " 1 | of " | 4 | " | | 740.55 |
| In | " 2 | of " | 4 | " | | 3,802.99 |
| In | " 3 | of " | 4 | " | | 379.23 |
| In | " 3 | of " | 12 E. | Jeffersonville District | 2,367.78 |
| In | " 4 | of " | 12 | " | | 7,757.78 |
| In | " 5 | of " | 12 | " | | 11,552.47 |
| In | " 6 | of " | 12 | " | | 2,552.00 |

Making the total number of acres— 142,343.42 which being divided by 640, the number of acres in a Square mile, gives 222 41/100 Square miles in the County.

It will be seen that there is but one full congressional Township in the county, the others being fractional townships, and parts of townships. It will also appear by the above Statement that the two first townships are East of the principal meridian, which is a line running north and South from the mouth of the Great Miami river.

This land is divided into fine farms—and some part of it has been laid out into town lots, and some of the towns are still in existance and some have been been vacated.

In 1813 John Francis Dufour and Daniel Dufour laid out the town of Vevay, since which additions have been made to it by John Sheets and Daniel Dufour, John F. Dufour, Corporation of Vevay, John Sheets and Vincent Dufour, Francis G. Sheets, Perret Dufour and David Armstrong.

In 1814 a number of out lots were laid out above and adjoining the Inlots. These out lots were of three and five acres each.

In 1815 Peter Harris, laid out the Town of Jacksonville, and in 1817 William Gerard laid out an addition.

In 1815 Edward McIntire laid out the town of Erin, opposite to Carrollton, which was vacated.

In 1816 Peter Demaree laid out the town of Allensville.

In 1816 Philo Averil laid out the town of Mount Sterling, and additions have been made thereto by Henry Cotton & and Lyman W. Mix, Samuel Beal and Robert Rosebrough.

In 1817 Benjamin Drake laid out the town of New York, the name has since been changed to Florence. Additions have been made thereto by Joseph Malin, James Campbell, and Benjamin L. Robinson.

In 1820 Elisha Wade laid out the town of Troy, which has since been changed to Patriot, and additions have been made thereto by, James Herrick, Martin R. Green, Bela Herrick and Hicks and Herrick.

In 1822 Patrick Donahue laid out the town of Montgomery, on his land above Patriot, but caused it to be vacated some years after.

In 1847 Daniel W. Loudon laid out the town of Bennington. Some years ago the town of Moorefield was laid out by some person, but the name is not certainly known, but is believed to be Franscis Lansdale. Fairview and East Enterprize, in Cotton Township, Soapville in Pleasant Township, and Quercus Grove, in Posey Township, which are small towns or villages, if ever laid out and platted into lots, those plats are not on record

# HISTORY OF SWITZERLAND COUNTY 145

in the Recorder's office, neither is the plat of the town of Moorefield on record.

Center Square was laid out by William Lawrence in 1835; and at one time candidates for the legislature were nominated, who favored the re-location of the County seat at that place. Mr. Lawrence remarked to the writer that he had spoiled a fine farm in trying to have a town built up.

In 1829 the office of Probate Judge was created by act of the Legislature,[1] and the first Judge elected under that law in the County was William C. Keen.[2] Keen continued to serve as Probate Judge until some time in the winter of 1839, when he was charged with purloining a letter containing a $20. bank note from the Post office at Printer's Retreat, at which place he was Post Master. He adjourned his court on Friday evening, and the Constable having the warrant was directed to arrest him, after the adjournment of the court on that evening, as that was the end of the term; he was accordingly arrested and brought before the writer, who was at the time an acting Justice of the peace in Vevay. Keen wishing to make some preparations for his defence wished the case continued until the following Monday. The case was continued, the defendant entering into recognizance for his appearance at that time.

On Monday the case was commenced, and by Thursday evening the case was decided by requiring Keen to enter into recognizance for his appearance before the Circuit Court, and the Judges of the Circuit Court recognized him to appear before the United States district Court for Indiana—an indictment was found against him in that Court, and he was tried, found guilty and sentenced to the penitentiary at Jeffersonville where he remained some time and was pardoned by President Van Buren— he returned to the County, and erected a small steam Mill at Florence—finally went east, and died at Germantown near Philadelphia.

At the Feby term 1839 the Judge of the Probate Court not appearing Elisha Golay one of the associate Judges held the court—(at one other term of the court held in the Spring of 1839 the Judge not appearing Elisha Golay and Newton H. Tapp associate Judges held that term of the Court.)

The August term 1839 of the court was held by John F. Dufour who was commissioned by the Governor to act until a successor could be elected.

An election was held, and John F. Dufour was elected and the first term of the court over which he presided after that election was in November 1839 and [he] continued the Judge of that Court until the August Election 1846 when Robert Drummond was elected and the first term of the court held by him was the November term 1846   the term for which he was elected expired in 1853—but upon the adoption of the present constitution and the laws passed by the legislature after its adoption the Probate Court was abolished and the Court of Common Pleas was organized[1]—and Robert Drummond was at the October election 1852 elected the first Judge of the Court of Common Pleas and continued in the office until the April term 1858. At the July term 1858 Judge Drummond not being in attendance on account of Illness the clerk, Auditor, and Sheriff appointed Scott Carter Judge pro. term. At the January term 1859 John J. Hayden commenced his Services as Judge and continued to serve until July term 1860.

At the February term 1861 Francis Adkinson served as Judge and continued until June term 1864.

At the November Term 1864 Robert N. Lamb served as Judge and continued to serve until March term 1868.

At the September term 1868 there being no regular Judge in attendance the Clerk, Auditor and Sheriff appointed Scott Carter as Judge pro. tem. who continued to serve until the 11th or 12th day of the term when he resigned—and the Clerk, Auditor, and Sheriff appointed

# HISTORY OF SWITZERLAND COUNTY 147

John Schwartz Judge pro. tem. who continued to serve from the 12th day of the term until the end of the term.

At the March term 1869 Scott Carter commenced serving as the regular Judge and continued to serve until the September term 1872, when the Court of Common Pleas was abolished by act of the Legislature.[1]

Judge Berkshire held a Special term of the Court in June 1872.

During the terms of Service of Drummond and Hayden Ohio, and Switzerland Counties formed the Judicial District—and afterwards, Dearborn and Jefferson Counties were added to the district, so that during the term of service of Scott Carter, and at the time of the abolishing of the court, Dearborn Ohio, Switzerland and Jefferson Counties composed the Judicial district. The circuit Court of the County during the Territorial government consisted of one President Judge and two associate Judges—the latter Judges being authorized by law to transact county business and also business pertaining to the settlement of decedents estates. The president Judges from the organization of the county in 1814 to the organization of the State Government were the following—

Elijah Sparks from 1814 to 1815. James Noble from 1815 to 1816—Jessee L. Holman from 1816 to 1818. After the adoption of the constitution, the following named persons, have occupied the bench as President Judge assisted by two associates up to 1851 when by the present constitution the office of associate Judge was abolished. John Test from 1818 to 1819, John Watts from 1819 to 1820—Miles C. Eggleston from 1820 to 1844 Courtland Cushing from 1844 to 1850.

Alexander C. Downey from 1850 to 1858, serving two terms of four years each—for one or two terms having associate Judges on the bench with him.

Joseph W. Chapman from 1858 to 1864.

John G. Berkshire from 1864 to 1876, the term of four years which he is now serving expiring this fall after the

## 148  INDIANA HISTORICAL COLLECTIONS

October election, at which his successor will be elected or he be re-elected.[1]

The November term 1849 was presided over by William Wick president Judge of the 5th Judicial circuit.

Robert N. Lamb was appointed by Judge Chapman to preside at the May term 1864, and also by the Clerk Auditor and Sheriff for the November term 1864.

Judges from other circuits have been called at various times to hold Special terms to try cases in which a change of Judge had been granted, among whom may be mentioned Judges Bicknell, Claypool, Cullen, New, Emmerson and Cravens.

The first associate Judges of the County [who] were appointed by the Governor of the Territory at the organization of the County in 1814 and continued to serve until 1820 were William Cotton and James McClure.

Abner Clarkson and Ralph Cotton were elected and their term of service commenced in 1820. Clarkson served untill 1825—and Cotton until 1822 in the fall when he resigned having been elected to the legislature at the preceeding August election.

John Wilson Served from 1822 to 1829—John F. Dufour from 1824 to 1827 when he resigned and became administrator of the estate of his brother John James—the business of the estate having to be settled before the associate Judges he thought it proper to resign—William Bradley was elected his successor and served until 1829 when he was induced to become a candidate for the legislature and was elected—Joseph Malin served from 1829 to 1836  Elisha Golay served from 1831 to 1845, Newton H. Tapp from 1836 to 1845, David Cain from 1845 to 1851, Walter Armstrong from 1845 to 1850—and died before the expiration of his term of service—John F. Dufour commenced a term of Service at the spring term (May) 1850, was taken sick while attending court and died June the 10th 1850.

George H. Kyle served from 1850 to 1851 when the office was abolished on the adoption of the present con-

# HISTORY OF SWITZERLAND COUNTY 149

stitution. Among the aspirants for the office of associate Judge may be named, John K. Walker of Cotton Township John Gibbons of Posey Township Alexander Sebastion of York Township, Caleb Mounts and Sylvanus Howe of Posey Township. At one time when Sebastian was a candidate for Judge, he came to Vevay in a farm waggon drawn by two horses. It was on a public occasion perhaps the 4th [of] July and the town was full of people from the country. Sebastian imbibed too freely of the ardent and took refuge in his waggon and fell asleep, and while fast asleep some mischievously disposed persons drew the waggon to the brow of the hill on Liberty Street between the lots belonging to the Kessler family and the residence of John Louis Thiebaud and let it run down the hill with Sebastian in it—he was awakened by the rapid progress of the waggon and supposing that the horses were running away, commenced calling out at the top of his voice to stop the supposed flight of the horses to the great merriment of all those who witnessed the affair. Sebastian after that affair declined being a candidate.

About the year 1818-1819 & 1820 candidates for office who resided in other Counties that [than] Switzerland, frequently visited Vevay on electioneering tours—on one occasion there was present in Vevay Gov. Jonathan Jennings, Harbin H. Moore and some others from abroad with [who] together with some of the Vevay "boys" visited "Switzerland" to taste some of father Morerods and Bettens wine, and the Gov. and one or two others from abroad not being used to the wine became considerably fuddled as well as some of the Vevay boys on the way up to town they had to pass through the "dog fennel" which grew very thick over the commons, and was at the time in full bloom and they having white pants and vests, they presented the spectacle of a pair of yellow pair of pants and yellow spotted vests.

About 1826 or 1827 a person named Thomas Ramsey who was addicted to inebriation was induced (by some of those who wished to get their liquor without paying) to become a candidate for representative. These *friends* of his after getting him about "half seas over" would get him on a dray, and hawl him in triumph to "Switzerland" and back to town after drinking several bottles of wine —this occurred several times. On one evening these *friends* instead of getting him on the dray got him on their shoulders and started for Mr. Dalmazzos who was selling "the ardent" on Main Cross Street, on the Corner of the lot owned by John Dickason, on the corner of the alley—they started from the corner of Main and Ferry Streets and wandered out of the way and over about where Clarksons, Thiebauds, and Todds houses now stand which was rather a low place, and where there was quite a pond of water, they stumbled and fell with Ramsey, and some of them taking Ramsey by the feet dragged him through the water to Dalmazzos. Ramseys clothing was well saturated with water and mud, the very picture of despair—in the sport of the *friends* Ramsey lost his watch and some small amount of money— this occur[r]ed about a week before the August election —the *friends* after this exploit turned against Ramsey, and Ramsey declined being a candidate.

It has occurred to the writer that he has not given any account of some of the Block houses that were built within the limits of the County as protection against hostile Indians. One was built in the McKay settlement about the time the Craigs came over from Kentucky—one was built some where on the hill not far from where French's Mill on Grants Creek stands. One was built on Log Lick creek about half a mile above where the road crosses the Creek above where Whites mill stood. William White and his neighbors, were among the active men in those times in guarding the Settlements

# HISTORY OF SWITZERLAND COUNTY 151

against Indian depredations—and it is said that William White spent Seventy five days, in assisting to build Block houses and "scouting" or "ranging" on the frontier to protect the settlement from Indian surprises and depredations. It is thought that William White was a leader among the persons who were called upon to guard the frontier and was Captain.

As the anniversary of our National Independance is no longer celebrated by the citizens of Vevay and vicinity, as in the days of the past, it may not be uninteresting to the readers of these reminiscancies of the past to hear how the day was celebrated by the Swiss Colonists and their American neighbors in the early days of the Colony and until within a few years past.

Perhaps as early as 1805 the year before John James Dufour returned to Europe, he was on a visit from the First Vineyard to his brothers and Sisters in New Switzerland, in the latter part of June of that year, and as the citizens had decided to celebrate the coming birth day of their adopted Country in the most appropriate manner the means at their disposal would permit, they prevailed on John James Dufour to remain and deliver the Oration on that occasion, accordingly the day came,—the neighbors of the settlement were invited—all the Swiss, the Cottons, Dickasons, Stewarts, of this side of the river, and the Sanders', Craigs, Neals, Bledsoes and Tandys from the Kentucky side of the river were present, and all met in a grove, or rather forest near where the Morerod house stands. William Cotton was reader of the Declaration of Independance, John James Dufour delivered the Oration, a Dinner had been prepared and eaten, toasts were proposed, drank and cheers, given, then the dancing commenced on the green, when married and unmarried joined in the dance which was continued untill near Sun down when each departed for their home, well pleased with the festivities of the day—

the writer has seen the manuscript of the oration delivered on that occasion, but is at present unable to say what has become of it—the recollection of it is, that it was not very lengthy, but full of the most patriotic sentiments towards the adopted country of the orator of the day.

These celebrations were observed every year by the Swiss colonists—and the writer well remembers that on one or two of those National celebrations about 1811 and 1812, the meeting was on a level spot under the shade of several large elms whose spreading branches protected those assembled from the rays of the hot sun, on the bank of the river just below where the ware house of U. P. Schenck and sons now stands—and there are no doubt some four or five of the descendants of the Swiss colonists, still living who were old enough to remember the good cheer, the lively motions of, perhaps father, mother, aunt uncle and their neighbors while engaged in dancing on the green grass in the shade of those elm trees. On one of those occasions Samuel Mennet the father of Francis E. Mennet was reader of the Declaration of Independance, and John Francis Dufour orator of the day. For a number of years the 4th of July was celebrated on that *then* lovely spot—but such scenes have passed, and if not, committed to writing, in a few more short years no one will be left to record these scenes and incidents of the past.

From the earliest recollection of the writer down to within the past Twenty years the 4th of July had been observed and celebrated in an appropriate manner. Frequently a barbacue was given, by some half dozen persons joining, together buying a fat ox or cow, butchering it and having the meat cut up and barbacued, and on such occasions, Vevay was sure to be filled with people from the country, an invitation, being generally extended to all. Lest some of the younger readers of these reminiscences may not understand the manner of cooking the meats at these barbacues—the following is given as the manner of thus cooking meat—a Ditch about 4 or 5 feet wide, about 2½ or 3 feet deep, and as long as may be deemed necessary, is dug this ditch is filled up with the best wood, to make the best of live coals when burned—after this wood is burned to a coal the meats being arranged on sticks of such a length as to reach completely across the ditch, thus placing the meat directly over the live coals in the ditch, and by turning the meat on these sticks frequently, it becomes thoroughly cooked in from one to three hours. It costs too much labor to prepare a dinner for a large crowd it [in] that manner to Suit us in these times of ease and comfort.

At one of these Barbacues in Vevay—the ditch was dug on the west side of the court house square near the west corner and the table was arranged on the east side of the court house forks being placed in the ground—poles placed in the forks and green bushes hawled from the neighboring forests to make a covering—each person who resided in Vevay and its immediate vicinity were to prepare themselves with such plates, knives, forks spoons and glasses as they needed—and these articles for persons from a distance was furnished by the citizens of the town. On this occasion Jean Daniel Morerod had a Turner by the name of Raymond to make him a wooden plate, fork spoon and goblet, these articles of table furniture were a great curiosity and were inspected by many who were present—such were the eccentricities of Mr. Morerod. To still further illustrate his eccentricities a clause of his last will and testament will be given in this connection—it is as follows.

"8th. And though it may appear singular to some "it is my will and pleasure, that no costly clothing, nor "a costly coffin, be buried to rot with my body but if I "should die at home I wish my body to be wrapped up in "a plain white sheet and put in a plain coffin made of "pine or other cheap boards the cost of which shall not "exceed two dollars and that the difference in price be- "tween this equipage of mine and that usually afforded

"in Vevay to travellers, to that place whence no one re-
"turns, be dealt out to those who shall meet at my house,
"to accompany my body to the grave, in the best wine
"that may then happen to be in my cellar." The will
was signed on the 14th day of February 1829 and was
proven and admitted to probate Novr 3rd 1838.

The children of Mr. Morerod lived in this county. The eldest Henriette L. was born on the home farm adjoining Vevay in 1804 and was the Second child born in the Swiss colony—in 1824 or 1825—she was married t Rodolph Morerod, her own cousin, who some few years later together with the members of the Swiss artillery Company were firing the cannon in commemoration of the marriage of Edward Patton, to the daughter of George Craig—and by a premature discharge of the gun so injured him that he died a few days after, leaving his bereaved widow and a little son now Doctor Eugene R. Morerod of Nevada City Missouri—Mrs. Morerod some years later Married John F. Tandy—she was well known by the ladies of Vevay and Surrounding Country as a good dress maker and modiste. She died during the present Spring of 1876—She became a member of the Methodist Episcopal Church of Vevay during the great revival in 1841—of which she continued a consistent and energetic member—contributing of her labor and means to promote the welfare of the church and she will be missed by none, so much as by the members of that church, with whom she worshipped for about thirty five years—she was a kind and generous friend, ready at all times to attend the bed side of the sick, and do all in her power to relieve, the sick, the suffering, and those who were called upon to mourn, departed friends. She was in every respect a consistent and devoted christian and died in the Hope of meeting that reward which is reserved for the people of God.

The second Daughter Lucy Detraz has lived so long in

JEAN DANIEL MOREROD HOME

LATER PICTURE OF MOREROD HOME

# HISTORY OF SWITZERLAND COUNTY 155

this Community that her life is her best history. Of The third Daughter Louisa Golay wife of Constant Golay the same may be said as of Mrs. Detraz.

The fourth daughter Mrs. Julia LeClerc proprietress of the LeClerk house, is widely known and respected. The fifth daughter Mrs. Josephine Hill resides in Arkansas.

The two sons Aime and Rodolph or John R. which is his proper name are and were well known to the residents of Switzerland County.

John R. Morerod was Sheriff of this County for two years and Treasurer of the County for two terms of two years each.

Mrs. Lucy Detraz was relating to the writer a short time since, her recollections of Lorenzo Dow preaching in this Section of the Country. She states that Lorenzo Dow preached in Vevay at a very early day perhaps in 1814 or 1815 and again about the year 1817 or 1818— the writer has a distinct recollection of a very eccentric person preaching in Vevay in 1814 the year that the town was illuminated on account of McDonoughs victory over the British during the war of 1812, and again in the Court house during a Session of the Circuit court and it is his impression that, that was during the fall term of the Court in 1817. The recollections of Lorenzo Dows Preaching in Vevay by the writer are that he was a very eccentric man whether in the social circle or in the pulpit.

From the organization of the County in 1814 to 1840 the sheriff of the County and occasionally other persons who were appointed by the Board doing county business for the purpose were the Collectors of the Revenue, under the laws then in force—in 1841 our present laws requiring the county Treasurer to collect the taxes or revenue first came in force,[1] consequently since 1841 the county Treasurer being the Collector it will not be necessary to give the names of the Treasurers who have had the collection of the Taxes. Only the collectors for the several years from 1814 to 1840 will be named in this connection. From 1814 to 1820 John Francis Siebenthal for the year 1820, 1821, & 1822 Israel R. Whitehead for the year 1823 Garret Perkins—for the years 1824, 1825, 1826, 1827 John Francis Siebenthal—for the year 1828 Henry Banta—for the year 1829 William McCullough—for the year 1830 Henry Banta—for the year 1831 Pruit Harvey—for the years 1832, & 1833 Henry Banta—for the year 1834 Ralph B. Cotton—for the years 1835-1836-1837-1838-and 1839 Daniel L. Livings the grandfather of Theodore Livings Esqr of this place for the year 1840 Henry McMakin. Of those who during the later years of the Collectors [served] prior to 1840 Daniel L. Livings served in that capacity continuously for a longer period than any of his predecessors. There lived in the North East corner of Jefferson Township a man named Enoch Shuff who had not paid his tax for several years—this man Shuff generally attended the polls of Cotton Township at Allensville, Mr Livings residing adjoining to Allensville determined to get if possible the Tax due by Shuff accordingly on the morning of the August election Mr Livings went to the polls, he had not been long at the polls before Shuff came up and offered to vote, when Mr. Livings called out "I challenge that vote"

"On what grounds" demanded the Inspector, "because he has not paid his tax for the last two or three years" responded Livings "A man who refuses to pay his taxes, shall not vote at an election when I am present if I can prevent it."

As early as 1816 and 1817 there appeared to arise a rivalry on the part of the Citizens of the upper end of the county and the lower end as, to who should fill the Several offices of the County. The leaders in this rivalry in the upper end of the County, denominated those of the lower end of the County as the "Swiss and Cotton party" and the strife for office for some years was quite ani-

# HISTORY OF SWITZERLAND COUNTY 157

mated—in 1818 the question of removing the county seat from Vevay was originated by some of the upper end folks and by 1820 the contest for members of the legislature was carried on, with that object in view.

In 1824 on the 19th of June a meeting was held at Jacksonville, "for the purpose of considering the propriety of relocating the County Seat and making it central. Linus Scoville was called to the chair and Isaac Chamberlin appointed Clerk"   "Moved that the ayes and nays be taken, when it appeared, that ninety were in favor of re-location, opposed to four in the negative."

"Resolved, that to effect the object of this meeting "two candidates only be supported to represent the Coun- "ty at our next Session. William Brandenburg, William "Gard and Linus Scoville were nominated, but Mr. "Brandenburg declined being considered a candidate and "agreed to give his interest to Gard and Scoville."

"LINUS SCOVILLE chairman"
"ISAAC CHAMBERLIN clerk."

Thus was the first perfect organization of those who favored a relocation of the County Seat, effected.

The election was held on the first Monday in August and resulted in the election of Stephen C. Stevens and William Gard—there were Seven candidates voted for, Stephen C. Stevens who received 358 votes, William Gard 319 votes   Newton H. Tapp received 204 votes Linus Scoville received 126 votes, George Teague received 55 votes   Robert McCorkle received 45 votes, William Brandenburg received 27 votes and Scattering 12 votes.[1]

There were very bitter and hostile feelings manifested by the friends of Scoville against Gard and his friend Gard was charged with bargaining with the friends of Stevens to secure his election and defeat Scoville.

During the Session of the legislature to which Gard was elected no move of any kind was made toward the relocation of the County Seat.   The next

agitation of the question of relocation was in 1844 or 45 A meeting was held at Center Square during the Summer or Spring. Thomas T. Wright who was a candidate for the legislature, and was supported by the Democrats, in Company with the writer and several prominent Democrats attended that meeting from curiosity to see what would be the result of the meeting— Martin R. Green and several prominent Democrats from the upper end of the County were present and taking an active part in the proceedings of the meeting. Mr. Wright was accosted by Green and some other persons from Posey Township and asked if he would "favor a re-location of the County Seat if he was elected to the Legislature, provided a majority of the voters of the county petitioned for that purpose. Wright declined making any pledges on the subject, one way or the other but said he "I am a candidate for the Legislature and expect to continue one until the close of the polls on the first Monday in August next, without making any pledges whatever." Green then Stated to the meeting that they would have to make nomination of a candidate favorable to their cause—after some little time for deliberation the name of Israel C. Smith was placed before the meeting and he was unanimously nominated—
On leaving the house Green remarked, "We now have pitted against Wright a good man Israel C Smith."

The impression of the writer is that Smith declined being a candidate before the day of election—however Wright was elected. The next move of those who wished a relocation of the County Seat, was to take Posey and Cotton Townships from Switzerland County and attach them to Ohio County. Accordingly in 1852 [1846] the friends of that measure selected as their candidates Martin R. Green for Senator from Ohio and Switzerland Counties[1] and John Tait of Ohio County for Representative the two counties forming a Senatorial and Representative district. The opponents of the measure by consent supported John A. Beal for Senator and

# HISTORY OF SWITZERLAND COUNTY 159

Perret Dufour for representative—Green and Tait were elected. The opponents of that measure committed an error, for they should have had Democrat opposed to Democrat and Whig against Whig. Beal and his Whig friend had a consultation about the matter with Dufour and his Democratic friends about making the change but at too late an hour in the canvass to result in any advantage to those opposed to taking off the two Township[s] and attaching them to Ohio County.

Petitions were circulated and Signatures obtained to them in Ohio County and in Posey and Cotton Townships, praying the legislature to attach those two townships to Ohio County.

Petitions were circulated by the opponents of the measure praying the Legislature if in their wisdom they deemed a change desirable, and for the public good that the Counties of Ohio and Switzerland be united together as one county and the County seat established in the Geographical center of the County thus formed—this turn in the matter rather checked the ardor of the Representative who lived in the Rising Sun.

The writer has overlooked a movement that was made in 1848 for the removal of the County Seat and asking the Legislature to appoint Commissioners to relocate the County Seat. Remonstrances [were made] against the re-location by commissioners, but asking the Legislature "Should you in your wisdom however be of a different Opinion from your remonstrators and grant a re-location of the said seat of Justice, in that case they would humbly suggest the propriety of leaving the selection of the scite to the voters of the County and that a majority of all the votes should be necessary to a choice."

In 1852 the question of re-location was again agitated, at the Session of the Legislature which Commenced January 6th 1853 a bill was introduced and became a law authorizing an election to be held at the several places of holding elections at which the voters were to vote No re-location and Relocation to *Florence* or any other point the voter wished—and if no one place had a majority of the Votes or "No re-location" had a majority of the votes —a second election was to be had at which No relocation and the point having the greatest number of votes for re-location should be voted for, and the majority to decide the matter.[1] The election was held, Mount Sterling —Center Square, Loglick and Florence were the points voted for at which to relocate—at the first election "No re-location" lacked a few votes of having a majority and Florence had the highest vote for "Relocation". At the second election "No Relocation" had a majority of 150 or 175 votes over Florence—and thus has ended one of the most, abused hobbies on which men ride into the legislature over those who have ten fold the talents and brains, that the successful candidate has.

The first election held in the County was held in May 1816 to elect a Delegate to the Convention to form the Constitution for the State Government. The next was held on the 3rd February 1817 to elect County Officers the Constitution having been adopted by the Convention on the 29th day of June 1816 after a Session of nineteen days the convention having met and organized on the 10th day of June 1816.

The first election for officers of the state and members of Congress was held on the first Monday in August 1816 the state being entitled to one member of Congress until the next census should be taken which would be in 1820. The elections until 1823 or 1824 were not so exciting as at the present day, there being so few voters perhaps being the cause.

The representation in the Convention to form the constitution was fixed by an act of Congress, and the time for the election of delegates and for the meeting of the convention was also fixed by the act of Congress[2]—the representation was as follows:

# HISTORY OF SWITZERLAND COUNTY 161

The county of Wayne four, the county of Franklin five the County of Dearborn three, the County of Switzerland one, the County of Jefferson three, the county of Clark five, the County of Harrison five, the County of Washington five, the County of Knox five, the county of Gibson four, the County of Posey one, the County of Warrick one, and the County of Perry one representative, in all forty two delegates.

It appears that between the passage of the act of Congress authorizing the election of the delegates (April 19 1816) and the close of the Session of the Convention (June 29th 1816) two new Counties Orange and Jackson had been organized. Switzerland County was not entitled to a Senator separately or as part of a senatorial district until after the first enumeration in 1820. The Senate of Indiana was composed of nine senators at the first meeting of the General Assembly and Twenty-Eight representatives, and had the Same number of Senators and Representatives untill 1818 or 1820.

In 1824 the elections in Indiana were quite spirited For Congress Switzerland County being in the third district, which included Henry, Rush, Decatur, Randolph, Wayne, Franklin, Fayette, Dearborn, Union Switzerland Ripley and Allen 12 counties.

John Test, Daniel J. Caswell, and James B Ray were the candidates. Test and Caswell were in favor of John Quincy Adams for President, but Test pledged himself, that if the choice of President should be thrown upon the house of Representatives, he would be governed by the vote of the people of the state or his district as expressed by the voters—Ray was in favor of Henry Clay for president.

Test was elected, the vote of Switzerland County being Test, 238; Ray, 197; Caswell, 186. The vote of the district, with the vote of one county (Randolph not included)[1] Stood Test, 4,522;[2] Ray, 2,936; Caswell 1,457.

In the second district the Candidates were Jeremiah Sullivan, and Jonathan Jennings, Jennings was elected receiving in Harrison county in which he resided a majority of 994 while Sullivan received in Jefferson County in which he resided a majority of 800—The Second district was composed of 16 counties, Jefferson, Clark, Jackson, Washington, Harrison, Crawford, Floyd Scott, Bartholomew Jennings Marion, Hamilton, Johnson, Shelby Madison and Delaware.

The first district was composed of 25 counties to wit: Orange, Posey, Spencer Warrick, Vanderburg, Posey [Perry], Gibson, Pike Dubois Knox Daviess, Martin Sullivan, Vigo, Parke, Monroe, Lawrence, Wabash Greene, Owen, Morgan, Putnam, Vermillion Hendricks and Montgomery, the candidates in this district were, William Prince, Ratliff Boone, Thomas H Blake, and Jacob Call.

Prince was elected, but having no data from which to give the vote let this statement Suffice.

The contest for President in 1824, was perhaps no more, exciting and Spirited in any locality in the State perhaps than in Switzerland County, for on the 31st of January 1824, the friends of Henry Clay met at the house of Thomas Armstrong in Vevay and organized by the appointment of Colonel John F. Siebenthal Chairman and Captain George G. Knox secretary—General William C. Keen, Stephen Whitcher Jr, and Nathaniel Cotton were appointed a committee to draft a suitable address to the voters of the third Congressional district. The meeting nominated Henry Clay as a candidate for President, and Andrew Jackson for vice President.

In conclusion of the address to the people Henry Clay is thus spoken of "In the language of the children of Israel on a certain occasion we say" "Let this good man rule over us."

On the same day a meeting favorable to the election of Dewitt Clinton to the Presidency met at the Court House in Vevay and organized by the appointment [of]

## HISTORY OF SWITZERLAND COUNTY 163

Hon Abner Clarkson as chairman and Israel R. Whitehead Esqr. as secretary. The meeting nominated Dewitt Clinton for President and Andrew Jackson for Vice President. A committee was appointed to draw up an address to the people, calling their attention to the great interest they had in using every proper measure in their power to procure the nomination and election of Clinton and Jackson.[1] That committee was composed of Simeon Slawson Stephen Greenleaf, Dr James Welsh, John Dumont John Gilliland, John Wilson, Israel R Whitehead, Aaron Chamberlin, Dr Lawton Richmond and James Rous.

On the 21st day of February 1824 at a large and respectable meeting of the Citizens of the County who were friendly to the election of Andrew Jackson to the presidency Daniel Dufour was called to the Chair, and Edward Patton and William McCullough appointed secretaries. The meeting was addressed by Isaac B. Kinsman, who in a few remarks explaining the object of the meeting, said "Mr. Chairman. The object of this meeting is I presume, to take into consideration the Qualifications of General Andrew Jackson to fill the office of President of the United States. In order therefore to bring the subject directly before the meeting I move that the following resolution be adopted viz. *Resolved* that this meeting pledge themselves to support General Andrew Jackson for the office of president of the United States."

In his further remarks in support of his motion to adopt the resolution, the speaker, among other statements said "always devoting his life to the service of his count[r]y" then stating, that "at the age of fifteen he is marshalled in our armies by the side of our revolutionary fathers, fighting and bleeding for the liberties we now enjoy" He is next found at the head of volunteers in the unknown forests of Tennessee driving the savages to more distant regions—then at the head of the Tennessee and Georgia militia striding from Victory to Victory, through the swamps of Alabama and Florida until the supremacy of his government was acknowledged alike by the Savages, and the haughty Spanish Don, who sought his own safety under the American Banners. The Speaker continued "He is a man with habits qualified to command freemen."—"Bold and intrepid in the field, and decisive in Council, he forms his plans with the Velocity of *Lightning* and executes them with the treméndous energy of *Thunder*."

The resolution offered by Mr. Kinsman was unanimously adopted. The following resolution was also adopted by the meeting— *Resolved* that our high consideration and respect for the Services and abilities of Henry Clay entitle him to our Support for the office of Vice-President of the United States.

The meeting appointed John Miller, George Tague, James D. Kirby, Joseph Brown, William McCullough and Thomas Armstrong a committee of corréspondence to promote the object of the meeting.

On the 19th of March 1824 the following notice was published in the Vevay Paper. William H. Crawford" The members of congress having nominated William H. Crawford for President and Albert Gallatin for Vice-President, it beho[o]ves all the steadfast friends to be up and doing. The friends of Mr. Crawford are requested to meet at the Court house in Vevay on Monday next, at 2 oclock P. M. to take such measures as will be advisable to advance the interests of said persons.

*Nobility*

March 10.

Whether the meeting was held is not known, but in the next issue of the paper the following appeared

"William H Crawford, Monday last was fixed on by the friends of Wm. H. Crawford to meet at the Court house in Vevay to adopt measures to advance the interests of Messrs. Crawford and Gallatin. The day came, it passed, not a soul approached the edifice.

The prominent men and aspirants for office in this part

# HISTORY OF SWITZERLAND COUNTY 165

of Indiana, particularly in the third Congressional District were opposed to the candidates for President on different grounds. Some opposed Clay and Jackson because of their being Slaveholders and living in Slave States. Some opposed Mr. Adams because of his residing in Washington City and [because he] was said to be a slave owner. Some of the aspirants for Congress were said to favor the election of Jackson, while here in Switzerland County and when in other counties where Clay or Adams were thought to be more prominent, they advocated the election of the one or the other as the one or the other was thought to be the most prominent.

At length election day came and it would appear that outside of Jefferson Township the people cared but little who was President. The unusual small number of votes cast was owing to several causes. Polls were opened in three townships only—Jefferson, Posey and Cotton Townships, and the votes of but one counted —Jefferson. The returning Judge from one township came in without the return. The other brought his return but not being in legal form it was rejected. However the Judges reported it to the Secretary of State specially. The vote of Jefferson Township was as follows—Jackson 161—Clay 108   Adams 28. The Vote of Posey Township—Jackson 66—Adams 46, Clay *none*. Cotton Township—Jackson 25, Adams 23—Clay 18— The election over, every body [was] glad "on it" as Brother Jonathan said. The friends of the several candidates who previous to the election could scarcely say a civil word to, or of each other, soon became reconciled to the voice of the Voters, and began to harmonize and associate together as was their usual custom before the canvass commenced.

As the result of the presidential election of 1824 was not decided by the people at the Polls neither of the candidates having a majority of the electoral votes, it devolved on the house of Representatives to name the President. John Quincy Adams was elected by the House of Representatives although he had by [but] 84 to 99 electoral votes for Jackson. Clay had 37, and Crawford 41 electoral votes.

It may not be generally known to the younger readers of these sketches that after the election of John Quincy Adams by the House of Representatives and his having appointed Henry Clay Secretary of State—the charge was made that Clay sold the vote of Kentucky for the office of Secretary of State—that circumstance caused nearly all of the original friends of Henry Clay in Switzerland County to become Jackson men.

At the presidential election 1828, Jackson and Adams were the opposing Candidates—the parties being named respectively the Jackson Party and The Adams party. The electioneering in Switzerland County was quite lively —the Adams party charging Jackson with being a cold blooded murderer, for having the two or three men in Alabama or Florida executed as spies—and hand bill[s] decorated with coffins were put in circulation by the Adams party, with a view of causing votes to be cast for Adams instead of Jackson—these handbills were denominated "Coffin Handbills". Jackson however carried Switzerland County and the State of Indiana, which caused the saying of "As goes Switzerland County so goes the State of Indiana."

At the presidential election in 1832, Jackson was the Democratic Republican Candidate and Clay the National Republican candidate. Jackson was elected carrying Switzerland County and the State—there was much opposition to Jackson because of his Veto of the Bill chartering the United States Bank, many who supported him in 1828 were his bitterest opponents—and when the Whig party was organized in 1836 they went over to the Whigs.

At the presidential election 1836, Martin Van Buren was the Democratic Candidate and William H. Harrison the Whig Candidate. Harrison Carried Switzerland

# HISTORY OF SWITZERLAND COUNTY 167

County and the State of Indiana, yet Van Buren was elected.

At the Presidential election 1840 Van Buren was the Democratic Candidate and William Henry Harrison the Whig Candidate—the canvass was the most exciting of any that had preceded it in Switzerland County, both parties rallying their forces in mass meetings and Barbacues. In Switzerland County the strife was very fierce. Before the August election of that year both parties arranged for a mass meeting and Barbacue, and both on the same day. The Democrats had their meeting and barbacue in a beech Grove that Stood back a short distance from the river—just below the foot of Vevay Island and the Whigs had theirs on the top of the hill, above Gramers Slaughter house—the Democrats engaged a Band of Music from Cincinnati, had a Six pounder cannon "Old Betz"[1] which the Swiss artillery company had in their charge which was fired in the morning early, and during the day a grand procession was formed and marched through the town and down to the Grove—where the speeches were made and the barbacued meats were eaten.

The Whigs procured a six pounder cannon and Band of Music from Cincinnati. Early in the morning the Whig, cannoneers commenced firing their gun The whigs from the back part of the County and from the Southern part of Ripley county came into town with a large Canoe on waggon wheels, filled with ladies. A procession was formed, marched through town, and went up the hill to the place where the speeches were made and the Barbacued meats were eaten. The Democrats in the bottom commenced firing their gun very rapidly, the whigs on the hill firing more rapidly than before; all at once the manager of the gun in the bottom, having paid attention to the firing on the hill suddenly exclaimed "Some one has been hurt, for that gun was prematurely discharged." It was not many minutes until the news spread throughout the town that two of the gunners on the hill were killed and one seriously wounded, which proved to be true, for those serving the gun wishing to fire as rapidly and [as] those in the Bottom, neglected swabbing their gun, leaving brands of fire unextinguished in the gun So that when the Cartri[d]ge came in contact with the fire it caused an explosion before it was rammed to the bottom of the gun—and killing one or two of those engaged in ramming and wounding another. At once all in the bottom started for the scene of the disaster, and met some from the hill conveying the dead and wounded into the town—this sad affair rather dampened the ardor of the opposing parties for the balance of the day and for some time afterwards. The captain of the Cincinnati Company in Conversation with the Captain of the Vevay Company informed him that they wished to fire as fast as the Vevay Company, and it was thought by them they could not do it without omitting the usual Swabbing. The Captain of the Vevay Company informed him that the Vevay Company had and could fire twenty nine rounds in three and one-half minutes—(this was done by the Vevay Company) at Cincinnati at the reception of Genl Lafayette in 1825). The battle cry of the Whigs during this Campaign, was "Tippacanoe and Tyler too" and their chief emblem was "Log Cabin and Hard Cider."

In this Conflict the Democrats were badly beaten in Switzerland County, the State and the Union Switzerland County giving Harrison and Tyler a majority of over four hundred.

At the presidential election of 1844 the Candidates were Polk and Dallas Democrats—and Clay and Frelinghuysen Whigs. The nomination of Polk was as much of a surprise to the Democrats of this County as the Nomination of Tilden at Saint Louis during July 1876. It was almost the usual exclamation "Who in h—ll is Polk" "I'll be d——d if I vote for a man nobody knows" and such like expressions. The canvass in Switzerland County was quite spirited. The cry of "Pork and dol-

## HISTORY OF SWITZERLAND COUNTY 169

lars" was frequently heard, and the emblem of the party was a large "Poke stalk" stuck in every waggon coming into town or travelling the roads, occupied by Democrats. Switzerland County gave Polk forty five majority, and he was elected.

At the presidential election in 1848 the candidates were Lewis Cass and Zachary Taylor, the canvass in Switzerland county was not very spirited. Cass it is believed carried the County by a Small majority. Taylor was elected.

At the presidential election 1852 Pierce was the Democratic Candidate and Genl. Scott the Whig candidate. Pierce had a majority in Switzerland County and was elected. General Scott was the last Whig Candidate as the Whigs as a party became disbanded.

At the presidential election 1856 James Buchannon was the Democratic, Millard Fillmore the American and John C. Fremont the Republican Candidate. Buchannon had a plurality in Switzerland County—Fillmore having the next highest number of votes.

At the presidental election 1860 Stephen A. Douglass was the regular Democratic Candidate, John C. Breckenri[d]ge the Candidate of the Democrats of Southern proclivities, and John Bell of Tennessee the Candidate of the American party—and Abraham Lincoln the Republican candidate. The vote of Switzerland County was divided between the several candidates as follows, Douglass 476  Breckenridge 499  Bell 510  and Lincoln 734 votes.

In 1864 the Candidates for President were James B. McClellan Democratic Candidate and Abraham Lincoln Republican Candidate. Lincolns majority in Switzerland County was 585 he receiving 1440 votes & McClellan 855.

In 1868 the candidates for president were Ulysses S. Grant republican and Horatio Seymour Democratic Candidate. Grants majority in Switzerland County was 257 he receiving 1466 votes and Seymour 1209 votes.

In 1872 the Presidential Candidates were Ulysses S.

Grant Republican and Horace Greel[e]y as the Democratic Candidates. Grants majority in Switzerland County was 328 he receiving 1444 votes and Greeley 1116 votes. It is said that politics sometimes make strange "bed fellows" but of all the Strange political freaks, ever performed by a powerful party or organization, such as the Democratic party of 1872 proved to be in the nomination or the endorsement of Horace Greel[e]y, the life long and bitter opponent of the Democratic party and the principles advocated by that party was the strangest political stroke of policy ever performed in this or any other age or country.

In 1823 the voters of Indiana voted "for" and "against" calling a Convention to amend and revise the Constitution of the state a large majority voting against the calling of a convention. The vote of Switzerland county was 40 for Convention and 602 against Convention—while in 28 counties the vote was for Convention 2601 and against Convention 11,991. The clerks of the remaining 20 counties failed to make returns according to Law. For that neglect of duty they were liable to forfeit and pay the sum of One hundred dollars each, recoverable by presentment or Indictments.

A strange feature in politics has been presented in Switzerland County since about the year 1830 or perhaps 1832 until about the year 1860 at nearly every election held when state officers were to be elected with perhaps the exception of 1843 and 1846 the whigs or opponents of the Democrats carried the County for their candidates for state officers—while the Democrats with perhaps the exception of 1840 carried the county for their candidates for County officers.

The district to which Switzerland County has been attached for electing members to Congress has been the "Third" untill the last districting of the State,[1] and has

## HISTORY OF SWITZERLAND COUNTY 171

been represented in congress by John Test, Amos Lane Oliver H. Smith George H. Dunn Thomas Smith, John L. Robinson, James H. Cravens, James H. Lane,[1] Cyrus L Dunham, James Hugh[e]s, Morton C. Hunter Ralph Hill, Henry W. Harrington, William S. Holman, and Jeptha D. New the present representative[2] John Test, George H Dunn Oliver H. Smith, James H. Cravens, Ralph Hill, and Morton C. Hunter being Whigs, and Republicans, and the remainder being Democrats. For representation in the State Senate, since the organization of the State Government, Switzerland County has been attached first, to Jefferson County as a senatorial District, and then to Ripley County—then to Ohio County—and at this time to Ripley County and Ohio counties.

Switzerland and Jefferson [were] represented in the State Senate by John Paul from 1816 to 1819—by Samuel Merrell from 1820 to 1821. In 1821, part of a term by William Cotton[3]—for 1822-1823 and 1824 by George Craig—for 1825, 1826 and 1827 by William Cotton—for 1828, 1829 and 1830 by Stephen C. Stevens—Ripley and Switzerland Counties forming the senatorial district from 1822. In 1831-1832, 1833, 1834, 1835 and 1836 by John Dumont being two term[s], for one of which he was opposed by James H. Cravens—the last term of Dumonts service in the Senate he represented only Switzerland County and Thomas Smith represented Ripley county—and it was during the last term of Dumonts service that he and Tom Smith (as he was familiarly called) made the record that made Dumont a candidate for Governor and Tom Smith for congress —by their advocacy of the classifying of the public works. Switzerland county was represented in the Senate in 1837-1838 and 1839 by Martin R. Green—in 1840 and 1841 by Joseph C. Eggleston, who resigned during the session of 1841-42 and in 1842 by Daniel Kelso—[in] 1843, 1844 and 1845 by David Henry— about 1845 Ohio and Switzerland Counties were formed into a Senatorial District and in 1846-1847 and 1848 was represented by Martin R. Green, and in 1849, 1850 and 1851 by John Woods—In 1852 and 1853 by William H. Powell.

The new constitution having been ratified by the people and the sessions of the legislature to be held under it biennially Senators having to be elected for four years— in the Sessions of the Senate commenced in 1855 and 1857, Philander S. Sage represented Switzerland and Ohio counties.—In the Sessions commencing 1859 and 1861 Benjamin L. Robinson was the Senator for the two Counties. In the session commencing in 1863 and 1865 Alexander C. Downey, and in the Sessions Commencing in 1867 and 1869 Flavius J. Bellamy represented to [the] district in the senate.

The district was again changed and Ripley attached to Switzerland County as a Senatorial District—at the Sessions that Commenced in 1871 and 1873 Moses K. Rosenbrough, was the Senator—At the' session commenced in 1875 William Culbertson was the Senator, and will continue as such until his successor is elected in 1878.[1] The foregoing is believed to be the names of all the Senators, who have represented Switzerland County in whole or in part since the organization of the State Government to the present time.

In the house of Representatives Switzerland County has been represented by the following named persons and at the sessions indicated by the date.

In 1816 by John Dumont—1817, 1818, by Ralph Cotton —1819 Samuel Merrill[2]—1820, 1821 by John Dumont— 1822 by John Dumont and Linus Scoville—in 1823 by Stephen C. Stevens and Ralph Cotton—in 1824 by Stephen C. Stevens [and] William Gard—in 1825 by William Gard and William C. Keen—in 1826 by Stephen C. Stevens and William Chamberlin—in 1827 by William Campbell—in 1828 by John Dumont and John F. Dufour —in 1829 by Samuel Jack—in 1830 by John Dumont— in 1831 by William Cotton—in 1832 by William Bradley in 1833 by Daniel Kelso—in 1834 by Daniel Kelso

# HISTORY OF SWITZERLAND COUNTY 173

in 1835 and 1836 Joseph C. Eggleston—in 1837 and 1838 James M. Cotton—in 1839 by Elwood Fisher—in 1840 by Hosier J. Durbin—in 1841 by Samuel Howard —in 1842 by Perret Dufour—in 1843 and 1844 Thomas T. Wright    in 1845 by Edward Burns.

The legislature at the session of 1845 attached Ohio County to Switzerland and the two have since that time composed a representative district—and at the August election 1845 John Tait Jr. was elected, and at the session of 1846 represented the two counties—1847 by Samuel F. Covington and Charles T. Jones—in 1848 by Daniel Kelso—in 1849 by John W. Wright and John W. Spencer—in 1850 by Thomas Armstrong—in 1851 by Samuel Porter and John W. Spencer—after this session the legislature met biennially and met in January instead of December as under the old constitution—in 1853 the district was represented by Oliver Dufour and Hazelett E. Dodd—in 1855 by George W. Harryman and David Cain—in 1857 by John W. Wright and John J. Hayden—in 1858 by William H. Gregory in 1859 by William H. Gregory the session held in 1858 being a Special session—in 1861 by Hugh T. Williams   in 1863 by Robert N. Lamb—in 1865 by Augustus Welch—in 1867 by James North  in 1869 by Stephen H. Stewart—in 1871 by William G. Holland—in 1873 by Benjamin North—and in 1875 by William T. Pate   the foregoing list of the names of persons who have represented Switzerland County from the organization of the State government to the present time is believed to be correct.

Of those representing the County in whole or in part in the Senate from 1816 to 1866 a period of forty years only three are known to be living, Martin R. Green, David Henry and Philander S. Sage.[1]

Of those representing the County in whole or in part in the house of Representatives for the same period only ten are known to be living: William B. Chamberlin Perret Dufour, John Tait Jr. Samuel F. Covington,

Charles T. Jones, John W. Wright, Thomas Armstrong, Samuel Porter, Oliver Dufour, Hazelett E. Dodd. It will be seen Martin R. Green was in the Senate in 1837, 1838 & 1839. David Henry in 1843, 1844 and 1845 and P. S. Sage in 1855 and 1857. That William B. Chamberlin was in the house of Representatives in 1826 fifty years ago and is now living with a married daughter in Covington Kentucky.

It was in 1846 that the question of attaching Posey and Cotton Townships of Switzerland County to Ohio County—the Candidates for Senator that year were Martin R. Green, John A. Beal and Daniel Kelso and for Representative John Tait Jr Nicholas Vineyard and Perret Dufour—the vote in Switzerland County Stood for Senator  Green 783—Beal 737—and Kelso 290. In Ohio County Greens Majority was 318—the vote for representative in Switzerland County was—Tait 761—Vineyard 231 and Dufour 762. Taits majority in Ohio County was 435. This statement is here made at the Suggestion of Martin R. Green who has called the writers attention to the unintentional error in referring to this election heretofore in these reminis[c]ences, in which the writer or the printer makes it read *1852* instead of 1846. Green was not a candidate for Senator in 1852.[1]

The writer has no data by which he can state with certainty who represented Switzerland County in the Territorial Legislature in the winter of 1814 and 1815 two Sessions after the County was organized, until the Sessions of 1816 which was the first after the organization of the state, but he has repeatedly heard Elisha Golay say that he was the representative in the territorial legislature, from the organization of the county until the state government was effected—he has also frequently conversed with John F. Dufour John F. Siebenthal and other public men of the county of that period on the Subject and all state the [that] Elisha Golay was that representative. There is nothing in the State Libra-

# HISTORY OF SWITZERLAND COUNTY 175

rians office to show the fact, as the Librarian has informed the writer.[1]

Just before the presidential election of 1832 persons were talking about the election, its probable results and arguing the merits of the Candidates, when some one in the crowd remarked that Jackson would be elected without doubt. Joseph Malin in his jocular manner remarked "I wish the snow would fall a foot deep the night before the election" "What do you make that wish for Squire" someone enquired, to which Malin replied—"So that these barfooted Jackson men could not get to the election." This created a great deal of merriment.

In January 1824 there was a meeting of the citizens of Vevay called to take into consideration the propriety of incorporating the town. The meeting was held and there was twelve votes cast for Incorporation and Seventeen votes against Incorporation—so at that time a majority [of] the citizens of Vevay who participated in that meeting were opposed to having the town Incorporated. A correspondent giving a history of that meeting and his opinion in regard to the question says "It was urged, that we were really in need of better regulations in our town. Thinks I to myself that is a fact. Likewise that a corporation at this time would be beneficial. Thinks I to myself, thats what puzzles me. There was sarcastic and pretty keen, sharp cutting on both sides of the question, then the vote was taken. The people will get their eyes open by and by and SEE what they are about, for it is manifestly for the general good of society, that regulations of a proper kind be adopted among them." "W"

In those days if a man and his wife parted if the husband saw proper, he advertized her. Different husbands did it in different language as the Following will show

"Matrimonial Disquietude."

"The undersigned forbids all persons from harboring

or trusting my wife Clarissa Cole who has this day forsaken his bed and board, without cause or provocation."

DANIEL COLE.

"VEVAY August 20"

"*Notice*" "All persons are hereby notified not to trust "or harbor Margaret Boyle my wife who has left my bed and board without any just cause as I am determined not to pay any debts of her contracting after this date."

January 20 "JAMES BOYLE."

"*Notice*" "All persons are hereby notified not to harbor or trust my wife Madeline Cler who left my bed and board on the 31st of July last and now lives in adu[l]tery with Michael Routin, as I am determined not to pay any debts of her contracting, and have petitioned for a divorce—I forbid the said Madeline from entering my house again."

"JOHN D. CLER."

"VEVAY September 15"

In answer to the above notice on the 1st of October the following appeared in the Indiana Register

"Attention" "The public are particularly requested to suspend their opinion for the present respecting the publication signed by "John D. Cler". I have employed the woman he calls his wife to reside in my family as a Servant or house-keeper and do not harbor her as he states."

"MICHAL ROUTEIN."

"September 24, 1824"

Another notice of "Matrimonial difficulty" appeared in the Vevay papers which read about as the one given above signed by James Boyle, and was ornamented with a dog worrying a Goat—and was signed by Francis L. Raymond.

In the *Indiana Register* of September 1824 appeared the following advertizement—"County orders for sale at this office. County orders will pay all debts due the County, including tax on lands, tax to the Clerk for certificates and seal and on writs."—"Price 50cts on the Dollar."

During the spring and Summer of 1824, there appeared in the *Indiana Register* three prospectus' for three different publications by three different persons to wit

William D. M. Wickham proposed "publishing by subscription a Gazeteer of the State of Indiana, containing a full and comprehensive view of the Counties, towns villages and boroughs and the number of their inhabitants. The Gazeteer was to be printed in pamphlet form and contains between forty and fifty medium octavo pages and delivered to subscribers at 25 cents per copy and to non-subscribers at thirtyone and a fourth cents per copy.

One other being "A treatise on the subject of Slavery in which the evils of slave holding will be shown forth both from the law of nature, and from the volume of divine revelation; as also the duty pointed out, of all the free Inhabitants of the United States relative to the practice" "The work, it is supposed will contain 150 pages."[1]

Price to Subscribers 50 cents per copy.

By James Duncan.

"The above treatise has been highly recommended by several gentlemen of Kentucky and Indiana   the letter of Hon. Jessee L. Holman Judge of the Supreme court of Indiana is given for the present"

"I have, been favored, for a few hours, with the manuscript of a "Treatise on Slavery" by the Rev James Duncan, and from a hasty perusal of the greater part of its contents, and the well known, abilities of the Author I conceive it to be  executed with a depth of thought and force of argument that well deserves the attention of all enquiring after moral truth and justly merits the patronage of the public.

JESSEE L. HOLMAN

DECATUR June 18, 1823

The author was a Presbyterian Minister and came to Vevay about the year 1822 or 1823, he was the father of the Hon. Alexander Duncan who represented to [the] Congressional district in Ohio, of which the City of Cincinnati, formed part, about the years 1837 to 1840 or about that period.

The other was the "proposal for publishing by subscription a Religious paper semi-monthly to be called the *Christian Herald.*"

"The object of the paper will be to diffuse religious Knowledge in an abridged form, so as to present to the public the principal interesting facts, relating to the progress of the Redeemers Kingdom in the world in a few pages semi-monthly."—"Price 50 per year."

This was to be published by Samuel Beal who then resided in Mount Sterling was a licensed preacher of the Gospel and Justice of the peace for Jefferson Township for many years. In his capacity of Minister and Justice of the peace he was called on to solemnize the marriage of many couple[s]. It was his uniform practice to present the newly married couple with a copy of the Word of God and if the Bride Groom paid him money for his services he always made a present of the same to the Bride. At the first establishment of the Post office at Mount Sterling in June 1824 he was appointed the first Post master.

In the *Indiana Register* published in Vevay, of the 3rd December 1824 appears—a notice of the sale of lands and town lots in Dearborn county, for taxes of 1822, 1823 and 1824 and the notice is given by John Spencer Sheriff and collector for Dearborn county,—the notice of sale comprises in and out lots in Rising Sun, Henry,

## HISTORY OF SWITZERLAND COUNTY 179

New Hanover Lawrenceburg Hardinsburg, Hartford Wilmington Decatur, New Lawrenceburg and Harrison, and all lands of Residents and Non residents in Townships 3, 4, 5, 6, and 7 in range 1—Townships 3, 4, 5, 6, 7, and 8 in Range 2—and Townships 4, 5 and 6 in Range 3—and the tracts of land advertised for sale vary in the number of acres from 10 to 1207 acres—the smallest, 10 acres the reputed owner was Isaac Lunger, and the reputed owner of 1207 in fractions 14, 15 and 16 Township 4 of Range one, was Jonathan Dayton—the reason for advertizing in a paper published out of the county in which the lands were to be sold, can be accounted for that there was no paper published in Dearborn county at the time which would appear Strange.

In the same paper of the 24th December 1824 the Sheriff and Collector of Switzerland County John F. Siebenthal, has a notice of sale of "tracts of non resident" lands for Sale for road taxes—that on Saturday the 15th day of January 1824 [1825], he would expose to pu[b]lic sale at the Court house door according to law so much of each tract, as will pay the road taxes due thereon and costs of sale.

There are Seventy two tracts of land advertised varying in the number of acre[s] each tract contains—145—155—160—219—308—321, 428—635 being the highest, and lowest number of acres in the tracts mentioned—yet the tax for which each tract was to be sold, was 4 days work three dollars and fifty cents. It would appear from that notice of sale that 635 acres of land paid no greater road tax than 145 acres did. That seems to be a very unjust mode of assessing road tax, or any other tax, but such was the law in those days.

In the same paper of Friday the 28th January, 1825, appears the following notice of a Show, or menagerie:

"Living Animals"—To be seen at Wm. Bradley's "tavern in Vevay, on Tuesday next; a number of curious "animals amongst which are a Camel, two tigers, a lama, "and a guanicus.—Price 12½ cents."

William Bradley's tavern stood on the Corner of the lot on which John Melcher's residence now Stands, and the barn, or Stable stood, back on the lot next the alley. In that Stable or Barn the animals to be exhibited were kept, and many were curious to see these natural curiosities, and the people from the Surrounding Country came to town to see them. The writer was of the number attracted by curiosity to invest 12½ cents to see the sight. As the notice states the "Price 12½ cents, some of the boys from the country thought—they were cheap, and one or two in the hearing of the writer and some of his young town boy friends, much to the merriment of the crowd when the writer or one of his companions called to the keeper and informed him that one or two boys from the country wished to buy an animal. The keeper informed the boys that it would be impossible for them to control the animals, and that they would have to hire a man to take care of them, when they declined purchasing.

At the Session of the Legislature of Indiana, 1823-24, in the bill relative to crime and punishment the following section was inserted—this may be found on page 145 of the journal of the proceedings of the Senate of that session:

Sec. 42.—Every person, who shall make, print or publish any slanderous or ridiculous writing, picture or sign, with a malicious or mischievous design or intent towards the government, majistrates or individuals, shall on conviction be fined not exceeding five hundred dollars."

As the above obnoxious section was inserted in the revised bill, and was no where to be found in the statutes before in force in this state, it was presumed at the time that William Hendricks, the revisor, could explain to the

## HISTORY OF SWITZERLAND COUNTY 181

people the motives for introducing it. The bill passed through all the readings, in both houses, to the last reading in the Senate, when John H. Thompson moved to strike it out, and the ayes and noes being called for were as follows: Ayes—William Graham, of Jackson County; James Gregory, of Marion; Eli Harrison, of Vanderburg; John Jenckes, of Vigo; Samuel Milroy, of Washington; Isaac Montgomery, of Gibson; Frederick Sholts of Daviess; James B. Slaughter, of Harrison; and John H. Thompson, of Clark— *Noes*, Samuel Chambers, of Orange; Daniel Grass, of Perry; John Gray of Dearborn; Lewis Johnson, of Fayette; James Raridon, of Wayne; James B. Ray, of Franklin; and Milton Stapp, of Jefferson. What would be thought of such a law at this day? It goes much farther than the gag law, passed by Congress in the reign of terror, during the administration of the elder Adams.

Sometime about the year 1818, a person from Jefferson County, on Indian Kentucky, came to Vevay with a fat steer to sell to the Butchers. It would appear that he was a man in the habit of using profane language. The law in relation to using profane language at that time was a fine of one dollar for each oath, but no more that [than] ten dollars fines could be assessed against a person for profane Swearing in any one day. Something happened to the Indian Kentucky man which caused him to swear, and he swore at such a terrible rate that the Justice of the peace, William C. Keen imposed fines to the amount of ten dollars, issued an execution and the fat steer was levied on to make the Judgments. The steer was sold but failed to bring a sufficient amount to to pay the fine and costs. Whether the balance of the Judgments was ever collected the writer is not prepared to say.

About the year 1824[1] there was a public well at the north Corner of the intersection of Main Cross and Market Streets, which was about 75 or 80 feet deep. The water was drawn with a windlass. Children frequently came to that well to draw water, which was a difficult matter for some small children to do. On a certain occasion a number of small girls of from 6 to 12 years of age were at the well for water. One girl named Elizabeth Hare attempted to draw the bucket on to a platform, lost her balance and was precipitated headlong into the well, falling the full depth of the well. The alarm was given, and a crowd assembled about the well consulting how best to get the girl out of the well. Edward Patton came up and seeing the hesitation on the part of those around, pulled off his coat vest and boots and taking hold of the rope made his way down to the bottom by sticking his toes in the cra[c]ks between to [the] stones and reached the bottom—took the girl set her in the bucket and with a handkerchief and a suspender he fastened her to the rope and gave the signal to hoist up, which was done, Patton following up by holding with one hand to the rope and placing the other against the wall, and sticking his toes in the interstices between the stones arrived safely to the top. The poor girl still alive was taken to her almost frantic parents where she lingered a few days and died. It is questionable whether there was any other person in the crowd besides Edward Patton who would have attempted to rescue the girl in the manner he did.

To give some idea of how plenty game was in Switzerland County the following incidents will be given here—About the year 1824 the writer accompanied his father John Francis Dufour to see something relating to a quarter section of land in the Southern edge of Cotton Township where we were to meet Heathcoat Picket at a place called the "Bear Wallow"   After getting through with the business—Picket said to Mr. Dufour "John stay here while I go over towards the lick, maybe I can get a

## HISTORY OF SWITZERLAND COUNTY 183

saddle of venison for you to take home with you." Picket went over from where we were (the quarter section now owned by one of the Peabodys which he bought of Benjamin Luster) to a lick on or near a piece of land owned by the Imiel family, about the fourth of a mile from where we were. It was not exceeding half an hour until we heard the crack of Pickets rifle, we went over where he was and found him in the act of taking the hide off of a fine Buck—we had a fine saddle of venison to bring home with us to Vevay. This was perhaps in the month of October.

During that same winter Heathcoat Picket brough[t] many saddles of Venison to Vevay for which he found a ready market and a fair price.

As late perhaps as 1832 Heathcoat Picket and his son Benjamin lived near Hiram Peabody—on land that has since been owned by James Gibb—while living there Benjamin Picket had a horse to get out of the stable during the night—he went to hunt for the horse, through the woods, and continued his search for the horse for two or three days without finding it—during these Searches for the horse he saw many deer but had no gun with him —so one morning he took his gun with him and during that day he killed two or three fine deer and come home with his horse and the deer meat in the evening. This circumstance has been recently related to the writer by Benjamin Pickett.

Sometime about the year 1835 the family of the Keeneys came to the county, the father and his son William J. Keeney made great numbers of scythe snaths and sold them throughout the County and went occasionally to towns along the river with them—the writer has purchased many of them while in Business from 1835 to 1842. In 1839 On one of the excursions of the father Keeney and his son William J. Keeney, on the river they were floating quietly down the Stream near Vevay Island, in a small open flat Boat, when an ascending Steamer ran over their small craft the father was drowned but William being a good Swimmer dove under the steamer and came off without the loss of life—this was in 1839. William J. Keeney was perhaps the first person to take a bale of hay into the town of New York (now Florence) and that bale of hay was pressed on a press of his own invention and make and he loaded the first baled hay into a flat boat at Florence for the lower country market. It remained however for Samuel Hewitt to invent, make, & put into successful operation the most useful hay press ever used in this or any other Country. Mr. Hewitt received a patent for his invention—which after Mr. Hewitt joined the *Mormons* received the appellation of the Mormon beater press—which in a few years superseded the old Screw press and all other hay presses, throughout this and the adjoining hay raising Counties in Southeastern Indiana. It is not necessary to say anything more in favor of the Mormon beater press for every hay raising farmer along the Ohio river and in fact over the whole great West has tested its usefulness and can best appreciate its work.

Sometime about the year 1829 or 1830 a young man who had studied medicine came to the County and located at Mount Sterling—and taught school, and at the same time pursued the Study of Medicine and in a few short years became one of the most extensive and successful practitioners in the county—in 1833 he was married to Miss Clarissa Golay daughter of Judge Elisha Golay—he removed to Greensburgh about the year 18— where he acquired an extensive and lucrative practice—his wife died about the year 1850 leaving three sons.[1] The widowed husband again married at Greensburgh and died about the year 1860. That young man lived to a tolerably advanced age,—That man was Doctor William Armington.

Some years after William Armington came to the county his Brother John L. Arming[ton] came to Mount

# HISTORY OF SWITZERLAND COUNTY 185

Sterling, commenced teaching School, at the same time studying medicine. He commenced the practice of medizine sometime in 1837, was married to Eliza B. Lee a daughter of Mrs. Rachael Whitehead. He practiced medicine at Mount Sterling, and at Vevay for some years, when he removed to Greensburg and practiced medicine there for some time. Then went to Minisota where he is still living and engaged in his profession. His son Charles L. Armington is also a practiceing physician at Northfield Minnisota.

John L. Armingtons first wife died at Greensbu[r]gh and Charles L. Armington is the only living child by that marriage.[1]

The first Silversmith and clock and watchmaker of Vevay was one William Paxton who was in the business in the year 1816 or 1817, and had his shop in a log house that stood [in] the lot on the hillside, south corner of Market and Union Street, being the lot on which John W Banta now resides—he made a sett of table and a sett of teaspoons for the mother of the writer, while he carried on the business in Vevay—he left Vevay about the year 1819 but where he went to is not known—not very far from the same time William Norrisez, a clock and watchmaker came to Vevay, opened his shop in the house now occupied and owned by James Torrence on Ferry Street, where he continued in business for a few years—his wife died after which he left Vevay and removed to some point in Kentucky abbove Cincinnati where he remained until about the year 1842 when [he] returned to Vevay, bought the farm on which the widow and children continued to reside for some years. About the year 1854 on his way home from Vevay carrying a bottle or can of coal oil—he accidental[l]y let it fall near the fire—the oil igniting instantly, he was so badly burned that he died in a Short time from the effects of the burn. At the time of his return to Vevay he had abandoned the clock and watch making business, and was a practising

Dental surgeon—he had an extensive practice throug[h]out the surrounding county and in Decatur county.

About the year 1819 or 1820 a Swiss by the name of Francis L. Flotron came to Vevay and commenced his occupation of Silver Smith, and clock and Watchmaker. His shop was in several different parts of the town but he became dissipated and at last recollections of him he was a mere sot and left the town without the regrets of any one. He left about 1824 or 1825. Several persons afterwards came to Vevay with a view of Starting in the business of Silver Smith and Clock and watch maker; but none of them made a permanent settlement in the business, until 1857 when Frederick A. Boerner came to Vevay and opened his shop in the store now occupied by F. A. Boerner and Brother which firm was formed in 1864 the time that Charles G. Boerner came from Cincinnati and formed a partnership with his brother Frederick A Boerner. William H: Ruggles was in the business here for a few years but finally left the place. One other person came to town opened a Shop in the small brick [building] at the north corner of Ferry and Pike Street—and was [able] to monopolize all the business, sell and work lower, than any one else, but a few short months passed and the new "Silversmith" left town leaving all that business that was to be done in Vevay to the firm of F. A. Boerner, and Brother to perform. This is as correct an account of the Silver Smith and clock and watch making business in Vevay as the writer can give from present recollections.

The physicians of Vevay were not blessed with the facilities of a drug store until about the year 1819 when Doctor James Welsh in partnership with his son George W. Welsh commenced the business in the Ell of the Brick build[i]ng—on the corner of Market and Main Cross Street, where they kept an assortment of the drugs and medicines used in those days, and continued until the death of his son George, when the business was continued by the Doctor and his son Joseph S. Welsh, the business terminating with the death of the Doctor in the year 1826—this was the first drug Store kept in Vevay—about the year 1827 or 1828 Abner Clarkson commenced the Drug business and continued under his own name and in connection with his son Doctor Samuel W. Clarkson and then with Perret Dufour until about 1852 or 53.

John L. Thiebaud Commenced the business in 1834 or 36 on a small scale, and continued enlargeing until he has attained his present prosperous and extensive business in that business.

In 1852 or 53 Isaac Stevens engaged in the business and continued in it, in connection with his son Edward M. Stevens, until 1873 when they sold out to Charles O. Thiebaud, son of John L. Thiebaud.

In 1871 Lawrence W. Golay and Ulysses P. Schenck Jr. engaged in the business, and continued until 1874 when Mr. Schenck sold his interest to Edward M. Stevens —the business of this house is still continued under the firm of Golay and Stevens.

So Vevay has at the present time three extensive drug stores which all appear to be doing a good business. This is believed to be as correct an account of the drug Stores of Vevay as can be given from the present recollections of the writer.

The farmers in and near Vevay until about 1814 had the services of Francis Louis Siebenthal as their black Smith. His shop stood not far from the Brick dwelling on the Norrisez farm below Vevay—he was a good workman and worked at his trade until about 1820 or 1821. The writer has at this time in his possession a two pronged potatoe hook made by him about the year 1811 for John F. Dufour—it was used chiefly to loosen the earth around the grape vines. In 1819 Frederick L. Grisard the father of F. L. Grisard of Vevay came to the neighborhood of Vevay and settled on the lands now owned by Peter LeClerc—and commenced working at Blacksmithing. In 1826 or 1827 he removed to Vevay and he and his son F. L. carried on the business for some time, until the old gentleman's advanced age compelled him to abandon the work.

About the year 1814 or 1815 John Harper built a shop on the lot now owned by Mrs. Julia LeClerc near Joshua D. Griffiths residence. He worked but a short time became dissatisfied and returned to Kentucky. About the time of his leaving Rufus Scott and Garret Perkins commenced the blacksmith business in Vevay and continued until about 1830 but as they did not work steadily they did but little work. Frederick L. Grisard Jr carrying on the business quite extensively and having a good number of hands employed, engrossed nearly the entire business for many miles throughout the surrounding country so that other shops with a small force did but little business. After Mr. Grisard quit the business about the year 1838, Hatch and Detraz—Joseph Jagers, Henry Hatch and others not now recollected were the principal Blacksmiths of Vevay until about 1860, since which Rutherford Rogers Boulton and Murphy have been the principal persons engaged in that business.[1]

About the years 1830 to 1835 the owners of the lands in the northern part of the County, began to turn their attention to sowing timothy, for meadows for hay—which in a few years, became the most important crop raised in the County. Daniel Sisson owning a farm on the eastern side of Pleasant Township had the timber standing on the land, girdled so that in a few years he had nothing to do but roll the timber together and burn it when his land was ready to be sown to meadow without breaking up—the seed was sown and harrowed in—others in the oak flats did the same—about the year 1834 Sisson was delivering his hay in Vevay—he remarked that if hay would always command the price it was then selling for (about 8 and 10 dollars per ton) the farmers of the county would get rich in a few years—about that time the hay was pressed on a wooden Screw press, and it required more work to press on one of those presses than on the more modern improvement in hay presses of

## HISTORY OF SWITZERLAND COUNTY 189

the present day. About the same period many hay farms were commenced throughout Cotton Township and in fact through out every section of the county—and in a few years the hay crop of the county, probably brought as much or more money into the County as all the other crops combined.

Until about 1851 or 1852, the greatest difficulty the farmer had to contend with in getting the surplus productions of his farm to market, was the need of good roads. In 1850 the Vevay Mount Sterling and Versailles turnpike Company was chartered and the road as far as the foot of "Davis," or "Shulls" hill was completed in 1852 as also the branch up as far as Jonathan McMakins. The completion of the road thus far, induced the farmers to enlarge their meadows—and consequently had larger crops of hay to deliver at Vevay the terminus of the road on the river—for before the making of that turnpike, the steep hill at Mount Sterling on the State road, and the mirey clay along the ridge between Mount Sterling and Vevay made it impossible, in the winter and Spring to draw with four horses, what can now be drawn with perfect ease with two horses.

This road has completed a Branch from the main road at Mount Sterling to Fairview, which gives the farmers of the hay producing portion of the County a good road to get their produce to market at Vevay.

This road was made and completed by a company composed of citizens of Vevay and the farmers and owners of land along and near to the line of the road owners of large tracts of land along the line of the road and near its terminus Subscribing from 500 to 2000 Dollars towards the Capital Stock of the company—Benjamin Wilson of Ohio County who was the owner of an entire Section (640 acres) of land one mile South of the terminus of the road at Fairview subscribing and paying forty shares of fifty dollars each, David Lee owning a large body of land near the same terminus Subscribing and pa[y]ing forty one Share[s], Asa Newton about 1½ or two miles west of the terminus at Fairview subscribing and paying ten shares and other farmers living two and three miles from the terminus subscribing and paying from two to Six shares—in that manner the company has built a good road, with a road bed 26 feet wide, on the center of which is spread broken limestone Sixteen feet wide, twelve inches thinck in the center and Six inches at the sides—the grade intended to be three degrees.     If all the six other turnpike roads which have been projected, built, and partly built in the county under the general law authorizing the formation of 'Gravel' and "Turnpike" road companies had, been built under a charter such as that of the Vevay Mount Sterling and Versailles Turnpike was built—it would have saved the people of the county thousands of Dollars, which have been spent in litigation, and evaded the ill feelings which have been produced in some parts of the county on account of misunderstandings about the road in one manner or other. If for instance those who commenced to build the Allensville, Center Square and Vevay turnpike had subscribed stock to an amount sufficient to have constructed the branch of the Vevay Mount Sterling and Versailles road from James Brown to Allensville and the branch from Center Square to East Enterprize the[y] would long since have had a good road from Allensville, and from East enterprize, and the[y] would have accomplished that, at an expence not exceeding, that which they have been at already, without their road being built—and if those who commenced the Pleasant Grove and Indian Creek road through Bennington had subscribed their money to an amount sufficient to have built the road from Shulls, to Pleasant Grove, they would now have had a good road—and saved the time, expence, and ill feelings engendered among the citizens along the line of that road and by which much litigation has been caused, the road not built, the company in debt, and the road placed in the hands of a receiver, with no power to collect tolls on that part of the road finished, with no favorable prospect of getting out of the difficulty into which the company is now placed, and no likelyhood of the bickerings and illfeelings, engendered among neighbors who were heretofore friends, being healed.

This may seem a very great departure from the design of this Historical Sketch—but may it not, at the next centennial be some insight given to those who may then be on the stage of action into the manner things wer[e] managed "One hundred years ago."

The Pleasant Grove & Indian Creek, and the Allensville Center Square & Vevay, roads are mentioned in this connection, as they appear to be the roads that are at present in a worse condition than the other roads without intended in the least to cast any reflection on the conduct of any person whether a citizen or acting in an official capacity in connection with said roads.

Of the Cabinet makers who have carried on that business in Vevay—may be mentioned George G. Knox who was the first, and who continued in the business from about the year 1815 to 18— when the business did not remunerate him for the labor performed. Joshua Smithson carried on the business for some years. Thomas Cole learned the trade with him. John L. Danglade carried on the business a few years. Charles Henderson was engaged in the business for several years—about 1833 Joseph Peelman came to Vevay and engaged in the business, which he continued to carry on for several years. One Robert Peck carried on the business for a short time—as furniture factorys began to be put in operation in Cincinnati the business was abandoned by those in Vevay who had been engaged in that business.

The time was when if a suit of clothes for a man or boy were wanted a tailor or merchant Tailor was not at hand to furnish the material and cut and make the garments, but the goods were procured, a tailor or tailoress was sent for to come to the house to work up the materials into such garments as wanted—in those early times many females went from house to house to make up garments for both male and female   About Vevay there were several females who were in the business and made a mans whole suit, by cutting making, and fitting—perhaps not quite as stylish in fit and workmanship as the "travelling" tailors of this period, but certainly as comfortable to both body and "purse"—throug[h]out the whole county in those days were, females who made it their entire business to cut, fit, and make, such clothing as their customers wished them to make.—there was back of Vevay a lady by the name of Andrews, or Andrus who was called on in the neighborhood of the Cottons on Indian Creek, and throughout the entire settlements about Mount Sterling, Jacksonville and Allensville to cut, fit and make men[s] apparel which work she performed in a good, Substantial and workmanlike manner—and in which apparel the men who wore them were considered "gentlemen." That lady afterwards, became the wife and companion of Stephen R. Tinker, who departed this life but a short time since. In Vevay we had the services of John Scott the father in law of James Cole, and Mrs. Manville the mother of Mrs. Julia L. Dumont from about the year 1814 to the time of Mr. Scotts removed [removal] from Vevay to a farm in the neighborhood of the Sticklers on the right hand fork of Indian Creek. Mrs. Manville quit the business about the year 1823 or 1825, except in her immediate family.

In the early days of the settlement of the County, the settlers had not the facilities for getting their Boots and shoes as at present—neither was there to be obtained the finer and the present fashionable styles of ladies Bootees shoes and gaiters or the mens fine shoes and "French Calf Boots."

It was customary for the head of the family to get a

# HISTORY OF SWITZERLAND COUNTY 193

common tanned Calf or kip Leather for the ladies and lasses shoes and a good side of upper leather for mens and Boys boots and Brogans, and have a Shoemaker to come to the house and make such shoes and Boots as the family were in need of—here in Vevay we had for shoemakers in the early settlement of the town as Shoemakers one Blaney, Kelley, Chaudet and Johnston, and about 1825 or 1826 Charles Thiebaud came to Vevay purchased the lot where Rodolph F. Grisards dwelling stands on which was two log houses not very far apart, he commenced a small business in his line there and continued in business in Vevay until his death in 186— during which period he built up a good business, amassed quite a competency and at his death his sons continued the business—others have during the last 25 or 30 years commenced the business in town, Benjamin F Smith and _____ Braun now being engaged in the business.

In the saddle and Harness making business, about the first establishment of that business in Vevay was commenced by Joseph Malin who now resides near Madison Indiana—his was an extensive business and his Saddles were in great demand all over the country for many miles around, and throughout the bordering counties in Kentucky—after Malin quit the business his brothers in law Miles Mendenhall and James W Cole continued the business and finally his son Ira N Malin carried on the business alone for a while and then in partnership with one Browning.

Joseph Kern the father of Edward Kern came to Vevay and either carried on a shop in that line of business or brought ready made saddles and harness with him. James Todd the father of Henry Todd, came to Vevay at an early day and engaged in the business which he continued for some years.

George Kessler, commenced the business at an early day, and continued in it with his son Victor Kessler until his death some five or six years since.

The tanning business was first established in the immediate vicinity of Vevay as early as 1815 by Francis S. Lindley and was continued by him untill about 1860.

John Louis Siebenthal started a small tanning [establishment] on the farm now owned by John L. Danglade and carried on the business on a small scale for a time. Lindley did a very extensive business in that line for many years and sent his leather to different points in this[1] Ripl[e]y and Jefferson Counties to be sold or bartered by his ágent for hides or cash  Other Tannerys were in operation for a long time at Allensville by Daniel K. Harris, and on the farm owned by Solomon Walden at the foot of the Mount Sterling hill on the lower side of the Turnpike by one ———— Wright and in Pleasant Township by one Banta, who was generally named "Tanner Banta" when being spoken of. One Robinson also had a tannery in Cotton Township between East Enterprize and Aberdeen in Ohio County.

It is believed that at the present time there is not a tannery in Switzerland County that is being carried on, with any great amount of stock.

As the School in Vevay has recently commenced, in the neat and comfortable school house, that has been built with the free will offerings of the citizens (taxpayers) of the town, each contributing in proportion to his property it may not be uninteresting to the boys and girls, young gentlemen, and young ladies, who have commenced attending the School on the 1st Monday of September 1876 to learn the kind of schoolhouses [in which] the writer and those of his age and some younger than he were taught, the rudiments of the English language. In the first place, there was once a horse mill stood on the lot on ferry Street about the Spot where Thomas Delanys Saloon stands[2]—that horse mill had gone out of use—the house in which the mill stones were placed was a round log house about 14 by 18 feet. Into this house a loose floor was laid  a piece of timber roun[d]ing on one side flat on the other—with two, two inch auger holes bored in each end on the rounding side and legs made with an axe driven in the auger holes, was a bench for the Scholars to sit on. The teacher had a split bottom chair and a small table or stand in front of him on which to lay his books, was the first School house in which the English language was taught in Vevay. This School was taught by John Wilson a Baptist minister.

From this School house the Scholars of the School in Vevay were promoted to the Seminary of Vevay which Stood on the lot on Ferry Street where Joseph Peelmans dwelling stands. This was a one story hewed log house perhaps 16 by 30 feet, 7 foot story, windows made by leaving one log out, on each side, which made a window the whole length of the building and wide enough to take two lights of Eight by ten window glass, in h[e]ighth a door, in the end coming into the alley—a board so arranged on each side, for those who were far enough advanced to begin writing as to be of the proper h[e]ighth to receive the light of the windows.

In that seminary the writer then about 8 years of age and others of his age both male and female were instructed in spelling, reading and writing for one or two years by James Rous the father of Zadig and Percy Rous.

One James Brown was a teacher some [time] later and kept his school in a one Story, round log, house that stood on the lot now owned and occupied by Rodolph F. Grisard. There was taught reading writing, arithmetic and Grammer. At one time Mrs. Julia L. Dumont was teaching School in the house now owned and occupied by Mrs. Lucy Detraz, the house not being plastered it began to be rather too cool for comfort so Mrs. Dumont proposed to some of her male pupils that if they would do the work, she would procure the lumber to ceil the room, which was done, and the room was more comfortable. Among those male members was Amie Morerod and others not recollected.

At another period a school was taught in a two Story frame building, that stood on the lot where John Melchers residence stands, by Mrs. Julia L. Dumont, and a year or two later a school was taught in the same room in the upper Story of that building by one Isaac B. Kinsman. The writer attended both schools.

Such were the Schoolhouses in Vevay in which the youth of Vevay and vicinity were instructed in the rudiments of the branches of a Common English, education in the days when the writer received his education.

How thankful should the youth of the present day be that the generations of the past have perfected our common School System, so that they have good comfortable buildings in which, to receive an education to fit them for the performance of the duties that may devolve upon them as citizens of this great and mighty nation.

The time was when some of those now living who are mothers and grandmothers and were born and reared in this county not only made their own dresses but, picked the cotton, hetcheled the flax, spun the wool, and wove the cloth of which the cotton and wo[o]llen dresses were made, some such mothers and grandmothers are now living in our midst—and many have gone to that "Bourne from whence no traveller returns."

Robert Bakes had a carding machine on Board of a Boat, which was moored in the Swift water of the Ohio river about where Schenk & Sons warehouse now stands so arranged that the current of water in the river turned the wheel and did the carding of Wool—he afterwards removed it into town and it was run by horse power this was about 1813 or 1814—he after that established a mill with carding attached where Siebenthals mill on Long Run now Stands—Several years after that he erected his carding machine at Mount Sterling.

## HISTORY OF SWITZERLAND COUNTY 197

Joshua Smithson erected a carding machine on the lot where Gills mill stands, and attached to it a Cotton Gin, which was run for some years, quite a large quantity of Cotton was raised in several neighborhoods in the County and in Kentucky opposite the county which was brought to Vevay to be ginned on Smithsons gin. George G. Knox also erected a carding machine on the lot corner of Main and Main Cross Street opposite the Court house square being part of the lot now owned by Robert A Knox he afterwar[d]s attached a mill for grinding corn & wheat.

Here is a small statement that may be of interest to the publishers of and Subscribers to newspapers of the present time. In the *Indiana Register* of Novr. 10, 1824 appears the following.

### "Look this way"

The following articles will be received in payment of debts due this office viz: Butter 10 cents—lard 5 cents. Tallow 8 cents—Feathers 25 cents—Beeswax 25 cents—Flax 18¾ cents Flax linen 25 to 31¼ cents—Pork 2 cents—Tow linen 12½ to 20 cents—Honey 75 cents per gallon, Cheese 12½ cents, Oats 10 cents per bushel—Flour $1.75 per hundred, Chickens 62½ cents per dozen—Wood $1.00 per cord. The price of the *Register* at that time was $2.00 for 52 numbers or a year.

In the same number of the paper appears the following "The tanners of Wayne county were to meet on the 30th ult. to consider the propriety of reducing the price of leather &c. I hope the tanners generally will follow the example. The farmer has long and justly complained of the extravagant charges of the Tanner"—the foregoing is an editorial.

After the adjournment of the legislature in February 1824 Stephen C. Stevens, gave to his constituents (the people of Switzerland County) a detailed Statement of the acts of that session in a published statement in the *Indiana Register*. In that statement he says "The "treasury department at the beginning of the Session "was much embarrassed and pressed for payment, and "the legislature was compelled to provide either by the "reissue of of treasury notes or by loan, the sum of "about $20,000 to meet the payments of the State debt "which were then due and daily becoming due. The "Governor had recommended a loan and that plan was "without hesitation adopted and an act accordingly "passed authorizing a loan of any sum not exceeding "$19,000. To have authorized the further issue "of Treasury notes, when it was well known that there "were no funds to redeem them, would have countenanced "the odious principle of banking without capital and "would have been an indirect species of Swindling. Such "a policy would have compromitted the integrity of the "state and reduced the Credit thereof below the dignity "of an honest and free people,—And further the print-"ing, stationary, transportation of the laws and Journals "and fuel if paid in specie would cost about $4,500—but "if paid for in treasury notes would cost about $6,000, "therefore in every point of view in which the subject "could be viewed it appeared to be impolitic and ruinous "to authorize a re-issue of Treasury notes. It was sup-"posed that the system of loaning might at first be un-"popular, but firmly believing that it was the only true "policy which could be adopted, and that it would stand "the test of honesty, wisdom and time it was adopted "without a dissenting voice."

The legislature of that period was not composed of "Greenback" members—the house of representative[s] Mr. Stevens says in his address to his constituents "con-"sisted of 26 farmers¹ 3 mechanics 5 doctors one private "gentleman 4 merchants and 6 lawyers making in all 46 "members—the senate consisted of 11 farmers, 2 tavern "keepers 1 doctor 1 merchant and 3 lawyers making

# HISTORY OF SWITZERLAND COUNTY 199

"in all 18 members including the lieutenant governor."

This account of the proceedings of the legislature as given by Mr. Stevens is here given that the "Greenback" and Anti "Greenback" parties may take note of what was thought by our public men without respect to party of the issue of irredeemable promises to pay by the Government of the State of Indiana—will not the same be the result of the General Government issuing "Green Backs"?

It appears that at that session of the legislature an act was passed changing the law in regard to executions and proceedings thereon.[1] The stay of execution in no case was to exceed Six months—real and personal property sold on execution, in all cases, to be sold for the best price it would bring—fifty dollars worth of property exempt from execution and articles exempted named in the act. The representatives from Switzerland County, Stephen C. Stevens and Ralph Cotton opposed the change of the law. The passage of that law created much excitement in some portions of the State—different modes of relief were spoken of. In Jefferson and Clark Counties much excitement existed.

A relief Society was formed in Madison,—There were Seventy Eight persons present Sixty four of whom were in favor of petitioning the governor to convene the legislature to repeal the law.

In Clark county a meeting was held at Charlestown professedly for the same purpose. There wer[e] 162 persons present only Sixty one of whom voted in favor of petitioning the governor to convene the legislature to repeal the law.

A large majority of the citizens of Switzerland County were opposed to the calling of an extra Session of the legislature.

At the celebration of the 4th of July 1824 after Stephen C. Stevens and Ralph Cotton had served in the legislature during the Session preceeding that celebration the following toast was offered by Dr James Welsh

"Col. S. C. Stevens the agreeable and usefully instruc-
"tive orator of the day, with his respectable Colleague
"Judge Ralph Cotton who were our last representatives
"in the legislature of Indiana—May Switzerland County
"have the continued happiness of so respectable and Ju-
"dicious a representation."

The loan authorized by the Legislature, mentioned in this sketch in 1824 was made in part to the State by the Harmo[n]ites, at Harmonie (New Harmony) and it appears that the *Indiana Register* edited by Wm. C. Keen in April 1824 contained an editorial reflecting or intending to reflect upon, the Legislature and the treasurer of state, for the expence incurred in getting the money or a part of it into the Treasury of the State. That article is as follows.

"Paying for the whistle."

"In the act of the last legislature making specific ap-
"propriations I find the following items viz.

| | |
|---|---|
| "To Samuel Merril, treasurer of State "for expences and horse hire for ten days "going to and returning from Harmonie | 22.50 |
| "To James S. Ewing, for ten days serv-"ice, and expences in going to and re-"turning from Harmonie | 23.50 |
| | $46.00 |

"I have looked in Vain, over the laws and resolutions
"for one authorizing those gentlemen to go to Harmonie,
"such a one in [is] not to be found. I suppose however,
"that it was on the loan business, if so we will pay pretty
"dear for that whistle   If five thousand dollars the
"amount borrowed from the Harmonites, costs us forty
"Six dollars in expences besides the interest we may ex-
"pect to pay several hundred before the time is ended
"In vain may the people expect to have their taxes
"reduced."

# HISTORY OF SWITZERLAND COUNTY 201

At the time the above was printed it appears that the editor used the pronoun "I" instead of the plural pronoun "We" as [do] the editors of newspapers of the present day—the suggestion is made that in those days the printer had no devil, therefore it was not necessary for him the [to] say "We" as the printers of the present day who have a "devil" and in speaking of themselves have to associate their "devil" with themselves hence the necessity of saying "We".

In the above extract the reader will observe that the editor was in favor of a reduction of the taxes judging from the manner he speaks that "In vain may the people expect to have their taxes reduced"—that the reader may see the difference between the rate of taxation in 1824 and in 1875, the taxes assessed in Switzerland County for 1824 may be stated as follows

| | | | | |
|---|---|---|---|---|
| on every 100 acres first rate land | $1.50 | state | 75 cts | county |
| on " poll | 50 | state | 00 | Co. |
| on every horse mule or ass 3 years old | 00 | " | 37½ | " |
| on every ox | 00 | " | 18¾ | " |
| on every silver or pinch back watch | 00 | " | 25 | " |
| on every gold watch | 00 | " | 75 | " |

now let the reader select 100 acres of land say in Egypt Bottom in Posey Township, owned by a man under 50 years of age with a span of good horses and a yoke of good oxen to work that land, his state tax would be $2.00, his county tax $1.87½ in all $3.87½ tax as in 1824, including his poll tax.

Now take that 100 acres of land valued for taxation
at thirty five dollars per acre, would make     3,500
a span of good horses valued at                  100
a yoke of good oxen valued at                    100
a poll tax of two dollars—the whole tax for 1875 being $1.50 on each one hundred dollars would with the two

dollars poll tax amount to Sixty dollars and Eighty three cents—nearly fifty seven dollars more than in 1824.

In January 1825 the Board of Justices, who transacted the County business appointed William B. Chamberlin of Posey Township, lister of taxable property for Switzerland County.

### "Indian Summer"

As connected with the history of the Western Country and the fear of a visit from the Indians to the settlements it may not be amiss to give an explanation of the words "Indian Summer" as termed by the first settlers. This expression, like many others, has continued in general use, althou[gh] its original import may have been forgotten. A backwoodsman seldom heard this expression without feeling a chill of horror, because it brought to his mind the painful recollection of its original application.

The reader must be reminded, that during the continued Indian Wars, and Indian depredations to which the first settlers of this part of our now prosperous country were subjected they enjoyed but little peace excepting in the winter season, when owing to the severity of the weather the Indians were unable to make their raids or excursions into the settlements. The onset of winter was therefore hailed, as a Jubilee by the early inhabitants of the Country, who throughout the Spring and early part of the fall had been hemmed in uncomfortable forts, and subjected to all the anxiety and distress of an Indian raid upon the Settlement.

At the approach of winter therefore, the farmers excepting the owner of the fort, removed to their farms, with the joyful feelings, of a tenant of a prison, on being released from his confinement All was bustle and hilarity in preparing for winter by gathering in the corn, digging the potatoes fattening the hogs, and repairing the cabins. To our forefathers, the first settlers of the west, the gloomy months of winter were more

## HISTORY OF SWITZERLAND COUNTY 203

pleasant than the balmy air of Spring or the flowers of May. It however sometimes happens that after the onset of winter the weather became warm; the Smokey time or Season commenced and continued for a considerable number of days. This was the Indian Summer, because it afforded the Indians another opportunity of visiting the settlements with their destructive mode of warfare. The melting of the snow saddened every countenance, and the warmth of the sun filled every heart with horror. The fear of another visit from the Indians, and of being driven from their cabins back to the detested fort was painful, to the highest degree, and this distressing apprehension was frequently realized.

Toward the latter part of February there is commonally a fine spell of open warm weather during which the snow melts away. This was denominated the "Powwawing" days, from the supposition that the Indians were then holding their war councils for the purpose of planning their spring campai[g]ns into the settlements. Sad experience in many cases, taught the early Settlers, that in this conjecture, they were not often mistaken.

The reader has no doubt often during his time witnessed the fine "Indian Summer" of this locality during the fall months—the foregoing is said to be the origin of the term "Indian Summer" as used by the present generation.

At an early day the manufacture of spiritous liquors was carried on in the County on a small scale at several points—about 1817 or 1818 Samuel Mennet commenced distilling on his farm now owned by his Son Francis E. Mennet, with a small copper-still he having a horse mill for the purpose of grinding the grain for distillation, what quantity was made by Mr. Mennet is not known. Another of the early distilleries was near Cottons mill on the farm now owned by Solomon Walden, the date of its erection is not known to the writer—although in 1824 a party of squirril hunters was to meet at "cottons still house" to count their game—not later perhaps than 1820 or 21 one of those small distilleries was erected and operated on the farm now owned by the wife of Hugh H Lamb near Mount Sterling. John Wilson while he owned the Mill now owned by John Bakes, erected a distillery near the mill on a larger scale than any (save one) that had ever before been erected in the County and that larger one was erected by a firm under the name and Style of Whitemore Barnes and Dufour—the persons composing that firm were Nathan M. Whitemore, Francis Barnes and Daniel Dufour—it was erected on the lot of ground where Charles Grammers Slaughter house now Stands—it was supposed its capacity would by [be] about 20 barrels of whiskey every 24 hours   it was run for a short time making a few barrels of whiskey, and was finally abandoned as an unprofitable investment, and all three of the partners were bankrupted in the operation. Daniel Dufour gave a deed to the firm for five acres of land, furnished $1000—in money and in return before the final closing up of the partnership, he received three or four barrels of whiskey.

Louis Gex Oboussier who owned the farm which John J P. Schenck owned at the time of his death—distilled the Lees of his wine and made brandy—he also made peach, Apple and Cherry Brandy, to the latter a German name was given something like "Keirshwas[s]er"—this was all distilled with a small copper Still.

Jean Daniel Morerod for a short time had a small copper still and made wine, apple and peach brandy, all on a small scale.

John James Dufour on his farm above the mouth of Log Lick creek had planted a large peach orchard and not Knowing how to turn them to profit procured a Small copper still, had a trough dug out of a large poplar log in which the peaches were thrown, mashed up, and the Juice drawn off into the still, and made into Brandy

WINE CASKS IN MOREROD HOME

TRUNK IN WHICH DUFOUR PAPERS WERE STORED

which was made in quite large quantities for two or three years, and was abandoned finally as he found a purchaser for his crop of peaches in the person of David H. Blunk who became a famous hay dealer through this county in a few years afterwards. Mr. Blunk in his life time informed the writer that the first trading he ever did was the purchasing a crop of peaches from John James Dufour on his Loglick farm for $100 to be paid as he made sales of the fruit—about the beginning of the peaches ripening he commenced shipping to Cincinnati, the two or three first shipments selling at a good price, and later shipments not selling so well—for his time and trouble after paying the $100 he had a clear profit of about Sixty dollars.

John Detraz had a small copper still at an early day and distilled brandies, and a liquor named "Absceinte" which from its green color was vu[l]garly called "pondwater" by many who frequented his place and drank of it—it was distilled from annis and some other herbs and had a very pleasant taste. Mr. Detraz also brewed and made beer, which was said by Judges to be of an excellent quality—but the quantity he made was very Small. Gabriel Hall the father of John and Will Hall erected a distillery on Halls Branch on the farm now owned by Dudley Leap—a[nd] run it for some years, he also had a mill sufficient to grind the grain for distillery, he made a large quantity of whiskey.

The writer has no recollection of any other distilleries in the county in those early times and none until the large distillery at Patriot was started and now owned by William T. Pate.

It has been repeated time and again as the writer now believes, that the annexation of Texas was carried in the United States Senate by one vote—that Edward A. Hannegan then United States Senator from Indiana was elected to the Senate by one vote, and that that one vote was given Hannegan by Daniel Kelso then Senator from Switzerland County, who was elected by one vote majority.

This is an error—for Kelso when he voted for Hannegan as United States Senator, represented Switzerland County by virtue of a majority of about 150 of the voters of the county over Samuel Howard at the August election of 1842, in 1843 David Henry was elected over Kelso by one majority. Kelso contested the election—and the Senate declared that neither was elected and sent them back to the people for decision, and at the August election 1844 Henry was elected by a small but decided majority—the writer is of the opinion that had Kelso voted for Tighlman A. Howard instead of Edward A. Hannegan he would not have been defeated by David Henry in 1843. Kelso's vote would have elected Howard but he chose otherwise. The writer states this of his own knowledge and observation, as he was one of the members of the House at the time.

In the early days of Methodistism in the Vicinity of Vevay it was customary to hold quarterly meetings alternately at the residences of the brothers in the Church who could furnish the best accommoditions—at one of those quarterly meetings which was being held at the house of Stilwell Heady, who then resided on and owned the farm on which John Bakes now resides on Indian Creek—the presiding elder or the preacher in charge, announced to the Congregation that it was then in order to name the place for holding the next regular quarterly meeting—at the same time paying quite a compliment to those brethren who in the kindness of their hearts, and for the love they had for the Redeemers Kingdom had furnished the place for holding their quarterly meetings, and entertained the brothers and sisters from a distance

He enquired "Has any one thought of the place for holding, the next Quarterly meeting" there was silence for some minutes, when a sister in a distant corner of the room by the name of Prewit "Aunt Polly Prewit" as she was familiarly styled, rose in her place and said "I move that our next quarterly meeting be held at Brother Stilwell Headys" for said she "He always feeds the hungry with the best he has and the chickens he has cooked for us are the best I have eat at any other brothers where I have attended quarterly meetings." It is needless to say that "Aunt Polly Prewits" voice had the effect of causing every one of that congregation to vote for the holding of the next quarterly meeting at Brother Stilwell Headys.

In those early days, every year during the summer or fall the Methodist brethren held Camp meetings in various part[s] of the Country within from three to Eight miles of Vevay—at those camp meetings it was usual for some one to have a stand, where cakes, and other dainties were sold. It chanced that at one of those camp meetings Otis Waldo, the father of Otis S. Waldo of Vevay and Frederick J. Waldo of Rising Sun who was in the baking business in Vevay had a stand from which he sold ginger cakes and other cakes—at that mee[t]ing there was a great deal of religious interest manifested and many persons were convicted of their sins, and made a profession of religion. Among the number thus professing to have found the Savior was Mr. Waldo—when the persons were requested to come forward Mr. Waldo was one of the first to approach near to the stand occupied by the ministers—one of the ministers recognizing Mr. Waldo exclaimed with a loud voice "Thank God even our ginger cake man has got religion." Mr. Waldo from that time forward lived a consistent and exemplary member of the church, his father mother, and sisters being long before members of the same church.

At one of those camp meetings held near the residence of Judge Cotton on Indian Creek, there was a great awakening, and many converts    one lady was so much overcome, that she fainted and a great crowd gathered around her—the weather being warm Jean Daniel Morerod seeing such a crowd around the fainted lady made his way to the crowd, and urged them to stand back and let her have the fresh air—many were disposed not to heed the request, but some fell back. Mr. Morerod seeing the pale face of the lady exclaimed "My God she is dead or dying" and drawing from his pocket a bottle with some whiskey or brandy in it stepped forward to wet her face with the liquor when he was drawn back by one of the preachers and told not to attempt such a thing as that. Mr. Morerod said "the woman will die if you do not do something for her soon."

These incidents are related without the least intention of casting any censure on any of the acts related but simply that they may be preserved for the coming generations.

The changes in the roads leading to and from Vevay to and from different parts of the County have been so changed that it would be almost impossible for a new comer to realize, that to reach such a point in the County from Vevay such a course and such a road must be travelled—as for instance one will be given Ross Township extended up into Ripley County perhaps to or beyond Olean—the road to reach that part of the county was called the "Ross Township Road"—that road turned to the left from the road going up to Jacksonville, about where the Fairview Branch of the V[evay] Mt. S[terling] and V[ersailles][1] turnpike leaves the road, and ran up by Elijah Dickasons, the Lees, and on to Bear Creek—at a later date after Ross Township was detached from the county, the Napoleon State Road was located, and ran a few miles west of the Ross Township road and onto Cross Plains.

About 1827 and 1828 there was quite exciting times in Aurora, Lawrenceburgh, Vevay and Madison, in relation to the location of a road from Lake Michigan to the Ohio

# HISTORY OF SWITZERLAND COUNTY 209

river, each of the foregoing, places contending that the terminus should be at their place—it was finally decided by the Legislature that the terminus of the road should be at Madison.[1] It was related by some of the Commissioners who were appointed to locate the road, that the Indians, who were then numerous along the Wabash, in Cass, Clinton, and the "Miami Reserve" had informed them that the best and most convenient route for that road to be located on was to proceed in a straight direction and reach the Ohio river at Vevay Island for they (the Indians) said that was the route they always took to reach the Ohio river. Who more likely to have a correct knowledge of the route and the place to strike the Ohio river than they who had traveled it for, many very many years—some of the first settlers of the Colony of Swiss here, have related in the hearing of the writer that there was an "Indian Trail" to be distinctly seen for some years after the[y] came here, up to the year 1810.

Up to the year 1820, 22, the road from Cincinnati to Vincennes was thus recorded in the almanacs of that time   "From Cincinnati to Vincennes."

Burlington 15 miles—Rising Sun 10—Judge Cottons 20 Madison 20, New Lexington 17, Salem 32, French lick 34, East fork White river (Shouts) 17, North fork White river (Hawkins) 20—Vincennes 16. Total 201 miles.

The reader will perceive that the road ran back from the river, Judge Cottons four miles back of Vevay being the only point named in this county.


With a view of giving publicity to the readers of these historic reminescenses, especially to those who are emulous to become proficient in the elegant and correct style of letter writing, an accomplishment so highly becoming every man, and for which so many lengthy essays, have been written in vain, the following specimen of all that is elegant, chaste and correct, that could be expected even from the pen of a Johnson or a Walker is here inserted. It is much to be regretted that so many fugitive pieces of this kind have been suffered to be lost, to the injury of literature—to atone in part for this neglect, a letter from a Quandam magistrate or Justice of the peace of former days in Switzerland County is here inserted. It is as follows

BOEN COUNTEY, Kentuky July 18, 1824.

MR. WMS. PERSON Senr. SER—I am informed you and your famley have truspassed in Cutting of timber and takin of Stone of the land of Elizabeth Campbell. I Am much sepersed that men will take such liberteys that they wold not give them Selves—Esqr. Smith Gives him Self the trouble to inform the peopel thare is no persons apinted who Can punish person for so doing if Up on that Ground Sir You have gon to work you will find that yaur tupiney Smith Judgment will not Save you from Damage and you may erest ashurd that you Shall pay for Shuch libertey's and that in Justises

JOSHUA PETTY

Joshua Petty was for m[an]y years a Justice of the peace of Posey Township in this county.

Of all those who have given instruction to the (now grown up) youth of Vevay, none perhaps ever gained so deep a hold on the love and affections of their pupils as did the Reverend Hiram Wason and his estimable lady Mrs. B. R. Wason, who taught the youth of Vevay and the immediate vicinity of the place from about the year 1843 or 1844 to 1856 or 1857, about thirteen years—Mr. Wason preached to the presbyterian Church and congregation from about 1844 to 1857 when he left Vevay and removed to West Creek Lake County Indiana where he is at present residing on a farm. Mr. Wason was not one of your flowery speaking ministers, but was a plain spoken and sensible minister of the Gospel—it was because he was beloved as a teacher, minister, and neighbor, by all that he, was called on to Baptise the children, stand by the bedside of the sick and Dying, and to marry the young—his lady was no less beloved by the youth of Vevay than he. On the occasion of the visit of Mr. and Mrs. Wason to Vevay at the time of the dedication of the Presbyterian Church a few years since, the ladies who had received instruction from Mr. & Mrs. Wason, manifested the Kind feelings and love they entertained towards them, by having a reception for them at the residence of the writer on the occasion of the meeting of the "Social Circle" of the Presbyterian ladies—all denominations joined in making that a grand reception on a small scale—Many valuable presents were presented to them by their former pupils, members of his old church and old neighbors.

Just think of the great changes that have been made in every branch of business and industry since the first years of the Settleing of Switzerland County. Then wedding tours were not fashionable or had not been thought of.

Then the farmers did not cut their legs off with mowing machines.

Then our mothers did not worry over disordered sewing machines.

Then horses which could trot a mile in 2.14 were somewhat scarce, or their speed had not been tested.

Then it required several days to procure a divorce and find a congenial spirit.

Then there were no disputes about the politeness of hack drivers.

Then every young man was not an applicant for a position as a clerk, storekeeper or bartender.

Then kerosene lamps did not explode and assist women to shuffle off their mortal coil.

Then men did not commit suicide by going up in balloons and coming down without them.

Then there were no third term millionaire bishops to stir up the waters of partisan politics.

Then there were no Turkish harems at Salt Lake and no Ann Elizas sueing for the 19th part of a divorce.

Then England was not very far behind the United States in all that tends to make a nation powerful and progressive.

Then the "Dutch" had taken Holland but they had not made France "come down" with a great pile of Smart money.

Then a young lady did not loose caste by wetting her hands in dishwater, or rubbing the skin off her knuckles on a washboard.

Then a physician who could not draw every form of disease from the system by tapping a large vein in the arm was not much of a doctor.

Then men were not running about over the country with millions of Fish eggs to be hatched to order, fish superintended their own hatching in those days.

Then the Condition of the weather on the 1st day of January was not telegraphed all over this continent on the evening of the 31st day of December. Things have changed.

Then People did not worry about rapid transit and their transportation, but threw their grain crop across the backs of their horses and uncomplain[in]gly "went to mill.

Then every man cut his coat according to his c[l]oth —every man was estimated at his real value, shoddy was not known—no person had "struck ile" and true merit and honest worth were the only grounds for promotion.

Then every boy who wished to go to the show had to get twelve and a half cents to pay his way in to see the Elephant, Lion and tiger.

About the year 1822 or 1823 there resided in the town of Warsaw then (Fredericksburg) a Baptist minister

## HISTORY OF SWITZERLAND COUNTY 213

(John Pavy) and the owner and Keeper of a Store, where goods were sold and all kinds of country produce and poultry was taken in exchange for goods whose name was Yates, the father of "Dick" Yates, as he was familiarly called—Mr. Pavy had left home on a tour for preaching, leaving his family and two Sons James, and Samuel at home—during his absence a show or menagerie visited Fredericksburg the admittance to which was twelve and a half cents   James and Samuel had but one Twelve and a half cent piece (a cut one at that). James being the eldest had to have that piece. Samuel was then left to his wits to raise the needed $12\frac{1}{2}$ cents to pay his way into the show. He had a fine chicken cock, which he caught, filed his spurs sharp and calling on Dick Yates accosted him with "Dick I've got a rooster that can whip yours". "Dick responded "I'll bet you ninepence he can't." The bet was taken, the chickens set down together   the second strike of Samuels chicken knocked Dicks chicken over, so Samuel got his $12\frac{1}{2}$ cents, was happy and went to the show.

These two lads located in after life in different localities. Samuel settled in this county and is the Samuel H Pavy of Craig Township.   Dick settled in Illinois and was the Richard Yates Governor of the State of Illinois now dead.

About the year 1819 a man named Moése Deserens was taken sick with Billious fever and was confined to his bed at John F. Siebenthals who then lived on the farm owned by the Norrisez family in a double log house that stood about or near to where the house occupied by Victor Norrisez now stands—during the night the sick man left his bed, the room, and the house and was no where to be found—a day or two afterwards some person found his body hanging to a tree up the branch or hollow that comes down from the right of the road as one goes to the upper Indian creek bridge out of the Norrisez lands and empties into the pond—before the making of the turnpike along that route the hill coming toward town was quite Steep and was termed "Moese hill" the title or name was given in consequence of this man having hung himself up that branch.

In early days an Irishman by the name of John Willis and his wife settled on a farm in Craig Township on Pendleton run    the road from Vevay to his farm, was desolate in the night time, and any night in travelling that road, owls could be heard hooting in all directions— it chanced that for a year or two after he had settled on that farm, he had frequent occasions to come to town, and return home in the night time    on some one or more of his nightly journey[s] home after he had reached the top of the hill back of town the owls commenced their hooting and it appeared to Willis that the owl said "and "who! who! are you. Willis replied Jo[h]nny Willis—the owl repeated "who! who! are you, when Willis enquired "and who are you be Jabbers" the owl again repeated "and who! who! are you." when Willis answered "Jo[h]nny Willis from Ireland" the owl again repeated "Who! Who! are you when Willis answered Jo[h]nny Willis from Ireland and be d—n to you" Willis in after years used to relate the circumstance with a great deal of merriment after he had ascertained who it was that thus accosted him, on his way home through the woods.

During the days in which Camp meetings were annually held in this part of the country there lived an old man by the name of Abraham Parkinson in the neighborhood of Vevay    he was a son of the Emerald Isle. At one of those camp meetings a friend and neighbor of his experienced religion, and in relating what he had experienced and seen—he said among other things that he "saw the Spirit of God descend in the shape of a dove."

Parkinson was standing by listening very attentively to the relation of what his neighbor had seen and felt— he asked the converted neighbor "was it a bird of a greyish cast"    the reply was "Yes"—then said Parkinson, "I lay you a guinea it was an owl sir."

As the writer has about exhausted his recollections of incidents that would be in any way interesting or instructive he will now bid the readers of these hortoric [historic] sketches farewell, and if by any thing he has written of individuals he has giving [given] cause for offence he begs pardon, and if any have been interested by their perusal he will have attained the object he had in view when the task was undertaken—to those who have given him words of encouragement by informing him that they were much interested in the reading of the "sketches" he returns his heartfelt thanks, and hopes that some person will commence with this centennial year to keep a daily record of such occurrences as may transpire in the County, and that they and others may continue that record so that when the next centennial year shall roll round, there may be a better record of events to give to those who may then be on the stage of action, than the writer has been enabled from his own Knowledge and information derived from others to give in these sketches. Then gentle readers farewell! farewell!

# APPENDIX

Au nom de Dieu Amen:

Moy Jean Jaques Dufour père declare par les presentes, que comme mes Enfans, savoir Jeanne Marie, Anthoinette, Jean François, Susanne Marguerite, et Jean David Dufour sont dans l'intention de partir pour aller joindre leur Frère ainé mon Fils Jean Jaques Dufour Vigneron a Frères-vignard au Kintucki dans les Etats Unis de l'Amerique, or comme mes sus nommés cinq Enfans n'ont pas attaint l'age de majorité et qu'ils ont encore besoins d'instruction, je les envoye et remets a mon susdit fils ainé Jean Jaques Dufour, en lui transmettant par les presentes mon autorité paternelle que j'ay sur eux, et le declare leur second père, pour pouvoir agir sur eux, et faire son possible pour avancer leur bonheur; pour ce faire, il agira avec eux comme si en étoit le veritable père, leur aprendra a travailler chacun a la portée de son age et de son sexe, les accoutumera a l'afsiduité et diligence, fera son possible pour les détourner de la paresse, l'oisiveté, la fenéantise, l'orgoeuil, la débauche, et autres pafsions vicieuses qui entrainent facilement les jeunes gens dans le malheur, que si quelcun ou quelcune sont appelés au saint état du mariage, il leur aidera et fera leurs conditions, mais sur tout fera ses efforts pour les instruire et leur persuader la verité de la Religion Chrétienne, et pour cela addrefsera souvent des ferventes prieres au Dieu de Misericorde, comme je le fais aufsi, qu'il lui plaise leur ouvrir l'entendement et le Coeur a la vraye foy chrétienne, seul et unique moyen pour avoir le bonheur dans ce Monde, et s'afsurer la vraye félicité dans la viequi est a venir, amen!

Par contre je constitue mes cinq Enfans sus nommés, et les afsujettis a leur sus dit Frère ainé a lui porter honneur, respect, soumifsion, obeifsance, et fidelité, en un mot a tous les devoirs que les Enfans doivent a leurs vrais pére et mére, jusques au tems qu'il croira pouvoir les declarer l'un apres l'autre majeurs et capable de se conduire par eux memes; mettant toute ma confiance en lui qu'il fera ma susditte volonté, je prie Dieu qu'il ayes en sa sainte Garde, pour foy de quoy je me suis souscrit

a Sales de Montreux le 13ᵉ Janvier 1801          Jean Jaques Dufour père

COMMISSION OF JOHN JAMES DUFOUR TO HIS ELDEST SON

## Patent for Jean Jaques Dufour, Jr.

In the name of God, Amen!

I, Jean Jaques Dufour, Sr. declare by these presents, that as my children, namely:—Jeanne Marie, Anthoinette, Jean Francois, Susanne Marguerite, and Jean David Dufour have the intention of leaving to join their oldest brother, my son, Jean Jaques Dufour, a vine-dresser in Fiersnewyard ["First Vineyard"]—in Kintucky in the United States of America, now since my above-mentioned five children have not reached their majority and since they still need guidance, I send and intrust them to my above-mentioned oldest son Jean Jaques Dufour, transmitting to him by these presents my paternal authority which I have over them, and declare him their second father, to be able to act with authority over them, and to do his utmost as if he were their true father, will teach them to work, each one according to his age and sex, will accustom them to industry and diligence, will do his best to keep them from indolence, idleness, sluggishness, pride, debauchery, and other vicious passions which easily lead young people to misfortune; that if any one of them is called to the holy state of matrimony, he will help them and will determine their conditions [in the marriage contract] but above all, will strive to instruct them and to convince them of the truth of the Christian religion, for which purpose he will often offer fervent prayers to the God of Pity, as I do also, that it may please him to open their understanding and their hearts to the true Christian faith, the one true happiness in the life which is to come, Amen!

On the other hand, I give my five children above-named, and subject them to their above-mentioned oldest brother, that they may show him honor, respect, submission, obedience and fidelity, in a word, all the duties which children owe to their true father and mother, until the time when he shall believe that he can declare them, one after the other, to be of age and capable of taking care of themselves; placing all my confidence in him that he will do my will, as above stated, I pray God that he will have [them] in his holy care, as evidence of which I have subscribed myself at Sales de Montreux, the 13th of January, 1801

JEAN JAQUES DUFOUR, Sr.

RECONNOISSANCE DE COMUNAGE DE NOVILLE & RENNAR

En faveur de monsieur L'ancien Juge et Sin Jean Jaques Rodolp DuFour de montreux & de Jean Jaques son fils.

Du 24 Juin 1762

Le President et Conseil des honorables Communeautés de Noville et Rennar cejourd'hui assemblés pour Vaquer aux affaires desdittes Communeautés, Il l'y est presenté monsieur l'ancien Juge & Sindic Jean Jaques Rodolph DuFour de Montreux et Jean Jaques son fils qui à paru c'y devant endit Conseil avec sondit pére, lequel à humblement requis que suivant l'acte de Communage du Sieur Daniel Dufour son grand pére quil à produit sous la datte du 9 Mars 1678: Signé Jaquemin notaire, Duquel Daniel est né Adam, et dudit Adam est né Pierre David, Jean Jaques Rodolph, et Etienne Pierre André, comme fait foi l'acte de Batistère produit end. conseil signé Chavanne pére, & Chavanne fils Pasteur à Montreux, outre le Contract de mariage dud. Daniel Dufour signé Poisat notaire, du 1.7b. 1687, demême que son testament par luy signé, et comme par ce testament il est nommé Lieutenant, et que l'on à requis dans la derniére assemblée quil prouvat comment il étoit parvenu au poste de chatelain, ce qui à été demontré par son Livre d'admodiation du Chatelard comme en fait foy la signature du Seigneur De Blonnay;—Ensorte que par deliberation desdits Conseils et suivant les actes que led. Sieur Juge Dufour nous à produit, nous avons reconnus iceux trois fréres, savoir Pierre David, Jean Jaques Rodolph, et Etienne Pierre André, qui sont tous trois Isseus dud. Adam Dufour qui étoit fils dud. Daniel Dufour, pour nos Communiers & Compatriotes le tout conformément audit acte de Communage à nous produit et sus designés, avons encore reconnu ledit Jean Jaques fils dudit Jean Jaques Rodolph qui s'est presenté endit Conseil;

## APPENDIX

RECOGNITION OF COMMON RIGHTS IN NOVILLE AND
RENNAR

In favor of the former judge and mayor, Jean Jaques
Rodolph Dufour of Montreux and of Jean Jaques his son.

June 24, 1762

The President and Council of the honorable communities of Noville and Rennar, this day assembled to attend to the affairs of the aforesaid communities, There presented themselves the former judge and mayor, Jean Jaques Rodolph Dufour of Montreux and Jean Jaques his son, who appeared before the council with his father, who humbly requested that according to the act of communage [common rights] of Monsieur Daniel Dufour his grandfather, which he produced under the date of March 9, 1678, signed Jaquemin, notary, from which Daniel, Adam was born, and from the aforesaid Adam were born Pierre David, Jean Jaques Rodolph and Etienne Pierre André, as proven by the baptismal record produced in the aforesaid council, signed Chavanne the elder, and Chavanne his son, Pastor at Montreux, besides the marriage contract of the aforesaid Daniel Dufour signed Poisat, notary, the 1st of July, 1687, as well as his will signed by him, and since by this will he is called Lieutenant and because they have required in the last assembly that he should prove how he had reached the position chatelain which was shown by his book of *admodiation*[1] as is proven by the signature of the Seigneur de Blonnay:—so that by the deliberation of the abovementioned councils and in accordance with the documents which Judge Dufour produced, we have recognized those three brothers, namely, Pierre David, Jean Jaques Rodolph and Etienne Pierre André, who are all three sons of Adam Dufour, who was the son of Daniel Dufour, as our commoners and compatriots, all in conformity with the act of common rights produced for us and abovementioned; we have also recognized the aforesaid Jean Jaques, son of the said Jean Jaques Rodolph, who pre-

Desquelles ont à fait Expedié le present acte de reconnoissance aud. Sieur Jean Jaques Rodolph Dufour sous le sceau armorial du Sieur Justicier Pierre Des Lameru President endit Conseil près la signature du Curial soussigné dud. Noville, le tout pour faire foy des presentes Donnés dans nôtre ditte assemblée ordinaire de Conseil le 24 Juin 1762.

### INSTRUCTIONS POUR MR. JEANFRANÇOIS DUFOUR

Le 26 mai 1792, en presence du Gouverneur Morris, Ambassadeur des Etats-unis, qui a Signé à l'acte, les Srs. Pierre Le Roi Dallarde et James Swan ont vendu au Sr. J. Payenboisneuf et à la famelie Vincendiere un terrein Situé sur la Riviere Ohio à lembouchure de Leotre Creek de la Contenance de 12500, acres, suivant le plan annexé à l'acte de vente et Signé par les Vendeurs. les acquereurs leur payerent Cette Terre Comptant aussi qu'on le Voit dans l'acte de Vente

Les acquereurs se rendirent en amerique où, peu de tems àprès, arriva Mr. Swan. alors les acquereurs lui demandirent de les mettre en possession de la dite Terre; Mr. Swan leur repondit, par lettre, qu'il alloit chargér un agent de la recherche de cette terre; et après un Long tems il leur écrivit que la terre qu'il avoit vendue appartenoit à divers particuliers. il proposa divers arrangments qui tous, constatant sa mauvaise foi, furent refusér. Vingt Lettres du Sr. Swan écrittes au Sr. Payenboisneuf constatent que les Sr. Dallarde et Swan n'ont Jamais été proprietaires de la terre vendue Suivant le plan signé et annexé à l'acte de Vente. Les acquereurs ont fait faire une consultation à Paris et voulant faire une nouvelle tentative pour éviter un procès desagréable aux Srs. Dallarde & Swan, leur ont fait communiquer cette Consultation. il paroit par la réponse des Vendeurs que pour éloigner le terme d'un Jugement qui les Condamneroit à rembourser, ils voudroient prendre

sented himself in the council; as a result of which things, the present act of recognition has been sent to Jean Jaques Rodolph Dufour under the seal of Judge Pierre des Lameru, President of the Council, beside the signature of the undersigned clerk of Noville, all in order to give faith to these presents given in our ordinary assembly of the council, the 24th of June, 1762.[1]

### INSTRUCTIONS FOR MR. JEANFRANÇOIS DUFOUR

The 26th of May, 1792, in the presence of Gouverneur Morris, ambassador of the United States, who signed the document, Messrs. Pierre Le Roi Dallarde and James Swan have sold to Mr. J. Payen-boisneuf and to the Vincendiere family a tract of land situated on the Ohio River at the mouth of Otter Creek, containing 12500 acres, according to the map attached to the bill of sale and signed by the vendors. The purchasers paid them for this land in cash as is shown by the bill of sale.

The purchasers went to America where Mr. Swan arrived soon after. Then the buyers asked him to give them possession of the aforesaid land; Mr. Swan answered them by letter, that he was going to commission an agent with the investigation of this land, and after a long time he wrote to them that the land which he had sold belonged to various individuals. He proposed various arrangements all of which, his bad faith being apparent, were refused. Twenty letters from Mr. Swan written to Mr. Payen-boisneuf show that Messrs. Dallarde and Swan have never been owners of the land sold according to the map signed and joined to the bill of sale. The buyers had a consultation at Paris, and wishing to try once more to avoid a lawsuit, disagreeable to Messrs. Dallarde and Swan, had this consultation communicated to them. It appears by the response of the vendors that in order to put off the execution of a judgment which would condemn them to pay back the money, they would like to take advantage of the fact that the purchasers

Avantage de ce qui les Acquereurs n'ont pas fait faire d'acte Juridique pour être mis en Possession.

Comme il faut se mettre en garde Contre la chicanne qui est la Seule resource des gens de mauvaise foi, il s'agit de faire Constater d'une Maniere Légale que le terrein désigné dans le dit plan Signé par Dallarde & Swan et vendu par eux au Sr. J. Payen Boisneuf et à la famille Vincendiere n'appartient pas aux Srs. Dallarde & Swan et quils n'ont Jamais delivré ni pu délivrer un terrein qui ne leur appartient Pas.

### Compte des avoirs de la Famille Dufour en Amerique, rendu au père

Compte que rend Jean Jaques Dufour des Proprietés qu'il a reçu de son Père lors qu'il est allé en Amerique, et de celles reçues lors qu'il y étoit ayant larrivée de ses frères vers lui en 1801, avec lesquels il est demeuré pendant 3 ans pour travailler a la première vigne en Societé avec la Compagnie pour létablissement de la vigne en Kentuky. En 1796, je me suis fait un fond de L2736, pour mon voyage en Amerique d'ont L1100 apartenoient à mon Pere provenant de la vente de son bien de Songi qui me les fournissoit parce que les interets de toute sa famille entroient pour beaucoup dans le plan de mon voyage—ci recu              L 1100–bz[?]

Pour l'interet depuis le 28 Fevrier 1796, que j'ai retire cette somme de chez Ms. Kinkelin et Roupp a Berne ou elle avoit été placée au 5% jusquau 1° Juillet que mes frères sont entrés chez moi, ci pour 5 ans 4 mois                 293. 3

# APPENDIX

have not had the judicial order made out to be put into possession.

As it is necessary to be on guard against the chicanery which is the only resource of people of bad faith, it is necessary to establish in a legal way that the land designated in the aforesaid map signed by Dallarde and Swan and sold by them to J. Payen-boisneuf and to the Vincendiere family, did not belong to Messrs. Dallarde and Swan and that they have never delivered and never could deliver a piece of land which did not belong to them.

### ACCOUNT OF THE POSSESSIONS OF THE DUFOUR FAMILY IN AMERICA, RENDERED TO THE FATHER

Account rendered by John James Dufour of the properties which he received from his father when he went to America, and of those received while he was there before his brothers joined him in 1801, with whom he stayed for 3 years to work at the first vineyard in association with the company for the establishment of the vineyard in Kentucky. In 1796 there was made up for me a fund of 2736 livres for my American journey, of which 1100 livres belonged to my father, coming from the sale of his property of Songi, which he contributed to me because the interests of his whole family were greatly involved in the project of my journey thus received........L 1100

As interest, since February 28th, 1796, when I withdrew this amount from the house of Messrs. Kinkelin and Roupp at Berne where it had been placed at 5% until July 1st when my brothers joined me,—that is, for 5 years, 4 months....  293.3

| | | |
|---|---:|---:|
| 1801 En Juin j'ai reçu par le canal de Mr. Gouffond de Philladelphie le produit de la vente d'une Caisse de marchandise envoyèe de la Suisse par Daniel, mais ayant été mal adressèe, est restée a la Douane de ditte Ville jusqu'ace quelle la fait vendre pour les droits d'entrée, lequel produit apres deduction des fraix et droits pour une autre Caisse que j'ai reçu se monte a $210.18 cents voyez la lettre a Mr. Gouffond. a 111 piasters pour L 400 de suisse................ | 757. | 3 |
| Jai pu avoir vendu avant larrivée de mes frères des Marchandises contenues dans le Caisse que j'ai reçu apres deduction des fraix de transport j'usqu'en Kentucky le reste a été vendu en Commun. $40 au taux ci dessus...... | 144. | 1 |
| Total des reçues | L 2294 | 7 |

Livrées

| | | |
|---|---:|---:|
| 1797. Daniel a reçu d'Obersteg de Boltigue pour moi, porte en reçues a mon Pere.. | 16 | 2 |
| 1801 Livré a Boralley par rencontre de ce que me devoient Ms. Mennet et Cart. | 619 | 8 |
| Livré a sa veuve apres la separation d'avec mes fréres, un Cheval provenant de Stuart pour $80. le reste de ce qui etoit du a Boralley lui a été paye par ensemble ........................ | 288. | 3 |
| 8bre le 16. Recu de Mr. Gouffond et employé au profit de la famille, le relicat de ce quil me devoit pour vente de mes marchandises en commission $112.57 cents ........................... | 405. | 6 |

Daniel a reçu a Lausanne 25 louis des parents de Mr Mennet auquel je les ai

## APPENDIX 227

1801    In June I received through Mr. Gouffond of Philadelphia the proceeds of the sale of a case of goods sent from Switzerland by Daniel, but having been badly addressed it stayed in the custom house of that city [Philadelphia] until it had to be sold to pay the import duty. It brought, after deducting these expenses and duties for another case which I received; it amounted to $210.18, as per the letter [of] Mr. Gouffond, at 111 dollars for 400 Swiss livres...................... 757.3

I was able to bring about the sale, before the arrival of my brothers, of some of the goods contained in the case which I received, after the deduction of the expense of transportation to Kentucky, the balance was sold jointly. $40 at the above rate     144.1

                     Total receipts    L 2294.7

### Payments

1797    Daniel received from Obersteg of Boltigue for me, carried on receipt to my father ........................... 16.2

1801    Paid to Boralley, out of the return of what Messrs. Mennet and Cart owed me    619.8

Delivered to his widow after separation from my brothers, a horse coming from Stuart, for $80. The balance of what was due Boralley was paid him jointly..    288.3

Oct. 16th.    Received from Mr. Gouffond and invested for the benefit of the family, the balance of the amount due me for the sale of my goods on commission $112.57    405.6

Daniel received at Lausanne 25 louis from the relatives of Mr. Mennet, of

| | | |
|---|---:|---:|
| rencontré sur ce qu'il me devoit apres deduction des fraix de transport dune malle .......................... | 316 | – |
| Rembourcé a Louis Sanders 50 piastre emprunté par Daniel a Pittsburg sur quoi est a deduiré 17 piastres ¾ que Daniel ma remis de cet argent $32¼— | 116. | 2 |
| Rembourcé a Morerod et a Boraley pour argent avancé par eux a mes frères en route et porté en reçue par Daniel a mon père........................ | 134. | 8 |
| Du moment de notre jonction j'avois en caisse au moins 83 piastres compris les 17.¾ que Daniel venoit de me remettre voyez le livre de la vigne | 299. | 1 |
| et ce que j'avois dépencé pour la famille avant davoir ouvert aucun compte pour balance de ce compte porte au credit des compte avec mon père en Suisse....... | 98 | 7 |
| total des livrees | L. 2294. | 7 |

debité a Jean

Omis un cheval venant de Stuart remis a Jean François quand il est allè porté le vin au President je crois en 1804. $60. L 216 2bz et quil a vendu pour pouvoir revenir il me seroit ainsi redu par la famille L 216.2bz que j'espere je pourai prelever sur ce qui reviendra de la 1° Vigne ainsi que les 136 piastres et 47 Cents que j'avois avance a la Societe de ditte Vigne avant larivee de mes freres.

Partage entre les enfans de Jean Jaques Dufour des proprietes quils ont en Communion dans les Etats Unis d Amerique fait ensuite de leur separation arrivee a First vineyard au Mois d'Octobre 1804, d'un consentement mutuel.

Les Copartageants sont Jean Jaques, Daniel, Jeanne

## APPENDIX 229

| | |
|---|---|
| which I returned those above what was due me after the deduction of expense for the transportation of a trunk...... | 316 |
| Repaid to Louis Sanders 50 dollars borrowed by Daniel at Pittsburgh from which is to be deducted 17¾ dollars of that sum, which Daniel turned over to me $32¼ .......................... | 116.2 |
| Repaid to Morerod and to Boralley for money advanced by them to my brothers en route and taken on receipt by Daniel to my father....................... | 134.8 |
| From the time of our uniting I had on hand at least 83 dollars, including the 17¾ which Daniel had just given me, as per the book of the vineyard........... | 299.1 |
| and my expense for the family before having opened my account, carried as a credit balance from this account to my account with my father in Switzerland | 98.7 |
| Total in livres | L.2294.7 |

Debit to John

Omitted, a horse coming from Stuart sent to John Francis when he went to carry the wine to the President, I believe, in 1804 ($60 L 216.2) and which he sold to enable him to return There would thus be due me by the family L 216.2 which I hope I can realize on the returns from the first vineyard, as also the 136 dollars and 47 cents which I advanced the society of the said vineyard before the arrival of my brothers.

Division among the children of John James Dufour Sr. of the properties which they held in common in the United States of America, made after their separation, brought about at the First vineyard in the month of October, 1804, by mutual consent. The copartners are John James, Daniel, Jane Maria, Marie Antoinette, John

Marie, Antoinette, Jean Francois, Susanne, David, et Aimé, ce dernier étant alors encore en Europe.

1°. Chacun des Copartageants aura un lot de terre en Suisserland de celles que le Congres des Etats Unis a concédée a Jean Jaques Dufour fils et ses Associes par acte du 1° May 1802. Comme suit. (les Nos. sont continués d'Ouest a l'Est sur ceux que Sibentals pere et fils, Betens et Morerod ont eu a titre d Associes.). No 4 appartiendra a Daniel No 5 a Jean Jaques, No 6 a Daniel Vincent fils de Jean Jaques, No 7 a Jean François, No 8 a David, No 9 a Aimé No 10. a Antoinette, No 11 a Susanne No 12. a Jeanne Marie. Daniel Vincent fils de Jean Jaques est reçu ici simplement comme associes de la même maniere que Betens, Morerod et les Sibentals. Jean Jaques Dufour ayant acheté a l'ouest du tract pour pouvoir redresser les portions et faire celle a François Sibental ainsi qu'il avoit été convenu entre les Associes. De cet aquis une portion a été cedée a Ms. Gex, Raimond et Stuart, le reste demeure *in Statu quo* jusquace qu'il soit definitivement paye. Le tout sera Mesuré et place dapres le plan dresse a ce Sujet.

Chacun des Copartageants sengage ici de payer sa part des terres qu'il aura lors quelles deviendront dues au Congres, et a ne pas les vendre quelles ne soyent payées ainsi que de remplir les angagements auquels se sont assujetté les Coassocies dans lacte de partage entre la famille Dufour, les Sibentals, Betens et Morerod.

2° Les Copartageants ayant travaillé en Commun pendant environ trois ans a létablissement de la premiere Vigne en Communion avec la Societé de dite Vigne avec laquelle Jean Jaques est engagé pour neuf ans dont six d'iceux sont fait: La proprieté aquise par ce travail dans la Societé de la Vigne sera partagée a proportion du tems et de sa valeur que chacun deux y a mis, mais

Francis, Susannah, David, and Aimé, the last being then still in Europe.

1st. Each of the copartners shall have a parcel of land in Switzerland out of those which the Congress of the United States granted to John James Dufour, Jr., and his associates by Act of May 1st, 1802, as follows. (The numbers are continued from west to east in order, after those which the Sibenthals, father and son, Betens and Morerod held by virtue of being associates.) No 4 shall belong to Daniel, No 5 to John James, No 6 to Daniel Vincent, son of John James, No 7 to John Francis, No 8 to David, No 9 to Aimé, No 10 to Antoinette, No 11 to Susannah, No 12 to Jane Maria. Daniel Vincent, son of John James, is herein regarded simply as one of the associates, in the same manner as Betens, Morerod and the Sibenthals. John James Dufour, having bought to the west of the tract so as to be able to straighten out the portions and make that of Francis Sibenthal as it had been agreed upon among the associates. A part of their purchase has been granted to Messrs. Gex, Raymond, and Stuart, the rest remains *in statu quo* until the final payment has been made. The whole will be measured and arranged according to the plan drawn up for this matter.

Each of the copartners hereby pledges himself to pay for his share of the lands which he shall have, when the same shall be due to Congress, and not to sell them until they are paid for, and likewise to fulfill the pledges which the associates have taken on themselves in the instrument of division among the Dufour family, the Sibenthals, the Betens and Morerod.

2nd. The copartners having worked jointly during nearly three years at the establishment of the first vineyard in common with the society of the aforesaid vineyard, to which John James was contracted for nine years, six of which have passed. The property acquired by this work in the vineyard society shall be divided in proportion to the time and its value, which each of them

pour prévenir les difficultés qui pouroient selever dans lestimation du dit tems on fixe ici que le tier de ditte proprieté apartiendra a ce partage, et les deux autres tiers a Jean Jaques Seul. Ainsi tout ce qui reviendra a la famille Dufour de la ditte compagnie apres sa liquidation sera partagé entre les copartageants dapres la proportion ci dessus. bien entendu que les $136.47 cents que la Societé de la vigne devoit a Jean Jaques Dufour par compte' régle avant larrivée de ses freres, seront comprises dans la liquidation de cette Societé comme une dette particuliere en faveur du dit Jean Jaques.

3. Chacun des Copartageants aura cinquante piastres à retirer de ce que doivent Sibentals père et fils, Betens et Morerod l'an 1814. Jean Jaques & Daniel auront ce que Doit Betens. Jean François et David ce que doit Gollay au nom de Sibental pére, Aimé et Susanne ce que doit Sibentals fils, Antoinette et Jeanne ⸺Marie ce que doit Morerod.

4° Chacun des Copartageants sengage solemnellement par les présentes de tenir les articles ci dessus comme regle entre nous, et comme une partie de nous sont mineurs Jean Jaques s'engage particulierement de présenter Une Copie du present partage sitot apres son arrivée a Montreux a Notre père Jean Jaques Dufour pour obtenir son aprobation paternelle fait a First vineyard ce 8me Novembre 1804.

J'aprouve tout cequi est ci devans pour ce qui me conserne
        atteste JEAN JAQUES DUFOUR, *père*

has put into it, but to prevent difficulties which might arise in estimating the said time it is hereby agreed that a third of said property shall be subject to this division, and the other two thirds to John James alone. Thus all that shall come to the Dufour family from the aforesaid company after its liquidation shall be divided among the copartners according to the above proportion. However, it is understood that the $136.47 which the vineyard society owes John James Dufour according to the account adjusted before the arrival of his brothers, shall be included in the liquidation of that society as a personal debt owed to the aforesaid John James

3. Each of the copartners shall have fifty dollars to be taken out of what the Sibenthals, father and son, Betens and Morerods owe in the year 1814. John James and Daniel shall have that which Betens owes. John Francis and David that which Gollay owes in the name of Sibenthal Sr., Aimé and Susannah that which Sibenthal Jr. owes, Antoinette and Jane Maria that which Morerod owes.

4th. Each of the copartners by these presents solemnly pledges himself to observe the above articles as binding among us, and as some of us are minors, John James personally pledges himself to tender a copy of the present division, as soon as he reaches Montreux, to our father John James Dufour in order to get his paternal approval done at the first vineyard this 8th of November, 1804

I approve all the foregoing so far as I am concerned

attest JEAN JAQUES DUFOUR, Sr.

1 Broillard de Voyage pour Jean Jaques Dufour
 de Sales a Montreux, au Bailliage de Vevey.

[The denominations of money in which accounts are entered in this daybook vary somewhat irregularly with the time and place concerned. The following explanations are only approximate, and the amounts here given as equivalents, when they differ from values given in numismatic manuals, are based on the actual usage in this daybook.
Batz, batzen (Swiss=10 rappen), 2.8 cents
Crown (English=5 shillings), $1.10
Denier (French), .077 cent: (Swiss), .116 cent
Ecu, Gros ecu, $1.10
Escalin or scalin (Dutch), 12-30 cents
Franc (French), 17–19 cents
Guilder (Dutch=20 stivers=320 pennings), 38.5 cents

Commencé le jour de mon depart pour les Etat Unis de l'Amerique.
 Montreux le 20° Mars 1796.

| | | |
|---|---|---|
| Compte de Voyage. | Doit | |
| A Compte de fond pour celui que je me fais pour ce Voyage savoir | | |
| Pour argent pris en Caisse [livres, sous, deniers] | L 736 | – – |
| Pour papier de Valeur pris en Portefeuille savoir deux reconnoissances contre Isenchmid Kinkelin et Roupp de Berne lune en datte du 31° Janvier 1796 du Capital de L 1400. avec interet au 5% et l'autre du 26 Fevrier 1796, de L. 600, au meme interet ce qui fait............. | 2000 | – – |
| 2  Du 20° Mars 1796. | | |
| Compte de Harde et Nippe | Doit | |
| A Compte de fond pour celui que je me fais pour mon Voyage savoir en harde et Nipe que je prend en Malle, a forme de l'inventaire que j'ai dans mon portefeuille et que j'estime valoir | 151 | – – |

## APPENDIX

1 DAYBOOK OF JEAN JAQUES DUFOUR OF SALES OF MONTREUX, BAILIWICK OF VEVEY, ON HIS TRAVELS.

Guinea (English=21 shillings), $4.62
Livre (Swiss=20 sous=240 deniers), 27–28.6 cents
Livre Tournois (French, equivalent of franc=20 sous), 18–19 cents
Louis (French, used with various values), in this daybook, $4.18
Piastre, used interchangeably with dollar
Pence, penny (English), 1.3–1.8 cents
Pound (English=20 shillings=240 pence), $4.40
Rappe, rappen (Swiss), .28 cent
Rixdollar (Dutch), $1.00
Scalin, variant of escalin
Shilling (English), 22 cents
Sol, sous (French, Swiss=12 deniers), .92 cent (French), 1.3 cents (Swiss).]

Begun on the day of my departure for the United States of America
  Montreux, March 20th, 1796
Traveling Account
To Funds Account, for the funds I am getting together for this journey, to wit:                    Debit
for money taken in cash [livres, sous, deniers]                                                    L 736  00  0
For bankable paper in portfolio, to wit: two notes against Isenschmid, Kinkelin and Roupp of Berne, one dated January 31st, 1796, principal L1400, with interest at 5%, the other dated February 26th, 1796, for L600, at the same interest, which makes    2000  00  0

2          March 20th, 1796
Clothing Account                                                                                    Debit
To Funds Account, for the supply of clothing I am carrying in my trunk for my journey, according to the inventory in my portfolio, and which I value at                                                             151   0   0

|  |  |  |  |
|---|---:|---:|---:|
| dudit | | | |
| Doit caisse a Voyage pour arg: mis en caisse pour [*Illegible*] | 736 | – | – |
| Berne le 22° dit | | | |
| Compte de Voyage        Doit | | | |
| A Compte de Caisse pour erre que j'ai donné au Domestique du Voiturier Lentz de Berne qu'il ma promi de me transporter mon bagage jusqua Paris, moyenant un louis que j'ai promis de lui livrer, dont les erres sont a compte.......... | 4 | – | – |
| le 25° dit | | | |
| Doit Compte de Harde et Nipe | | | |
| A Compte de Caisse pour une montre que jai achetè de Henny de Berne maintenué pour L 34 et la chaine et assortiment 16s [?] | 34 | 16 | – |
| 3    Du 11 Avril 1796 | | | |
| Doit Compte de Voyage | | | |
| A Compte de Caisse pour les fraix que jai fait jusqua Paris ou jarive ce jourdhui | L 45 | 16 | |
| dudit | | | |
| Doit idem | | | |
| Pour bagatelle que jai acheté et mise dans mon caisson | 6 | 10 | – |
| item pour solde de Compte au voiturier qui a mené mon équipage a forme de larrengemt. pris avec lui a Berne le 22° de Mars passe........................ | 12 | – | – |
| du 22 dit | | | |
| item pour boire au Voiturier sus dit pour mavoir laissé assoir sur le Siege........ | 2 | | |
| du 5 May | | | |
| Doit            Hardes et Nipes pour avoir fait repasser me Montre | 2 | – | – |

# APPENDIX

do.
Debit Cash     To Traveling [Account]
for money taken in cash [*Illegible, see however, p. 1*]      736   0   0

Berne, March 22nd
Traveling Account          Debit
To Cash Account, for earnest money I gave to the hired man of the carrier Lentz of Berne, who promised to transport my baggage as far as Paris, for one louis that I promised to pay him, the earnest money being on account.      4   0   0

March 25th
Debit Clothing Account
To Cash Account, for a watch I bought of Henny of Berne [valued at?] L34 and the chain and accessories 16 sous [?]      34   16

3          April 11, 1796
Debit Traveling Account
To Cash Account for the expenses I incurred as far as Paris, where I have arrived this day      L 45   16

do.
Debit idem.
For notions which I bought and put in my chest      6   10

Item for settlement with the carrier who hauled my belongings according to the agreement made with him in Berne on March 22nd last.      12   0   0

22 do.
item.—for tip to above-named carrier for having allowed me to sit on the driver's seat      2

May 5
Debit          Clothing Account
For having had my watch overhauled      2   0   0

4　　　　　Du 14° May 1796  
Doit . . . Compte de Marchandise  
A Compte de Caisse  Pour celle que jai  
acheté a Paris ce jourdhui de Monsieur  
Giroud payée Comptant Savoir  
42 montres dargent à 22 L. la  
piece　　　　　　　　　　　　　　L 924  
9 idem de Chasse a 30 L　　　　　270  
8 idem en Or a 72 L´　　　　　　　576  

　　　　　　　　　　　　　　　　1770　1770　—　—  
　　　　　dudit  
Doit　　Compte de traite et remise  
A Mr. Isenchmid Kinkelin et Roup a  
Berne pour la traite que je fais sur eux  
ordre Vincent Dufour, de la Somme de  
Deux milles livres: laquelle jai employe a  
payer les montres ci dessus et 230 L en  
numeraire　　　　　　　　　　　　　　　　2000　—　—  
　　　　　dit  
Doit **Harde et Nippes**  
A Compte de caisse pour une houpeland  
que jai achété a Paris　　　　　L 12  
une paire de soiller　　　　　　　　3  

　　　　　　　　　　　　　　　　　15　　15　—　—  
5　　　　　Du 14° May 1796  
Doit　　　　　　　　　Marchandises  
A Caisse pour celles que jai achété a  
Paris pour envoyer a Ma femme pour re-  
mettre au Justicier Yaux  savoir 8 Vol-  
ume d'un livre intitule Lagriculture de  
lAbe du Rosier paye comptant.........　　44　—　—  
　　　　　dudit  
Doit　　　　Compte de Caisse  
A Traites et Remise pour le comptant  
que jai reçu sur celle fournie aujourdhui

# APPENDIX

| 4 | May 14th 1796 | | | | |
|---|---|---|---|---|---|

Debit                Merchandise Account
To Cash Account, merchandise I bought in Paris this day of Mr. Giroud for cash, to wit:

42 silver watches at 22L. apiece,     L924
9 idem, hunting [watches], at 30 L.,    270
8 idem, gold, at 72L.               576

                                 1770    1770   0   0

                    do.

Debit            Drafts and Remittance
To Mr. Isenschmid, Kinkelin and Roup of Berne for the draft I am drawing on them to the order of Vincent Dufour for the sum of two thousand livres: which I have used to pay for the above watches, and 230L in coin                                          2000   0   0

                    do.

Debit                Clothing Account
To Cash Account, for an overcoat which I bought in Paris               L 12
A pair of shoes                       3

                                     15     15   0   0

5            May 14th, 1796
Debit                      Merchandise
To Cash, for the purchase I made in Paris to send to my wife for delivery to Judge Yaux, to wit: 8 volumes of a book entitled "L'agriculture de l'Abbé du Rosier," paid for in cash                                       44   0   0

                    do.

Debit                 Cash Account
To Drafts and Remittance, for the cash I received on the draft I drew today in favor

| | | | |
|---|---:|---:|---:|
| a Vincent Dufour sur Isenchmid et compe. a Berne .................... | 2000 | – | – |
| du 15 dit | | | |
| Doit            Compte de Voyage | | | |
| A Compte de Caisse pour les fraix que jai fais a Paris soit pour vivre ou pour acheter les bagatelles nécessaires ayant été Nouri et Logé chez Vincent Dufour des le 11° Avril júsqua aujourdhui et méme jusquau 18° que je crois de partir | 42 | – | – |
| 6        Du 18° May 1796 | | | |
| Doit           Hardes et Nipes | | | |
| A Compte de Caisse, pour une paire de Soillers que jai acheté a Paris......... | 1 | 16 | – |
| item un petit miroir et un cuir a rasoir | 2 | – | – |
| dudit | | | |
| Doit           Marchandises | | | |
| A Caisse pour une Malle pour Serrer mes effets et marchandise aquise pour comptant a Paris.................... | 5 | 8 | – |
| item pour 6 paires de pandant doreille doré ............................ | 1 | 18 | – |
| item 4 coliers demails............... | 1 | 10 | 9 |
| 8 paires de pendant d'oreille d Email... | 3 | 1 | – |
| 7 paires de boucles d'oreilles.......... | | 5 | 9 |
| 2 Colliers verts ..................... | | 8 | – |
| item 4 douzaines bas de Soye blanc de gange du Citoyen Allain rue St Martin no 5 a Paris—254 8 de fr | 169 | 12 | – |
| item 5 douzaines a chainette de Lion a 52 la douzaine..................... | 173 | 6 | 8 |
| 7         Du 18° May 1796 | | | |
| Suite de la facture ci devant | | | |
| item 5 paires bas de Paris blanc a 5 10 la paire ........................... | 18 | 6 | 8 |
| item 5 paires idem de Nimmes a 4 5... | 14 | 3 | 4 |
| item une marmite economique et un bidon | 8 | | |

APPENDIX 241

of Vincent Dufour on Isenschmid and Company of Berne                    2000  0  0

    15 do.
Debit    Traveling Account
To Cash Account, for what I expended in Paris, either for living or to buy necessary small articles, having been boarded and lodged at Vincent Dufour's from April 11th, till today, and even till the 18th when I expect to leave.   42  0  0

6   May 16th, 1796
Debit    Clothing Account
To Cash Account, for a pair of shoes I bought in Paris                  1  16  0
Item, a small mirror and a razor strop                                  2   0  0

    do.
Debit    Merchandise
To Cash, for a trunk to hold my belongings, and the merchandise I purchased for cash in Paris                                                           5   8  0
Item, for 6 pairs of gold-plated earrings                               1  18  0
Item, 4 enamel necklaces                                                1  10  9
8 pairs of enamel earrings                                              3   1  0
7 pairs of earrings                                                         5  9
2 green necklaces                                                           8  0
Item, 4 dozen white silk stockings, gauged, from Citizen Allain, rue St. Martin, No. 5, in Paris—254 fr. 8                                            169  12  0
Item, 5 dozen chain-stitch stockings of Lyons at 52 fr. a dozen       173   6  8

7   May 18th, 1796
Continuation of above invoice:
Item, 5 pairs of white Paris stockings, at 5 fr. 10 a pair             18   6  8
Item, 5 pairs idem of Nîmes, at 4 fr. 5                                14   3  4
Item, a fuel-saving pot and a can                                       8

                    Du 25° May
Doit                Compte de Voyage
A Caise pour ce que jai depencé a Paris
en Outre de ce qui est marque devant
layant quité ce jourdhui                    10   -   -
                    Du 27° dit
Doit                Compte de Voyage
A Caise pour ce qui ma couté de Paris au
Havre tant pour la nouriture que pour le
transport étant arive aujourdhui a 5
heure du Soir au Havre                      22  14   -
                    Du 1° Juin
Doit                Harde et Nipes
A Caisse pour un Pentalon de toille que
jai achete au havre............5 Tou.
Achette de 1 aunes ¾ flanelle   3
la façon pour avoir fait redoubler mon
habit musque                  1–10
                              ─────
                              9 10         6   6   8

8           Du 7° Juin 1796
Doit                Compte de Voyage
A Caisse pour les fraix que ma causé une
malheureuse maladie que je ne connois
pas javois mal a la tette et jettois altére
Savoir
Consultation d'un Medecin      3
La 2° pour theriaque fleur de tilleu
et un lavement.................  1 10
le 3° Pruns et Sene............       9
le 4. 4 Citrons ½ Lb. cassonnade
pour limonade .................  1 17
un lavement ...................     12
le 6° un lavement..............     12
et une emettique mais que je nai
pas pris                            10
                              ─────
                              8 10         5  13   4

## APPENDIX

### May 25th

Debit                Traveling Account

To Cash, for what I spent in Paris in addition to what is given above; having left this day        10  0  0

### May 27th

Debit                Traveling Account

To Cash, for what I spent from Paris to Havre both for food and transportation, having arrived today at five o'clock in the evening at Havre      22  14  0

### June 1st

Debit                Clothing Account

To Cash, for a pair of cotton pantaloons that I bought in Havre    5 fr. Tournois

Bought 1¾ ells of flannel    3

For having had my musk coat relined                 1 10

                        9 10    6  6  8

### 8        June 7, 1796

Debit                Traveling Account

To Cash, for expenses caused by an unfortunate illness new to me (my head ached and I was thirsty), to wit:

Consultation of physician    3 fr.

The 2nd, for a theriac, a lime-tree flower, and an enema        1 10

The 3rd, prunes and senna      9

The 4th, 4 lemons, ½ lb. brown sugar for lemonade           1 17

An enema                         12

And an emetic, which however I did not take                      10

                        8 10    5  13  4

Dudit

Doit             Compte de Voyage
A Caisse pour suitte de fraix que ma maladie ma cause laquelle s'est trouvée être la fievre tierce

| | | |
|---|---:|---:|
| pour 2 Lavements pris le 8-10 | 1 | 4 |
| une medecine prise le 10° | | 12 |
| un opiat et de la rubarbe pris abord par precaution.......... | 1 | 4 |
| Au Medecin pour ses visites..... | 3 | |
| | 6 | 0 | 4 — — |

9         Du 7° Juin 1796

Doit             Compte de Voyage
A Caisse pour le payement de mon passage au Capitaine Mitchel commandant le Brig la Sally destiné pour Philadelphie, et ce pour être rendu en ditte ville avec mes malles et être nouri a la 2° Table savoir la Somme de.........50 piastres L 175 — —
item pour les aprovisionnements que jai pris a bord pour adoucissemt

| | | |
|---|---:|---:|
| Savoir 1 pot eau de vie de cidre | 1 | 10 |
| ½ pot de celle de vin......... | 2 | 5 |
| dz bouteilles pour le contenir... | | 18 |
| deux gobelets de fer blanc et 3 verres ..................... | | 14 |
| un matlas et une couverture grossier ..................... | 16 | — |
| 3 Lb Cassonnade.............. | 3 | |
| 4 Citrons ................... | 1 | 4 |
| Siro de vinaigre et de Capilaire | 3 | |
| douza bouteilles et le vin pour en remplir onze un setant cassée.. | 12 | 4 |
| une bouteille de vinaigre....... | — | 16 |
| un pot de Ch: et une corbeille p: le m: ................... | | 15 |

# APPENDIX

do.

Debit                    Traveling Account
To Cash, for further expense caused by my
illness, which turned out to be tertian
fever:

| | | | | |
|---|---|---|---|---|
| For 2 enemas taken the 8th-10th | 1 fr. | 4 | | |
| A medecine taken the 10th | | 12 | | |
| An opiate and rhubarbe taken at once as a precaution | 1 | 4 | | |
| To the physician for his visits | 3 fr. | | | |
| | 6 fr. | 0 | 4 | 0 0 |

9          June 7th, 1796
Debit                    Traveling Account
To Cash, payment of my passage to Captain
Mitchell, commanding the brig *Sally* bound
for Philadelphia, I to be landed in said city
with my trunks and to be boarded at the
2nd table, to wit:

| | | | | |
|---|---|---|---|---|
| The sum of 50 dollars | | | L 175 | 0 0 |

Item, for the provisions I took on
board to supplement my food, to
wit:

| | | |
|---|---|---|
| 1 pot of cider brandy | 1 fr. | 10 |
| ½ pot wine brandy | 2 | 5 |
| A dozen bottles to hold same | | 18 |
| 2 tin goblets and 3 glasses | | 14 |
| A mattress and a coarse blanket | 16 | 0 |
| 3 lbs. brown sugar | 3 | |
| 4 lemons | 1 | 4 |
| Syrup of vinegar and maiden-hair | 3 | |
| Twelve bottles and wine to fill eleven, one having been broken | 12 | 4 |
| One bottle of vinegar | 0 | 16 |
| A Ch[ina] pot and basket for the same | | 15 |

quelque cotte dail.............  5

|  |  | 42 | 11 | L 28 | 7 | 4 |

10   Du 11 Juin 1796
Doit                Compte de Voyage
a Caise pour les fraix suivants
A la blanchisseuse au Havre    2  16
Pour transport de mes malles   5   9
pour bagatelles achettè au Havre
port de lettre et comedie         15
pour mon compte chez Madam le
grix demain le jour étant fixé
pour Mettre a la voille......... 32   —
avec les tringuel
                               41   0  L 27   6   8
       Du 4° Juillet
Doit                     Voyage
a Caise pour fraix et refraichissement
achette aux Isles Acores ou nous avons
relaché ..........................  12   —   —
       Du 22 dit
Doit                       Caise
A Marchandise pour trois paires de bas
vendu a lequipage du vaisseau a 2
piastre 1/3 la paire, la piastre a 35 1/2   21   6
bz [?]
item une paire, les a chainette          3  11
11         12° Aoust 1796
Doit                  Marchandise
A Caise pour les droits d'entrée que jai
paye pour les entrer en Amerique a Wilminton .........................  L 59  14   —
       Du 20° Septembre
Doit                      Caisse
a Marchandise pour la vente de deux
montre d'or que jai vendu a Wilminton..  273   —   —
item 6 d'argent dont deux quantieme et
une de Chasse....................  280   —   —

## APPENDIX 247

| | | | | |
|---|---|---|---|---|
| A few cloves of garlic | 5 | | | |
| | 42 fr. 11 | L 28 | 7 | 4 |

10        June 11, 1796
Debit                Traveling Account
To Cash, for the following expenses:

| | | | | |
|---|---|---|---|---|
| To the washerwoman at Havre | 2 fr. 16 | | | |
| For transfer of my trunks | 5    9 | | | |
| For notions bought in Havre, letter postage, and comedy | 15 | | | |
| For my bill at Madame Le Grix tomorrow, the day being fixed for setting sail, including tips | 32   — | | | |
| | 41    0 | L 27 | 6 | 8 |

July 4th
Debit                Traveling
To Cash, for expenses, and refreshments bought at the Azores, where we put in           12   0   0

July 22nd
Debit                Cash
To Merchandise, for three pairs of stockings sold to the crew of the ship at $2 1/3 a pair,                                                21   6
the dollar at 35 1/2 batzen[?]
Item, one pair of chain-stitch stockings           3   11

11        August 12th, 1796
Debit                Merchandise
To Cash, for customs duties I paid for bringing same into America at Wilmington  L 59  14  0

September 20th
Debit                Cash
To Merchandise, for the sale I made of two gold watches at Wilmington                273   0   0
Item, 6 silver watches; two telling dates, and one with hunting case                 280   0   0

| | | | |
|---|---:|---:|---:|
| item au detail 3 d'argent dont 1 quant. | 162 | 15 | – |
| item les bijoux | 15 | 15 | – |
| item 7 paires de bas de Soye blanc | 49 | – | |
| item 7 paires de couleur | 45 | 10 | – |
| item 4 douzainnes de couleur.......... | 252 | – | – |

     Du 22° dit
Doit      Compte de voyage
a Caisse pour la depense que jai fait
jusqua ce jour dans mes diferent voyages
de Lancastre Reding et Baltemr     91 – –

12   Du 22° Septembre
Doit      Harde etc
a Caisse pour les habilements que je me
suis acheté savoir

| | | | |
|---|---:|---:|---:|
| une paire de Souiller................. | L 4 | 7 | 8 |
| pour me faire un pentalon 1½ aus. de drape ............................ | 4 | 7 | 8 |
| pour façon dudit.................... | 5 | 5 | – |
| une paire de calesson............... | 3 | 10 | – |
| un Dictionnaire anglais et fr:......... | 7 | 15 | 8 |
| deux cartes geographique............ | 15 | 3 | – |

     Dudit
Doit      Caisse
a Marchandises pour une douzaine de bas
blanc remis a Mr Tiller pour prix dacquis 44 10 –

     Dudit
Doit      Jos: Jm Obersteg
a Caisse pour les argens qu jai debource
pour lui             7 – –

     Dudit
Doit      Caisse
a Marchandise pour les bas de soye de
couleur vendu a Baltimore contre la Marchandise a page Suivante

13   Du 22° Septembre 1796
Doit      Marchandise
a Caisse pour celle que jai achetées a Bal-

## APPENDIX 249

| | | | |
|---|---|---|---|
| Item, at retail, 3 silver watches; one telling dates | 162 | 15 | 0 |
| Item, the jewels | 15 | 15 | 0 |
| Item, 7 pairs of white silk stockings | 49 | 0 | |
| Item, 7 pairs of colored | 45 | 10 | 0 |
| Item, 4 dozen colored | 252 | 0 | 0 |

September 22nd
Debit            Traveling Account
To Cash, for the expense I incurred up to this day in my various trips to Lancaster, Reading and Baltimore    91   0   0

12       September 22nd
Debit            Clothing, etc.
To Cash, for the clothes I bought for myself, to wit:

| | | | |
|---|---|---|---|
| A pair of shoes | L 4 | 7 | 8 |
| 1½ ells of cloth to make me pantaloons | 4 | 7 | 8 |
| For making same | 5 | 5 | 0 |
| A pair of drawers | 3 | 10 | 0 |
| An English and French dictionary | 7 | 15 | 8 |
| Two maps | 15 | 3 | 0 |

                   do.
Debit            Cash
To Merchandise, for 1 dozen white stockings furnished to Mr. Tiller at cost price    44   10   0

                   do.
Debit            Jos. Jm. Obersteg
To Cash, for the money I paid out for him    7   0   0

                   do.
Debit            Cash
To Merchandise, for the colored silk stockings sold at Baltimore in exchange for the merchandise on following page

13       September 22nd, 1796
Debit            Merchandise
To Cash, for merchandise I bought in Balti-

timore en echange des bas de Soye de couleur savoir
une piece indiene couleur fauve

| | | |
|---|---|---|
| N° 1 tirant ............ | 14 liardes | |
| une ditto N° 2 | 15 | |
| ............3° | 14½ | |
| ............4° | 14 | |
| a fond blanc 5° | 7 | |
| ............6 | 14 | |
| ............7 | 10½ | |
| a fond fauve 8 | 10 | |
| | 99 liardes a | |
| | L 1-18-2½ | L 189 – – |
| item | 8 mouchoir blancs | |
| | 5 fond blanc et raye | |
| | 8 ...... blancs | |
| | 21 a L 1-15 la piece | 36 15 – |
| item 4 pieces de nanquens de China a L 3-18-9 ......................... | | 15 15 |
| item 60 echevettes de fil de couleur de Londre a 3s 6d. la echevette.......... | | 10 10 |

14      Du 27° Septembre 1796

Doit                Marchandises
a Caise pour celles que jai acheté de Mr. Notnagel et Montmolin a Philadel pour comptant Savoir

| | | Dolars | Cen. |
|---|---|---|---|
| 3 Mouchoirs de Soye de Couleur a ................................. | 7/6 | 3 | – |
| 6 Mouchoirs de Soye dit Schaale | 12/6 | 16 | – |
| 1 Douzaine bas de laine pour h. | – | 5 | 63 |
| 1 dito | 54/ | 7 | 19 |
| ½ dito | 60/ | 4 | – |
| 1 dito pour enfant | 21/ | 2 | 79 |
| 2 douzaines gants de laine p:h | 51/ | 13 | 60 |
| 10 mouchoirs de Soye noir | 8/4 | 11 | 11 |

## APPENDIX

more in exchange for colored silk stockings,
to wit:
One piece of printed calico, fawn-colored
No. 1 measuring 14 yards
one ditto, No. 2, 15 "
" " " 3, 14½ "
" " " 4, 14 "
white back " 5, 7 "
" " " 6, 14 "
" " " 7, 10½ "
fawn back " 8, 10 "

99 yards
at L 1–18–2½   L 189   0   0

Item, 8 white handkerchiefs
5 white and striped back
8 white back

21 at L 1–15 each                36  15   0
Item, 4 pieces of China Nankeen
at L 3–18–9                      15  15
Item, 60 skeins of colored London thread
of London at 3 sous 6 deniers per skein   10  10
14           September 27th, 1796
Debit                            Merchandise
To Cash, for merchandise which I bought
from Messrs. Notnagel and Montmolin in
Philadelphia, for cash, to wit:

|  | | Dollars | Cents |
|---|---|---|---|
| 3 handkerchiefs of colored silk, at | 7/6 | 3 | 00 |
| 6 handkerchiefs of so-called shawl silk, | 12/6 | 16 | 00 |
| 1 dozen woolen stockings for men, | — | 5 | 63 |
| 1 ditto | 54/ | 7 | 19 |
| ½ ditto | 60/ | 4 | 00 |
| 1 ditto for children | 21/ | 2 | 79 |
| 2 dozen woolen gloves for men | 51/ | 13 | 60 |
| 10 black silk handkerchiefs, | 8/4 | 11 | 11 |

| | | | |
|---|---|---|---|
| 1 douzaines miroirs de Poche | – | | 87 |
| 1 dito | | – | 51 |
| ½ Lb. soit 22 paignettes divoire | 70/lb | 4 | 79 |
| une douz: dito de corne | | | 54 |
| 1 piece dentelle blanche 8⅓ Aune | 2/6 | 2 | 70 |
| 1 piece ditot 22⅞ | 2/7 | 7 | 90 |
| 1 —— ditot 9 | 1/8 | 2 | – |
| 7 pieces rubans fleuretes | 8/4 | 7 | 76 |
| 7 dito | 3/2 | 2 | 96 |
| 3 dito | 4/2 | 1 | 67 |
| item d'un autre Md. deux mouchoir de madras | | 2 | |
| 15 | | | |
| 2 pieces ruban .................... | 6/4 | D. 1 | C. 66 |
| 2 pieces ruban noir................12/6 | | 3 | 66 |
| 1 dito ............................. | | 1 | 13 |
| 1 ................................. | | 1 | |
| 6 p dito peintes ....................10/ | | 8 | – |
| 3 p ......noires ................... | 6/6 | 2 | 60 |
| 6 ................................. | 1/6 | 1 | 20 |
| 6 ................................. | 2/6 | 2 | – |
| 4 ................................. | 3/ | 1 | 60 |
| 2 pieces dito faveur................ | 9/6 | 2 | 66 |
| 4 ...... dito ................... | 8/6 | 4 | 57 |
| 4 Mouchoirs Shaals p: femme.......12/6 | | 6 | 66 |
| ce qui fait aprés deduction du 5% | | 121 | 40 |
| Du 29 dit | | | |
| item de Monsieur John Carrell | | | |
| 3 douzaine de clefs de montres à | 3/ | 1 | 20 |
| 2 d: chaines N° 35581.............16/6 | | 4 | 40 |
| 1 dito 25034.............30/ | | 4 | – |
| ¾ dito 36589.............18/ | | 1 | 84 |
| dudit | | | |
| item de M. John Plasants | | | |
| 4 miliers daguilles | 11/5 | 6 | – |
| 1 gros de de a coudre | 9/ | 1 | 20 |

## APPENDIX

| | | | |
|---|---|---|---|
| 1 dozen pocket mirrors, | | – | 87 |
| 1 ditto | | – | 51 |
| ½ lb., or 22 ivory combs, | | 70/Lb. | 4 79 |
| 1 dozen horn combs, | | | 54 |
| 1 piece white lace, 8⅛ ells, | | 2/6 | 2 70 |
| 1 piece ditto 22⅞ | | 2/7 | 7 90 |
| 1 —— ditto 9 | | 1/8 | 2 00 |
| 7 pieces flowered ribbon, | | 8/4 | 7 76 |
| 7 ditto | | 3/2 | 2 96 |
| 3 ditto | | 4/2 | 1 67 |
| Item, from another merchant, two madras handkerchiefs | | | 2 00 |
| 15 | | Dollars | Cents |
| 2 pieces ribbon | | 6/4 | 1 66 |
| 2 pieces black ribbon, | | 12/6 | 3 66 |
| 1 ditto, | | | 1 13 |
| 1 | | | 1 |
| 6 ditto, printed | | 10/ | 8 00 |
| 3 pieces black, " | | 6/6 | 2 60 |
| 6 pieces " " | | 1/6 | 1 20 |
| 6 " " " | | 2/6 | 2 00 |
| 4 " " " | | 3/. | 1 60 |
| 2 pieces ditto favor | | 9/6 | 2 60 |
| 4 ditto | | 8/6 | 4 57 |
| 4 shawl handkerchiefs, for women | | 12/6 | 6 66 |
| (which makes after deducting 5%) | | | 121 40 |

September 29

Item, from Mr. John Carrell

| | | | |
|---|---|---|---|
| 3 dozen watch keys at | | 3/. | 1 20 |
| 2 dozen chains No. 35581 | | 16/6 | 4 40 |
| 1 ditto 25034 | | 30/. | 4 |
| ¾ ditto 36589 | | 18/. | 1 84 |

do.

Item, from Mr. John Plasants:

| | | | |
|---|---|---|---|
| 4 thousand needles | | 11/5 | 6 00 |
| 1 gross thimbles | | 9/. | 1 20 |

1 douzaine de Lunette N°. 1      37/6    5   00
1 d   dito           N°. 2       15/     2   –

16        Du 29° September 1796
Doit                              Caisse
A Marchandises pour celles que jai vendue
comptant savoir, cinq pair de bas de Soye blanc
a 2 piastres la pair...........................  10   –
item dans la route depuis Philadelphie a
Pittsbourg, deux montres a quanti... 37½ ⎫
deux de chasses................... 37    ⎬ 110  –
deux communes .................. 35½ ⎭
une commune .................... 18  ⎫
reçu pour une d'or echangée contre    ⎬ 36  –
une dargent a l'angloise............. 18 ⎭

              Du 30° dit
Doit                              Hardes &c
a Caisse pour une paire de Souillé que je
me suis achété a Ph:             1 3/16
une ecritoire ......................  3/16
deux cadenats pour fermer mes males  3/16
                                 ─────    1  56

              dudit
Doit                              Marchandise
a Caisse pour refactures que jai fais faire a
quelques montres par M. Sandos............  4  50
item pour avoir fait peser mes males a fin de
les envoyer a Pittsbourg et les faire charger    50
item pour le transport jusqua Pittsbourg ayant
pesè 162 Lb gros poids                      15  50

17         Du 30° Octobre
Doit                              Caisse
A Marchandise pour celle que jai vendues pour
comptant a Pittsbourg a un françois savoir 4
montres dargent a chasses et 8 communes a 22
dolars la p                                264  –

## APPENDIX 255

| | | | | |
|---|---|---|---|---|
| 1 dozen spectacles No. 1 | | 37/6 | 5 | 00 |
| 1 d. ditto " 2 | | 15/. | 2 | 00 |

16 September 29th, 1796
Debit                                    Cash
To Merchandise, for what I sold for cash, to wit:

| | | | |
|---|---|---|---|
| 5 pairs white silk stockings at $2 a pair | | 10 | 00 |
| Item, on the way from Philadelphia to Pittsburg | | | |
| two watches, telling date | 37½ ⎫ | | |
| two, hunting-case | 37 ⎬ | 110 | 00 |
| two, common | 35½ ⎭ | | |
| one, common | 18 ⎫ | | |
| received for a gold watch exchanged | ⎬ | 36 | 00 |
| for an English silver watch | 18 ⎭ | | |

September 30th
Debit                          Clothing, etc.
To Cash, for a pair of shoes which I

| | | | |
|---|---|---|---|
| bought at Philadelphia | 1 3/16 | | |
| An inkstand | 3/16 | | |
| Two padlocks to lock my trunks | 3/16 | | |
| | | 1 | 56 |

do.
Debit                                 Merchandise

| | | |
|---|---|---|
| To Cash, for repairs I had made on some watches by Mr. Sandos | 4 | 50 |
| Item, for having had my trunks weighed to forward them to Pittsburg, and put on board | | 50 |
| Item, for transportation to Pittsburg, weight being 162 lbs. gross | 15 | 50 |

17              October 30th
Debit                                   Cash
For what I sold for cash at Pittsburg to a Frenchman, to wit:

| | | |
|---|---|---|
| 4 silver hunting watches and 8 common watches at $22 apiece | 264 | 00 |

### Du 30° Septembre

Doit                        Voyage
a Caisse pour ma pension a Phil: jusqua ce
jourdhui que je part pour LOest.............    4    25
pour blanchissage ........................         75

### Du 11° Novembre

Doit                        Voyage
pour frais de route et Pension des le 30° de
Septembre passé a ½ d. par j    20    50

### Du 15 dit

Doit                        Caisse
a Marchandises pour montres que jai vendue a
Pittsburgs argent comptant savoir 12 a des
françois a 22 la piece [this entire item is
crossed out in the original]    264
bisé pour etre porte 2 fois

### Dudit

Change a Marietta 1 montre a quantiemme
contre un rifle recu de tourne...............    2    –
18

1796         ### Du 15° Decembre

Doit                        Caisse
pour Marchandises pour la vente des Suivantes
savoir
une montre a Marietta    24
item a Monsieur Marechal payable aux Illinois
par Mr. Menard [the two preceding items were
crossed out with the note "porte ailleurs"]    22
deux [montres] a Monsieur Ogule    36

1797          Janvier le 20°
Doit                        Marchd.
a Caisse pour rabillage fait faire a mes montres    4    80
item pour lacquis de 38 pioches a mais a raison
de 7/. la pieces    35    48
item pour 1 lb de Salpettre..................    1    33

# APPENDIX

September 30th
Debit　　　　　　　　　　　　　Traveling
To Cash, for my board in Philadelphia up to
the present day, when I leave for the East,　　4　25
For laundry　　　　　　　　　　　　　　　　　75
November 11th
Debit　　　　　　　　　　　　　Traveling
For traveling expenses and board from the
30th of September last... at ½ dollar per day　20　50
November 15th
Debit　　　　　　　　　　　　　Cash
To Merchandise, for silver watches which I
sold at Pittsburg for cash, to wit: 12 to some
French at 22 dollars a piece [this entire item
is crossed out in the original]　　　　　　　264
stricken out; entered twice.
do.
Exchanged at Marietta 1 watch telling date
for a rifle. Received to boot　　　　　　　　2　00
18
1796　　　December 15th, 1796
Debit　　　　　　　　　　　　　Cash
To Merchandise, for the sale of the following,
to wit:
A watch at Marietta　　　　　　　　24
Item, to Mr. Marechal payable in Illinois
by Mr. Menard [the two preceding items
were crossed out with a note, "entered
elsewhere"]　　　　　　　　　　　　22
Two [watches] to Mr. Ogule　　　　　　　　36
January 20th, 1797
Debit　　　　　　　　　　　　Merchandise
To Cash, for repairing done to my watches　　4　80
Item, for the purchase of 38 corn hoes at the
rate of 7/. apiece　　　　　　　　　　　　35　48
Item, for 1 lb. of saltpetre　　　　　　　　　1　33

                    Du 30°
Doit                                    Marchd.
a Caisse pour les suivantes que jai acquise savoir
18 aches                                          22   —
un marteau une douzaine de grayon autant de
lime                                               1    3
  19
1797            Du 1° Fevrier
Doit                                         M:
a Caisse pour les suivantes que jai aquise a Pis-
bourg de Mr. Ogule savoir 2½ douz. cardes de
cotton n° 10 a 81/. la d.
2½ douzaines idem n° 9 a 72/.
1 douzaines idem n° 7 a 66/. la d.
plus 2 paires n° 9......9/.                       61   —
item pour 8 boites de roues de Chars               3   —
item de Tomas et Samuel Magues 2 douzaines de
chapeaux a                          22/6
ce qui fait avec 4/.6 pour embalage               72   30
item de Benjamin Herr
4 pot a cuisine n° 120    a   10/.
3 item            n°   16.....12/.
3 ide                  20    14/6.
ce qui fait apres deduction du 5%½                15   44
item pour une carabine a Maride avec son at-
tirail                                            22   —
  20
1797            Fevrier le 18°
Doit                           Conte de Voyage
a Caisse pour ma pension et fraix dès le 11°
Novembre passé jus que aujourdhui que je part
de Pbts. pour les Illinois sur la riviere a ½ p.
par jour                                          48   50
                  Dudit
Doit                           Monsieur Menard
A Caise pour argent a lui preté payable aux
Illinois ................................... 200      —

## APPENDIX

January 30th
Debit       Merchandise
To Cash, for the following articles I bought,
to wit:
18 axes            22 00
a hammer, dozen pencils [?], and as many files 1 30

19
1797    February 1st
Debit       Merchandise
To Cash, for the following I bought at Pittsburg of Mr. Ogule, to wit:
2½ doz. cotton cards, No. 10 at 81/. a doz.
2½ dozen the same, No. 9 at 72/.
1 dozen the same, No. 7 at 66/. a doz.
plus 2 pairs, No. 9.............9/...... 61 00
Item, for 8 wagon wheel boxes    3 00
Item, from Thomas and Samuel Magues
2 dozen hats at       22/6
which makes, with 4/6 for packing   72 30
Item, from Benjamin Herr:
4 cook pots No. 120 at 10/.
3, the same, No. 16  12/.
3, the same, " 20  14/6
which makes after deducting 5½%   15 44
Item, for a rifle *a Maride* with its accessories 22 00

20
1797    February 18th
Debit      Traveling Account
To Cash, for my board and expenses from November 11th last till today, when I leave Pittsburg for Illinois by river, at ½ dollar per day              48 50
      do.
Debit       Mr. Menard
To Cash, for money lent him, payable in Illinois             200 00

item a marchandise pour Une montre vendue a
Marechal .................................. 22
pour autant quil paye pour Marechal
                dudit
Doit                       Harde et Nipe
A Mr. Menard pour une paire de Blankettes a
3 point ................................... 4  28
                dudit
Doit                     Com. de Voyage
A Mr. Menard pour mon passage et Nouriture
jusque au Kasquaskias
  21
1797         Du 18° Fevrier
Doit                     Mr. Menard
a Caisse pour autant a lui livre en espece    8  44
              Du dit
Doit                     M: Menard
A Marchandises pour celles vendue a Galipolis
a Mr. ——— lesquelles il doit payer savoir 3
montres d'argent a 22 p. la pieces............ 66  —

            Du 8° Avril
Doit                     Mr: Menard
A Marchandise pour la tourne que me revient
de Sénégal pour le Change de ma Carabine.... 1  —
ou 20 lb de Plomb..........................
item pour deux paires de lunettes remises a sa
belle merè ................................ 1  20
              Dudit
Doit                 M François Moreau
a Marchandise pour celle a lui vendues savoir
22 paignettes d'ivoire a 45 bz la piece......... 9  90
item 6 idem de corne......................     40
  22        Du 18° Avril 1797
Doit                     Mr. Menard
a Marchandise pour celles remises aux Suivant
et portée a son compte a Mr. Peira un chapeau
fin                              6

# APPENDIX 261

Item, to merchandise, for a watch sold to Marechal (inasmuch as he pays for Marechal)    22

do.

Debit     Clothing
To Mr. Menard, for a pair treble-stitch blankets    4   28

do.

Debit     Traveling Account
To Mr. Menard, for my passage and board to Kaskaskia

21

1797     February 18th
Debit     Mr. Menard
To Cash, for amount handed him in coin    8   44

do.

Debit     Mr. Menard
To Merchandise, for the goods sold at Gallipolis to Mr. ———, which he is to pay for, to wit:
3 silver watches at $22 apiece    66   00

April 8th

Debit     Mr. Menard
To Merchandise, for the difference coming to me from Senegal for the exchange of my rifle for 20 lbs. of lead    1   00
Item, for two pairs of spectacles delivered to his mother-in-law    1   20

do.

Debit     Mr. Francis Moreau
To Merchandise, sold to him, to wit:
22 small ivory combs at 45c apiece    9   90
Item, 6 horn combs                 40

22     April 18th, 1797
Debit     Mr. Menard
To Merchandise, delivered to the following and charged to his account:
To Mr. Peira, a fine hat    6

a Mme. Menard idem................ 6
a Mr. Reiner 2 idem................12
item a Rohl 1 idem................ 6
a M: Reiner 6 cent aiguille............ 2
et 1 douzaine dèz a coudre           ¼
a M: Menard 3 cent aiguilles         1
                                    ─── 33  25
            Du 20° dit
Doit                  Monsieur Menard
a Marchandise pour celles remise a Madame
savoir un Mouchoire Shaal de Cotton et un idem
de Soye                                  6  66
            Dudit
Doit                  Monsieur Dubardeau
a Marchandise pour les suivantes savoir
une piece de ruban................ 2p
14 verge indiene...................11
2 Schaals indienne............ 6 2/3   19  66
23          Du 4° May 1797
Doit                        Menard
a Marchandise pour les suivantes
7 mouchoirs de soye noir a 2p¼..   15¾ ⎫
un idem de couleur............à 2   2  ⎪
un chapeau remis a Anthoine            ⎬  26  20
la Chapelle ................à 6    6  ⎪
une paignette ivoire ........45 bz  45 ⎪
deux paires de lunette n°........   1¾ ⎭
            Du 6° dit
Doit                   Joseph Prat
et lautre de Soye   134 lb plomp         6  66
            Du 8° dit
Doit                   M. Menard
a Marchandise pour les suivantes

# APPENDIX

| | | | |
|---|---:|---:|---:|
| To Mrs. Menard, idem | 6 | | |
| To Mr. Reiner, 2 idem | 12 | | |
| Item, to Rohl, 1 idem | 6 | | |
| To Mr. Reiner, 6 hundred needles | 2 | | |
| and 1 dozen thimbles | ¼ | | |
| To Mr. Menard, 3 hundred needles | 1 | | |
| | | 33 | 25 |

April 20th
Debit                         Mr. Menard
To Merchandise, delivered to Madame, to wit:
a cotton shawl handkerchief and one of silk      6   66

do.
Debit                        Mr. Dubardeau
To Merchandise, for the following, to wit:

| | | | |
|---|---:|---:|---:|
| 1 piece of ribbon | $2 | | |
| 14 roods of calico | 11 | | |
| 2 calico shawls | 6 2/3 | 19 | 66 |

23          May 4th, 1797
Debit                        Menard
To Merchandise, for the following:

| | | | | |
|---|---|---:|---:|---:|
| 7 black silk handkerchiefs | at $2¼ | $15¾ | | |
| One idem, colored | at 2 | 2 | | |
| One hat delivered to Anthoine la Chapelle | at 6 | 6 | $26 | 20 |
| one ivory comb | at 45 bz. | .45 | | |
| Two pairs of spectacles No. | | 1¾ | | |

May 6th
Debit                        Joseph Prat
To Merchandise, for two Shawls, one of cotton and the other of silk, 134 lbs. lead......    6   66

May 8th
Debit                        Mr. Menard
To Merchandise, for the following:

| | | | | |
|---|---|---|---|---|
| une douzaine de Miroirs | 1 p | ½ | | |
| un idem plus grand | 2 | ½ | | |
| une hache remise a Sl. Warley | 3 | ½ | 21 | 75 |
| 8 aunes indienne a une femme du Cap Girardo .................. | 12 | – | | |
| un mouchoir de Soye noir pour envoyer a St Louis | 2 | ¼ | | |

24        Du 8° May 1797
Doit                                        Turcot
a Marchandise pour un chapeau fin...........   6  –

                Du 6° Juin
Doit                            Harde et Nipe
a Menard pour façon d'une paire de culote et recomodage de Chemise                          1  00
Compte de voyage
item pour la traverse sur la riviere trois fois...  1  50

                Du 8° dit
Doit                                  Menard
a Marchandise pour celles qu'il a recu pour descendre aliance a la Grece [?]
savoir une piece de toile        22
et un Chapeau fin....................  6
item un mouchoir de Soye noir reçu quand jetois a St. louis...................  2¼  30  25

                Du dit
Doit Menard payant pour Richard cure a la prairie
a Marchandise pour trois montres dont une de Chasse ..............................  70  –

25        Du 8° Juin 1797
Doit                              Harde et N.
a Marchandise pour celle employées a me vetir savoir une paire de bas de Soye de couleur deux paires de blanc...........  3p
un Chapeau .......................  3
une piece de nankin pour pentalon.....  1
deux paires de bas de laine...........  1  66
deux douzaine de boutons.............  –  50

# APPENDIX

| | | | |
|---|---|---|---|
| One dozen Mirrors | $1½ | | |
| One idem, larger size | 2½ | | |
| One hatchet delivered to Sl. Warley | 3½ | 21 | 75 |
| 8 ells calico to a woman of Cape Girardeau | 12.00 | | |
| One handkerchief of black silk to send to St. Louis.............. | 2¼ | | |

May 8th, 1797
Debit                          Turcot

| | | |
|---|---|---|
| To Merchandise, for a fine hat | 6 | 00 |

June 6th
Debit              Clothing Account

| | | |
|---|---|---|
| To Menard, for making a pair of breeches, and mending shirt | 1 | 00 |

Traveling Account

| | | |
|---|---|---|
| Item, for crossing the river three times | 1 | 50 |

June 8th
Debit                        Menard

To Merchandise, which he received to go down aliance a la Grece [?], to wit:

| | | | |
|---|---|---|---|
| A piece of cloth | 22 | | |
| And a fine hat | 6 | | |
| Item, one black silk handkerchief received when I was in St. Louis..... | 2¼ | 30 | 25 |

do.
Debit Menard, paying for Richard, parish priest at La Prairie

| | | |
|---|---|---|
| To Merchandise, for three watches, one a hunting [watch] | 70 | 00 |

June 8th, 1797
Debit                          Clothing

To Merchandise, used for my own wear, to wit: one pair of colored silk

| | | | |
|---|---|---|---|
| stockings, two pairs of white | $3 | | |
| One hat | 3 | | |
| One piece of nankeen for pantaloons | 1 | | |
| Two pairs of woolen stockings | 1 | 66 | |
| Two dozen buttons | | 50 | |

|  |  |  |  |
|---|---|---|---|
| | Dudit | | |
| Doit | Caisse | | |
| a Marchandise pour celles vendues content a St. Louis savoir trois montres dor a 50 p. la piece .................................................. | | 150 | – |
| | Dudit | | |
| Doit | Mr. Soulard | | |
| a Marchandise pour une montre de Ch: | | 25 | – |
| | Dudit | | |
| Doit | Voyage | | |
| a Caisse pour les fraix faite a mon Voyage de St Louis ............................................... | | 1 | 50 |
| 26 | Du 11° Juin 1797 | | D |
| Doit | Beguin | | |
| a Marchandise pour un chapeau demis a Ortubise ............................................... | | 6 | – |
| | Du 24° d | | |
| Doit | Beguin | | |
| a Marchandise pour un mouchoir de Soye dit Schal .................................................. | | 3 | 34 |
| | Dudit | | |
| Doit | couk | | |
| a Marchandise pour le restant apres une peau de loutre d'un Chapeau | | 2 | – |
| | Dudit | | |
| Doit | Harde &c | | |
| a Marchandise pour une paire de pentalon de Nankin | | 1 | – |
| | Dudit | | |
| Doit | Monsieur Pirous | | |
| a Mar: pour six haches que je lui ai envoyee 21p. | | 21 | – |
| | Du 25° | | |
| Doit | Menard | | |
| a Marchandise pour une piece de fleuret remis a Madam ............................................ | | 2 | 25 |
| item deux yards de ruban fleurets............ | | | 60 |

### APPENDIX

|  |  |  |
|---|---:|---:|
| do. | | |
| Debit — Cash | | |
| To Merchandise, sold for cash at St. Louis, to wit: three gold watches at $50 apiece | 150 | 00 |
| do. | | |
| Debit — Mr. Soulard | | |
| To Merchandise, for one hunting watch | 25 | 00 |
| do. | | |
| Debit — Traveling | | |
| To Cash, for expenses incurred on my St. Louis Trip | 1 | 50 |

26      June 11th, 1797      D

| | | |
|---|---:|---:|
| Debit — Beguin | | |
| To Merchandise, for a hat delivered to Ortubise | 6 | 00 |
| June 24th | | |
| Debit — Beguin | | |
| To Merchandise, for so-called shawl silk handkerchief | 3 | 34 |
| do. | | |
| Debit — Couk | | |
| To Merchandise, for the remnant of an otter skin used for a hat | 2 | 00 |
| do. | | |
| Debit — Clothing, etc. | | |
| To Merchandise, for one pair Nankeen pantaloons | 1 | 00 |
| do. | | |
| Debit — Mr. Pirous | | |
| To Merchandise, for six axes I sent him, $21 | 21 | 00 |
| June 25th | | |
| Debit — Menard | | |
| To Merchandise, for one piece of fleuret delivered to Madam | 2 | 25 |
| Item, two yards of fleuret ribbon | | 60 |

27          Du 29° Juin 1797
Doit belle Rose             a Marchandise
pour une Verge ½ de ruban noir............    —   50
item pour une gramaire angloise.............    2   —
            dudit
Doit                        Harde et:
a Menard pour façon d'une paire de pentalon..   1
item pour demi mains de papiers............    "
          Du 29 Juillet
Doit                        Voyage
a Caisse pour les fraix fait en allant et revenant
de St Louis.................................    1   50
            dudit
Doit             Compte dArpentage
A Soulard pour la demi de celui que j'ai fait au
Cap Girardo                       36   25
            dit
Doit                        Soulard
a Caisse pour solde de son compte paye comptant    10   25
            dudit
Doit                        Sonnette
a marchandise pour le restant de deux piastres
que je lui devois sur une piece de nanquen....       50
28          Du 29° Juillet 1797
Doit                        Harde &c
a Lorimier pour deux peaux de chevreuil
passées pour une paire de culote...... 4p
deux douzaine de boutons............. 1
¼ daune de toile.................... — 50
du fil de laiton pour agrandir une chain 1     6 50
            dudit
Doit                        Harde &c
a Marchandise pour la façon d'une paire de
culote de peau............................    1   —
            dudit
Doit                        Lorimier
a Compte d'arpentage pour cellui que jai fait de
sa terre au cap Girardo...................    72   50

## APPENDIX

27         June 29th, 1797
Debit Belle Rose         To Merchandise
For 1½ rods of black ribbon               50
Item, for one English grammar         2   00
              do.
Debit               Clothing
To Menard, for making a pair of pantaloons   1
Item, for a half quire of paper            1
            July 29th
Debit               Traveling
To Cash, for expenses incurred in going to
St. Louis and back               1   50
            do.
Debit         Surveying Account
To Soulard, for one half of the survey I made
at Cape Girardeau               36   25
            do.
Debit               Soulard
To Cash, for settlement of his account in cash   10   25
            do.
Debit               Sonnette
To Merchandise, for the balance of two dollars I owed him on a piece of Nankeen           50
28         July 29th, 1797
Debit             Clothing, etc.
To Lorimier, for two buck skins,
dressed, for a pair of breeches,   $4
Two dozen buttons            1
¼ ell of cloth                 50
Copper wire to lengthen a chain   1        6   50
            do.
Debit            Clothing, etc.
To Merchandise, for making a pair of buckskin breeches               1   00
            do.
Debit               Lorimier
To Surveying Account, for the survey I made
of his land at Cape Girardeau         72   50

|  | dudit | | |
|---|---|---|---|
| Doit | Harde. | | |
| a Menard pour une paire de souiller sauvage... | 1 | – | |

|  | do | | |
|---|---|---|---|
| Doit Menard payant pour Richard le Cure a marchandise pour une carte geograp: un dictionnaire de Boyer un item de geografique..... | 7 | | |

29        Du 10° Aoust 1797

Doit                                  Voyage
a Menard pour les articles suivants pris a son compte chez Morisson 1 once de quinquina                                      1p
Don une paire de soulier.............. 3     } 4   50
Bienvenu une chopine de vinaig:          50
Doit                                  Menard
a Marchandise pour les suivantes quil a vendue a divers 38 pioches a mais a
2 p ................................ 76
4 pots de Cuisine n°. 12..........2¼   9
3 idem .........n°. 16........a 3   9
3 idem .........n°. 20..........3¼   9¾
item 8 boites de roues de Char........ 6
5 aches et une herminette             18      127   75

18° dit

Doit                                  Menard
a Caisse pour 130 piastres en bon du roi d Espagnes a lui remis pour me les negocier.... 130   –

30        Du 23° Aoust 1797

Doit                                  Menard
a Marchandise pour celles qu'il a vendues pour mon compte a divers.................... 123   92
Doit                                  Menard
a M: pour la rente de 200 p. quil a jouis lesquelles je lui ai remis a Pittbourg, et quil me donne de sa bonne volonté................... 100   –

## APPENDIX

do.

Debit                              Clothing
To Menard, for one pair of moccasins      1 00

do.

Debit     Menard, paying for Richard the Priest,
To Merchandise, for a Map, a Boyer dictionary and a geographical dictionary      7

29         August 10th, 1797

Debit                          Traveling
To Menard, for the following articles bought for his account at Morrison's

| | | |
|---|---|---|
| 1 ounce Peruvian bark | $1 | |
| Don, a pair of shoes | 3 00 | 4 50 |
| Bienvenu, a pint of vinegar | 50 | |

Debit                            Menard
To Merchandise, for the following which he sold to divers persons:

| | | | | |
|---|---|---|---|---|
| 38 corn hoes | at | $2 | 76 | |
| 4 Kitchen pots No. 12 | | 2¼ | 9 | |
| 3 idem No. 16 | at | 3 | 9 | |
| 3 idem No. 20 | | 3¼ | 9¾ | |
| Item, 8 wagon wheel boxes | | | 6 | |
| 5 axes and one adze | | | 18 | 127 75 |

August 18th

Debit                            Menard
To Cash, for 130 dollars in bonds of the King of Spain, delivered to him to sell for me      130 00

30         August 23rd, 1797

Debit                            Menard
To Merchandise, for the goods he sold for my account to divers persons............... $123 92

Debit                            Menard
To Merchandise, for the interest on $200 of which he has had the use, which I lent him in Pittsburg, and which [interest] he gives me of his own free will      100 00

27°

Doit                            Marchandise
a Menard pour les Suivantes qui ma remis
savoir
13372 Lb de Plomp...............
dont 4500 Lb a 5 Cts............ 225p.
et   8872 Lb a 6 Ct............. 532  32
item pour 300 Lb lard a 25 Ct..... 75
item...554 Lb biscuit a 8 p le Cent  44
item 4 minots de gris a 1½p: Cwt..   6
item 2 minots de pois a 3 p. Cwt...   6
item pour le chariage du plomb au
bord de l'eau ...................    6
                                   ─────
                                    894  32

31
Suite de la facture ci devant transport    894  32

item pour les gages de six rameurs jusqua Cin- 360
cinati  jusqua la Chute 40 p Cha.
item pour les gages du patron............... 70  –
et le patron aura 50 p: a la Chute         ─────
            entout                          1324  32
item pour le louage de la berge............. 50
item pour ½ Lb de Clouds                         25

        dudit
Doit voyage a March pour une montre d'or
donnee pour ma pension aux Illinois......... 50  –

        dudit
Doit                            Menard
a Marchandise pour le resta de celle qui me
reste a forme de linventair que je lui laisse, lesquelles ont coute a Ph: et Pitbourg 159—12
lesquelles il prend en compte pour         200  –

# APPENDIX

### 27th

Debit                               Merchandise
To Menard, for the following which he delivered to me, to wit:
13,372 lbs. lead

| | | | | |
|---|---|---|---|---|
| 4,500 lbs. of it at | 5c | $225 | | |
| and 8872 lbs. at | 6c | 532 | 32 | |
| Item, for 300 lbs. bacon at 25c | | | 75 | |
| Item....554 lbs. biscuit $8 per cwt. | | 44 | | |
| Item, 4 minots [cwt] of grits [?] at $1½ per cwt. | | 6 | | |
| Item, 2 minots of peas at $3 per Cwt. | | 6 | | |
| Item, for cartage of the lead to the river | | 6 | | |
| | | | 894 | 32 |

### 31

| | | |
|---|---|---|
| Continuation of foregoing Invoice, carried over | 894 | 32 |
| Item, for the wages of six oarsmen as far as Cincinnati. Up to the Falls $40 each | 360 | |
| Item, for the wages of the captain, and the captain will receive $50 at the Falls | 70 | 00 |
| in all | 1324 | 32 |
| Item, for the hire of the barge | 50 | 00 |
| Item, for ½ lb. of Nails | | 25 |

do.

Debit                               Traveling
For one gold watch given for my board and lodging in Illinois      50   00

do.

Debit                               Menard
To Merchandise, for the remainder of the goods I still have according to the inventory I leave him, which goods cost in Philadelphia and Pittsburg 159.12 and which he takes on account for      200   00

### 14° 7bre.

| | | | |
|---|---|---|---|
| Doit | Voyage | | |
| a Caise pour mes fraix de route jusqua Louis Ville ou je suis aujourd'hui | | 15 | – |

### 24°

| | | | |
|---|---|---|---|
| Doit | Marchandise | | |
| a Caise pour le portage de mon Plomb au passage de la Chute.......................... | | 12 | 75 |

32
### Du 26 Septembre

| | | | |
|---|---|---|---|
| Doit Caise a | Marchandise | | |
| pour 94 Lb de Plomb vendu | | 8 | – |

### 28°

| | | | |
|---|---|---|---|
| Doit Voyage a | Caisse | | |
| pour ma pension et fraix a Louis Ville........ | | 12 | 75 |

### Du 4° Octobre

| | | | |
|---|---|---|---|
| Doit Caisse a | Marchandise | | |
| pour 18 Lb plomb......................... | | 3 | – |
| item pour une montre..................... | | 25 | |

### Du 8°

| | | | |
|---|---|---|---|
| Doit | Menard | | |
| a Caisse pour le Solde de son compte que je lui ai envoye soit en Ouiski ou en argent par le retour de la berge.................... | | 61 | 5 |

### Dudit

| | | | |
|---|---|---|---|
| Doit Caisse a | March: | | |
| pour 1005 de plomb vendu a Cincinati a M. Ramsey a 11.1 Lb. | | 111 | 72 |
| item pour une montre..................... | | 27 | – |

### Dudit

| | | | |
|---|---|---|---|
| Doit Caisse a M......................... | | | |
| pour 100 Lb de Plomb a Snodgras........... | | 12 | – |

33
### Du 8° Octobre

| | | | |
|---|---|---|---|
| Doit Marchandise a Caisse | | | |
| pour du biscuit que jai achetes pour remplacer du pouri 114 Lb | | 10 | 25 |

# APPENDIX

### September 14th
Debit                                Traveling
To Cash, for my expenses on the way as far as Louisville, where I am this day     15   00

### September 24th
Debit                            Merchandise
To Cash, for the portage of my lead around the Falls     12   75

32         September 26

Debit Cash                To Merchandise
For 94 lbs. of lead sold     8   00

### 28th
Debit Traveling               To Cash
For my board and lodging, and expenses in Louisville     12   75

### October 4th
Debit Cash                To Merchandise
For 18 lbs. of lead     3   00
Item, for a watch     25

### 8th
Debit                                Menard
To Cash, for the settlement of his account which I sent him, part in whisky, part in money by return of the barge     61   05

### do.
Debit Cash                To Merchandise
For 1005 [lbs.] lead sold at Cincinnati to Mr. Ramsey at 11.1 a lb.     111   72
Item, for a watch     27   00

### do.
Debit Cash                To Merchandise
For 100 lbs. of lead to Snodgrass     12   00

33         October 8th

Debit Merchandise               To Cash
For biscuit I bought to replace some damaged 114 lbs.     10   25

Du 24° 10bre.
Doit            Voyage            A Caisse
pour ma pension chez M: Mennecier a Cincinati
des le 5°Octobre......................... 16   25
item pour faire racommoder mes habits...... 2    –
                dudit
Doit          Marchandise         A Caisse
pour transport de mon plomb................ 1   50
              du 29° dit
Doit            Voyage            a Caisse
pour fraix de route de Cincinati a Lexington... 5 –
            Du 2° Fevrier 1798
Doit            Voyage            a Caisse
pour ma pension et fraix a Lexinton        23    –
                du 13°
Doit            Voyage            a Caisse
pour ma pension et fraix a Francft          4    –
34          Du 16° Fevrier 1798
Doit            Voyage        a        Caisse
pour fraix de route de Francfort a Birdtoun  2  75
                Du 17°
Item pour frais au dit lieu................. 3
                Du 19
item pour fraix de route jusqua Rolinfork.....   66
                Du 23°
item jusqua Greentown.....................     25
                Du 26
item jusqua Rolinfork de retour............     50
                Du 28
item jusqua Sprinfield......................     50
              Du 3° Mars
item jusqua Harisbourg                       2   –
                Du 4°
item jusqua Danville......................      60

## APPENDIX

October 24th
Debit Traveling            To Cash
For my board and lodging at Mr. Mennesier's in Cincinnati from October 5th    16  25
Item, to have my clothing mended               2  00
                  do.
Debit Merchandise          To Cash
For transportation of my lead                  1  50
               October 29th
Debit Traveling            To Cash
For expenses on the way from Cincinnati to
Lexington                                      5  00
             February 2nd, 1798
Debit Traveling            To Cash
For my board and lodging and expenses in
Lexington                                     23  00
                  13th
Debit Traveling            To Cash
For my board and lodging and expenses at
Frankfort                                      4  00
34           February 16th, 1798
Debit Traveling            To Cash
For expenses incurred on the way from
Frankfort to Birdstown                         2  75
                  17th
Item, for expenses in said town                3
                  19th
Item, for traveling expenses to Rolling Fork      66
                  23rd
Item, to Greentown                                25
                  26th
Item, return to Rolling Fork                      50
                  28th
Item, to Springfield                              50
               March 3rd
Item, to Harrodsburg                           2  00
                  4th
Item, to Danville                                 60

                    Du 5°
item jusqua Lexinton                                    1
                    Du 12°
item jusqua Millersburg                                 1
                    Du 14°
item jusqua Lexinton derechef                              75
                    du 16°
item pour ma pension a Lexinton de le 5°..... 6
35          Du 20° Mars 1798
Doit             Voyage        a    Caisse
pour ma route a Cincinati...................  3   –
                    dudit
Doit        Harde
pour une paire de Souiller                          1  75
                    Du 1° Avril
Doit     Caisse     a Marchandise
pour la vente de 22 Lb de plomb..............  5  25
                    Du 4°
Doit  voyage       a       Caisse
pour blanchissage et un Crayon                      –  50
                    Du 23°
item ....        a lui meme
pour ma pension A Cincinati donné mon livre
de Geometrie celui de Gnomonique, et un ther-
mometre .................................  5   –
item                a       Caisse
pour 22 Lb ½ de biscuit pour ma provision de
voyage ..................................  2
pour consulte et droge d'un Medecin..........  3  75
                    du dit
Doit  Mar:                           à Caisse
pour faire transporter mon plomb a la riviere
a bord d'un batteau......................  1  16
36          Du 24° Avril 1798
Parti de Cincinati pour remonter la riviere
Doit voyage a                    Marchandise
pour diferentes choses pour provision de bouche
que jai achete en route pour du plomb........  8   –

# APPENDIX 279

|  |  |  |
|---|---|---|
| 5th | | |
| Item, to Lexington | 1 | |
| 12th | | |
| Item, to Millersburg | 1 | |
| 14th | | |
| Item, to Lexington again | | 75 |
| 16th | | |
| Item, for my board in Lexington from the 5th | 6 | |

35            March 20th, 1798
Debit            Traveling            To Cash
For my expenses on the way to Cincinnati            3   00
            do.
Debit            Clothing
for a pair of Shoes            1   75
            April 1st
Debit            Cash       To Merchandise
For the sale of 22 lbs of lead            5   25
            4th
Debit            Traveling            To Cash
For laundry and one pencil            50
            23rd
Item       [Traveling account]       To itself
Given for my board in Cincinnati my book on geometry, the one on gnomonics, and a thermometer            5   00
Item                        To Cash
For 22½ lbs. of biscuits for my traveling supply            2
For consultation and drugs from a doctor            3   75
            do.
Debit Mdse.            To Cash
To have my lead hauled to the river and on board a boat            1   16

36            April 24th, 1798
Left Cincinnati to go up the river
Debit       Traveling       To Merchandise
For various provisions which I bought on the way in exchange for lead            8   00

### Du 15 May

Doit Caisse a Mar:
pour plomb vendu a Marietta en passant...... 28 –

### Du 25° May

Doit Mar: a elle meme
pour 1628 Lb de plomb que jai donné pour faire
transporter le reste a Pittsbourg ou je suis arrivé ce jourdhui

item a Caisse
pour faire emmagasiner 96 lingot du dit plomb 3 –

### dudit

Doit voyage a Caisse
pour un pain de 2½ Lb............. 12c ⎫
pour frais faits en epayant de faire de ⎬ 1 12
la grenaille ...................... 1 – ⎭

### Du 12° Juin 1798

Doit Voyage a Caisse
pour ma pension a Pittsbourg et pour quelque
racomodage a mes habit.................. 6 –

### Du 13°

item pour frai de route jusqua Washington... 33

### Du 14°

Doit Mar: a lui même
pour le change de 4 Montres argents contre une
juments sellee et bridée qui jai faite a Redstone

### dudit

Doit M: a Caisse
pour tourne donné sus la jument susdite...... 8 50

### du 15°

Doit voyage a Caisse
pour frai a Geneve........................ 1 –

### du 17°

Doit item pour route jusqua Pittsbourg ou jarrive derechef ................................ 1 56

## APPENDIX 281

### May 15th
Debit   Cash            To Merchandise
For lead sold at Marietta on my way through        28  00

### May 25th
Debit   Merchandise            To Itself
for 1628 lbs. of lead which I gave to have the remainder transported to Pittsburg where I arrived this day.

Item,                           To Cash
For having 96 pigs of said lead stored.......      3   00

### do.
Debit Traveling                 To Cash
For a 2½ lb. loaf of bread.......... 12c   ⎫
For expenditures incurred in trying to     ⎬   1  12
make small shot                     1  00  ⎭

### June 12th, 1798
Debit Traveling                 To Cash
For my board and lodging in Pittsburg, and
for some mending on my clothes                     6   00

### 13th
Item, for traveling expenses to Washington
[Pa.]                                                  33

### 14th
Debit Merchandise               To itself
For the exchange at Redstone of 4 silver
watches for a saddled and bridled mare

### do.
Debit Merchandise               To Cash
For the money given to boot on the aforesaid mare                                          8   50

### 15th
Debit Traveling                 To Cash
For expenses at Geneva                             1   00

### 17th
Debit, item, for traveling expenses to Pittsburg where I arrive again                      1   56

38           Du 23° Juin 1798
A Pitsburg laissé a M. Wrenshall Mon Plomb a vendre en Comission
Doit   Marchandise   a                    Caisse
pour 262 Lb de plomp vendu par M. Larwill a
10 p. ct. [?] la Lb.......................... 29   11
Doit   Marchandise a                  lui meme
pour un Cheval change contre du plomb velue a  80   –
Doit voyage a Caise....................... 3   10
savoir pour la pension de ma jument.... 1–50
et pour la mienne Chez Mary........... 1–60
parti pour Philadelphie

         Le 4° Juillet
Arrivé a Philadelphie avec mes deux chevaux
Doit voyage       a              Caisse
pour frai de route......................... 18   –

         le 11°
Vendu la Jument en vente poublique pour 42 $ a recevoir dans 3 jours
Doit Voyage      a                     Caise
pour la pension de mes Cheveaux et pour en faire ferrer un...................... 7   25

39           le 13me Juillet 1798
Doit Voyage     a             Marchandise
pour une piece de Corderoi pris chez Peacok associes de Wrenshall en payement du plomb laisse a ce dernier 23 yard a 7/10.   24   –
Doit voyage a                  Caisse
Pour Ma pension des mon Arrivée.. $3
deux paires de Souillers........... 2   75
une Chemise .................... 1   87
une paire de bas................. 2   50
fruit et autre fraix............. 2        12   12

## APPENDIX

38    June 23rd, 1798
At Pittsburg left to Mr. Wrenshall my lead to
be sold on Commission
Debit Merchandise            To Cash
For 262 lbs. of lead sold by Mr. Larwill at
10%[?] a lb.                                    29   11
Debit Merchandise            To itself
For a horse exchanged for lead valued at [?]   80   00
Debit Traveling              To Cash           3   10
To wit: for keep of my mare         1   50
And for my [board and lodging] at
Mary's                              1   60
Left for Philadelphia
   July 4th
Arrived in Philadelphia with my two horses
Debit Traveling              To Cash
For expenses on the way                        18   00
   11th
Sold the Mare at public sale for $42 to be
paid me in 3 days
Debit Traveling              To Cash
For the keep of my horses and to have one
shod                                            7   25
39    July 13th 1798
Debit    Traveling       To Merchandise
For a piece of Corduroy bought at Peacock's,
Wrenshall's partner, in payment of the lead I
let the latter have, 23 yards at 7/10          24   00
Debit Traveling              To Cash
For my board and lodging from my
arrival                             $3
Two pairs of Shoes                  2   75
One shirt                           1   87
One pair of stockings               2   50
Fruit and other expenses            2
         ———
            12   12

### 14
Doit Caisse a Marchandise
pour le prix de la jument vendue le 11° dit   42   –
Ecri une longue letter pour mes Parens et mis
a bord le vaissau la liberte pour Bourdeau, et
méne mon cheval a 8 milles hors de ville

### 16
Doit voyage a Caisse
pour ce que jai payé a ma bourjoise a Camp   2   –
parti pour New Yorck par le Pakboat de Burlington

### 18°
Arrivé a New Yorck a une heure du Matin, a
quelle houre une grande incendie se manifesta
et brula tout un square

40           le 18me Juillet 1798
Doit voyage a Caisse
pour fraix de route de Philadelphie a New Yor   3   75

### le 19°
Doit voyage a Caisse
pour une paire de bas et deux mouchoirs de
Mousseline ................................   5   –
Demeuré Chez Monsieur Rossier
Ecris deux lettres pour mes parens lune par
Hambourg et lautre par Copenhague

### le 25°
Parti de New Yorck pour revenir a Philadelphie

### 28°
Doit Voyage a Caisse
pour fraix de New Yorck a Philadelphie our [?]
jarrive aujourdhui ........................   2   –
Doit Marchandise à Caisse
pour une Malle...........................   3

### le 31°
Doit Voiage a Caisse
pour une piece de toille pris chez Nollnaguel [?]
de 64 yard...............................   24

## APPENDIX

### 14

Debit Cash          To Merchandise
For the price of the mare sold the 11th inst.    42
Have written a long letter to my parents and mailed it on board the ship *La Liberté* bound for Bordeaux, and took my horse 8 miles out of town

### 16

Debit Traveling          To Cash    2 00
For what I paid my landlady in the County
Left for New York by the Burlington packet

### 18th

Arrived in New York at one o'clock in the morning, at which hour a great fire broke out and burnt a whole square.

40       July 18th, 1798

Debit Traveling          To Cash
For traveling expenses from Philadelphia to New York    3 75

### 19th

Debit Traveling          To Cash
For a pair of stockings and two muslin handkerchiefs    5 00
Living at Monsieur Rossier's.
Written, two letters for my parents, one via Hamburg, and the other via Copenhagen.

### 25th

Left New York to return to Philadelphia

### 28th

Debit Traveling          To Cash
For expenses from New York to Philadelphia, where I arrived today    2 00
Debit Merchandise          To Cash
For one trunk    3

### 31st

Debit Traveling          To Cash
For one piece of cloth bought at Nollnaguel's, 64 yards    24

laquelle piece jai remise a Ma Boujoise Madame Warthman proche le marche dans le nord liberties pour me faire 12 Chemises et 3 draps.

41           le 31° Juillet 1798
Doit Caisse           a           Marchandise
pour les bas de Soyes que javois laisse a Gouffond pour vendre en Commission............ 51 —

          le 1° Aoust
Doit voyage et harde           a           Caisse
pour divers livres et cartes geographiques..... 8    79
pour façon de 2 paires de Culote et un habit... 8    —

Doit Marchandise           a           Caisse
pour avoir fait mettre le quantieme a une montre d'or .............................. 5    —
Donne une Caisse a Thomas Moors pour Pittsburg

          2°
Doit voyage           a           Caisse
pour ma pension a Philadelphie............... 2    25
pour cella mon cheval hors de ville........... 3
parti pour le Kentucky
          le 12°
Arivé a Pittsburg
Doit voyage           a           Caisse
pour fraix de route moi et mon Cheval    12    —
          le 13°
Doit Voyage           a Marchandise
pour une couverture de Laine pris chez Wrenshall a compte de plomp    5

42           le 16° Aoust 1798
Doit voyage           a           Caisse
pour ma pension et celle de mon cheval chez Mary ................................... 2
Parti de Pittsburg

APPENDIX

Which piece I gave to my landlady, Mrs. Warthman, near the market on North Liberty, to make me 12 shirts and 3 sheets

41        July 31st, 1798
Debit Cash        To Merchandise
For the silk stockings that I had left with Gouffond to sell on commission      51   00

August 1st
Debit    Traveling and Clothing    To Cash
For various books and maps      8   79
For the making of 2 pairs of breeches and a coat      8   00
Debit Merchandise        To Cash
For having altered a gold watch so it would show the date      5   00
Given a box to Thomas Moors for Pittsburg.

2nd
Debit    Traveling        To Cash
For my board and lodging in Philadelphia      2   25
For that of my horse in the country      3
Left for Kentucky.

12th
Arrived at Pittsburg
Debit    Traveling        To Cash
For traveling expenses of myself and horse    12   00

13th
Debit    Traveling      To Merchandise
For a woolen blanket bought at Wrenshall's and paid for in lead      5

42        August 16th, 1798
Debit    Traveling        To Cash
For my board and lodging and that of my horse at Mary's      2
Left Pittsburg

## 18°

Arive a Wheeline ..........................
Doit voyage               a       Caisse
pour fraix de route et ferry................ 2   50

### le 19°

Doit voyage               a       Caisse
pour provision pour passer les desserts........ 2   50

### le 26

Arive a Washington en Kentucky fraix        50

### le 28

Arrivé a Lexington fraix de route............ 2

### le 29°

Doit voyage               a       Caisse
pour 3 yards de toille pour une Chemise...... 2   75
pour un boisseau d'avoine..................     25

### 6me. September

Doit Caisse               a      Marechal
pour argent empreunte..................... 5   –

43        le 10me September 1798

Arrivé a Franckfort fraix................. 1

### le 11°

Couru aux allentour de Frankfort avec M. Brown le Senateur pour chercher un emplacement pour la vigne sur la riviere

### le 12°

Parti pour cotoyer la Riviere du Kentuky pour chercher un emplacement a la vigne

### le 13

Arivé Chez Steel—fraix.................... 1   –

### le 14

Arivé Chez Anderson proche General Scott fraix .....................................     75

### le 15

Arrivé proche de Cords ferry...........fraix   –   50

### le 16

Arrive Chez David Waker proche de la Route d'Hicman et nayant rien trouvé qui me plu

## APPENDIX

#### 18th
Arrived in Wheeling
Debit    Traveling              To Cash
For expense on the way, and ferry      2  50
#### 19th
Debit    Traveling              To Cash
For provisions to cross the wilderness    2  50
#### 26
Arrived at Washington in Kentucky, expense    50
#### 28
Arrived in Lexington, expenses on way    2
#### 29th
Debit    Traveling              To Cash
For 3 yards of linen for a shirt      2  75
For a bushel of oats                      25
#### September 6th
Debit    Cash              To Marechal
For money borrowed              5  00
43        September 10th, 1798
Arrived in Frankfort—expenses        1
#### 11th
Went over the country around Frankfort with Mr. Brown, the Senator, to look for a place on the river for the vineyard.
#### 12th
Started out to skirt the Kentucky River to find a place for the vineyard
#### 13
Arrived at Steel's, expenses        1  00
#### 14
Arrived at Anderson's, near General Scott's, expenses        75
#### 15
Arrived near Cord's Ferry, expenses    50
#### 16
Arrived at David Waker's near the Hickman road, having found nothing which pleased me,

exepte proche de francfort mais le prix étant trop haut pour moi

44          le 18me 7ber 1798
Arrivé derechef a Lexington fraix........... 1 50

le 20me

Laisse mon Cheval a Lexington et jai été a pied jusqua Cleaveling landing la on ma donne un conot et je suis dessendu la riviere jusqua lembouchure d'Hicman ou je suis arrive

le 30me

Doit voyage          a      Caisse
pour fraix de route...................... 2 -

le 2° October

Arrive derechef a Lexington ou jai raporte a la Societé de la vigne que javois vu 3 ou 4 place qui me plairois pour établir la vigne, et ils conclurent d'acheter dans le big bend 4 milles en dessus de lembouchure d'Hicman un tract de 630 acres d'un James Haselrig

5

Doit Saugrin a          Marchandise
pour une montre a lui remise pour avoir une machione Electrique et autre chos          30 -

45          le 13° October 1798
Jai vaque avec lagent de la Societé pour acheter le terrain pour la vigne de James Hazelrig et préparé pour aller commencer de travailler

le 14°

Doit Voyage et harde          a Marchandis
pour une Montre dor Changée a Nancaron pour étofe pour m'habiller et autre objet necessaire.. 55 -

le 19°

Doit harde          a Marchandise
pour une montre d'argent remise au tailleur King pour me faire des habits.............. 23 -

## APPENDIX

except near Frankfort, and that too high-priced.

44    September 18th, 1798
Arrived again in Lexington, expenses                1  50

                20th

Left my horse in Lexington and went on foot to Cleveland landing, where I was given a skiff and went down the river as far as the mouth [of the creek at] Hickman's, where I arrived

              the 30th

Debit    Traveling           To Cash
For expenses on the way                              2  00

           October 2nd

Arrived again in Lexington where I reported to the Vineyard Company that I had seen 3 or 4 places which would suit me for laying out a vineyard, and they concluded to buy in the Big Bend 4 miles above the mouth [of the creek at] Hickman's, a tract of 630 acres from James Haselrig.

                5

Debit        Saugrin        To Merchandise
For a watch given to him to procure an Electric machine and some other things          30  00

45    October 15th, 1798
I was busy with the Company's agent buying the land for the Vineyard from James Hazelrig, and preparing to go and begin work.

                14th

Debit Traveling and Clothing
                To Merchandise
For a gold watch given in exchange to Nancaron for goods for my clothing and other necessities                                      55  00

                19th

Debit Clothing           To Merchandise
For a silver watch given to tailor King to make me clothing                          23  00

le 5° November
Preparé pour aler commencer louvrage sur le terrein de la Societé et tenu journal depuis ce jour pour la dite Societé dans un livre qui depose a Firstvineyard nom done a la place ou on fait la vigne

46        le 1° Fevrier 1799
Arivé aujourdhui ici a Baltimore alant a Philadelphie et Newyorck pour ramasser et achetter des Chapons de vigne pour planter pour la Societe pour arriver ici (ayant quitte Firstvineyard le 2° de Janvier) jai passé par Craborchard, les Willderness, Powels valée, Clinich River, Russel courthouse, Rockgapp, wolf creek, Wakers creek, Botelour Lexington, Charlottesville, Monticello Richemont, Fredericksburg Alexandrie & Washington City.
Doit Compte de Ferme a        Caisse
pour 36 arbres a fruit acheté ici pour etre envoyé en Kentuky        12 —
L'argent pour la vigne a été porté a compte a la Societé de la vigne

47        le 10° Fevrier 1799
Arivé a New York porté tous mes fraix de route a la Societe de la vigne

le 19
Doit Compte de Ferme        a Caisse
pour 7 Couteaux serpetes.................. 4 —

le 1° Mars 1798
Doit harde        a Caise
pour façon des chemises et draps de lits remis a Madame Warthman vide ci devant page 40    6   40

2°
Doit voyage        a Caisse
pour une malle et corde acheté a Philadelphi... 3 —

## APPENDIX

### November 5th
Prepared to go and begin the work on the Company's land, and from that day have kept the journal for the said Company in a book which remains at Firstvineyard, name given to the place where the vineyard is being established.

46      February 1st, 1799

Arrived today here in Baltimore on my way to Philadelphia and New York to pick up and buy grapevine slips to be planted for the Company. To get here (having left Firstvineyard on the 2nd of January) I passed through Craborchard, the Wilderness, Powel's Valley, Clinich River, Russel Courthouse, Rockgap, Wolf Creek, Waker's Creek, Botelour, Lexington, Charlottesville, Monticello, Richmond, Fredericksburg, Alexandria & Washington City.

Debit    Farm Account      To Cash
For 36 fruit trees bought here to be sent to Kentucky      12   00

The money for the grapevines has been charged to the account of the Vineyard Company.

47      February 10th, 1799

Arrived in New York—charged all my traveling expenses to the Vineyard Company.

### 19
Debit Farm Account      To Cash
For 7 pruning knives      4   00

### March 1st, 1798 [sic]
Debit Clothing Account      To Cash
Given Mrs. Warthman for making shirts and bed sheets—see above, page 40      6   40

### 2nd
Debit Traveling      To Cash
For a trunk and rope bought in Philadelphia      3   00

pour blanchissage ....................... − 25
     le 5°
Doit Caisse       a Marchandise
pour ce que Peacok ma donne a compte du plomp
remis a Wrenshal...................... 35 −
     le dit
Doit Compte de ferme     a Caisse
pour diferente espece de graine    2 50
[47$^1$]    le 6me Mars 1799
Parti derechef de Philadelphie pour le Kintucky ayant avec moi un Char Charge de Chapon de vigne de plus de 35 diferentes especes en ayant acheté d'un Legau 10000 a 4 piastres et a 8 piastres le 0/0 tous les fraix porté au compte de la Societé de la vigne
     le 19
Doit hardes et voyage     a Caisse
pour une paire de Souillers indien acheté a Pittsburg ............................. 3 −
     le 5° Avril
Doit Marchandise      a Caisse
pour mettre a bord d'un batto 39 lingots de plomp ............................... 75
     dit
Doit Marchandise a      lui meme
pour echange de 150 Lb de plomb contre 203 Lb de fer en bare
[47$^2$]    le 5° Avril 1799
Doit Caisse      à    Marchandise
pour 2016 de plomb que Wrenshall ma vendu et dont il me paye ce jour    77 −
Echange chez M. Beelens 93 Lb de plomb pour 3 1/2 boisseau de graine de timotee.. 4 3/9
un Chapeau .................... 30/.
4 feve de Tonce................. 7 6
la graine de timotée a été chargée a la Societe de la vigne

## APPENDIX

For laundry 25

5th
Debit Cash                 To Merchandise
For what Peacock paid me on account of the
lead left with Wrenshall              35 00
                    do.
Debit Farm Account            To Cash
For various kinds of seed            2 50

[47¹]          March 6th, 1799
Left Philadelphia again for Kentucky, taking with me a wagon loaded with grapevine cuttings of more than 35 different varieties having bought of one, Legau, 10,000, at 4 dollars and at 8 dollars a hundred, all costs being charged to the account of the Vineyard Company.

                 19th
Debit Clothing and Traveling     To Cash
For a pair of Indian shoes bought in Pittsburg                               3 00

               April 5th
Debit Merchandise              To Cash
For putting on board a boat 39 pigs of lead     75
                 do.
Debit Merchandise              to itself
For exchange of 150 lbs. of lead for 203 lbs. of iron in bars

[47²]          April 5th, 1799
Debit Cash                 To Merchandise
For 2016 [lbs.] of lead which Wrenshall sold for me and for which he paid me this day    77 00
Traded at Mr. Beelens 93 lbs. of lead for 3½ bushels of timothy seed           4 3/9
One hat                             30.
4 Tonka beans                   7.6
The timothy seed has been charged to the Vineyard Company.

Doit harde a Marchandise
pour un Chapeau—contre du plomb     4   –
une petite bouteille de benjoin          –  50
Doit Caisse a Marchandise
pour 986 Lb de plomb a 8ct.            78  88
Doit Bracken a March.
pour 2448 Lb de plomb a lui vendu a 11Ct la Lb
payable dans 6 mois                   269  28

48            5 April 1799
Doit Voyage          a Marchandise
pour une bride.................. 1
un Sacc ....................... 1
une Couverture de laine.......... 3   75
3 pairs de souillers.............. 5    –
un tincup ...................... –   14
                                         10  89

            dudit
Doit Marchandise          a lui meme
pour commission payé a Wrenshal et port de
lettre ..........................................  1  50
parti de Pittsburg

            le 14me
Arrivé a Limestone par la riviere
Doit Marchandise          a Cash
pour paier le fret de 39 lingots de plomb...... 15  10
Doit Fraizer a          Marchandise
pour 114 Lb de plomb a lui vendu a un Mois
de Credit ........................................ 13  68
Doit Caisse          a Marchandise
pour 50 Lb de plomb vendu en route        6  50

49        le 16me Avril 1799
Doit Vimond de Millersburg[?]     à March.
pour 9 lingots quil a recu a vendre en Comission a 5%
Doit Scott & Edward de Paris
a Marchandise pour 192 Lb de plomb vendu a
eux a 9d                                 24   –

# APPENDIX

| | | | |
|---|---|---|---|
| Debit Clothing | To Merchandise | 4 | 00 |
| For a hat—for lead | | | 50 |
| A small bottle of benzoin | | | |
| Debit Cash | To Merchandise | 78 | 88 |
| For 986 lbs. of lead at 8c | | | |
| Debit Bracken | To Merchandise | | |
| For 2448 lbs. sold to him at 11c a lb., payable in 6 months | | 269 | 28 |

48           April 5, 1799

| | | | |
|---|---|---|---|
| Debit Traveling | To Merchandise | | |
| For a bridle | 1. | | |
| A sack | 1. | | |
| A woolen blanket | 3.75 | | |
| 3 pairs of shoes | 5.00 | | |
| A tincup | .14 | 10 | 89 |

do.

| | | | |
|---|---|---|---|
| Debit Merchandise | To itself | | |
| For commission paid to Wrenshall and letter postage | | 1 | 50 |

Left Pittsburg.

14th

Arrived in Limestone via the river

| | | | |
|---|---|---|---|
| Debit Merchandise | To Cash | 15 | 10 |
| To pay for the freight of 39 pigs of lead | | | |
| Debit Frazier | To Merchandise | 13 | 68 |
| For 114 lbs. of lead sold to him on one month's credit | | | |
| Debit Cash | To Merchandise | 6 | 50 |
| For 50 lbs. of lead sold en route | | | |

49           April 16th, 1799

| | | | |
|---|---|---|---|
| Debit Vimond of Millersburg To Merchandise | | | |
| for 9 pigs [of lead] he received to be sold on commission at 5% | | | |
| Debit Scott & Edward of Paris [Ky.] To Merchandise | | | |
| For 192 lbs. of lead sold to them at 9d | | 24 | 00 |

### 15 May

Doit Marchandise　　　　　　　a Caisse
pour le voiturage de 33 lingots de plomb jusque
chez Jonson　　　　　　　　　　　　　　　44　4

### 16

Doit Caisse　　　　　　　　a Marchandise
pour 716 Lb de plomb vendu a Trotter a 9d....　89　50

### dudit

Doit Saugrin　　　　　　　a Marchandise
pour 4 lingots de plomb a lui vendu a 9d......　50　—
50　　　　le 16me May 1799
Doit Caisse　　　　　a　　Marchandise
pour la vente de 3380 Lb de plomb vendu a
Divers marchants a Lexington Leavy en ayant
eu 1852 Lb..................................　422　50

### 23°

Doit Marchandise　　　　　　　a Caisse
pour le restat du voiturage de mon plomb par
Jonson ....................................　1　96

### dit

Doit Marchandise　　　　　　　a Caisse
pour le plomb donne a voiturer depuis Jonson a
Lexington .................................　10　—

### 14 September

Doit Caisse　a　　　　　　　　　Fraser
pour ce qu'il a paye a Joseph Lion a qui jai
donne un ordre et porte le tout a compte de la
Societé de la vigne pour travail que le dit Lion
a fait pour elle...........................　13　68
51　　　15 November 1799
Doit Caisse　　　　　　　a Scot et Edward
pour ce que Bank ma paye pour eux..........　24　—
　　　　　　　le 10 Xber
Doit harde　　　　　　　　　a Caisse
pour une paire de Souiller　　　　　　　　　2　25
　　　　　le 14 Janvier 1800
Doit harde　　　　　　　　　a Caisse
pour ce que jai acheté a Lexington Chez Anderson Bashop et Mecbean...................　2　41

## APPENDIX

### May 15

Debit Merchandise     To Cash
For cartage of 33 pigs of lead to Johnson's    44 40

### 16

Debit Cash     To Merchandise
For 716 lbs. of lead sold to Trotter at 9d.    89 50

### do.

Debit Saugrin     To Merchandise
For 4 pigs of lead sold to him at 9d.    50 00

50     May 16th, 1799
Debit Cash     To Merchandise
For the sale of 3380 lbs. of lead sold to various merchants in Lexington, Leavy having received 1852 lbs.    422 50

### 23rd

Debit Merchandise     To Cash
For the balance of the cartage of my lead by Johnson    1 96

### do.

Debit Merchandise     To Cash
For the lead I had carted from Johnson's to Lexington    10 00

### September 14

Debit Cash     To Fraser
For what he paid Joseph Lion to whom I gave an order and charged the whole to the Vineyard Company for work which the said Lion did for them    13 68

51     November 15, 1799
Debit Cash     To Scott and Edward
For the amount Bank paid me for them    24 00

### December 10th

Debit Clothing     To Cash
For a pair of shoes    2 25

### January 14, 1800

Debit Clothing     To Cash
For what I bought at Lexington at Anderson Bashop and Mecbean's    2 41

### 15 Mars

| | | | |
|---|---|---|---|
| Doit harde | a Caisse | | |
| pour racomodage d habit payé a M. Louis..... | | – | 25 |

### 23

| | | | |
|---|---|---|---|
| Doit harde | a Caisse | | |
| pour un Chapeau achete de Mecbean.......... | | 5 | – |

52      le 6me Avril 1800

| | | | |
|---|---|---|---|
| Doit harde | a Caisse | | |
| pour une piece de triege pour faire des pentalon | | 7 | 50 |
| Doit compte de Ferme a Caisse pour 2 crayons et 4 Couteaux serpettes..................... | | 4 | 75 |

### 15 May

| | | | |
|---|---|---|---|
| Doit hardes | a Caisse | | |
| pour ce que jai acheté chez Parker | 2–38 | | |
| une Paire de Souiller chez Nancarron | 1–66 | 4 | 4 |

### 7me Juin

| | | | |
|---|---|---|---|
| Doit harde | a Caisse | | |
| pour façon d'habillement................... | | 1 | 50 |

### 23

| | | | |
|---|---|---|---|
| Doit Marchandise | a Caisse | | |
| pour les Emoluments dune procure envoyee a Goufon pour retirer largent dune Caisse de Marchandise venant de Suisse et laissee a la Douane de Philadelphi jusquace | | | |

53

| | | | |
|---|---|---|---|
| que la ditte Douane a fait vendre la Caisse.... | | 3 | 33 |

### 24 Juin 1800

| | | | |
|---|---|---|---|
| Doit harde | a Caisse | | |
| pour ce que Jai acheté chez Jourdan.......... | | 2 | 25 |

### 3 Juillet

| | | | |
|---|---|---|---|
| Doit harde | a Caisse | | |
| pour ce que jai achette chez Parker........... | | 9 | 88 |

### 17 Aoust

| | | | |
|---|---|---|---|
| Doit Marchandise | a Caisse | | |
| pour ce que ma couté une experience de vouloir faire du vin de peche dans une cistern de bois qui a coule............................... | | 15 | – |

# APPENDIX

### March 15

Debit Clothing        To Cash
Paid to Mr. Louis for mending clothes     25

### 23

Debit Clothing        To Cash
For a hat bought of Mecbean     5 00

### 52     April 6th, 1800

Debit Clothing        To Cash
For a piece of goods [?] to make pantaloons     7 50

Debit Farm Account        To Cash
For two pencils and 4 pruning knives     4 75

### May 15

Debit Clothing        To Cash
For what I bought at Parker's    2.38

One pair of shoes at Nancarron's    1.66    4 04

### June 7th

Debit Clothing        To Cash
For clothes made     1 50

### 23

Debit Merchandise        To Cash
For fees for a proxy sent to Goufon to collect the money on a box of merchandise from Switzerland left at the Customs Office of 53 Philadelphia until the Customs Office had the box sold     3 33

### June 24th, 1800

Debit Clothing        To Cash
For what I bought at Jourdan's     2 25

### July 3

Debit Clothing        To Cash
For what I bought at Parker's     9 88

### August 17

Debit Merchandise        To Cash
For my expense in an experiment in which I tried to make peach wine in a tank that leaked     15 00

### 20 9ber

| | | | |
|---|---|---|---|
| Doit harde | a Caisse | | |
| pour ce que jai acheté..................... | | 2 | 84 |

### 6 May 1801

| | | | |
|---|---|---|---|
| Doit Caisse a | Goufond | | |
| pour ce que jai tiré sur lui par Jourdan....... | | 80 | |

54　　　　　le 6 May 1801

| | | | |
|---|---|---|---|
| Doit harde | a Caisse | | |
| pour 10 yards de toille..................... | | 5 | – |
| Doit Compte de Ferme | a Caisse | | |
| pour ce que jai paye a Compte de 795½ acres de terre achetée du Congres a la derniere vendue a 2 piastres lacre un quart a payer comptant outre les Emoluments | | 405 | 20 |
| pour fraix et depens pour aller voir les terres, attendre a la vendue et porter largent a Cincinaty ............................... | | 30 | – |

### 9 Juin

Ayant reçu la nouvelle que mes freres venoient je parti pour aller a leur rencontre et jalai jusqua Marietta ou je les rencontrai le 18me et redescendi la riviere avec eux et arriverent le 3me Juillet a Lexington....................

55　　　　　le 6me Juillet 1801

Mes freres et toute leur compagnie fesant en tout 17 personnes arrivere a Firstvineyard et jentrai en compagnie avec mes freres et Soeurs pour travailler la vigne des lors tout a été en Commun cependant ce qui ce trouve a moi avant la reunion doit se prelever apres.

| | | | |
|---|---|---|---|
| Doit voyage | a Caisse | | |
| pour les fraix fait dans ce voyage............ | | 30 | – |
| Doit Caisse | a Mon Pére | | |
| pour les interets de la moitie des 2000 Livres suisse porte a compte devant page 1, qui lui apartiennent, jusqua aujourdhui que jentre en Societé avec la famille...................... | | 68 | 75 |

# APPENDIX

|  |  |  |  |
|---|---|---|---|
| November 20 |  |  |  |
| Debit Clothing | To Cash |  |  |
| for purchases |  | 2 | 84 |

May 6, 1801
Debit Cash                 To Goufond
For my draft on him through Jourdan    80   00

54          May 6th 1801
Debit Clothing             To Cash
For 10 yards of cloth                5   00

Debit Farm Account        To Cash
For what I paid on account for 795½ acres of land bought of Congress at the last public sale, at two dollars per acre, one fourth cash, besides the fees            405   20

For expenses in going to see the lands, in attending the sale, and in taking the money to Cincinnati            30   00

June 9th

Having received news that my brothers were coming, I started to go to meet them, and I went as far as Marietta, where I met them on the 18th, and returned down the river with them, and the party arrived in Lexington on the 3rd of July.

55          July 6th, 1801

My brothers and all their company, making in all 17 persons, arrived at Firstvineyard and I entered into a partnership with my brothers and sisters to work the vineyard. From this time on all has been in common. However, what was mine before the partnership is to be deducted after.

Debit Traveling            To Cash
For the expenses incurred on this trip    30   00

Debit Cash             To my Father
For the interest on one-half of the 2000 livres Swiss entered in account above, page 1, which belong to him, up to the present day, when I enter into partnership with the family    68   75

56 le 6° Juillet 1801
Doit Caisse a Mon Pere
pour la moitie des 2000 Livres Suisse que je
porte a compte de fond dans la page 1.° pour me
les avoir pretée pour faire mes fonds en piastres
10 gros ecus pour 11 piastres.................. 275 –
Doit Caisse a Goufon
pour le restat de largent qua produit la vente
dune Caisse de marchandise venant de Suisse
apres avoir paye les droits fraix et transport
dune autre Caisse 136 18
Doit Caisse a Braken de Pittsburg
pour ce que jai retire en diverse fois par Parker,
Jourdan et Anderson la balance de son compte.. 269 28
Doit Caisse a Mon Pere
pour ce que je peu avoir vendu des marchandises envoyee de Suisse avant larrivee de mes freres 40 –

57 le 6me Juillet [1801]
Doit la Societé de la vigne a Caisse pour ce que
je leur ai avance jusqua ce jours conste le
compte ave elle........................... 136 47
item pour mes salaires jusqua ce jour outre le
40 actions que jai pour les deux 1° annees 1000 –
Doit Mon Pere a Caisse
pour une ordre tire sur moi en faveur de
Boralay et accepte........................ 550 –
Doit Caisse a Mon Pere ou a ses fils tous ensemble pour ce que nous avons paye en
Comunion de lordre ci dessus moi ayant paye
le reste par Mennet Cart et une Jument....... 298 –
Doit Daniel ou Mon Père a Caisse pour ce que
Daniel a reçu de M. Mennet pere pour porter ici
a son fils et que jai paye 110

## APPENDIX 305

| | | | |
|---|---|---|---|
| 56 | July 6th, 1801 | | |

Debit Cash            To my Father
For one-half of the 2000 livres Swiss, which
I have entered on the funds account on page 1,
for having lent them to me to make up my
funds; in dollars, 10 gros écus for 11 dollars      275    00
Debit Cash            Goufon
For the balance of the money from the sale of
a case of merchandise from Switzerland, after
paying for the customs dues and for the
transportation of another case      136    18
Debit Cash            To Braken of Pittsburg
For what I collected on various occasions
through Parker, Jourdan and Anderson; the
balance of his account      269    28
Debit Cash            To my Father
For what I was able to sell of the goods sent
from Switzerland before my brothers' arrival      40    00

57            July 6th [1801]
Debit The Vineyard Company            To Cash
For the amounts I advanced to them up to
the present day, according to my account with
them      136    47
Item, for my wages down to this day, besides
the 40 shares that I have for the first two
years      1000    00
Debit My Father            To Cash
For a draft drawn on me in favor of Boralay,
and accepted      550    00
Debit Cash            To my Father, or
to his sons together, for what we have paid
in common on the above draft, I having paid
the balance by Mennet—cart and a mare—      298    00
Debit Daniel or my Father            To Cash
For what Daniel received from Mr. Mennet,
Sr., to bring here to his son; which I have
paid      110

58          le 6me Juillet 1801
Doit la famille de Mon Pere a Caisse pour ce que
javois quand nous nous somme reunir.......... 50  –

### 15 October
Doit Caisse a                    Saugrin
pour ce que jai recu a diferentes fois.......... 53  84
Doit la famille              a Caisse
pour ce que jai reçu de ce que dessus depuis la
reunion ................................... 35  60
Doit la famille              a Caisse
pour ce que jai reçu de Goufon depuis la reunion
et employe a son profit..................... 112  57

### October 1804
La famille a cesse detre en Comunion Daniel
voulant aller sur ses terres et Jean François
étant majeur ne veut plus rester unis..........

59          8° November 1804
ensuite de notre separation Jai dressé un plan
de partage par lequel chacun des Enfans de
Jean Jaques Dufour Senior auront un Lot dans
le tract de Terre que le Congres ma consedes et
a mes Associes, mon fils Vincent Dl. aura aussi
un lot comme associe. Jen ai fait larpentage et
la division sur le plan aussi exactement que possible, les deux Sibentals, Betens et Morerod qui
etoien venu avec mes frères sont aussi reçu
comme associes, Mais comme larpentage étoit
en diagonale avec la riviere et quil nous convenoit de redresser nos lots jai acheté un tract
a long du premier de 1111. acres jen ai remis
319 a M. Gex 150 a Raimont et 160 a Stuart et
fait une portion pour changer avec Francois
Sibental ainsi quetoit convenu, ce qui previent de
ce redressement et de cet echange je lai marque
sur le plan en trois lots de 162 acres chacun que
je men reserve la disposition

# APPENDIX 307

| 58 | July 6th, 1801 | | |
|---|---|---|---|
| Debit my father's family | To Cash | | |
| For what I had when we formed the partnership | | 50 | 00 |
| | October 15 | | |
| Debit Cash | To Saugrin | | |
| For what I received on various occasions | | 53 | 84 |
| Debit Family | To Cash | | |
| For what I received on the above since the partnership | | 35 | 60 |
| Debit Family | To Cash | | |
| For what I received from Goufon since the partnership and employed for its benefit | | 112 | 57 |

October, 1804

The family has ceased being in partnership, Daniel wishing to go on his land and Jean François, being of age, does not wish to remain any longer in partnership.

59            November 8th, 1804

In consequence of our dissolution of partnership I have drawn up a plan of division by which each one of the children of Jean Jaques Dufour, Senior, will receive an allotment in the tract of land which Congress granted me and my associates. My son Vincent Dl. will also receive an allotment as an associate. I have surveyed and apportioned it on the plan as exactly as possible. The two Sibentals, Betens and Morerod who had come with my brothers are also admitted as associates. But as the survey was diagonal to the river, and as it was advisable for us to straighten our plots, I bought a tract alongside the first 1111 acres. Of this I turned over 319 to Mr. Gex, 150 to Raimont, and 160 to Stuart and set off a plot to exchange with François Sibental as was agreed upon. What comes to me from this straightening and exchange I have marked out on the plan in three plots of 162 acres each, the disposal of which I reserve for myself.

**60**
Par le susdit partage Chacun de mes frères et Soeurs aura sa portion du tier de ce que la Societé avec la Societe de la vigne en Kintucky rendra, jy ai travaille seul 6 ans et nous tous 3. deplus chacun de mes freres et Soeurs auront 50 piastre que Doivent Sibentals père et fils Betens et Morerod pour mindemnifier de mes fraix pour obtenir la concession du Congress, Une Copie de mes Compte avec Mon Père et du partage mensionné ci dessus ainsi que du plan des terres sus mensionnees est deposé a la maison de Firstvineyard au Soin de Jean Francois Dufour et une autre copie sera, sil plait a Dieu présentée a Mon Père en Suisse...

**61**     1° Janvier 1805
Jai fait un arrangement avec Hart et Brown pour faire du Salpetre pour eux dans la Caverne de Madisson

20°
Jai laissé la vigne au Soin de Jean Roux et ai été a la dite cave

22
Doit harde              a Caisse
pour racomodage et facon dhabillemt. par Susanne ............................................  6  –

22 Avril
revenu de la Cave ne pouvant pas me sauver et repris le soin de la vigne

1° May
Doit Caisse           a Hart & Brown
pour ce quil mont Donné pour avoir travaille pour eux a la Cave                              80  –

**62**     2° May 1805
Doit Ferme                a Caisse
pour ce que Jai payé a Roux pour le tems quil ma representé ............................  30  –

# APPENDIX 309

60
By the above division each one of my brothers and sisters will receive his portion of one-third of the products of the partnership and the Vineyard Company in Kentucky, for which I have worked alone 6 years, and all of us, 3 [years]. In addition, each of my brothers and sisters will receive 50 dollars owed by Sibental, Sr., and his sons, Betens and Morerod, to indemnify me for the expense incurred by me in obtaining the grant from Congress. A copy of my accounts with my father and of the above mentioned division, and also a copy of the plan of the lands above mentioned is kept at the house at Firstvineyard in the care of Jean François Dufour, and another copy will be given, if it so please God, to my father in Switzerland.

61          January 1st, 1805
I have made arrangements with Hart and Brown to make saltpetre for them in the cave at Madison.

### 20th
I left the vineyard in care of Jean Roux and went to the said cave.

### 22nd

| | | |
|---|---|---|
| Debit Clothing | To Cash | |
| For mending and making of clothing by Susanne | 6 | 00 |

### April 22nd
Returned from the cave, not being able to get away [from the vineyard], and have resumed the care of the vineyard.

### May 1st

| | | |
|---|---|---|
| Debit Cash | To Hart & Brown | |
| For what they paid me for having worked for them at the cave | 80 | 00 |

62          May 2nd, 1805

| | | |
|---|---|---|
| Debit Farm | To Cash | |
| For what I paid Roux for the time he represented me | 30 | 00 |

1 Aoust

Remis la vigne aux soins de Jean François pour le terme de 4 ans pendent que jyrai en Suisse chercher ma famille

4°

Jai compte quayant fait diferent voyages depuis que jai ouvert un Compte a la Societé de la Vigne, et cella pour mon propre Compte ou Cellui de la famille, Comme cellui dUper blue lick en 1801. cellui de goos Creek lannee suivante cellui de Red bank Saline river et Poste Vincennes En October 1803. et cellui aux trois fourches du Kentucky dans tous les voyages je charchois a me procurer une Saline pour faire du Ser [Sel], dune nouvelle maniere

63        4° Aoust 1805
Doit Voyage                a Caisse
pour les frais des diferents voyages mentiones ci devant .................................. 100   —

5°

Jai été en Suisserland avec deux charpentiers pour batir un Moulin sur l'Ohio Golay devant se joindre a Moi pour le faire faire mais ayant change d'Avis jai aussi renoncé

Doit Compte de Ferme             à Caisse
pour les frais de lexpedition ci dessu.......... 19   —

10°

Doit Gex           a Compte de ferme
pour sa part des fraix et depens fait pour acheter les terre que nous avons paremsemble.. 30   20

dit

Doit Gex           a   Compte de ferme
pour 319 acres de terre que je lui ai remis du tract pour etre paye en quatre instalements savoir ¼ le 1° Dec 1803; Xber 1805; '6 et 7     638

# APPENDIX

### August 1
Have placed the vineyard in care of Jean François for a period of 4 years, while I go to Switzerland to get my family.

### 4th
I consider that, in making various voyages since I opened an account with the Vineyard Company, and those voyages on my own account or on account of the family, such as the one to Upper Blue Lick in 1801, the one to Goose Creek the following year, the one to Red Bank, Saline River, and Post Vincennes in October 1803, and the one to the Three Forks of the Kentucky, in all these voyages I was trying to procure a salt pit to make salt in a new way.

63        August 4th, 1805

Debit Traveling         To Cash
For expenses of the different trips, mentioned above     100  00

### 5th
I went to Switzerland with two carpenters to build a mill on the Ohio, Golay intending to join with me to have it built, but he having changed his mind, I also gave it up.

Debit Farm Account         To Cash
For expense of above expedition     19  00

### 10th
Debit Gex         To Farm Account
For his share of expenses incurred in the purchase of the lands we own in common     30  20

### do.
Debit Gex         To Farm Account
For 319 acres of land of the tract that I turned over to him, to be paid for in 4 instalments, to wit: ¼ December 1st, 1803, December 1805; '6 and '7     638  00

64          6° September 1805
Doit Gex a                              Caisse
pour ce que jai paye pour lui au Charpentiers
Rector et Fowler                            10   –

                 dit
Doit Caisse                             a Gex
pour ce quil ma remis en Dexember 1803 a
compte des terres que je lui ai remis      214   –
Doit Caisse                             a Gex
pour Ce que Jean Roux lui devoit sur une
montre dont je me charge                    10   –

              29° November
Doit Caisse de Ferme                    a Gex
pour ce que Jean François lui doit que jai
pris a payer................................ 45  –
le quel est du en Aoust prochain avec interet a
6 pour %
Doit Rector           a Compte de Ferme
pour le surplus de la valeur du Chevall quil a
eu sur ce que [?] je lui devot              10  50

65           29 November [1805]
Doit James Steward      a Compte de Ferme
pour 160 acres de terre que Je lui ai vendu a
4 piastre l'acre payable 1/3 content 1/3 lanne
1805, et 1/3 en Juillet 1805              640
Doit, Compte de Ferme            a Steward
pour les Cheveaux et betails quil ma remis a
compte de la vente ci dessus              383  25
Doit Compte de Ferme          a M. Rossier
pour ce quil mont preté pour payer les terres
achettes avec Gex......................... 100
item                         au Land Office
pour les 3 derniers payements dudit terrain...1666 50
outre les interets.........................
pour les 3 dernier payements des deux fractions
sur Logglick Creek achettée ala vendue du mois

## APPENDIX

64      September 6th, 1805
Debit Gex      To Cash
For what I paid for him to the carpenters
Rector and Fowler      10   00

do.
Debit Cash      To Gex
For what he gave me in December 1803 on
account for the lands I sold him      214   00

Debit Cash      To Gex
For the amount Jean Roux owed him on a
watch, for the payment of which I assume responsibility      10   00

November 29th
Debit Farm Cash      To Gex
For what Jean François owes him, for which      45   00
I have assumed payment which is due next
August with interest at 6%

Debit Rector      To Farm Account
For the difference between the value of the
horse that he took and what I owed him      10   50

65      November 29 [1805]
Debit James Steward [Stuart]
         To Farm Account
For 160 acres of land I sold him at 4 dollars
an acre, payable 1/3 cash, 1/3 [at the first day
of] the year 1805, and 1/3 in July 1805      640

Debit Farm Account      To Steward
For the horses and cattle he gave me on account of above sale      383   25

Debit Farm Account      To Mr. Rossier
For what they lent me to pay for the lands
bought with Gex      100

Item      To the Land Office
For the last 3 payments on said land      1666   50
besides the interest
For the last 3 payments on the two fractions
on Logg Lick Creek, bought at the public sale

dAvril 1801 savoir 795 acres ½............1193  25
outre les interest
Doit la famille         a Compte de Ferme
pour le Cheval que Jean a eu pour aller a Was-
tinton porter le vin au President             60

66            29° Novembre 1805
Doit Daniel Dufour      a Compte de ferme
pour le Cheval et betail quil a eu de Steward
compris louvra que le Charpentiers Recter lui a
fait                                      121  27
pour 15 barils de corn quil a eu sur l'Ohio   15  –
Doit les Suivant        a compte de Ferme
Betens pour une vache de Steward      13
Sibental     dito                     12   25  –
Doit Compte de Ferme          a Caisse
pour ce que jai donné aux Suivant pour me faire
une Cloture a lautour de 16 acres de terres en
Suisserland pour planter un verge
a Sibental                       21–4/6
a Bell                           25        46  75

            dudit
Doit Compte de Ferme          a Caisse
pour une Action dans la societé de la vigne
achete de Wibel                            50  –

67         1° Janvier 1806
Doit la Societe de la vigne       à la Famille
outre ce que j'ai porte contraux pour moi
meme le page 57. le tout provenant de mes   4647  64
salaires de ceux a mes freres et Soeurs et
dargent avance
Doit Caisse              a la famille
pour les marchandises que j'ai vendue depuis
notre separation, et dont j'ai paye de mes
propre deptes ...........................   20  –
Doit la famille       a Compte de Ferme
pour l' erreur de larticle ci dessus

## APPENDIX 315

in the month of April, 1801, to wit: 795½ acres, besides the interest — 1193 25

Debit Family     To Farm Account
For the horse that Jean was given so that he could go to Washington to take the wine to the President — 60

66     November 29th, 1805
Debit Daniel Dufour     To Farm Account
For the horse and cattle he received from Steward, including the work that the carpenter Rector did for him — 121 27
For 15 barrels of corn that he got on the Ohio — 15 00

Debit the following     To Farm Account
Betens, for a cow from Steward    13.
Siebental    ditto    12. — 25 00

Debit Farm Account     To Cash
For what I paid the following to build me a fence around 16 acres of land in Switzerland to plant an orchard
To Sibental    21 4/6
To Bell    25. — 46 75
                do.

Debit Farm Account     To Cash
For one share in the Vineyard Company bought from Wibel — 50 00

67     January 1st, 1806
Debit The Vineyard Company     To Family
In addition to what I have debited them with for myself, page 57, for my wages, those of my brothers and sisters, and for money advanced — 4647 64

Debit Cash     To Family
For merchandise I sold since we dissolved partnership and with which I paid some of my own debts — 20 00

Debit Family     To Farm Account
For the error in the above entry;

parce que la Separation de la famille ayant eu lieu en Octobre 1804, le 21 Mars 1805 jai regle compte avec la vigne et la balance en ma faveur etoit .................. 683 47
dont il faut deduire ce que porte p 57 ........................ 134 47 [136 47]
et pour 3 ans de salaire fait..... 3000

3549 00

qui etoit la vraie Some que je devois porte ainsi pour ballancer je porte ici........... 1098 64
laquelle somme je me suis acquis et porte en debit de la Societe de la vigne depuis notre Separation
toutes ces entrees relativement a nos fonds dans la Societé de la vigne ne servent qua faire voir que ce n'est pas moi

68
moi qui suis en gain avec mes freres Car jai determine par le partage mentioné ci devant page 59, comment j'entends que nous nous partagions, ils peuvent etre utile en Cas que mes freres ou mon Pere refuse de signer ce partage

4° 1806
Doit Jean François      a Compte de Ferme pour miel quil a vendu a Robert Dow et le Cabaretier de Nicolasville                8 50

11° Janvier 1806
Doit la Societé de la vigne      a Jeanne Marie pour ce quelle me avancè pour elle dont je reste caution payable a mon retour................ 38 –
Doit Caisse       a       Jean François pour argent avancé pour paye Roux         2 94

## APPENDIX

for the termination of our partnership having occurred in October 1804, on March 21, 1805 I settled accounts with the Vineyard, and the balance in my favor was                                            $683  47
From which must be deducted what I have entered, p. 57,......   $134  47
And for 3 years of wages amounting to                            $3000

making ......................  $3549  00
which was the real amount I should have entered.
And so to balance I enter here                                          1098  64
Which amount I have earned, and I debit the same to the Vineyard Company from the termination of our partnership.
All these entries concerning our funds in the Vineyard Co. are merely intended to show

68

that I have not taken advantage of my brothers, for I have determined by the division of property mentioned above, p. 59, how I think we should share. These entries may be useful in case my brothers or my father refuse to sign that plan of division.

[January] 4th, 1806
Debit Jean François     To Farm Account
For honey he sold to Robert Dow and the saloon keeper of Nicolasville              8  50

January 11th, 1806
Debit Vineyard Company     To Jeanne Marie
For the amount she advanced me for it, for which I stand security, payable on my return     38  00
Debit Cash          To Jean François
For money advanced to pay Roux              2  94

69                Janvier 21° 1806
Doit Caisse              a              Weber
pour argent preté pour mon voyage.......... 4  50
item pour le fraix fait chez lui.............. 5  —
Doit Caisse              a              Robert
pour ce quil ma donné a compte des gants et
tabatiéres quil a avendre.................... 8
Doit Caisse              a              Clay
pour ce quil ma preté pour mon voyage...... 155
              13me Fevrier
Doit Caisse         a         Jean Francois
pour ce que monsieur Payen ma remis pour lui a 14  12
              le 16
Doit voyage              a              Caisse
pour les fraix de mon voyage de Lexington a
Washington City ou Jarrive ce jourdui Chez M.
Villard ..................................... 15  50

70
        Washington City ce 18me Fevrier 1806
Doit Voyage                         a Caisse
pour ce que jai payè pour faire publier mon invention et mon Cheval dans la Gazette........ 2  —
item pour 1½ boisseau de mayes et 1 main de
papier ...................................... 1  25
              20me
Doit voyage                         a Caisse
pour du mais pour mon Cheval.............. 1  87
pour du papier.............................     25
pour fruit ..................................     50
              23°
Doit voyage                         a Caisse
pour ma pension............................ 4
              25°
Doit Caisse              a Compte de ferme
pour ce que jai retire de la vente de mon cheval
a M. Bard, avec selle et bride              60
Doit voyage                         a Caise
pour ce que jai donné au Jeune homme     1

## APPENDIX

69    January 21st, 1806
Debit Cash       To Weber
For money lent for my voyage    4 50
Item, for expense incurred at his place  5 00
Debit Cash       To Robert
For what he gave me on account for the gloves
and snuffboxes he has for sale     8
Debit Cash       To Clay
For the amount he lent me for my voyage 15
     February 13th
Debit Cash    To Jean François
For what Mr. Payen gave me for him  14 12
     February 16th
Debit Traveling      To Cash
For the expense of my trip from Lexington
to Washington City where I have arrived
this day at Mr. Villard's      15 50

70
Washington City, this 18th of February, 1806
Debit Traveling      To Cash
For the amount I paid to have my invention
and my horse advertised in the Gazette  2 00
Item, for 1½ bushels of corn, and one quire
of paper           1 25
      20th
Debit Traveling      To Cash
For corn for my horse      1 87
For paper            25
For fruit            50
      23rd
Debit Traveling      To Cash
For my board and lodging     4
      25th
Debit Cash     To Farm Account
For what I received from the sale of my
horse to Mr. Bard, with saddle and bridle 60
Debit Traveling      To Cash
For what I gave the young man   1

et pour le foin pour mon Cheval 1 2
pour un dessein d'une poue a vapeur 1
pour du fruit et liqueur 50
71   Washington City 2 Mars 1806
Doit voyage a   Caisse
pour ma Pension chez monsieur Villard...... 4 –
         8me
Doit voyage   a Caisse
pour ma place dans le Stage de Georgetown 4 –
pour ma pension blanchisage et trinkgelt 5 50
Doit Clay   a Caisse
pour ce que jai remis a M. Thruston pour lui remettre .................................... 15 –
         9me
Doit voyage   a Caisse
pour fraix jusqua Baltimore ou j'arive ce jour 50
      Baltimore ce 10me Mars
Doit voyage   a Caisse
pour fraix dici et provision pour a bord du paqueboat ................................. 75
                                                                          63
pour mon passage jusqua Frenchtown 1 50
         11
Doit voyage   a Caisse
pour mon logement a Frenchtown 25
et passage dans le stage jusqua Newcastel 1 25
72   Philadelphie ce 12me Mars 1806
Doit voyage   a Caisse
pour mon passage sur le paqueboat depuis Newcastel ................................. 1 –
pour une pinte deau de vie.................. 19
         17me
Doit voyage   a Caisse
pour fruit, liqueur, papier pain & 1 50
pour racomodage d'habit.................. 1
         24me
Doit voyage   a Caisse
pour ma pension pendant mon sejour a Philadelphie ................................. 4 63

## APPENDIX 321

| | | |
|---|---:|---:|
| And for hay for my horse | 1 | 2 |
| For a drawing of a steam wheel [?] | | 1 00 |
| For fruit and liquor | | 50 |

71  Washington City, March 2, 1806
Debit Traveling                To Cash
For my board and lodging at Mr. Villard's     4 00

           8th
Debit Traveling                To Cash
For my fare on the Georgetown Stage          4 00
For my board and lodging, laundry and tips   5 50
Debit Clay                     To Cash
For the amount I gave Mr. Thruston to give
to him                                      15 00

           9th
Debit Traveling                To Cash
For expenses till I reached Baltimore today    50
       Baltimore, this 10th of March
Debit Traveling                To Cash
For expenses here, and provisions to take      75
on board the boat                              63
For my fare to Frenchtown                    1 50

           11
Debit Traveling                To Cash
For my lodging in Frenchtown                   25
and fare on the stage to Newcastle           1 25

72  Philadelphia, this 12th of March, 1806
Debit Traveling                To Cash
For my passage on packet-boat from New-
castle                                       1 00
For a pint of brandy                           19

           17th
Debit Traveling                To Cash
For fruit, liquor, paper, bread and          1 50
For mending coat                             1

           24th
Debit Traveling                To Cash
For my board and lodging during my stay in
Philadelphia                                 4 63

pour mon passage sur le paquet de Burlington .................................... 25
pour provision                                    33
pour mon Lit a Burlington.............. 12½ [?]

### 25
Doit voyage                a Caisse
pour mon passage par le Stage dAmboy.. 2 30
pour mon dejeune a Crambery.......... 47

### 26°
Doit voyage          ,       a Caisse
pour mon Lit a Amboy................. 15

### 27
Arive a Newyork a minuit payé le lit.... 13
et le dejeuné......................... 38
73    Newyorck ce 28me Mars 1806
Doit voyage                a Caisse
pour une Male........................ 4

### 1° Avril
Doit voyage                      a Caisse
pour les objets suivants come provision pour mon passage de la mer jusqua Bourdeaux
pour fermer une Caisse............. 50
56 Lb de biscuit................... 3 25
98—de ris ........................ 1 63
9¾ de fromage..................... 1 27
11½ de jambon.................... 1 75
20 sucre .......................... 2 50
14 de raisains..................... 1 78
6½ de chocolat.................... 2 12
deux emetique et 2 once de cremede tar   25
une casserole ⎫
un pot de fer blanc ⎪
deux tin cup ⎬ 1 80
une culliere ⎪
et une fourchette ⎭

APPENDIX

| | | |
|---|---|---|
| For my fare on the Burlington packet | | 25 |
| For provisions | | 33 |
| For my bed in Burlington | | 12½[?] |
| 25 | | |
| Debit Traveling      To Cash | | |
| For my fare on the Amboy stage | 2 | 30 |
| For my breakfast at Cranbury | | 47 |
| 26th | | |
| Debit Traveling      To Cash | | |
| For my bed in Amboy | | 15 |
| 27 | | |
| Arrived in New York at midnight | | |
| Paid for my bed | | 13 |
| and breakfast | | 38 |

73  New York, this 28th of March, 1806
Debit Traveling      To Cash
For a trunk                                  4

April 1st

Debit Traveling      To Cash
For the following articles provided for my passage by sea to Bordeaux

| | | |
|---|---|---|
| A lock for a box | | 50 |
| 56 lbs. of biscuit | 3 | 25 |
| 98 " of rice | 1 | 63 |
| 9¾ of cheese | 1 | 27 |
| 11½ of ham | 1 | 75 |
| 20 of sugar | 2 | 50 |
| 14 of raisins | 1 | 78 |
| 6½ of chocolate | 2 | 12 |
| two emetics and 2 ounces of creme of tartar | | 25 |
| a sauce pan ⎫ | | |
| a tin pot ⎪ | | |
| two tin cups ⎬ | 1 | 80 |
| a spoon ⎪ | | |
| and a fork ⎭ | | |

| un Matelas .................... | 2 | - | | |
|---|---|---|---|---|
| | | | 18 | 85 |

Outre les provisions ci dessus Madame Roulet et
Monsieur Rossier ont eut la bonté de me fournir
6 Lb de Beure  2 douz oeufs, 7 bouteilles de vin
et 6 deau de vie

74            Avril le 5me 1806
Doit voyage                    a Caisse
pour une paire de Souillé.................  2  -
pour laver le linge......................       50
      dit
Doit compte de ferme       a M Rossier
de Newyork pour balance de compte reglé ce
jourdhui .............................. 184 71
       dit
Doit Mon frere Daniel,   a Compte de ferme
pour port de lettres.....................  3  -
ainsi que les suivants pour meme objet
Louis Raimond .........................  1  50
Golay ................................     25
Morerod ..............................     25
Betens ...............................     50
Sibentals ............................     50
       le 8me
Doit ferme                    a Caisse
pour les livres ci apres que je me suis achété
Un Gazetier de Morse............. 3  25
le message du President sur la Louis-
siana ........................       56
le Franc Masson................       50
                4  31

75         Newyorck ce 9me Avril 1806
Doit voyage                    a Caisse
pour ce que jai donné pour boire aux domes-
tiques a M. Rossier ou jai demeuré tout le tems
que jai éte a Newyorck..................  1  50
pour ce que jai donne a M. Thibaut.
pour mon passage jusqua Bordeaux sur le Brig

APPENDIX 325

a mattress .................... 2 00
                                       18 85

Besides the above provisions, Madame Roulet and Monsieur Rossier were kind enough to furnish me 6 lbs. of Butter, 2 doz. eggs, 7 bottles of wine, and 6 of Brandy.

74            April 5th, 1806
Debit Traveling              To Cash
For a pair of shoes                     2 00
For washing linen                         50
              do.
Debit Farm Account      To Mr. Rossier
Of New York for balance of account settled
today                                 184 71
              do.
Debit My Brother Daniel   To Farm Account
For postage on letters                  3 00
And also the following for same object
Louis Raimond                           1 50
Golay                                     25
Morerod                                   25
Betens                                    50
Sibentals                                 50
              8th
Debit Farm                   To Cash
For the following books I bought for myself;
Morse's Gazeteer               3 25
the President's Message on Louisiana  56
The Free Mason                 50
                                        4 31

75   New York, this 9th of April, 1806
Debit Traveling              To Cash
For the tips I gave to the servants of Mr. Rossier where I lodged the whole time I was in New York                        1 50
For what I paid Mr. Thibaut for my passage to Bordeaux on board the brig *Young Ed-*

Young Edward Capitaine Paterson Moris, dans le Stirage .................................... 50 –
pour faire mener mon butin a bord........... – 32
a deux heures levé lencre et sorti du Port.
     Plimouth en Angletere ce 15° May
Doit voyage a                         Caisse
pour ports de lettres reçue de Londre de M. F. Perret ........................................... 44
a 100 lieues de Bourdeaux nous avons été pris par un vaisseau aglois et conduit a Plimouth le 4 de May ou nous somme arivé le 12 et reste en quarantaine jusquau 5° de juin
76        Plimouth ce 7me Juin 1806
Pris un Passeport pour me rendre a Londre
Doit voyage                     a Caisse
pour les article Suivant acheté et payé a Plimouth
de la regalisse........................... 4
pour pontonage ........................ 2
de la biere............................12
                                          —      18
             8 me
Doit Caisse         a M. Rossier de Newyorck
pour ce que jai tire sur eux en faveur du Capitaine Moris chez M. Coudere a Bourdeau...... 10 –
Doit voyage                     a Caisse
pour metre fait transporter a bord du Paket de Portsmouth ................................. – 23
pour ce que jai perdu avec un matelot a qui javois vendu a credit une paire de pentalon.... 1
             Portsmouth ce 11me
Doit voyage                     a Caisse
pour mon passage de Plimouth ici....... 2.37
item jusqua Londre dans la diligence.... 3.12
et pour ma male pesant 70Lb........... 1.68
pour aller a terre.................... .12
                                        —    7  29

## APPENDIX

*ward*, Captain Paterson Moris, in the steerage | 50 | 00
To have my belongings brought on board | | 32
At two o'clock weighed anchor and sailed out of port.

  Plymouth, England, this 16th of May
Debit Traveling       To Cash
For postage on letters received from London from Mr. F. Perret | | 44
A hundred leagues from Bordeaux we were captured by an English ship and taken to Plymouth on May 4, where we arrived on the 12th and remained in quarantine till June 5th.

76 Plymouth, this 7th of June, 1806
Secured a passport to go to London
Debit Traveling       To Cash
For following articles bought and paid for in Plymouth
Liquorice     4
For bridge toll   2
Beer      12 | | 18

       8th
Debit Cash   To Mr. Rossier of New York
For a draft I drew on them in favor of Captain Moris, through Mr. Coudere in Bordeaux | 10 | 00
Debit Traveling       To Cash
For having had myself carried on board the Portsmouth packet | | 23
For what I lost in selling a pair of pantaloons to a sailor on credit | 1 |

  Portsmouth, this 11th of June
Debit Traveling      To Cash
For my passage from Plymouth here   2   37
Item, to London in the stagecoach   3   12
And for my trunk weighing 70 lbs.   1   68
to go on land         12
            ——— | 7 | 29

77       Londre ce 12me Juin 1806
Doit voyage                          a Caisse
pour les fraix suivants fait aujourdhui ici ou
jarive ce matin.........................
au Coché .............................. 12
au porteur de mamale a lauberg......... 12
dejeuné ............................... 28
la Chambre ........................... 23
au valet ..............................  4
au porteur de ma male dans mon logement 40
                                         ——    1   19

       ce 15 et 27me Juin inclusi
Doit voyage                         a Caisse
pour les fraix suivant fait a Londre
pour de la piere............Sterl. - -  2
du papier et une brosse............. 2   -
pour 3 oranges.....................  -   3
au bureau des Rolls pour voir une
record ............................  3   6
pour 2Lb¾ de fromage............  1  10+
de la Biere........................      2
pour voir St. Paul.................      4+
pour du lait Caillé................      1
pour du bouillon...................      4
item et autre fraix................     11+
pour une Carte.................... 1     -
une bouteille de gome elastique...... 1  -
                                       ————
                                        11   7
78                          Transport de page 77
                    Sterlin -  11   7
pour 4 Lb de biscuit pour provision.  2   -
   3   de Jambon ............    1  10
pour blanchissage ...............   4   1
Logement pour 15 jour...........   18   -

## APPENDIX

77  London, this 12th of June, 1806
Debit Traveling                To Cash
For following expenses incurred here today,
where I arrived this morning—

| | |
|---|---:|
| To the coachman | 12 |
| To the porter who carried my trunk to the inn | 12 |
| Breakfast | 28 |
| Room | 23 |
| To the valet | 4 |
| To the porter who carried my trunk to my lodgings | 40 |

                                          1  19

This June 15th to 27th, inclusive
Debit Traveling                To Cash
For the following expenses in London:

| | | | |
|---|---:|---:|---:|
| For beer | Sterl. 0 | 0 | 2 |
| Paper and brush | | 2 | |
| For 3 oranges | | | 3 |
| To the Office of the Rolls to see a record | | 3 | 6 |
| For 2¾ lbs. cheese | | 1 | 10+ |
| Beer | | | 2 |
| To see St. Paul | | | 4+ |
| For clabbermilk | | | 1 |
| For bouillon | | | 4 |
| Item, and other expense | | | 11+ |
| For a map | | 1 | |
| An India rubber bottle | | 1 | |

                                         11   7

78        Brought forward from page 77
                           Sterl. 0  11   7

| | | |
|---|---:|---:|
| For 4 lbs. biscuit for provision | 2 | |
| 3 of ham | 1 | 10 |
| For laundry | 4 | 1 |
| Lodging for 15 days | 18 | |

| | | | | | |
|---|---|---|---|---|---|
| pour le transport de mes males a bord du paquet de Gravesend...... | | 1 | 8+ | | |
| | 1 | 19 | 2 | | |
| pour otre fraix omis............ | | 1 | 10 | | |
| a/50 pour 11 piastres | 2 | 1 | 0 | 9 | 2 |

Londre ce 27 Juin

Doit Caisse a  Monsieur Perret de Londre pour ce quil ma preté payable a M Colomb Johannot le 30me Aoust 1806 L 20 Sterlin a 16 L Suisse pour fait en piastre  88 —

Gravesend ce 27me Juin

Doit voyage  a Caisse

| | | | | |
|---|---|---|---|---|
| pour les fraix fait ici du pain....S | — | 1 | 3½ | |
| du beure 1½ Lb............... | | 1 | 8+ | |
| une vessie pour une bource....... | | | 3+ | |
| un fromage de Holande 7 Lb..... | | 2 | 1 | |
| pour mon passage de Londre ici.. | | 2 | — | |
| pour me mettre a bord dun vaisseau Hollandois pour aller a Roterdam.. | | 5 | 7+ | |
| Sterlin | | 13 | 0 | 2  86 |

79  Brile ce 28me Juin 1806

Doit Voyage  a Caisse pour les fraix fait ici ou je suis arrive aujourdhui et de tenu jusquau 7me Juillet......................

| | | | |
|---|---|---|---|
| pour vivre pendant la detention ................ | moneye d Hol Guild 4 | 4 | — |
| pour des cerise 2Lb a/4 la Lb....... | | 8 | — |
| pour du bouillon................. | | 8 | — |
| pour le vin au matelots........... | | 12 | — |
| pour me mettre a bord du batiment pour aller a Rotterdam........... | | 5 | — |

## APPENDIX 331

For putting my trunks on board the
Gravesend packet                              1  8+
                                           ─────────
                                            1 19  2
For other expenses omitted [above]          1 10
                                           ─────────
At 50 [shillings] for 11 dollars     2  1  0        9  02
         London, this June 27
Debit Cash              To Monsieur Perret
of London for what he lent me, payable to
Mr. Colombe Johannot, August 30th, 1806;
counting 20 livres [shillings] Sterling to 16
livres, Swiss; this is in dollars                  88  00
         Gravesend, this 27th of June
Debit Traveling            To Cash
For expenses here:
Bread          Sterling [shillings]  1  3½
Butter 1½ lb.                         1  8+
A bladder for a purse                    3+
A Dutch cheese, 7 lbs.                2  1
For my fare from London here          2  0
To take passage on a Dutch ship
to go to Rotterdam                    5  7+
                                     ─────────
                     Sterling 13  0              2  86

79    Brielle, this 28th of June, 1806
Debit Travel                    To Cash
For expenses incurred here where I arrived
this morning; will be detained till July 7th—
Living expenses during   Dutch money
my detention             Guilders    4  4  —
For cherries 2 lbs. at /4 per lb.    8     —
For bouillon                         8     —
For wine to the sailors             12     —
For getting on board ship to Rot-
terdam                               5     —

pour mon passage................  16   –
                                 ─────────
                         Guilder 6 13   –
la ginee a 12g[?] fait en piastre...........   2  56

     Roterdam 7 & 10 Juillet incl
Doit Voyage                           a Caisse
pour fraix fait ici pour la brouette..   4   –
pour mon voyage dici a la Haye et
revenir le 9m...................  1   3   6
une coefe de chapeau.............  1
pour voir un moulin..............      2   –
autre fraix .....................      –   6
pour un pain pesent apeu pres 1½ Lb   3   4
                                     ─────────
                                      2  10   –      96

80      Rotterdam ce 10me Juillet 1806
Doit voyage a                          Caisse
pour les fraix suivants fruit, argend
d H ............................      3   –
pour mes passeports chez le consul
Amé ...........................  5   –   –
Mes depends a Marechal de Turenne 5   6   –
pour visa de Mon passe port Chez le
C. françois ....................  2   –   –
pour du Geneivre................      1   –
pour mon passage a Dort avec mamale ..........................     14   4
a Dort pour un commissionaire.....    2
le Genievre ....................      1   –
                                     ─────────
                       Guilder   13   7   4     4  98

     Breda 12
Doit Voyage                           a Caisse
pour mon passage ici..............  1  16   –

## APPENDIX

| | | | |
|---|---|---|---|
| For my passage | 16 | – | |
| Guilders | 6 | 13 | |
| Counting the guinea at 12 guilders[?], this is in dollars | | | 2 56 |

Rotterdam, July 7–10 incl.
Debit Travel — To Cash

| | | | |
|---|---|---|---|
| For expenses here for the truck | 4 | | |
| For my trip from here to the Hague and return on the 9th | 1 | 3 | 6 |
| A lining for a hat | 1 | | |
| To see a mill | 2 | | |
| Other expenses | | 6 | |
| For a loaf of bread weighing about 1½ lb. | 3 | 4 | |
| | 2 | 10 0 | 96 |

80    Rotterdam, this 10th of July, 1806
Debit Traveling — To Cash
For the following (Dutch money)

| | | | |
|---|---|---|---|
| Fruit | 3 | | |
| For my passports from American Consul | 5 | | |
| My expenses at the Marechal de Turenne | 5 | 6 | |
| For viséing my passport at the French Consul's | 2 | | |
| For gin | 1 | | |
| For my passage to Dort with my trunk | 14 | 4 | |
| At Dort for a porter | 2 | | |
| For gin | 1 | | |
| Guilders | 13 | 7 4 | 4 98 |

Breda, [July] 12
Debit Traveling — To Cash
For my passage here        1 16 –

pour la diligence a moitie chemin
dAnvers ........................ 1   7  –

le 13me
pour logement et depends a Breda        9
pour ma malle jusqua Anvers      1   16
le 14 Arrivé a Anvers. resté chez M.
Obousier jausquau 18me matin
payé pour mon passeport..........       4
pour vin a la Servante............      8
                                   ─────────
                        Guild. 6   0         2   30

81      Boon ce 18me Juillet 1806
Doit Voyage                     a Caisse
pour fraix ici.....................  –   6   4
pour mon Passage a Bruxelle.......      10   –
le 19 mon Logement a Hall.........      14   –
                                   ─────────
                        Guild. 1   10  4    –   59

              Hall ce 19me
Doit Voyage                     a Caisse
pour les fraix de route Suivant,
compte argent de france, mon dejeune 1   1   4
autre fraix ....................         1   6
Diné a Mons....................          6   4
le 20r. paye mon Logement a Jemape      14   –
fruit, pain et fromage............      12   –
eau de vie a Moucheau............        1   4
le 21 Loge a Cambray............. 1      –   –
Dejeune a Maniere................       10   –
biere et fruit....................       5   –
Diné a Peronne..................        14   –
le 22 loge a deux lieues de Perronne..  14   –
Dejeune a Roy...................        10   2
du cidre en Route................        2   –

## APPENDIX

| | | | | |
|---|---|---|---|---|
| For stagecoach one-half the way to Antwerp | 1 | 7 | – | |
| 13th | | | | |
| For lodging and expenses in Breda | | 9 | | |
| For my trunk as far as Antwerp | 1 | 16 | | |
| On the 14th arrived in Antwerp and stayed at Mr. Obousier's until morning of 18th | | | | |
| Paid for my passport | | 4 | | |
| For wine to the maid | | 8 | | |
| Guild. | 6 | 0 | | 2  30 |

81     Boon, this 18th of July, 1806

| | | | |
|---|---|---|---|
| Debit Traveling | To Cash | | |
| For expenses here | 6 | 4 | |
| For my passage to Brussels | 10 | | |
| The 19th, for my lodging in Hal | 14 | | |
| Guild. | 1  10 | 4 | 59 |

Hal, July 19th

Debit Traveling         To Cash
For the following expenses, in French money,

| | | | |
|---|---|---|---|
| My breakfast | 1 | 1 | 4 |
| Other expenses | | 1 | 6 |
| Dinner at Mons | | 6 | 4 |
| The 20th, paid for my lodging in Jemmapes | | 14 | |
| Fruit, bread, and cheese | | 12 | |
| Brandy at Moucheau | | 1 | 4 |
| The 21st, lodging in Cambrai | 1 | | |
| Breakfast at Masmière | | 10 | |
| Beer and fruit | | 5 | |
| Dinner at Péronne | | 14 | |
| The 22nd, lodged two leagues from Péronne | | 14 | |
| Breakfast at Roye | | 10 | 2 |
| Cider on the way | | 2 | |

le 23 a Etray St Denis logement.... 1  8  –

7  19  6

82

Pond ce 23° Juillet 1806

Doit                                    Voyage
a Caisse pour les frais suivants
ici dejeune—argent de france....    –  10  –
Diné a Senlis....................       8  –
pour le diligence jusqua Paris....  10  15  –

L 11  13  –

A Paris le 24°
Doit Voyage et harde           a Caisse
Pour les habits que je me suis
achette une Culotte.............  11   –  –
une veste ....................    7
une paire de Bas..............    4  10  –
une Chemise .................     9   –  –
des boucles .................         10  –

L 32

le 29° Change a Paris 9 guinees un
rixtaller un Shelling Sterling et un
Escalin d'Hollande recu pour   L 241   6

le 2° Aoust
Doit Voyage et harde           a Caisse
pour les Livres suivant..................
Volney sur Lamerique..........  L 9   –
une pomme de cedre............    1

L 10

## APPENDIX

The 23rd, at Estrée St. Denis lodging     1   8

                                            7 19   6

82
Pont [Ste. Maxence], this 23rd of July, 1806
Debit                                Traveling
To Cash, for the following expenses (French money)

| | |
|---|---|
| Breakfast here | 10 |
| Dinner in Senlis | 8 |
| For the stagecoach to Paris | 10 15 |

                                        L 11 13

                     Paris, 24th
Debit Traveling and Clothing      To Cash
For the clothes I bought

| | |
|---|---|
| Pair of breeches | 11 |
| A coat | 7 |
| A pair of stockings | 4 10 |
| A shirt | 9 |
| Buckles | 10 |

                                        L 32

The 29th, changed in Paris 9 guineas one rixdollar, 1 shilling sterling, and 1 Dutch escalin, receiving for them                     L 241   6

                  August 2nd
Debit Traveling and Clothing      To Cash
For the following books

| | |
|---|---|
| Volney on America | L 9 |
| A cedar apple | 1 |

                                           10

83          Paris le 6° Aoust—1806
Doit Voyage                              a Caisse
pour les fraix suivants—
transport de ma malle a la Douane    1   6
pour droit pour malle..........      1   4
pour autre fraix a Paris........    12   —
                                    ─────────
                                    L 14  10
A Paris jai logè chez le bon ami Vincent Dufour
a qui jai causé beaucoup de fraix pour lesquels
je lui suis redevable......................
Parti pour Auxere paye pour le
Coche deau .................    L 9  10
pour mon passeport...........     5   —
pour deux mouchoirs..........     6   —
le 9 Arrive a Auxerre fraix......   1   5
a Rouvrai pour caleche........    5
fraix de bouche..............     1   —
le 10. pour logement..........        13
autre fraix ..................         9
pour pataches depuis vitau......  2  13
a Pont sur pan...............        10
loge a 3 lieues de Dijon........      6
                                  ─────────
                                  L 32   6

84          Dijon ce 11me Aoust 1806
Doit Voyage                              a Caisse
pour les fraix suivants dejeune ici...     15
pour vin ........................           2
pour un Char.....................          12
le 12 pour logement a Dole.........   1   12
pour dejeune et Boisson...........        10
pour aller a Char 3 lieus...........      10
pour voir la Saline a Salin..........      9
le 13 mon logement a Salin..........   1  12
Diné ..............................      15

# APPENDIX

83   Paris, August 6th, 1806
Debit Traveling                           To Cash
For the following expenses:
Transfer of my trunk to Customs Office   1   6
For duty on trunk                            1   4
For other expenses in Paris              12

                                         L 14 10

At Paris I lodged at the house of my good friend, Vincent Dufour, to whom I caused much expense, for which I am indebted to him.

Left for Auxerre
Paid for the barge                       L  9 10
For my passport                             5
For two handkerchiefs                       6
The 9th, arrived at Auxerre—expenses     1  5
At Rouvray for the barouche                 5
Expenses for food                        1
The 10th, for lodging                      13
Other expenses                              9
For stage from Vitteaux                  2 13
At Pont-sur-Pan[?]                         10
Lodged 3 leagues from Dijon                 6

                                         32  6

84   Dijon, this 11th of August, 1806
Debit Traveling                           To Cash
For the following expenses: break-
fast here                                  15
For wine                                    2
For wagon                                  12
The 12th for lodging at Dôle             1 12
For breakfast and drink                    10
To ride on wagon 3 leagues                 10
To see the salt pit at Salins               9
The 13th for lodging at Salins           1 12
Dinner                                     15

| | | |
|---|---:|---:|
| le 14 mon logement a 2 lieues de Pontarlier .................................. | 11 | |
| Dejeunè a Pontarlier................. | 9 | |
| pour etre a le a Char................ | 10 | |
| pour viser de mon passeport.......... | 12 | |
| Pris le Char du Postilion | | |
| Dine au ———.................... | 1 | 4 |
| a La Sara payé a Postilion........... | 12 | — |
| Le 15° Logé 2 Lieues de Lauzane[?].. | 12 | |
| Dejeune a Vevey.................... | 12 | |
| le Carosse de Lausanne a Vevey...... | 3 | — |
| Arivé Chez moi a Montreux en bonne Sante a 4 heure du Soir | | |

L 26  7   4 83

85   Montreux ce 20me Aoust 1806
Doit Caisse de Voyage a Monaye de Montreux pour les argents Suivants....................

| | L | |
|---|---:|---:|
| De Jean Pierre Dufour a Compte des Interet quil doit................argent d Suis | 16 | — |
| de la Caisse................................ | 64 | — |
| de diferente autre Chose.................... | 32 | |

112

28me
Doit Voyage                           a Caisse
pour les fraix du voyage de Lausanne fait en famille ...................................    16  —

2me 7bre
Doit Monsieur Perret de Londre a Caisse pour laquit de sa lettre de Change tirée de Londre sur moi a lordre de Collomb Johannoz du 27 Juin 1806 ............................................   320  —

86         Du 20° Fevrier 1816
Deposè chez Monsieur Ausset a Vevey

APPENDIX

| | | | |
|---|---|---|---|
| The 14th for lodging 2 leagues from Pontarlier | 11 | | |
| Breakfast at Pontarlier | 9 | | |
| For riding on a wagon | 10 | | |
| For having my passport viséed | 12 | | |
| Took the coach of the Postillon Dinner at " | 1 | 4 | |
| At LaSarraz paid the Postillon | 12 | | |
| The 15th, lodged 2 leagues from Lausanne | 12 | | |
| Breakfast at Vevey | 12 | | |
| The coach from Lausanne to Vevey | 3 | | |
| Arrived home in Montreux in good health at four in the afternoon. | | | |
| | L 26 7 | 4 | 83 |

85  Montreux, August 20th, 1806
Debit Cash for Traveling. Montreux
                                currency [?]

| | | |
|---|---|---|
| For the following sums: | | |
| From Jean Pierre Dufour on account for the interest he owes—in Swiss money | L 16 | 0 |
| From Cash | 64 | 0 |
| From various other sources | 32 | |
| | 112 | |

28th

| | | |
|---|---|---|
| Debit Traveling             To Cash | | |
| For expenses of the trip from Lausanne which was made accompanied by my family | 16 | 0 |

September 2nd

| | | |
|---|---|---|
| Debit Mr. Perret of London        To Cash | | |
| For the payment of his bill of exchange drawn from London on myself to the order of Colomb Johannoz, dated June 27th, 1806 | 320 | 0 |

86         February 20th, 1816
Deposited with Monsieur Ausset at Vevey

pour argent de route pour retourner aux Etats
Unis                                            L 1200
                    Mars 15
Acheté a Vevey de M. Hettich 28½ de toile
dAlsace pour me faire 11 Chemises pour L 51–
la façon des Chemises coute   5bz2r[?] la piece
                    Mars 26
Achete chez M. Moreillon a Vevey 5½ aunes de
toile des Indes de Coton pour 7 Chemisettes et
dont 2 Chemisettes pour mon fils a 23bz l'aune
et 3 mouch. et pour 6 mouchoirs de cou a 15 en
tout                                           L 21.6.5
jai echange ceci contre de la toille de coton du
pais
87            26 Mars 1816
Paye au tailleur pache pour façon d'un habit,
garde habit et pentalon de notre drap, ayant
fourni les boutons de fil et cordonnet.....L 12
                    "
Acheté chez Walter 4 aunes de drap gris, pour
une roupe et col. a L 8 laune............L 32
doublure ................................   4
                    "
Au tailleur Pache pour facon de la roupe et du
Col ...................................L 7
                  Avril le 20
Achette encore chez M Moreillon 3 aunes de
toille pour completter la 12ne de chemises, a
18bz laune
                  May le 2
Chez M. Hettich  19⅜ aunes de toile commune
de 42 pouces de large a 16bz laune.....L 30  4
on a fait des chemises pour mon fils
[88]            May le 2 1816
Chez Nicollier une brosse a savon...............  3bz
une paire de ciseaux.........................  12

## APPENDIX

for traveling funds to return to the United
States                                L 1200

### Mar. 15th

Bought at Vevey of Mr. Hettich 28½ of Alsatian linen to make 11 shirts for myself, for L 51 the making of the shirts costs 5 batzen 2 rappen [?] apiece

### March 26th

Bought at Mr. Moreillon's at Vevey 5½ ells of India cotton cloth for 7 shirt fronts, of which 2 are for my son, at 23 batzen an ell, and 3 handkerchiefs and goods for 6 neckerchiefs at 15 in all                         L 21.6.6

I exchanged this for homespun cotton cloth.

87         March 26, 1816

Paid the tailor Pache for making a coat, a coat protector, and pantaloons of our cloth, having furnished the buttons, the thread and the braid  L 12

### do.

Bought at Walter's 4 ells of gray cloth for a smock and collar at 8 livres an ell          L 32
Lining                                       4

### do.

To the tailor Pache for making the smock and collar                                    L 7

### April 20

Bought again at Mr. Moreillon's 3 ells of linen to complete the dozen of shirts at 19 batzen an ell.

### May 2

From Mr. Hettich 19⅜ ells of common linen, 42 inches wide, at 16 bz. an ell         L 30  4
made shirts for my son.

[88]         May 2, 1816

Bought at Nicollier's a scrubbing brush     3 batzen
A pair of scissors                          12

une brosse a dent.............................. 2.5
un pied de berne.............................. 4bz

le 4° Juin 1816

Chez M. Berdez 1⅞ de drap Bleu pour un habit a L 18 laune

3¼ de futaine olive a 38bz pour une paire de pentalon

2 aunes de toile de lin grise pour doublure à 8bz et 5 aunes ¼ de toile my blanche pour 2 grosse chemise a 14 bz

Chez M. Nicollier 6 bonnets de coton pour 51bz 2 de galette pour 18 bz

Chez Md. Doge 2 paires de bas de fil a 19bz et une paire de galette noir 30 bz

chez une autre marchande 2 paire de bas de fil a 20bz

[89] le 4 Juin 1816

Chez Madamne Moreillon—

4½ aune toille pour chemise a 16bz............ 7.6–2
¾ dito blanche à 18........................... 1.3–2
3 mouchoir de poche blanc a 9bz............... 2.7..

le 10° Juin

Chez Monsieur Mayor pour une paire de pentalon de cotone a 23bz laune 2¾

pour un gilet 50bz de swandown

le 12

pour le dernier dun gilet....13bz

de milaine 2 aunes de toile de lin a 15bz

une écharpe et une cocarde 18bz

le 20°

Pour acquité le tailleur Pache pour facon dun habit 3 pentalons, un gilet, et la founiture des boutons et fil............L 16.

[90] le 23° Juin 1816

Recu de M: Ducret Régent a Cherney la somme de L 1000. pour remettre a Marie Veuve de J. Dl Boralley

# APPENDIX

A toothbrush 2.5
A Bernese foot rule 4

### June 4th, 1816

Bought of Mr. Berdez 1⅞ of blue cloth for a coat at 18 livres an ell
3¼ of olive fustian at 38 bz. for a pair of pantaloons
2 ells of gray linen for lining at 8 bz. and 5¼ ells of half bleached linen for 2 coarse shirts at 14bz.

Bought of Mr. Nicolier, 6 cotton nightcaps for 51 bz., 2 of floss silk for 18 bz.

Of Mrs. Doge, 2 pairs of lisle stockings at 19 bz. and one pair of black floss silk at 30 bz.

Of another tradeswoman, 2 pairs of lisle stockings at 20 bz.

[89] June 4th, 1816

Of Madame Moreillon

| | | |
|---|---|---|
| 4½ ells of linen for shirt at 16 bz | | 7.6–2 |
| ¾ " " bleached linen at 18 | | 1.3–2 |
| 3 white pocket handkerchiefs at 9 | | 2.7 |

### June 10th

Of Mr. Mayor for a pair of cotton pantaloons at 23 bz. an ell, 2¾ for a vest, 50 bz worth of swansdown

### 12th

for a vest back, 13 bz. worth of half wool cloth, 2 ells of linen at 15 bz., a scarf and a cockade, 18 bz.

### 20th

To pay the tailor Pache for making a coat, 3 pantaloons, a vest, and furnishing the buttons and thread L 16

[90] June 23rd, 1816

Received of Mr. Ducret, schoolmaster at Cherney the sum of 1000 livres to deliver to Marie, the widow of J. Dl. Boralley.

dit
Recu de Juge Vuichoud pour Daniel la Somme
de L 33.1.5
A mon arrivé Jai payé les deux sommes ci
dessus

do.

Received of Judge Vuichoud, for Daniel, the sum of L 33.1.5

On my arrival I paid the above two sums.

# NOTES

## NOTES

[Page 1]  ¹ The confederacy was composed of five tribes of Iroquoian stock, the Mohawk, Oneida, Onondaga, Cayuga, and Seneca, to which the Tuscaroras were afterward added. [Ed.]

[Page 2]  ¹ Autographs in the Pennsylvania State Library show the correct spelling of this officer's name to be "Lochry," but the creek is known by the corrupt form "Laughery." Laughery Creek is not within the present Switzerland County, but through divisions of the original territory, has become the boundary between Dearborn and Ohio counties. A monument commemorating the massacre of Colonel Lochry and his men has been erected in Riverview Cemetery, near Aurora. [Ed.]

² The following paragraphs, given by Dufour as an extract from Lieutenant Anderson's journal, are not direct quotations as his punctuation suggests. For a reprint of the journal, see James McBride, *Pioneer Biography. Sketches of the Lives of Some of the Early Settlers of Butler County, Ohio,* 1:278 ff. (Cincinnati, 1869).

[Page 6]  ¹ The proclamation of Governor William Henry Harrison for the erection of Dearborn County was dated March 7, 1803. The date of the organizing act for Jefferson County was November 23, 1810. *Indiana Historical Collections,* 7:84 (Indianapolis, 1922); *Acts of the Indiana Territory,* 1810, pp. 14-15.

[Page 7]  ¹ *Acts of the Indiana Territory,* 1814, pp. 30 ff.

² "I will not promise that the style of composition will be so fascinating as to induce it to be read but that the incidents related, will enable the reader to learn of the hardships and privations as well as dangers endured by the early settlers.

"It has been suggested that in the presentation of these incidents I should not be too reserved and modest in giving a full history of the Dufour family who founded the Swiss Colony of 'New Switzerland.'

"I will necessarily have much to say of that family and their associates, who braved the voyage across the Broad Atlantic, leaving the ease, comforts and luxuries of an old and wealthy country, a country that dated its settlement back to the time of Ceasar, to [found] a new home in the then wi[l]derness of the great [land] of America, where the whoop of the Indian, [and] the howl of the Wolf would greet their ears, in[stead] of the sound of the Church bell, and the busy hum and clatter of men hurrying to and from the daily avocations of Civilized life.

"I hope you, and all who read this history will judge of the Style, and composition charitably.

"I will therefore commence with a short history of the Dufour family and of their settlement of 'New Switzerland' as their colony was named

"PERRET DUFOUR"

This introduction appeared in the original draft of the 1876 manuscript, but was omitted in its revision.

² Following the occupation of Switzerland by the French in 1798, the old cantonal system of government was abolished and the Helvetic Republic created. It existed, under the dictation of Napoleon, until 1803, when the cantonal system was reëstablished. *Cambridge Modern History*, 9:96-105 (New York, 1906).

[Page 9]  ¹ John Brown was senator from Kentucky from 1791 until 1805. [Ed.]

² See *post*, 13 ff.

[Page 15]  ¹ Dufour, *Vine-Dresser's Guide*, 7-10.

[Page 16]  ¹ United States, *Statutes at Large*, 6:47-48.

[Page 18]  ¹ "In crossing the Atlantic Ocean, the vessel in which he had taken passage, was captured by an English man of War and taken to Plymouth on the 4th of May 1806. He remained in England not being permitted to depart, until the 5th of June following—when he departed on his journey to Switzerland." 1869 MS., p. 19.

² "Which payment would become due in 1812." *Ibid.*, p. 19.

³ United States, *Statutes at Large*, 2:712.

[Page 21]  ¹ "Many persons have enquired, what the word 'Blanc' attached to the name Daniel Dufour meant. . . . .

"In Switzerland in Europe, and perhaps in some other countries of Continental Europe it is or was the comtom [custom] to attach the family name of the wife to the name of the husband; for instance Daniel Dufour married a woman whose family name was 'Blanc' so after his marriage to her he wrote his name 'Daniel Dufour Blanc, so with Mr Zelim Humbert, he married for his first wife a woman whose family name was 'Droz' after his marriage he wrote his name 'Zelim Humbert Droz', so with Mr Louis Gex, he married for his first wife a woman whose family name was Oboussier, after his marriage he wrote his name Louis Gex Oboussier; these three persons are believed to be the only instances among the Swiss who first settled here, who, conformed to that Custom, they having married in Europe." 1869 MS., p. 60.

[Page 22]  [1] "In 1803 some of these families came from the first Vineyard in Kentucky to these lands—Jean Dl. Morerod, and Philip Bettens moved into a cabin that had been erected by some 'squatter' on the public lands near where Charles Norrisez house stands—and remained there together, until they could build themselves, cabins on, their respective tracts of land, which lie adjoined." Ibid., p. 1.

[Page 24]  [1] "Improvements began to be made at other points along the river above where Vevay now stands—and the lands on which Vevay was laid out were being cleared up Daniel Dufour having commenced in 1804 to make an opening between where William Hall resides and U.P. Schenks Warehouse—and John F Dufour (who was yet at the first vineyard) had hired some person to commence an opening on his land, between where Vineyard and Liberty Streets now run." Ibid., pp. 4-5.

[Page 26]  [1] "He was one week in getting to Port William. The Ohio river was so high that the back water ran up the Kentucky river to Frankfort—making it necessary to row the small boat, in which the voyage was made. On arriving at Port William it was found impossible for him to get up the Ohio to the place of his destination alone so leaving the boat, with his wife, and only child, and what articles of household goods were on board he walked up to New Switzerland, to get some of his friends from there to go and help him up with the small boat. On the next morning they started up the river, and at night arrived at the mouth of Indian creek." Ibid., pp. 19-20.

[2] Buckner Thruston was senator from Kentucky from 1805 until 1811. [Ed.]

[Page 30]  [1] "As these colonists had been accustomed to use good cold spring water in their native country, which came gushing out of the mountains it was very natural, that they should in some manner furnish themselves, with, such a necessary beverage in this, their new home—and as there were no Springs they had to resort to the digging of wells. Mr Morerod had one dug near his house sometime in 1812 or 13, others were dug in the Settlement; the depth of the wells, in the river bottom near Vevay were from 85 to 90 feet. Mr Morerods was about 85 feet deep.

"On the 7th of August 1815 John Francis Dufour entered into a written Contract with William Scott and Samuel Smith, to dig, curb with timber, and wall up with stone a well at or near the corner of said Dufours dwelling house in the town of Vevay Indiana Territory—said well was to be of the same dimensions as to width, and thickness of the walls as that of Jean Daniel Morerod near Vevay, and to be of such a depth as always to have at least three feet of water in it,—in walling up that part where the water would rise to, moss was to be put between the stones to prevent the sand from getting through;—the curbing was to be commenced with the digging; as the well would be near the corner of said Dufours house, the said Scott and Smith obligated themselves to pay said Dufour all damages that might be occasioned to his house in case the said well or any part thereof should cave in before it was completely finished and for two years after wards. The well was to be completely finished by the 1st of November following, for which work said Dufour obligated himself to pay to said Scott and Smith two Dollars and Eighty Seven and a half cents per foot for every foot said well should measure in depth when completely finis[h]ed, to the depth of Seventy feet, and three Dollars per foot for every foot over and above Seventy feet. The well was finished and was at the North corner of Market and Main Cross Street, near the corner of the lot on which William Archer now resides; that well was used by the whole town for a number of years. It measured when completed 87 feet in depth, and was in constant use untill about the year 1839 or 1840, when cisterns began to be built in considerable numbers, in the town, when the use of the well was dispensed with and filled up." 1869 MS., pp. 103-105.

[Page 31] [1] "In the early days of Vevay, what few youth were about the town did not enjoy the privileges and benefits of having good Schools, such as the youth of Vevay have at the present day.

"In 1816, 1817 and 1818, the first School was opened, in which Greek and Latin, and the higher branches of English literature were taught. This school was conducted by Alexander Holton, who gave public notice of his school in the following card, published in the *Indiana Register,* in November, 1817.    'NOTICE'
'The Subscriber has opened a school in the Town of Vevay, State 'of Indiana, which he calculates, personally, to superintend. The 'branches of Literature he will teach, and the terms of Tuition 'per quarter, are as follows; to wit: Reading $3.00. Reading and 'writing, $3.50. Mathamatics, in its various branches—Geography 'and English Grammar, $4.00    Greek and Latin Languages $5.00.

## NOTES

'He flatters himself that from the long habit of teaching the above 'branches of literature, particularly the languages, and Mathe-'matics, that he shall be enabled to give Satisfaction to all persons 'who shall favor him with their patronage.'
" 'ALEXANDER HOLTON'

" 'VEVAY, Novr 18, 1817.

"Mr. Holton was an accomplished scholar, and his school was well patronized, considering the small number of scholars in the town and vicinity to be taught.

"A Mr Wilson, a Baptist preacher, taught a school in Vevay in a small log house which stood on Ferry Street, on the lower part of the lot on which the Russell House now stands. That house had previously been occupied as a horse-mill, but about the time of its occupancy as a place where the young idea was taught to shoot, the mill was removed from town. This was in the fall of 1815. In Mr Wilsons school, Orthography, reading and writing only were taught.

"James Rous, the father of Zadig & Percy Rous, in 1814 and 1815, taught school in the Seminary of Vevay, which was a one-story hewed log house, about twenty or twenty five feet long, by twelve or fifteen feet wide, with a door in one end, and for win-dows to give light, one log on each side, at the proper heighth, was cut out, and a sash with perhaps twenty or twenty five lights of glass in each, in a single row, was fitted into the opening made for the window. In this house the writer was a scholar for a year or more, and among his school-mates who attended that school, he can now name but few who are living: John Scott, now Dr Scott, of New York City, brother-in-law of James Cole, Rebecca Cole, now the wife of Enos Littlefied, Esqr, who left this place about one year ago for Texas, and perhaps William W. Huston, of York Township.

"Mrs Julia L. Dumont, whose reputation as a successful teacher is well known in this community, commenced, teaching perhaps about the year 1820, and for many years delighted to give in-struction and her kind advice to the boys and girls who were placed under her care for educational purposes. She was per-haps the most successful and efficient teacher that ever imparting [imparted] instruction in Vevay. This by no means is said to detract, from the merits of any who have been called to teach in our public Schools since she ceased from teaching. Many of the present fathers and mothers of Vevay, who were pupils under Mrs Dumont, and obtained their education under her teaching, lived to see their children receive their education, so far as the English language was taught, by her and under her instruction.

"A sister of the Hon John Dumont, Mrs Jane Steele, who afterwards married Mr Jessee Murphy, taught a school in a frame building on Pike street, not far from the corner of Union & Pike streets. She taught for some time. The writer attended her school, but cannot recollect how long, or who were his class mates, with one exception, a Miss Catharine Anderson, the wife of the Hon. Isaac Naylor, of Crawfordsville, Indiana.

"Sylvanus Waldo, a brother to the father of O.S. and F.J. Waldo, taught school here, but the length of time is not recollected, nor the year during which he taught. He was taken sick while his school was being carried on, and it is thought he died from the effects of that sickness.

"One James Brown taught a school in the log house which stood on the lots on Main Street now Occupied by R. F. Grisard. This school was kept for several years, and although Mr Brown was reputed a cross and severe teacher, yet his scholars improved rapidly under his tuition. In that school the writer made most of his advance in his studies. Most of his school mates in that School have removed from this place; but a majority of them have been called to that 'bourne from whence no traveller returns.' This school was taught perhaps in 1820, 21 & 22.

"At one time—the exact date not recollected—one Wick commenced a school in a frame building which stood on Main Street nearly opposite the Court House, which was continued but a short time, for want of sufficient patronage. Whether it was the Hon. Wm W. Wick, a brother of his, or a relative, is not now known. He came well recommended, but as there were several schools in progress in the town at the time, he did not on that account receive sufficient patronage.

"Some time during the year 1822 or 1823, Isaac B. Kinsman, a down-easter, from the banks of the Kennebec, river in the State of Maine, came to Vevay, and commenced school teaching. He was a good Scholar, and capable of teaching Latin, Greek and Hebrew. He continued teaching school at intervals until perhaps in the fall of 1825. He was in the habit of indulging too freely in the use of intoxicating liquors, which unfitted him at times for his avocation. He had a very good school, and gave general satisfaction in his teaching, for he never kept his school open while intoxicated. In 1824, in April of that year, he concluded to abandon school teaching, and turn his attention to trading. Accordingly he gave notice that he wished to purchase a large quantity of 'Turkeys,' 'Ducks' and 'Good chickens', to be delivered in Vevay on three certain days of the week following, for which he promised to pay in Specie, for chickens, fifty cents per Dozen, for a single dozen, or 62½ cents per dozen for five Dozen or more, brought at one time by the same person. Same price for Ducks, and 25 cents a piece for Turkeys.

"He collected together a good number of each, and took them down the river, making quite a good speculation by the operation. He was a ready writer, and the paper published in Vevay at the time was made interesting by his contributions. One of his articles published in the *Indiana Register*, September 17, 1824 reads thus:

"'MR KEEN—Report says the books belonging to the Auditor's 'office, under the territorial government have been lost. Will you 'have the goodness to let the people know if that is the fact? 'Who was the Auditor at the time, and what loss the State sus-'tained in Consequence of the loss of the books &c?'

"'Report also says that the legislature once authorized the Jef-'fersonville canal company to raise a certain sum of money by 'lottery—that managers were appointed—a Scheme published—'many tickets sold for cash—and the purchasers of tickets swindled 'out of their cash, as the lottery was never drawn; do tell the 'people, who were the managers and agents of this business—who 'were the Swindlers, and such other information on the subject as 'you may be in possession of ———.

"'Report says, that ——— will be a candidate for the Senate 'of the United States. The people have heard very strange Stories 'about his conduct towards his wife; that in consequence of his 'neglect, &c. she pined, sorrowed, and died    Please tell them 'How it is.'

"In September, 1824, a man and wife living near Vevay, not very harmoniously together, the wife left the husband and went to live in the family of a neighbor. As usual in such cases, the deserted husband gave notice in the public paper that his wife had left his bed and board, and was living in adultery with the neighbor, where she had gone to stay. Kinsman hearing of the affair, sought an opportunity to see the man with whom the truant wife was living, and advised him to publish a denial of the charges published by the deserted husband. It was agreed that Kinsman should prepare the notice, which appeared in the paper a short time after as follows:

"'Attention' The public are particularly requested to suspend 'their opinion for the present respecting the publication signed '———. I have employed the woman he calls his wife to reside 'in my family as a servant or house keeper, and do not harbor her'"  1869 MS., pp. 152-56.

² "Is . . . Vevay," is crossed out, and "died in 1877 or 78" is substituted.

[3] "Of the firm of Tandy and Detraz milliners of this place." 1869 MS., p. 12.

[4] "Who was in 1835 or 1836 Post Master here and was the first auditor of Switzerland County." *Ibid.*

[5] "As the best means for safety, at night several families would meet at Mr Morerod's, as the most central and convenient place—the women and children remaining within, with the door well barred, and the men, by turns, standing guard outside. How many anxious nights were passed in this manner, cannot now be told—but during the fall of 1810 and winter of 1810-11 this was kept up the men working through the day in their fields and clearings, not knowing at what moment they might be attacked by Indians and massacred, in the presence too, perhaps of their wives and little children. But fortunately they passed through the winter and spring without any hostile demonstration being made against the Settlement. Sometime before the Battle of Tippecanoe, in 1811 the Indians became more hostile and attacked a settlement somewhere north of Madison at a point, which gave to that event the *'Massacre of Pigeon Roost.'* This occurred sometime in the winter of 1811-12 and as that had taken place within less than thirty miles of New Switzerland the settlers were again thrown into dismay and consternation not knowing but that they would be attacked by these merciless savage foes who spared none regardless of age sex or condition. And this consternation was not confined to the settlers at New Switzerland but spread throughout the whole southern, and southeastern portion of the Territory. This state of uncertainty continued during the spring of 1812 when the authorities ordered the militia to be called out and orders were issued by the commandants of regiments to have men raised by voluntary Enlistment. Elisha Golay who had been commissioned a captain in the first Battallion in the first regiment of the militia of Jefferson County by William Henry Harrison, then Governor of Indiana Territory—his commission bearing date the fourth day of February 1811—received an order to enlist men in his company which order is in the following words:

"MADISON 10th May 1812. CAPTAIN ELISHA GOLAY: DEAR SIR—I have received orders from Colonel David Hillis, this day to have raised within this Battalion fifteen, privates, two, corporals and two sergeants, who are to be rendezvoused in Madison on Friday next at the hour of 12 Oclock. You are hereby authorized and required to convene your company on Wednesday next, for the purpose of raising by voluntary enlistment, three, privates and one sergeant, within your Company, to be equipped according to law and marched with two days, provision to Madison on Friday

the 15th of this instant as above stated. You are to hold the same number of men in readiness to March to Madison on Saturday 23rd of this instant as a relief to the first draft. But if volunteers cannot be had you will have to draft, and place your whole company in such order as to give relief every ten days to those who are in service. You are also notified that you are to command the company now raised, and will come prepared accordingly to serve until discharged by order of the Colonel or Commander in Chief. "JOHN VAWTER *Major*
"*1st Battalion 6 Regt Ind. Mil.*'"
1869 MS., pp. 13-14.

[Page 32] [1] "'CAPTAIN ELISHA GOLAY—You will proceed on the morning of the 16th instant with the detachment now under your command from the town of Madison to the Outside of the frontier Settlements of this County, and then to range East and west, as far as the settlements extend. On your arrival at the frontier you will proceed without delay to build a block house of such size and form as will most securely and conveniently accommodate a detachment of from thirty to forty men including officers. You will also keep a sufficient number of men on duty as rangers both east and west, of the spot on which you may erect the block house to watch the motions of the Indians and give timely notice of their approach, and in case of any alarm, either by an attack or otherwise, you will take the most speedy method of giving notice to the lieutenant Colonel of this regiment, and in every case of this kind you are referred for, further instructions, to the orders of the Commander in chief whose general orders are most implicitly to be obeyed. You will in all your movements be on your guard, and never allow any advantages to be taken of your forbearance, with the enemy, while on their frontiers and in all cases, when there is strolling and skulking parties of Indians within the boundaries of your command, with whom your men may meet, do not allow your men to run any risk by enquiring of them, respecting their friendship, towards us unless, circumstances will Justify it. You will also be held responsible for your conduct while on this command. Your present tour will be for ten days from the time of your departure from this place, and at the same time you, are not to come in with your men until, a relief arrives unless compelled by a superior force of the enemy. You will take care to give your orders to the men under your command, not by any means whatsoever to fire, after sunset unless, at an enemy or to give an alarm and at all other times it will be expected, that your orders, will be given, on this subject with prudence and exercised with caution. You will take care to keep on duty at all times a sufficient number of sentinels and no other orders will be given to them, but such as your prudence may by circumstances require "DAVID HILLIS "MADISON May 15th 1812.— "Lt Col. 6th R. I. M.

"See with what minute details the order specifies the duties of the commander of this detachment of hardy backwoodsmen, while on duty far from the more settled parts of the country, and on the enemies own ground. It was well known—they had a wily and treacherous enemy to deal with, and that it required prudence courage and fortitude, for so small a number of men to meet perhaps hundreds of the savage foe, whose mode of warfare was, to spare neither, age sex, or condition when they attacked the settlements of the white man. The duties assigned to this detachment were strictly carried out and these hardy backwoodsmen again returned in safety to their families and friends. After this time there were no more hostile Indian raids into the settlements along and near the Ohio river in this part of the territory. Among the names of those who composed this command, may be recognized the names of some who have been somewhat prominent in the affairs of the state. David Hillis, who represented Jefferson county in the legislature, and was Lieutenant Governor of the state. The Vawters were men of note in the state, after the formation of the State government. John Vawter, was a member of the Senate for many years, filled the office of United States marshall for the district of Indiana, and was an active and influencial friend and advocate of the System of internal improvements—and he and one of the other Vawters were the first Ministers of the Gospel who preached in this part of the territory. They were of the Baptist persuasion. Williamson Dunn was the father of Col. William McKee Dunn, who is well known, by the citizens of the County. Luke Oboussier, & Lewis Golay were residents of New Switzerland—the latter a brother of the Captain & father of Selden T. Golay—Stephen Rutherford was the father of Joseph Rutherford of this place. John Tague was the father of Joseph Tague who resides at Mt Sterling. James Picket was a brother of Heathcoat Picket, and uncle to Benjamin Picket. Abraham Cline lived below Indian Creek, and I believe was related to the Raymonds and Edward Violet. Daniel Demaree was a connection of the Demaree's living on Indian Kentucky in Jefferson County and those living in this County. Of the other members of that detachment the writer has no knowledge. These men were some of the instruments employed by God in making this (then) wilderness a suitable abode for civilized men that he might Honor and Glorify, the Creator and Preserver of their lives and healths and that we their decendants might have a 'goodly heritage' and give God the Praise for all the mercies and blessings vouchsafed to us as a people." 1869 MS., pp. 15-18.

² "In the summer of 1812 a family residing about where Lewis Schroeder lives consisting of a man and his wife, whose name is not now recollected but thought to be Rayles—the man being up in Switzerland (on this side of the Creek) working—the woman heard the firing of guns, up the Creek and supposed that Indians were in the neighborhood became alarmed for his safety—and there being no nearer neighbors that [than] at the mouth of the Creek she proceeded down to near where Edward Violet and his father were at work in the field, and crying out loudly for help the father directed his son Edward to go and see what was the cause of the noise they heard—when he came to where the woman was he found that she was very much frightened, saying that large numbers of Indians were coming down the Creek for she had heard the guns firing. She was set over the creek and proceeded up to where her husband was at work for safety." *Ibid.*, p. 21.

[Page 33] ¹ "The returns of elections, returns of overseers of Roads, Battallion and Regimental musters, and various other duties of officers and citizens was transacted and performed at Madison." *Ibid.*, p. 21.

² "Sometime after these rangers were dismissed from duty and it no longer required, their absence into the interior one of them in an evil hour was tempted to commit a crime, and yielding to that temptation, was prosecuted in the Court for stealing a Barrel of whiskey or cider—a trading boat having landed below the foot of the Island having among other articles whiskey on board to sell. This man whose name was Peter Lock, a very large robust young man managed to get a barrel of whiskey out of the boat and carried and rolled it into a thicket a short distance back from the river bank, by some means he was discovered as the thief or suspected, proceedings were instituted against him for the theft, and Amos Lane, then supposed to be the most able Lawyer among us, was employed to defend him—he was acquitted and the fee that Lane received for his services was the transfer of a certificate for the south half of a quarter section of land lying on Plumb Creek which Lane after ward sold to Amos Gilbert and is the land now owned and occupied by Thomas Huffman." *Ibid.*, p. 23.

³ "John James Dufour died in the spring of 1827, at his residence above Log Lick, leaving his property to his only son,

Daniel Vincent Dufour. Francis Louis Siebenthal died of a disease contracted in the lower Country, where he had gone with a boat load of produce, some time about the year 1824 or 1825. His son, John Francis Siebenthal, died near Cincinnati, about nine years since.

"The old gentleman Borallay died from the effects of the kick of a horse, some few years after coming to the Country. His widow lived to be a very old person. His son Peter died about the year 1854, on the old homestead in Garrard County, Kentucky. The daughter was married to a man named Mayfield, who removed to Monroe County in this state, where she died, leaving quite a large family, some of whom are still living in that County.

"Philip Bettens lived and died on his farm just below Vevay—the front part of the farm being now owned by his daughter Mrs Duplan and Samuel E Pleasants. His wife died a few year[s] after. His daughter, who married John Detraz, died about three years since. Daniel Dufour died in the winter of 1854, lacking a few days of 90 years of age. His wife died in the summer of 1865, aged about 88 years. John David Dufour died in 1845, leaving his land above Vevay—about 700 acres—to his children.

"John Francis Dufour died in June 1850, having been taken ill during the sitting of the Circuit Court, of which court he was, at the time, one of the associate Judges.

"Jean Daniel Morerod was married to Antoinette Dufour, and they lived and died on their farm below Vevay, on which John R. Morerod, their son, is now living—Mr Morerod died about the year 1838, and Mrs. Morerod in the winter of 1857.

"Jane Maria Dufour married John Francis Siebenthal, and lived for many years on their farm, being the one now owned by the widow and heirs of William Norrisez. Mrs Siebenthal died in the neighborhood of Cincinnati some years since, and shortly afterwards Mr. Siebenthal died.

"Susannah M. Dufour was married to Elisha Golay, and lived on their farm above Plumb Creek, untill both become of such an age as to make it adviseable for them to cease from the labors attendant on farming. They lived with their son, Constant Golay. Mrs Golay died in 1866, aged about 80 years, and her husband died about one year afterwards, aged 83 past.

"One member of the Dufour family, Aime Dufour, who was quite young when the Colonists left their native country, was not permitted to accompany them on account of his being too young. After he had grown up and completed his education, he came to the Country in 1816, residing in this neighborhood for some years, when he went to New Orleans, and finally settled at Vermillionville, Louisiana, where he was still residing about two years since.

"It is impossible to state with any degree of certainty the number of the descendants of the Dufour family but as near as can be ascertained at present, the number cannot be much under one hundred and seventy-five, or Eighty.

"At this time there is no one of those who were grown, at the time of their settleing in the Colony, now living, except the widow of John Francis Dufour who is still living, and is near 80 years of age." 1869 MS., pp. 24-25.

[Page 34] [1] "As the old persons, began to decline in years, and were no longer able to attend to the vineyards, and their children began to take charge of these matters, the culture began to be neglected, and their attention was turned more to raising corn and potatoes; so that at this time there is but little wine made on the farms where such quantities were made in by gone years." *Ibid.,* pp. 25-26.

[2] "During John James Dufour's absence in Europe, when writing to his brothers and sisters, he would invariably urge them to be industrious in the management of their vineyards, and gave directions about many of the particulars necessary to be observed to succeed in making good wine. And in writing about the laying off the town, he was very solicitous about the manner in which it should be done.

"The reason, no doubt, of his anxiety about the success of the colony in succeeding in their undertaking, was that his father, when they left Europe, had entrusted the care of his children to his eldest son. This was done by a writing, in which the father transferred his paternal care over his children to his eldest son, John James Dufour; and by that writing it was enjoined upon the said John James Dufour to learn them to be industrious, economical, & sober, and see that they did not become indolent, proud and haughty: and above all, that he should use his efforts to instruct and pe su[a]de them as to the truths of the Christian religion, and for that purpose he was directed fervently to pray the God of Mercy, as he (the father) would also himself do, that He would open their hearts and consciences to the true Christian faith, as the only means of making them happy in this world, and to assure true felicity in the life to come." *Ibid.,* pp. 26-27.

[Page 35] [1] "After the organization of the County, of Switzerland, it was necessary to select and elect some person, to represent the county in the territorial Legislature, the county not being, fully organized until October 1814 it is propable no one was elected for representative, until some time in 1815. Elisha Golay, was the first representative elected, and it is thought, the only one from Switzerland County until the organization of the State Government in 1816." 1869 MS., p. 65.

[Page 37] [1] "In the early settlement of this part of Indiana, there was a law of Congress in force, by which sections 21 and perhaps sections 22 in every congressional Township, were usually called, *reserved lands*, and the price was fixed on such lands at four dollars per acre—under that Law George Turner who lived on the Kentucky Side of the river, above the head of Vevay Island, became the purchaser of the South East quarter of Section 21, Township 2. Range 2. In 1818 he advertised that quarter section of land for sale—requiring one fourth of the purchase money in hand, the balance at the end of three years, with interest.

"Whether he sold that land at that time or soon afterwards is not known, but David Miller became the purchaser of that quarter section of land, but at what date is not known.

"However some of the heirs of George Turner have lately had a suit pending against David Miller in one of our courts for their interest in the land as an error was made in selling the interest of said heirs while miners, by the guardian perhaps by deeding a different quarter of land in a different section, from the quarter and section petitioned to be sold.

"At the time Mr Turner paid four dollars per acre for that land there was equally as good land in the neighborhood to be had at two Dollars per acre." *Ibid.*, pp. 117-18.

[Page 38] [1] "Bakes run his carding machine in Vevay for some years, when he built a mill on Long Run, where Siebenthals mill now stands, and Mr Rous remained in Vevay for some time, when he removed to the Country and located on the farm, which is now the pauper farm. Mr Bakes had his mill so arranged that he carded wool and ground grain; and Mr Rous built a horse mill, on the top of the Hill near to Mr Bakes'. Often in the summer and fall months, when there was not sufficient water to run Bakes' mill, Mr Rous' horse mill was running, and did all the neighborhood grinding. Often when clouds would arise with the appearance of rain, they would seem to part to the west of the Mill, and no rain falling, gave the opportunity to Bakes or some other person who wished to carry on a joke, for saying that Mr Rouse, by some necroman[c]y and raising a long pole, would part the clouds and prevent the rain from falling to raise the run, and thereby Bakes could not run *his* mill, so that Rous could have all the grinding to do on *his* horse mill." *Ibid.*, p. 29.

[2] "The courts were also held for a while at the house of Robert M. Trotter, who was a relative of Gabriel Johnson, whose house

was situated on Main Street, and occasionally at the house of Thomas Armstrong." 1869 MS., p. 29.

[Page 41]   [1] *Acts of the Indiana Territory*, 1813, pp. 39 ff.

[2] The commissioners appointed were James Dill, Alexander A. Meek, Jesse L. Holman, Jacob Short and Isaac Dunn. *Ibid.*, 1814, p. 32.

[Page 42]   [1] "George G. Knox, who had purchased a lot in Vevay, but who was still residing at Frankfort, Ky., proposed to give fifty dollars in carpenters work, or ten dollars in cash.

"As a farther inducement for the commissioners to locate the seat of Justice at Vevay, Daniel Dufour Blanc, and John Francis Dufour gave the following obligation

" 'SWITZERLAND COUNTY, October 28th 1814: We, the sub-'scribers, Oblige ourselves, our heirs, executors, &c., that We will 'be accountable to the agent that may be appointed, by the court, 'in and for said County, to pay and guarantee to him for the use 'of said county, the payment of Two thousand five hundred Dol-'lars, on account of the subscription referred to within, on this 'condition, that is to say, that the seat of Justice for said County 'shall be placed at Vevay, in said County. Witness our hands and 'seals the day aforesaid.

" 'DANIEL DUFOUR BLANC (Seal)
" 'JOHN FRANCIS DUFOUR' " (Seal)

1869 MS., p. 34.

[2] "The first term of the Circuit Court in and for the County of Switzerland was begun and held on Friday the 28th day of October 1814 and was composed of a Circuit or presiding Judge, and two associate Judges, appointed by the Governor, of the Territory.

"There was present at that term of the Court the Honorable Elijah Sparks circuit and presiding Judge in the third Circuit and the Honorable William Cotton and James McClure associate Judges of the Circuit Court in and for the County of Switzerland who produced their commissions as such Judges, with the certificate thereon, of the oaths of Office having been duly administered to them, and also John Francis Dufour, who produced his commission as Clerk of said Court, with a certificate endorsed thereon of the oaths of office having been duly administered to him, the court thereupon required the said John Francis Dufour to give bond with security in the sum of One thousand dollars, payable to his excellency Thomas Posey Governor of the Indiana Territory and his successors in office conditioned for the faithful performance of the duties of the office of Clerk of said Court, as directed by the act of assembly in such cases made and provided, there was also present John Francis Siebenthal who also produced his commission as sheriff of the County with a certificate endorsed thereon of the oaths of office having been duly administered to him, the Court required him to enter into bond with security in the sum of Four thousand dollars payable to the Governor of the Territory and his successors in office conditioned, for the faithful performance of the duties of the office of Sheriff for the County of Switzerland, as directed by the act of assemble in that cases made and provided.

"The following named persons having been summoned as Grand Jurors came into court: James Rous foreman, Stilwell Heady, Philo Averil, George Coggshell, Peter Harris Louis Gex Oboussier, John McClure, Amos Brown, Joseph McFall, Robert Gullion, Thomas Mounts, John Nelson, Philip Bettens, Nathaniel Cotton, Abisha McKay, Henry Hannas, Joshua Kains, and Peter Demaree, who after being duly, sworn and charged, retired to consult of the business before them.

"The following named persons were admitted to practice in this Court as attornies and counsellors at law: Amos Lane William Hendricks, John Test, and James Noble.

"The Court appointed James Noble Esqr. attorney at law. Prosecuting attorney for Switzerland County for and during good behavior.

"The court also ordered to be entered upon the records rules for the Government of the practice in said Court—which rules upon reflection it is thought proper to make more public, than they now are in the old musty records of the Court for the Terms of October 1814 and March 1815, which is only one half quire of foolscap paper sti[t]ched together.

"I. The attornies in managing business shall keep themselves within the bar.

"II. All motions Shall be made in the morning, before entering upon the docket and not afterward, except such as necessarily arise out of the opening or progress of a cause.

"III. Not more that [than] two counsels on each side will be heard in argument upon any motion whatever.

"IV. Not more than three counsel[s] on each side will be permitted to argue a cause to the Jury, except the same shall appear to the court to be of more than ordinary importance.

"V. All motions for continuance, and all motions for new trial grounded upon facts, shall be supported by affidavit and decided without argument.

"VI. When a cause is regularly called and postponed by the consent of parties, the same shall not be called again until the docket is gone through, and upon the second calling shall not be

## NOTES

continued for any ordinary cause of continuance arising, posterior to the postponement.

"VII. No time will be given to draw a plea after the cause is called for trial, provided the declaration was on file in sufficient time for putting in plea upon the rules.

"VIII. No agreement of the bar will be regarded by the Court unless the same is upon the record or assented to by each party.

"IX. Each cause when called in order must be immediately entered upon for trial, continued or postponed by consent of the parties, or placed at the foot of the docket by the plaintiff.

"X. No motion in arrest of Judgment or for a new trial will be heard after the expiration of three days from the rendering of verdict except the cause for a new trial shall have been discovered after the expiration of that period.

"XI. In no case shall more than one attorney be permitted to speak on the Closing argument.

"This completed the first days proceedings of this the first court held for Switzerland County.

"On Saturday the 29th of October 1814 the court met.

"The Grand Jury empannelled on the previous day returned into court with an Indictment against David Beebee for selling unwholesome provisions, and having no further business were discharged.

"The prosecuting attorney moved the court that a venire facias issue against David Bebee returnable on the first day of the next march Term of the court to answer to the Indictment.

"James Noble was allowed Sixteen Dollars for his services as prosecuting attorney during the term which was ordered to be certified to the sheriff for payment.

"The court then adjourned to meet on the 27th day of March 1815.

"At the March Term of the Court on the first day Honorable Elijah Sparks circuit Judge and William Cotton associate Judge were in attendance.

"On the first day of the term, the following named persons were sworn as Grand Jurors, John Gilliland foreman James Stewart James McKay, Adoat [?] Sample, William Harcoat, Norman B. McGruder, William Smith, Peter Lock, Nicholas Lentz, John Campbell, Zela Moss, Solomon Nighswonger Griffith Dickerson, [Dickason] William T. Huff, John Mills, John Rayl Thomas Gilliland, John Fenton and Philip Fry.

"John Lawrence and Pinkney James, were admitted to practice law in this court.

"In the case of the United States against David Bebee indicted at the Octr term of the court, was tried by a Jury which returned a verdict of not guilty.

"The grand Jury found and returned into court Eight indictments for Assault and Battery and affrays two for Larceny and one for retailing spirituous liquors without license.

"James McKay one of the grand Jurors, was arraigned for contempt of the court by being intoxicated, and the court being informed by him that he did not intend offering a contempt to the court, by getting and remaining intoxicated, the Court discharged him.

"Philip Fry also a grand Juror was arraigned for a contempt of court by absenting himself from the grand Jury without permission of the court he stated to the court that he had no intention of offering a contempt to the court upon which he was discharged.

"James Noble was allowed Twenty dollars for his services during the term as prosecuting attorney, and the Court adjourned until the next term.

"The next term of the court commenced on the 26th day of June 1815, with the Honorable James Noble as Circuit Judge and the same associates as at the other Terms.

"William Hendricks was appointed Prosecuting attorney.

"Stephen C. Stevens was on motion of Alexander A. Meek, allowed to practice as an attorney and counsellor at law at this court *ex gratia*.

"At the October term 1815 of the Court, the same Judges were on the bench as at the June term.

"At this term of the court Alexander Holton, Joseph F. Farley and Reuben Kidder were admitted to practice as attornies and counsellors at law in this court.

"At the March term 1816 the Honorable Jessee L. Holman having been appointed Circuit Judge, was present and presided, the associate Judges also being on the bench.

"William Hendricks was still prosecuting attorney.

"At this term of the court Stephen C. Stevens, was admitted to practice as an attorney and counsellor at law in this Court.

"Two cases for divorce were commenced at the March term 1816. George Millen against Eliza Millen, and Maria Wilson against William Wilson, in both cases it appeared that the defendants were non residents of the Territory, the court therefore ordered that a copy of the order should be inserted in the *Western Sun* Eight weeks successively; the *Western Sun* was published at Vincennes—at the June term of the Court these two divorce cases appear on the docket, and it was made appear to the Satisfaction of the Court that the defendants were not inhabitants of the Territory, the court ordered that notice of their pendency be inserted in the *Indiana Register* for Eight weeks successively. The *Indiana Register* was published in Vevay by William C. Keen, so it may be well to recollect this fact, for this is the best evidence that can now be had of the date of the commencement of a newspaper in Switzerland County namely between the first of April and middle of June 1816, for it is intended to give a history of the newspaper enterprize in this county in some future number." 1869 MS., pp. 49-53.

[Page 44] [1] "'That all that part of this County lying east of 'the section line which begins on the Ohio river at the corners of 'Fractional Sections 8 and 9, and runs north to the boundary of 'this county at the corner of sections 21 and 29, in Town 3, range '2, west, compose one Township, to be known by the name of '*Posey;* and that all that part which lies west of the aforesaid 'line, compose one Township, to be known by the name of Jeffer-'son'." *Ibid.*, p. 36.

[2] "The father of Mrs. Samuel Protsman and of Mrs. William Protsman." *Ibid.*, p. 37.

[Page 45] [1] "According to the provisions of an act of the Territorial legislature, approved March 2nd, 1813, entitled, 'An act for fixing the seats of Justice in all new Counties hereafter to be laid off.'" *Ibid.*

[2] "Said County Agent was also instructed 'to cause the corners 'of the Jail house to be cut down, and also such trees as are in 'danger of falling on said house, and pay for the same out of any 'money which may come to his hands, belonging to the County'.

"Persons at this day might probably suppose that there was not much use in putting a criminal in such a Jail, with only a stock lock and pad lock to keep those confined therein; from making their escape; and they might also wonder why it was ordered to cut down the corners of the Jail after it was built. In raising log houses in those days, the ends of the logs projected nearly one foot, and it was the cutting off the ends of those projections which is meant by having the 'corners of the Jail cut down'" *Ibid.*, p. 38.

[3] "Said house to be two stories high, thirty-six feet long, and 'thirty feet wide; the first story twelve feet between floors, and the 'second ten; and that on that day a plan of the building will be 'exhibited, and further conditions made known.'

"On the 2nd of May, 1814, the court met and were engaged most of the day in arranging a plan for said building, when it was thought advisable to alter the dimensions, which had been previously agreed upon, so as to make the house thirty-six by thirty-two." 1869 MS., p. 39.

⁴ "The court house was not finished so as to be used untill perhaps in 1816." *Ibid.*

[Page 46]   ¹ "She was buried in ... 1814." *Ibid.*, p. 40.

² She was buried in 1816. *Ibid.*

³ "This society was composed of members who paid a certain amount into the Treasury annually, which amounts were expended for the purchase of books. In Novr., 1814 the President and directors of the Society appointed John Francis Dufour, to solicit donations. The following appointment was given him by the officers:

" 'The President and Directors of the Literary Society of Vevay 'being anxious as far as in their power to place instruction within 'the reach of the rising generation, and considering their con-'tracted funds, do hereby solicit the patronage of Literary char-'acters who feel a spirit of benevolence towards our infant instu-'tition. We therefore do hereby authorize John Francis Dufour to 'receive donations in books and other things for said society, and 'we pledge ourselves for said society, and we pledge ourselves, that 'all donations, shall be recorded in our society Journal.'

" 'Vevay 5th Nov 1814.'

" 'JNO. DUMONT, *President*'
" 'GEORGE COGGSHELL' ⎫
" 'ROBT. M. TROTTER'   ⎬ *Directors.*
" 'DL DUFOUR BLANC' "  ⎭

*Ibid.*, pp. 40-41.

[Page 47]   ¹ "Of the inlots laid out in 1813 Eight were reserved and donated to the '*Seminary of Vevay*' which was afterward, in 1816, incorporated by the Legislature. On one of these lots a log school house was built in the fall of 1815, in which a school was maintained and kept up for some years. This house stood on the lot now owned in part by Joseph Peelman, on Ferry Street on the spot where said Peelmans brick dwelling stands. These lots, after the introduction of our present Common School system, were by the common consent of the Donor John Francis Dufour, The trustees of the Town and citizens, disposed of and the proceeds, merged into the common school fund in the building of a school house, and afterwards used in aid of the building of our present public school building." *Ibid.*, p. 41.

The law incorporating the Seminary of Vevay, was approved

## NOTES 371

December 26, 1815. *Acts of the Indiana Territory*, 1815, pp. 103 ff. The law incorporating the Literary Society of Vevay was approved August 31, 1814. *Ibid.*, 1814, p. 95.

² "Sometime in the fall of 1814 the news of McDonoughs victory over the British on Lake Champlain was received by the citizens of the young town of Vevay, who, to show their joy at the reception of the news of the Victory, decided to have an illumination of the Town. Every house, in fact every window in every house, was as brilliantly illuminated as could be with common tallow candles." 1869 MS., p. 42.

[Page 48] ¹ "The associate Judges who were by the laws in force in the Territory, authorized to transact the county business, such as causing roads and highways to be laid out, opened, and kept in repair, and also the appointing of Overseers of the roads, and assigning the hands, to each supervisor, the appointment of all Township Officers except Justices of the peace, were also authorised to, transact business pertaining, to decedents estates, granting licenses for keeping Taverns, and establishing rates to be charged by tavern keepers, had a great deal of business pertaining to opening highway to attend to for the first year or two." *Ibid.*, p. 44.

² "He obtained license on the 24th of November 1814, and on the 25th of Novr. 1814. The court established the following rates to be charged by tavern keepers in the County of Switzerland: For a meal of victuals 25 cents, for Lodging per night 12½ cents, for corn or oats per gallon 12½ cents for horse at hay per 24 hours 25 cents, for whiskey per half pint 12½ cents, for peach brandy per half pint 12½ cents, for Holland gin, French Brandy and Jamaica spirits per half pint 50 cents, for rum per half pint 37½ cents for imported Madiera wine per quart two Dollars, for Switzerland Madiera wine per quart or bottle one Dollar, for Switzerland red wine per quart or bottle 75 cents, for Domestic gin and cherry bounce per half pint 18¾ cents.

"In March 1815 license was granted to William Cooper to keep a tavern in Vevay, on the 30th March 1815 a license was granted to Peter Harris to keep a tavern at his house in this county, and in November 1815 he laid out the town of Jacksonville.

"In September 1815 license was granted to 'Uncle' Thomas Armstrong (as he was familiarly called) to keep a tavern in the town of Vevay for one year from the first day of July 1815 he having entered into bond with security at that time.

. . . . . . . . .

"The relations of an anecdote in which 'Uncle Thomas' was concerned may not be amiss, in this connection: At the time he was keeping his tavern in the log house corner of Main and Union street, James Hamilton (the father of Edward P., William, and John Hamilton who are well known among us) carried on the hatting business in a shop on the half lot on the alley back of the Baptist church, and as it was customary, with hatters in those days, to call in some of their friends during the night, while coloring, to partake of a 'chicken supper' on one of these occasions, Hamilton invited some of his friends and among the number 'Uncle Thomas' to take supper with him, 'Uncle Thomas' of course accepted the invitation, and with the other guests partook of a splendid 'Chicken supper', the next morning when Mrs Armstrong went to the coop for chickens, for breakfast lo and behold they had all 'vamoused', she called 'Uncle Thomas' and informed him that some one had stolen all the chickens, 'Uncle Thomas' at once suspected that he had the night previous been of the party, that devoured the chickens, which Mrs Armstrong had intended for breakfast, he said nothing, but afterwards gave Hamilton a cursing for the trick he had played off on him.

"David McCormick obtained licence to keep tavern in Vevay in September 1815, and kept his tavern in a part of the house in which George E. Pleasants now resides.

"In May 1816 license was granted to Samuel Fallis to keep a tavern in Vevay, the house in which he kept his tavern was a one story brick, standing on Main Street on the lot on which Charles Thiebauds dwelling house now now stands and occupied by him at this time.

. . . . . . . . . . . .

"Jonas Baldwin kept his tavern in the frame house now standing on the Corner of Ferry and Market Streets, now owned by the widow and heirs of the late Joseph Dalmazzo." 1869 MS., p. 44-47.

³ "Robert M. Trotter being perhaps to [the] first person to keep a house of public entertainment in the town." *Ibid.*, p. 119.

⁴ "To entitle a person, to obtain a license to keep tavern he was compelled by the law to have the petition of a certain number of persons praying the Court to grant the license, and also to prove to the satisfaction of the court that he was a person of good moral character. . . . . . . . .
he was required to enter into bond with security to keep his said tavern as required by law." *Ibid.*, p. 44.

⁵ "On the Corner of Main and Union Streets." *Ibid.*, p. 46.

⁶ "William Bradley kept the same house in 1819 and 1820 when he removed to a new house erected on the lot corner of Market and Union Street. . . . The present scite of the Le Clerc house,

was occupied by many others not now recollected, except Amos Gilbert who built the 'Russel House' who occupied it from 1827 to about 1832 or 1833." 1869 MS., pp. 119-120.

[Page 49] ¹ "Aime Dufour . . . came to this country in 1816." *Ibid.*, p. 25.
"During the year 1813 or 1814 Amie Dufour brother of the Dufour family embarked for the United States." *Ibid.*, p. 63.

² "Mrs. Morerod after the Arrival of her Brother Amie, hung the clothes he wore while travelling and in which he slept in the Barns, on a peach tree before the house, under that peach tree afterwards came up and grew some 'Orchard' grass, the first ever seen in the west, by the poineers of that day, the seed no doubt having attached to the clothes in one of the Barns and thus brought to the west." *Ibid.*

[Page 50] ¹ "The heads were made by placing one nail at a time in a vice and with a hammer, was f[l]attened out to make the head." *Ibid.*

[Page 51] ¹ "Among the early traders to New Orleans or the 'Mississippi' country' . . . may be named Charles F. Krutz." *Ibid.*, p. 64.

² "After selling out in the lower Country the hands who took the boats down as well as the owners, to get home traversed the Indian Country on foot, or if they preferred and had the means they purchased a 'Chickasaw poney' on which to make the trip, which required a few more hours, than are now required to make the trip from New Orleans to Louisville or Cincinanti." *Ibid.*

³ See *ante*, 38 ff.

[Page 52] ¹ "In the case United States against David Bebee for selling unwholesome flesh the indictment for which was found by the first grand Jury ever empanneled in Switzerland County and which was tried at the Second term of the circuit Court the following is the names of the persons composing the Jury which tried the case    Robert McKay Robert Bakes, Ralph Cotton Jr., Robert Cotton, John M. Johnson, William Campbell, Rawleigh Day, Thomas Paxton, Adam Cline, Walter Clark, John T. Deming and Luke Oboussier.

"The first Indictment found by the grand Jury for Larceny was at the Second term of the Court, and was against a female    her name was Isabel English, an Indictment for Assault and battery was also found against her.

"She was tried on the Indictment for Larceny by a Jury and acquitted,—on the Indictment for assault and battery she was fined by the court One Dollar, and the costs, and she was required to enter into recognizance in the sum of Twenty five Dollars for keeping the peace for six months, she came into court and her own recognizance was taken for keeping the peace 'toward all the good citizens of the United States and more especially towards the person and property of Viletta Richie for the space of six months.'

"It appears to have been the invariable practice in the Circuit Court under the Territorial government, that when a person was found guilty of an assault and Battery, they were required to enter into recognizance to keep the peace, this no doubt was required by the laws then in force; Would it not be a good provision to have incorporated into our statutes at this day? it would no doubt be the means of preventing the many complaints that are now brought into our courts for assault and Battery for it would no doubt deter persons from assaulting and beating those with whom they would become angry." 1869 MS., p. 54.

² "The court appointed William Campbell, John Campbell and Williams Pierson, commissioners to convey the land to Job Trusdell in compliance with the Conditions of a bond dated 26th February 1814, according to the 28th Section of an act of the Legislature entitled, 'An act authorizing the granting of letters testamentary and Letters of administration, for the settlement of intestate estates and for other purposes' approved September 17th 1807." *Ibid.*, p. 57; *Laws of the Indiana Territory*, 1807, pp. 68 ff.

[Page 53] ¹ "The School Sections, Section 16, in each congressional Township, which was reserved for School purposes, appears to have been under the Control of the Territorial Legislature as early as 1815, and before the organization of the State Government, for on the 28th of October 1815 at a Special Court, Amos Brown was appointed by the Court, a trustee to lease the School sections within the Township of Posey in this county as the law directs;—and John Francis Dufour was at the same time appointed a trustee to lease the School sections within the Township of Jefferson. . . ." *Ibid.*

² "A schedule of all debts owing, and all the property owned by the petitioner had to be made out and sworn to, and notice given to all his creditors, to appear on a certain day and shew cause if any they could why the petitioner should not be liberated.

"If the court were satisfied that notice had been given to all the Creditors, of the pendency of the petition and the time at which it would be acted upon by the court, and that he had delivered, all the property named in the Schedule to some person as trustee, he

## NOTES

could be set at liberty, and the court should order that the clerk issue his warrant to the officer, holding the petitioner in custody commanding him to set the petitioner at liberty, and the court also had to appoint a trustee to dispose of all the property of the petitioner for the benefit of his creditors, and that such trustee should make distribution of the proceeds of such sale according to law." 1869 MS., p. 58.

³ "The names of James Hastie, who was the father of, William, George, Charles, and John Hastie all four of whom reside in York Township, and Charles Muret, who was the father of Julius Muret, Mrs. Mary McCormick widow of John McCormick, and John Louis Muret, appear as early as 1814, their names are given as they were Europeans; Mr Hastie first settled on Plumb Creek, and in the early days of the settling of this county, he shipped his surplus produce down the river to find a market; for sometime he had a very large 'perouge', made by digging out a very large poplar tree (which might be termed a 'big dugout') in which he shipped his surplus Corn, and potatoes to Louisville." *Ibid.*, p. 61.

[Page 54] ¹ "The only one in the Colony from about 1809 or 10 to 1813." *Ibid.*

[Page 55] ¹ For further references to Henry Clay, see *ante*, 128-29 and 162 ff.

² "Years after Indiana became a state and began to go far ahead of Kentucky in increase of wealth and population, Mr. Dufour happened to be at Mr. Clays near Lexington, when in the course of conversation Mr. Clay remarked that in his opinion the people of Indiana were wise to excluding [exclude] slavery from the state, as he was convinced, that the rapid Growth of the State in wealth and population was attributable in a great degree to the fact that slavery was prohibited, while Kentucky with as fertile a soil as Indiana and a much older state, was, not increasing in wealth and population as fast, simply because slavery was tolerated in the State." 1869 MS., p. 66. For a sketch of Jennings life, see *Indiana Historical Collections*, 12:27-28 (Indianapolis, 1924).

³ "The publication of the news paper, . . . was commenced sometime in the spring of 1816 perhaps in the month of May or June . . . and continued untill one volume and a half of the paper was completed . . . on the Sixteenth of December 1817, the partnership . . . was dissolved." 1869 MS., p. 66. For a further account of early newspapers, see *ante*, 110-15.

## 376  INDIANA HISTORICAL COLLECTIONS

[Page 56]   [1] "In Novr or December 1823 recommenced the publication of the *Indiana Register*." 1869 MS., p. 67.

[2] Allen was printer of the *Annotator* under the editorship of Henry S. Handy as early as March 8, 1828; he became proprietor of the paper in the summer of that year. Upon the beginning of the third volume, in May, 1829, he changed its name to *Western Annotator*. Warder W. Stevens, *Centennial History of Washington County Indiana*, 387-88 (Indianapolis, 1916). [Ed.]

[3] "In 1832 or 1833." 1869 MS., p. 67.

[4] Printer's Retreat lay between Jacksonville and Vevay. It is listed among the post-office towns of Indiana in the *United States Official Register* from 1833 until 1837. [Ed.]

[5] "Where he and one Josephus B. Kent, published a paper for some time and Keen, purchased a steam mill in Vevay, of Joshua Smithson, giving his Printers Retreat lands in payment therefor." 1869 MS., p. 68.

[6] "A neutral paper in politics . . . during which time a very lively newspaper war was carried on between Randall and Keen and Co.—" *Ibid.*

[7] "Isaac Stevens Jr." *Ibid.*

[8] "Which was also neutral in politics." *Ibid.*

[9] "Joseph C. Eggleston, after Gray was dispossessed of the *Times* office, purchased a new press and materials, and started Wilson H. Gray in the publication of a Whig paper entitled the *Statesman* which was conducted by him, until sometime in 1841 or 1842 when the publication was entirely suspended and Eggleston disposed of the press and material." *Ibid.*, p. 69.

[Page 57]   [1] "A Democratic paper named *The News* which he continued for one or two years, during which time the *Revielle* published by F. J. Waldo was the organ of the opposition to the Democracy." *Ibid.*, p. 70.

[2] "Just . . . office" is crossed out and "continued its publication to May 1882 when he sold out the office to P. J. Hartford & F. J. Dalmazzo," substituted.

[Page 58]   [1] "All prosecutions which had been commenced before the organization of the State Government were in the name of the United States, some of which were dismissed—and some in which the sheriff made return '*non est inventus*' alias capias! were

## NOTES

ordered to be issued and the defendants to be held to bail in the sum of fifty dollars." 1869 MS., p. 81.

[2] "Stephen C. Stevens, Alexander A. Meek and Amos Lane were admitted as attornies and counsellors at law in the Switzerland Circuit court they having produced regular licences signed by the Honorable Jessee L. Holman and James Scott Esquires two of the Judges of the Supreme court of the state." *Ibid.*

[Page 59] [1] "It appears that James Rous was elected to serve untill the first Monday in August 1818, Isaac Stanley until the first Monday in August 1819, and Caleb Mounts until the first Monday in August 1820. It may not be out of place to say here that James Rous resided on what is now the pauper farm in Craig Township, Isaac Stanly in Vevay, where he was merchandizing, and Caleb Mounts in the upper end of the County near Grants Creek, and no doubt there are those in that part of Posey Township that may remember him the board having been organized on the first day, adjourned until the next day." *Ibid.*, p. 76.

[2] "All that part of the County lying east of the line dividing Ranges One and Two in the district of lands offered for sale at Cincinnati, to form one Township to be known by the name and style of Posey Township.

"All that part of the county which lies within the following bounds to wit: Beginning at the South East corner of Section 12, Town 2, Range 2 thence running west with the sectional line to the South west corner of Section Nine Town 3, Range 3, thence north to the County line, thence east with said line, to the range line dividing Ranges one and two, thence south with said Range line to the place of beginning to form one township, to be known by the name and style of Cotton Township.

"All that part of the County which lies in the Jeffersonville District north of the line dividing Townships five and Six to form and be one Township to be known by the name and style of Ross Township.

"All that part of the County which lies west of the Sectional line, which Strikes the Ohio river between Fractional Sections, thirty two and thirty three in Town 2, Range 3, in Cincinnati District and South of the line dividing Townships five and Six in Jeffersonville District, to form and be one Township to be known by the name and style of Craig Township.

"All that part of the County which lies within the following bounds to wit: Beginning where the line dividing Rang[e]s One and Two strikes the Ohio River,—thence running north with said line to the south east corner of Section 12 Town 2, Range 2, thence west with the sectional line to the South west corner of Section nine Town 3, Range 3, thence south with the sectional line to the Ohio River between fractional Sections 32 and 33, in Town 2 Range 3, thence up the river following the meanders thereof to the place of beginning to form and be one Township to be known by the name and style of Jefferson Township." 1869 MS., pp. 76-77.

² "The clerk was ordered to make out an extract of these proceedings, and cause one hundred copies thereof to be printed and delivered to the Sheriff to be by him distributed throughout the County. This was the notice given of the time and the place of holding the elections for Justices of the peace, and also the notice to the persons appointed as inspectors of elections in the several Townships of their appointment and this completed the business of the first meeting of the Board of County Commissioners, for Switzerland County." *Ibid.*, p. 78.

[Page 60] ¹ "The Board also appointed superintendants for the several School Sections No 16, in the several Congressional Townships in the County appointed Supervisors for the Roads, and allotted the hands to each supervisor, they also appointed, fence viewers, and overseers of the poor for the several Townships, and this being done, the arrangements for the tran[s]action of the County business was completed and put into active operation.

"All the business transacted by the commissioners for the first year or two, was of course very tedious and required much time to perfect all the business, as every thing was new, and all that was done, had to be done from the Knowledge the commissioners had of the different localities of the county." *Ibid.*, pp. 78-79.

² "On the 3rd day of the term the other associate Judge, James McClure appeared for the first time, produced his commission and the oath required by law was administered to him when he took his seat on the bench.

"On the 4th day of the term Reuben W. Nelson was admitted to practice in the Court, satisfactory evidence having been produced, that he had been admitted to practice in the Supreme court.

"On the last day of the term the court made the following order. 'Ordered that the device of the Seal of this court be the American 'Eagle with thirteen stars about its head, and immediately over 'its head two bunches of grapes, and the words "Switzerland Coun-'ty Circuit Court" engraved around it, as it appears above' just to the left and above the order is an impression made, with the seal, being the seal now used as the seal of the Circuit Court." *Ibid.*, p. 82.

At this term of court "Hezekiah B. Hull, John Lawrence, William Hendricks, Henry P. Thornton, Samuel Merrill, Alexander Holton and James Noble were admitted as attornies." 1869 MS., p. 82.

[3] "On that day . . . Alexander Gilliland and Daniel J. Caswell were admitted to practice as attornies . . . as were also Truman Richards, Miles C. Eggleston, and William Carpenter." *Ibid.*

[4] "On the first day of the term, John Dumont, William McCray, Isaac M. Johnston, and Nathaniel French were admitted ex gratia as attornies. John Test and James B. Ray were admitted to practice." *Ibid.*, p. 83.

[5] "Truman Richards was appointed prosecuting attorney during the term, at this term George H. Dunn was admitted to practice as attorney." *Ibid.*

[Page 62] [1] "From 1816 to 1826." *Ibid.*, p. 84.

[Page 65] [1] "Who is still supplying the pulpit of the church" is changed to read "and    Goldsmith who continued to supply the pulpit of the church untill 18    ."

[Page 66] [1] The statement quoted from the *Cincinnati Gazette* is obviously incorrect. Fenandez C. Holliday quotes from the autobiography of Peter Cartwright, who preached in southeastern Indiana in 1804 (*Indiana Methodism*, 23 ff. [Cincinnati, 1873]), and William W. Sweet mentions a Methodist organization in that locality as early as 1802 (*Circuit-Rider Days in Indiana*, 4 [Indianapolis, 1916]). Rezin Hammond seems to have been the first Methodist minister who preached in Indianapolis, but the date was probably 1821; the account rests only on early oral tradition. See *Logan's History of Indianapolis from 1818*, pp. 7, 14 (Indianapolis, 1868), written by Ignatius Brown; Berry R. Sulgrove, *History of Indianapolis and Marion County, Indiana*, 32 (Philadelphia, 1884); Jacob P. Dunn, *Greater Indianapolis*, 1:85 (Chicago, 1910).

[2] "1837 or 8." 1869 MS., p. 129.

[Page 68] [1] "Some of the services, were very impressive, as the sermons read were those which had been deliver[e]d in the 'Fatherland' by some of the most eminent ministers of that period, belonging to the Protestant Church, and perhaps their delivery had been heard there by some of the eldest persons present who heard the reading here, which must no doubt have recalled to their minds, recollections of their former home, the friends & companions of their youth, far away from them across the broad Atlantic." *Ibid.*, pp. 131-32.

[Page 70]   ¹ "And drink *water* alone evermore."   1869 MS., p. 107.

[Page 71]   ¹ "And Libra and Scorpio will gladly recede."   *Ibid.*, p. 108.

² "There is neither date, or any other mark by which it can be ascertained, at what date or at what place the foregoing lines were written, but it is known by some now living and who attended the school of Mr J. F. Buchetee, that he was residing here in New Switzerland in 1811 or 1812, and that while here he became acquainted with the Swiss colonists, hence it is inferred that while here he wrote the poem in Latin entitled 'Empire of Bacchus' It is also ascertained that at about the same period of time a person by the name of Priestly came to the colony and remained for a short time, it is also ascertained that 'Priestly' was a good latin scholar, hence it is thought that he translated this poem while in the Colony." *Ibid.*, pp. 108-9.

³ "The act incorporating the Company was passed January 14, 1818." *Ibid.*, p. 109; *Laws of Indiana* (special acts) 1817-18, pp. 57 ff.

[Page 72]   ¹ "In April 1818 . . . to receive subscriptions to the capital Stock of the company, and the Directors also appointed William Cotton and John Gilliland assistants to promote and facilitate the business.

"Subscribers to the stock were required to pay five Dollars at the time of Subscribing—the agent was requested to receipt for monies paid by subscribers, and to forward to the President of the Board at Jeffersonville a certified list of subscribers who had paid five dollars on each share.

"Subscribers thus certified were entitled, at the election for directors on the first Monday of July 1818, to vote either personally or by proxy—what success the agent met with in receiving subscriptions to stock in the company is not now known." *Ibid.*, pp. 109-10.

² " 'It is hoped the above arrangement will have the effect of expediting the lottery.' 'I am Sir your Obt Servt'
"JOHN F. DUFOUR Esqr                              " 'J. BIGELOW' "
*Ibid.*, p. 110.

³ "It appears that the regulation of the Board of Directors proposing to take notes for Lottery tickets sold, succeeded very much to the satisfaction of the Directors—as appears from the following letter from the President J. Bigelow.

# NOTES

"'JEFFERSONVILLE March 14th 1819.'

"'DEAR SIR'

"'Your favor of the 4th inst came safe to hand. We are happy 'to see you are succeeding so well in the sale of tickets; The form 'of the notes you are taking will I presume answer every purpose. 'The mode we had adopted here is to take them payable on the 'last day of the drawing of the lottery; we shall endeavor to give 'notice to every agent, when that day will be, for the purpose of 'facilitating the collection of his notes. If more tickets are wanting 'please to let us know, and we will send them to you. The first 'Monday in May is the day fixed for commencing the work of the 'Canal'

"'I am Sir your friend'

"'JOHN FRANCIS DUFOUR Esqr.'    "'J. BIGELOW'

"It may satisfy the curiosity of many by giving a sample of the tickets in this lottery, the following is a copy of one of the tickets

"'JEFFERSONVILLE OHIO CANAL LOTTERY'

"'First Class, No 4687.'

"'The holder of this Ticket will be entitled to receive such prize 'as may be drawn to its number, in the first Class of the Jeffer-'sonville Ohio Canal Lottery, if demanded within Twelve months 'after the drawing is finished, subject to a deduction of fifteen per 'cent on all cash paid'

"'CHRISTOPHER HARRISON, *manager*'

"'JEFFERSONVILLE, 1818'

others of the tickets now before the writer are signed by Saml. Gwathmey manager.

"The notes given by persons who purchased tickets on a credit read as follows. Copy of one of the notes signed by Lawrence Nihell

"'$210.'—'Five days after the completion of the drawing of the 'first class of the Jeffersonville Ohio Canal Lottery I promise to 'pay to William Bradley or order at the office of Discount and De-'posit of the Bank of Vincennes, the State Bank of Indiana at 'Vevay Two hundred and Ten Dollars, for value received this 27th 'day of January A. D. 1819.'    "'LAWRENCE NIHELL'

this note is endorsed by Wm Bradley, Robert Burchfield, J. Hamilton, Jacob Malin, Joseph Malin and Ira Mendenhall.

"Other notes of the same purport are before the writer while writing this account; one for *$60*, signed by A. B. Dumont and endorsed by G. Coggshell, I. R. Whitehead and Samuel Merrill; One for $60—signed by Thomas Armstrong endorsed by Daniel Dufour, William C. Keen H. Cotton, John F. Siebenthal, Lucien Gex, for E. Gex Lucien Gex, Jean D. Morerod and Margaret Armstrong.

"One for $60,—signed by Ralph Cotton and endorsed by Samuel Fallis, Charles F. Krutz Truman Richards, and James Dalmazzo.

"One for $60—signed by John Wilson and endorsed by Edward Patton.    One for *$102*, signed by John F. Dufour and endorsed by John James Dufour and one for $60, signed by Garrett Perkins and endorsed by Rufus Scott.

"These notes bear different dates some dated in February March April and May 1819. It would seem that the payment of these notes was never called for as they remained in the possession of John F. Dufour together with tickets not sold and came to the possession of the writer with other old paper which was thrown aside as waste paper.

"About the middle of April 1818 Mr Dufour received the following notice from J. Bigelow chairman of the Board of Managers of the Lottery

" 'JEFFERSONVILLE April 10th 1818'
" 'SIR

" 'The drawing of the Lottery having commenced, it is indis-'pensably necessary, that the managers should receive from the 'agents, correct and frequent account of the tickets sold, without 'which, they can form no idea how fast the drawing should pro-'gress. You are, therefore, requested to forward immediately a 'list of tickets sold by you, and to continue it in future at least 'once in two weeks; you will please to let your account shew the 'number of each ticket sold.'   " 'By order of the Board'

" 'JOHN FRANCIS DUFOUR Esqr'    " 'J. BIGELOW chairman'

"A statement of the Drawing of the Lottery up to the 15th of April 1818 shows that No 5816 drew a prize of $500.00 No 1638, $100.00. No 10118 $50.00. and 32 other tickets drew each a prize of $6.00, and 65 other tickets drew each Blank

"A Statement of the drawing up to the 20th of April 1818, shows the drawing of one prize of fifty Dollars, fourteen prizes of Six Dollars each and thirty five blanks.

"In transmitting the last named statement Mr. Bigelow writes to Mr Dufour the following:
" 'DEAR SIR'

" 'I enclose you $15 to purchase some Vevay wine    that which 'is unmixed by any kind of preparation would be preferred, please 'get the best you can of that description, it would be better to be 'put in a cask that had been used for wine before.    On 'the first Monday in next month we commence the Canal and I 'should be very glad to have a little wine of domestic manufactory 'to drink on the occasion if you could possibly get it down here by 'that time it would be a great favor. Your return of the number

# NOTES

'of tickets sold is received, I am glad to find you succeed so well in 'selling'
" 'Your Obt Servt.'
" 'JOHN FRANCIS DUFOUR Esqr' " 'J. BIGELOW'

"A statement of the drawing of the Lottery April 27th 1819, shows the drawing of two prizes of one hundred dollars each, thirty two of Six Dollars each, and Sixty Six blanks.

"A statement of the fifth drawing May 5th 1819 shows the drawing of one prize of One hundred Dollars thirty four of Six Dollars each and Sixty five Blanks

"At the time of Transmitting a statement of the fifth Drawing Mr. Bigelow acknowledges the receipt of the wine just as they were preparing for dinner.

"A statement of the Sixth drawing shows that drawing of on[e] prize of fifty dollars, twenty nine of Six Dollars each and Seventy Blanks, this drawing it appears took place on the 11th of May 1819. Mr Dufour received the following instructions in regard to unsold tickets

" 'DEAR SIR'

" 'The Tickets that are drawn and remain unsold in your hands 'you will of course hold subject to the orders of the managers un-'til your settlement.'
" 'Yours Respectfully'
" 'JOHN FRANCIS DUFOUR Esqr' " 'J. BIGELOW'

"The Seventh, Eighth, ninth, tenth and Eleventh drawings appear to have resulted about as those already given,—there being only two prizes of One hundred dollars each and one fifty Dollar prize drawn while the proportion of Blanks are about the same as in former drawings. The following was received by Mr Dufour.

"JEFFERSONVILLE 1st July 1819.

" 'SIR'

" 'If the ticket No 4765, is yet in your hands and unsold you will be so good as to preserve it for the benefit of the institution, as it was drawn on Tuesday last a prize of 50 Dolls'
" 'Yours Respectfully'
" 'Mr. J. F. DUFOUR' " 'ORLANDO RAYMOND *Secretary*'
" 'Vevay. " '*of Board of Managers*'

"It appears that the company by this time, began to be looking after the funds, due to them for Subscriptions of stock and on the sale of tickets by agents, for at a meeting of the Board of Directors on the 21st of September 1819 the following resolutions were adopted.

"1 Resolved, that the treasurer of the board be requested from time to time, to take the most effectual step to collect the sums due from the stockholders, and the monies in the hands of the Lottery agents; and that he be authorized to appoint an agent or agents for that purpose, and that the Treasurer of the Board of Managers be requested forthwith to pay over to the Treasurer of the Canal company, the money remaining in his hands.

"2nd Resolved, That if the Treasurer shall find it necessary to appoint an agent or agents, to settle with or collect money from Lottery agents, he shall be authorized to empower the agent or agents so appointed by him, to sell Lottery tickets, and to solicit further subscriptions to the capital stock of the company.

"3. Resolved, That the Treasurer be requested to forward a copy of the resolution of the 7th of December 1818 relating to the sale of tickets on a credit to each of the Lottery agents, and require their punctual observance of the same, and that they forward certificates of the cashiers of the Banks in which they may have made deposits in compliance of that resolution.

"Saml. Gwathmey Treasurer of the Board of Directors appointed Robert Wallace an agent for the purpose of collecting monies due the company, either on account of sale of Lottery tickets or of the subscription of stock in said company. On the 14th October 1819, the Treasurer notified Mr Dufour that the drawing of the lottery was progressing weekly, and was expected to continue in that way till completed and that he would be furnished from time to time with a statement of the drawing.

. . . . . . . . . . . .

"Whether any person made money by the operation or not is not now certainly known.

"It does not appear that any of the notes given for Lottery tickets ever were paid or fell into the hands of the Managers of the Lottery, or the Treasurer of the Canal Company.

"It appears as though every institution chartered by the State Legislature in the early days of the State, came to an untimely end, for example, the Bank of Vincennes the State Bank of Indiana the Canal Company and the Farmers and Mechanics Bank which was located at Madison with a Branch at Lawrenceburgh, all died a natural death long before the time [limit within which] they were by law permitted to transact business.

"In November 1817 The Grand Masonic Hall Lottery commenced drawing, and in December 1817 William C. Keen gave notice that a few tickets, warranted undrawn could yet be had at the original price of *Ten Dollars*; this lottery its believed also failed in realizing the exp[ect]ations of those who had the management of its affairs." 1869 MS., pp. 111-16.

[Page 74] [1] "After the termination of the War of 1812 with Great Britain many European emigrants came to Vevay and the

Neighboring Settlements in the County; during the years 1815, 1816, 1817 and 1818 great numbers from Europe seeking homes in the west came to this County many of whom purchased lands and permanently Settled among us." 1869 MS., p. 86.

² "From the Isle of Jersey." *Ibid.*

³ "Perhaps in 1818." *Ibid.*, p. 87.

[Page 75] ¹ "It would be a novel[t]y for some of your readers, to see a horse shod in the manner it was performed by Mr Grisard, for the writer on more than one occasion, it was performed perhaps by driving the nails in the usual manner, and for trimming the hoof after the nails were driven, the foot was placed on a sort of stool and while there was trimmed and rasped one holding the horse's foot on the stool." *Ibid.*

² "Mr Bolens married a Miss Pernet a cousin of David E. Pernet who resided so long at Mt. Sterling, he settled near Mount Sterling where the mound stood, and lived in a neat and comfortable looking log cabin for some time. He had brought with him to America a number of watches, and while living in the cabin alluded to, the watches were hung up against the wall near a window fronting the road, one night some thief in passing, removed a pane of glass, put his hand through and took some of the watches; in the morning the watches were missing, Mr Bolens mounting a horse rode to Vevay and secured the services of Jacob Malin, and another started down the river towards Madison in search of the thief, whom they overtook at or near Indian Kentucky still having in his possession the watches, the thief was placed on a horse, his feet tied under the horse and his hands behind his back and brought back as far as 'Uncle Morerods' gate where they halted, the thief was given his choice of being taken to town, put in jail, and kept there until court or take forty lashes on his bare back with a raw hide—he chose the latter—he was taken back of 'Uncle Morerods' barn, there tied to a tree his back made bare, a bottle of wine given him to drink which he swallowed when the forty stripes were well applied, when his back was washed with wine, his clothes replaced, led back to the gate on the river bank a bottle of wine given him to drink and he advised to leave, and never to show himself in the neighborhood again, he made his way down the road in the direction of Madison.

"In 1821 or 1822 Mr Bolens being at New Orleans with a cargo of Pork, stopped at a hotel. On entering he observed a person sitting with his face towards the door by which he entered, who so soon as Bolens entered turned his face and he could not get a fair chance to see his face, but that man left the hotel the next day and was not seen again by Bolens about New Orleans. Being unable to sell his pork at New Orleans he went to Havanna with it, and there he again encountered the man he had seen at the hotel in New Orleans, and again the man seemed to shun him, and left the hotel where they had stopped, Bolens was always of the belief that the thief who stole his watches, was whipped so unmercifully, and the man he met at New Orleans and at Havanna were one and the same, and that while in New Orleans and in Havanna, after he had seen him he was somewhat uneasy lest he might be waylaid and murdered by that man and fully prepared himself for any, thing of the Kind." 1869 MS., pp. 88-89.

[3] "And afterwards went to Bethlehem and entered into partnership with his brother in merchandizing." *Ibid.*, p. 89.

[4] "Who was so well and favorably Know[n] by the citizens of Mount Sterling and the surrounding Country, turned his attention to farming and keeping a retail store." *Ibid.*

[Page 76] [1] "He Kept a store, in which clothing, shoes, and every other article required by the laborers on the Canal was kept." *Ibid.*, p. 92.

[2] "The pecuniary aid he has extended to many of our farmers, in assisting them to buy and improve farms, whereby they were enabled to make for themselves comfortable homes, is a proof of his sagacity as a financier and business man, he may be said to be in the strictest sense of the word a sagacious and shrewd business man." *Ibid.*, pp. 92-93.

[3] "The names of many of those who went...from...his instruction as votaries of Vulcan...are here given. Henry Hatch, William Malcomson, Lemuel Siebenthal, Daniel Detraz, William Rochat, Joseph Jagers." *Ibid.*, p. 93.

[4] "In the fall of 1816 or Spring of 1817." *Ibid.*

[5] "Mr Malin had been merchandizing for a few years in connection with the saddle and harness making business, and turning his attention entirely to merchandizing, he entered into that business very actively and with much success. He occupied one part of the house in which Robert A Knox now resides on Main Street for a shop when he first came to the place, and then moved into a small two story frame [house] which stood on or near the spot, where the house to [now] stands, on Market Street, occupied by Mr. Shaw where he remained for several years when he re-

moved to a building on Main Street, about where the two story frame occupied by J. C. Wells & Co. and S. E. & J. K. Pleasant's, and adjoining to the house on the corner of Ferry and Main in which he carried on the mercantile business." 1869 MS., pp. 93-94.

[Page 78] [1] "To show the manner in which small change was secured, the following announcement to the public was made and the agreement of those in business in the town to take the small bills for their goods and wares.

"*To the Public.*

"Considering the scarcity of Small change and the solicitations of Some of my friends, I have been induced to issue small bills redeemable with current Bank notes. I intend keeping by me at all times three and five Dollar notes on the banks of Cincinnati or Kentucky or other good banks to the amount of the bills which I may have out. I will receive the said bills in payment of postages, fees or any other dues, to me or to other persons, which I am authorised to receive and I will redeem them, whenever the holder thereof will change one of the notes aforesaid if he has not [enough] of my bills to amount to three dollars I will receive small bills on the Banks of Kentucky, or Cincinnati, or other good Banks or specie to make up the balance.

"VEVAY August 5, 1816.                           "JOHN FRANCIS DUFOUR

"We the subscribers will receive in payment of any dues, John Francis Dufour's bills untill we notify to the contrary. Thomas Armstrong, Daniel Dufour Jonathan Reeder, David McCormick, Bazilla Clark Rawleigh Day, Joseph Noble, Isaac Stanley, Joseph Bentley, Jonas Baldwin, Charles F. Krutz, John F. Siebenthal.

"In accordance with the foregoing Statement of John Francis Dufour and the agreement of the business men who signed an agreement to receive the small bills, such small bills were printed signed num[b]ered and put in circulation, and they with those afterwards issued by Lucien Gex, Rawleigh Day and the Corporation of Vevay formed the small change used in this community for some years." *Ibid.*, p. 96.

[2] *Laws of Indiana*, 1816-17, pp. 185 ff.

[Page 79]  [1] "In December 1819." 1869 MS., p. 98.

[Page 80]  [1] "On the 7th of February 1820 a Statement of the condition of the branch Bank at Vevay was made and is as follows.

| | |
|---|---|
| Notes Discounted | 42,781.13 |
| Bills discounted payable at the Bank of Cincinnati | 1,872.00 |
| Vevay Branch notes in Bank | 29,715.00 |

| | |
|---|---:|
| Bills receivable as cash in payment of debts in Bank | 7,185.00 |
| Do       Do       Burnt | 6,760.00 |
| Change Tickets in Bank | 50.12½ |
| Do   Do   Burnt | 31.00 |
| Western Notes | 25.00 |
| Specie | 905.28½ |
| General expences | 285.30 |
| Due from V. Vairin | 18.00 |
| Deficit which includes the account on the Ledger which the Cashier has there entered against himself | 4,636.43 |
| | $94,264.27 |

| | |
|---|---:|
| Deposited to the Credit of the Bank of Vincennes | 30,506.31 |
| Bills receivable as cash in payment of debts signed and issued | 17,140.00 |
| Change tickets      do      do | 3,007.00 |
| Vincennes notes payable at Vevay | 41,900.00 |
| Deposited to credit of Miami Exporting Company | 107.06 |
| Balances in favor of Individuals | 785.38½ |
| Discounts | 818.51 |
| | $94,264.27 |

We the Undersigned, being a committee appointed for the special purpose, do hereby certify the above Statement to be correct and that the said branch Bank as it above appears was delivered over by the Cashier to John F. Dufour the president of said Bank on the said 7th day of February 1820. We the said committee further certify that all the property books and papers of said Branch Bank were all and singular then and there delivered to the said John F. Dufour by the said Cashier, except the two bills of exchange mentioned in the above statement which are in the Bank of Cincinnati for collection as appears per Bill Book.

"JOHN F. DUFOUR.
"JOHN GILLILAND.    } committee
"THOMAS ARMSTRONG."

1869 MS., pp. 99-100.

[2] "In these times of high taxes, and burdens upon the tax payers of the country, of which we hear so much said every day where, an assemblage of people, are met, and of which we read in every newspaper, published in our land, it may be interesting to those who read these articles, to know something about the burdens, and taxes borne by the people, forty or forty five years ago.

"These things can be seen by any person, who would take the trouble of examining the records of County affairs on file in the Auditors office at Vevay, so far as relates to the County of Switzerland, and the archives of State at Indianapolis so far as relates to the state finances—but that every person and tax payer of the County may have a glimpse at these matters, who reads the *Democrat* a few statements in relation to these matters will be given in these numbers from time to time. The first will be a 'Statement of the financial concerns of Switzerland County from the 16th of November 1822 to the 12th of November 1823 inclusive.'

It appears that that on the 15th November 1822 there was a deficit of $914.20, in other words the County was in debt to that amount at that date. The amount of the duplicate placed in the hands of the collector for the year 1823 amounted to the sum of $1,126.80, and the amount of other receipts were $288.64, making the total amount of receip[t]s for the county provided the whole amount on the duplicate was collected $1,415.44.

"The total amount of expenditures including the $914.20 the amount of the deficit for the year 1822 as above stated was $2387.05 [from] which it will be seen [that] the indebtedness of the County on the 12th November 1823 was $971.61, showing that instead of paying off the debt of the previous year, the indebtedness of the county was increased.

"This Statement shows that the whole amount of taxes collected and on the duplicate for that year amounted [to] $1415.43¾ for that one year; at the August Election 1824 the number of votes cast for the three candidates for congress, in the county was 621 votes, by dividing the amount of taxes imposed on the voters of the county for that year by the number of Voters, will show that the taxes was about $2.28 for each Voter—and yet there was a deficit of $971.61½ which would have required an additional tax of about $1.56 on each voter to pay that deficiency—and would have required a tax of about $3.84 on each Voter for that year.

"About this time county orders were offered for sale by those holding them at 50 cents on the dollar, without purchasers, except in Suitable amounts for tax payers to pay their county taxes; how very different from, what these matters are at this time—the amount of taxes, charged on the Duplicate, the receipts and expenditures of the County and the number of Voters in the County at present, only, can make the reader realize the difference.

"It appears that the receipts and expenditures of the State from the commencement of the State Government, in 1816 to the first of January 1823 made an aggregate of $113,230.34, received at the State Treasury during that period from taxes alone, to which is added revenue of the Territory, receipts on account of seat of Government, salt springs and incidental receipts to make the aggregate of receipts from all sources amount to $183,185.51 while the aggregate of expenditures amounted to $170,686.53 and leaving a balance in the treasury on the first of January 1824 of $12,498.53 which to the casual observer, would appear, to be a very satisfactory financial condition for the young state to boast of, after an existance of only seven years.

"But for all this good showing, the financial affairs of the State it is said were in a very unsatisfactory condition, for on the assembling of the Legislature on the first Monday in December 1823, the Governor communicated to that body the situation of the affairs of the State.

"On taking a view of the financial concerns of the State together with the situation of the departments of the auditor and treasurer, it was deemed advisable to make a thorough examination and exhibit of those departments from the beginning of the State government up to the first of January 1824. To do this would require the constant labor of a master book keeper, and accountant for something near thirty days. Numbers of the members of the legislature could have ably performed that service, but none of them were willing to leave the house, and their other business entirely to attend to that—hence it became necessary to employ some person to perform that service. The Hon. Isaac Blackford was called upon, and although the task was almost Herculean, yet he undertook it and in about thirty days, went through both departments from the first day of the state government up to the 1st day of January 1824, and made a detailed report in writing, exhibiting in a clear, plain, and satisfactory manner the true situation of the financial concerns of the State. The report was a document of great importance, inasmuch as it was the foundation of a new era in the management of the departments of the Auditor and Treasurer of State. The treasury department at the beginning of that session of the legislature was much embarrassed, and pressed for payment, and the legislature was compelled to provide, either by the reissue, of treasury notes, or by loan the sum of about $20,000 to meet the payments of the state debts which were then due and daily becoming due. The Governor had recommended a loan, and that plan for raising the required amount was adopted, without hesitation, and an act passed authorizing a loan of any sum not exceeding $19,000.

"The reissue of treasury notes was opposed on the ground, well known that there were no funds to redeem them, and that it would have been countenancing the odious principle of banking without capital, which in their opinion would have been an indirect species of swindling. It was supposed by some that the system of loaning might at first, be unpopular, but firmly believing that it was the only true policy, which could be adopted by which the credit of the state could be preserved, and that it would stand the test of honesty, wisdom and time, it was finally adopted without a dissenting voice.

"A law was passed by that legislature removing the seat of Government from Corydon to Indianapolis on the 1st day of January 1825: and the next general assembly was to convene there on the 2nd Monday in January 1825.

. . . . . . . . . .

"At that session of the legislature the votes cast for and against the calling of a Convention to change the constitution of the state were examined and officially announced as follows 'No convention' 11,991 votes 'convention' 2601 votes majority against a Convention 9,390 votes. Nearly half the counties neglected to make returns to the secretary of state.

"The financial operations of the State Treasury for the year 1824 were more successful than was anticipated by the most sanguine. Of the $19,000 supposed to be necessary to be procured by loan, only $5,971, was procured and of that sum $975 were seminary funds unemployed in the treasury. So beneficial to the treasury was the change of system, that the current expenditures were more easily and more promptly met with that amount, than the[y] were the previous year by a reissue of $15,000 of treasury notes; and with the additional advantage, that on the expenditures, authorized by the legislature of the previous year, the state paid interest on $5,971 only, while on that authorized by the legislature at its preceeding session interest was paid on $15,000. In addition, the public credit was maintained, the currency restored to soundness, and much of the public expenditure economized, in proportion as the currency was rescued from depreciation.

"The receipts into the treasury during the year 1824 amounted to $40,435.94 by which the treasury notes were redeemed in good faith, and the Audited Warrants paid and there was on the 10th of January 1825 in the treasury in available funds $12,508.

"The State debt amounted on the 1st of January 1824, to $27,044.19. On the 1st of January 1825 in [it] amounted to $17,499.17 exclusive of Interest. That indebtedness consisted of $4,655 treasury notes then in circulation $5,971 loan, $5,000 which the State owed to roads and canals, and $1,373.17 on bonds transferred to the treasurer of the United States. The State debt on the 10th January 1825 exclusive of interest, exceeded the actual cash in the treasury, $4,991.15.

"The revenue for 1824 after deducting the per cent for collecting amounted to $39,294.86. The current expenditures of the year 1825 were estimated not to exceed $21,000 and [a] reduction on [of] all contingent expences were [was] confidently expected." 1869 MS., pp. 162-66.

[Page 81] [1] "The next physician who came to the town was Dr. John Mendenhall who came in 1815 or 1816, who commenced the practice of his profession and had quite an extensive and lucrative practice for many years, in fact until his age prevented him from paying attention to calls from the country any distance from town, and going about at night.

"About the year 1816 or 1817 Dr James Welch who was also a Presbyterian minister came to Vevay, bringing with him a large stock of Dry goods; he commenced the mercantile business, as also the practice of his medical profession, preaching on the Sabbath in the Court house; about the year 1818 or 1819 he built the large brick building corner of Market and Main Cross streets, one room, in the corner of the main building, was occupied as a store room, the one immediately in its rear being used as the counting room, and one room in the ell as a Drug Store; the latter being attended to by his son George W. Welsh, who died about the year 1820. Dr Welsh it was said, was in the habit of using intoxicating liquors, as a beverage to excess, and often has the writer heard him tell his congregation, from the pulpit, during his sermons, 'Do as I tell you, and not as I do' referring no doubt to his habit of using intoxicating drinks frequently to excess, be that as it may, the church judicature, instituted proceedings against him sometime in the year 1825 or 26, and after an investigation of the case he was silenced as a minister, and shortly afterwards died, as was said by some, from mortification, at the decision made against him.

"The judicature that condemned Dr Welsh was presided over by Joshua L. Wilson of Cincinnati, who was so long connected with the first Presbyterian church at Cincinnati.

"Dr Edward Stall a regular physician formerly from Baltimore came to Vevay soon after and remained for several years, he finally left and removed to Cincinnati; one of his daughters married a Mr Wolf and resides in Rushville in this State; Her Husband was in the Service during the rebellion, and was killed or died, a son who is at present or was a short time since Auditor of Rush County was also in the service, and served as an officer, with distinguished honor to himself and the cause he espoused.

"Many other physicians of more recent date were residents of Vevay and regular practitioners some of whom were eminent in their professions. About 1827 Dr. Samuel W. Clarkson commenced practicing, and became a very skillful and successful physician. Dr. Joseph McCutchen a regular graduate of Dublin medical college came to Vevay 1832 or, 33, and had a very extended practice and became quite wealthy by attention to his practice." 1869 MS., pp. 121-22.

² The jury was composed of "Robert Cotton, John Shupe, Nathaniel Cotton, Isaac Richards, Daniel Haycock, Daniel Bray, David Winteroad, Francis Lonsdale, Ralph Cotton, Benjamin Cole, Marvin Backus, and Nathaniel Gerard." *Ibid.*, p. 75.

[Page 83]   ¹ Dufour in his manuscript of 1869 speaks of Joseph Bosseau as "being at this time 78 years of age, and residing on Bee-Tree Run, 2½ miles from Vevay, and his brother John, being his segnior by 5 years, resides in Wood County West Virginia."

² The sentence "Joseph Bosseau . . . year" is crossed out.

³ "It is said that in the very early days of navig[a]ting the Ohio and its tributaries, that the following dialogue, if it may be so termed occurred between a person on shore and the captain of a Keel boat out in the stream descending the Ohio 'Hallo the Boat' 'Hallo'. 'What is the name of that boat?' 'Yellow Stone' 'Where is it from?'   'red stone'   'Where are you bound to?' 'Lime Stone'   'What are you loaded with?'   'Grind stones' 'What is the Captains name?'   'Whetstone'." 1869 MS., p. 147.

⁴ "The boat on which he was employed up the Kentucky river, was in the service of Lewis Sanders, who about that time was engaged quite extensively, in manufacturing near Lexington Kentucky and in mercha[n]dizing.     It is said that John Sanders and Ab. Sanders, were engaged in running boats up the Kentucky river about this time but the exact year the writer has not been able to ascertain.

. . . . . . . . .

"At one time on leaving Pittsburgh a bet was made, by the Captain of the Keel 'Uncle Joe', was on board of and the Captain of another boat as to which would beat to Cincinnati. The boat on which 'Uncle Joe' belonged was to start one day ahead of the other boat. On arriving at Biffington's Island the water being quite low and not of a sufficient depth to admit the passage of the boat—about 100 barrels of whiskey were put over board, and with a rope made fast together by tacking the rope to the Barrells. They were sent ahead to their destination at the Mouth of Big Sandy, and yet the boat could not pass untill stone[s] at the bottom were removed to deepen the channel and the boat, by this means, was gotten through the shallow channel, but that their competitors might not profit by the channel being thus cleared of the obstruction to their passing, the stones thus removed together with others were thrown back into the channel from which they had been taken—thus making the channel perhaps shallower than, they found it, so when the other boat arrived at that point they could not pass and were compelled to deepen the channel which delayed them, and 'Uncle Joe' and his companions landed their boat at Cincinnati about three days in advance of their competitors.

"John and Joseph Bosseau are said to be the only survivors of those who were engaged in navigating the western waters in those early days, with Keel boats.

"These facts and incidents are here related, as related the writer by 'Uncle Joe' himself, some days since, not for any worth or merit attaching to them but with the thought, that perhaps fifty years hence some of those who may then be on the stage of action, may chance to read them and learn what those who preceded them in the Voyage of life had been called upon to do and to suffer that the necessaries of life might be conveyed from one point to another in this now great and prosperous valley of the 'father of Waters', and his numerous tributaries.

"It is said that John Bosseau is to visit this county soon and if so, let any who are curious, to hear from his and his brother Josephs own lips a recital of their trials, hardships, privations, and pleasures too, call and perhaps what is here written of them and much more may be learned." 1869 MS., pp. 147-150.

"In reading the accounts of passengers, arriving in San Francisco California, from New York city in Six and Eight days calls to the recollection of the writer, the travels performed by persons from this place to different points in the State years gone by—In 1817 or 1818 the trip from Vevay to Vincennes, was performed on horseback in the Spring of the year in about Six days, through mud, rain and across Swollen water courses, in many cases having to cross a stream through the water for the distance perhaps of some two, three and often times four miles.

"As late as the fall of 1832 the writer in company with others, were over three days in reaching Indianapolis from Vevay, which at that time was as great an undertaking as a trip to St. Louis or St. Paul would be in these days of fast travelling." *Ibid.*, p. 126.

[Page 84]   ¹ General Lafayette came to Cincinnati from Covington, Indiana. *Ibid.*, p. 137.

² "Sometime in 1818 or 1819, William C Keen, who was a Brigadier General of Indiana Militia, and resided in Vevay, received Two Six pounder Iron guns from the State authorities, being the

quota of that grade of arms to be distributed in his brigade. One of those guns was sent to Rising Sun, where an artillery company had been Organized. The other was retained at this place, and a company was organized, and Daniel Vincent Dufour was elected Captain of that Company. There was no person at the time who knew much if any thing of artillery practice, except the Captain, he having attended a military School in his native country. The company was organized, and were regularly drilled, So that in a short time, it was, what might be termed a No 1. company, So far as maneuvering with the Gun was concerned. The company was, after it had been organization [organized], three or four years, composed of young men from Switzerland, and Sons of the Swiss about Vevay, and a few Americans. The names of some of them as far as can be ascertained, were; Captain Daniel Vincent Dufour, privates Stephen C. Jones, William H. Jones, Charles Thiebaud, Abraham Raymond, Rodolph Morerod, Frederick Morerod, John Detraz, Benjamin Detraz, George Kessler, Frederick Deserens, Justus Vairin, Andrew Bornaud, Philip Bettens, Benjamin F. Siebenthal, Frederick L. Grisard. After the first organization of the company, many others became members, but none appear to have been near as expert gunners as some of the old members, who were drilled and exercised, in the management of the gun occasionally on Sunday afternoons

. . . . . . . . . .

"On introducing the General to the Swiss artillerists, John James Dufour took occasion to make a speech in which he referred to the services of the General during the War of the Revolution, and that the Swiss who then Stood before him, had come to the United States to enjoy the blessings of the Government he had been instrumental in securing for his fellow man.

"After firing their gun for Several hours, the Cartridges gave out, and they had to procure others. It is said that the members of the Cincinnati Company, chagrined on account of the correctness and the rapidity with which the Vevay company went through the exercise of loading and firing, made cartridges for the Vevay gun too large, with the view of retarding them in the rapidity of their firing; but still the Vevay company, although the cartridges were too large, were still able to fire twice or three times to the Cincinnati company's one.

"The two companies tried their skill in rapid firing on the following day, and bets of from one hundred to one thousand dollars were freely offered that the Vevay Company could fire two to one, none of which bets were taken.

"The Uniform of the Company was rather an awkward and heavy one for Summer wear. It consisted of a Blue dress coat trim[m]ed in Scarlet, a bear skin Cap about one foot high, rather bell-crowned, and trimmed with scarlet cord and tassel. Well does the writer, who in later years was a member of the company, remember how oppressive the great black cap and blue cloth coat buttoned up to the chin, were on fourth of July occasions, when drawn up in line in the hot sun. The uniform of the 'Old Specks' of 1862 & 1863, although very oppressive in warm weather, was nothing to compare with that of the Old Swiss artillery company.

"Among those members who took part in manning the gun on the Visit to Cincinnati, and participated in the festivities of the occasion, were the Captain, John and Benjamin Detraz, Stephen C. Jones, William H. Jones, Abm Raymond, Frederick Deserens. Others were of the number, but their names are not now recollected.

"Some members of the company were unexpectedly prevented by unforeseen circumstances from being present. Of that number, Rodolph Morerod, George Kessler, Justus Vairin and Frederick L. Grisard can be named, and it is said that some of them were very much disappointed in not being with their comrades.

"The occasion of the Visit of General Lafayette to Cincinnati was an event that was heralded in the papers of that place and the Surrounding country for months before the appointed time for his arrival there.

"After the ceremonies of his reception, and, the incidents attending, the newspapers of Cincinnati, Louisville, Lexington, and all the smaller towns, for weeks after, were filled with, accounts of the Ceremonies, and of the many incidents that occurred on that day; and all of them had to award the praise to the Swiss Artillery Company of Vevay for, the precision, and rapidity with which they managed and fired their gun; and it may be said that every member of that company felt proud of belonging to it, whether he was present or absent on the occasion, which elicited so much praise from Strangers.

"Many of the Statements made in this number are from personal recollection, and others from facts related by some members of the Company who took part in the management and fireing of 'Old Betz' on that occasion." 1869 MS., pp. 136-40.

[Page 88]   ¹ "The father of Mrs Ungler." *Ibid.*, p. 118.

² "The father of Francis Bonner." *Ibid.*

³ "Now" is crossed out and "lately" substituted.

[Page 89]   ¹ See *ante*, 56, note 1.

[Page 91]   ¹ "Certain persons who were opposed to his election, and wishing to defeat him, met together and determined on supporting Daniel Haycock as a candidate in Opposition to Mr. Merrill. The canvass was conducted with much spirit by the friends of both candidates. Mr. Merrill's claims on the score of qualifications for the position, were not in the least questioned by any, but his opponents urged against him that he was a Yankee adventurer; that their candidate was a man of the people, and ought to be elected; and all the usual appliances of those early days were used to induce the voters of the county to vote for Daniel Haycock, the peoples candidate, against Samuel Merrill, the Yankee adventurer, who had come among us only to get office, which, as was urged, he could not get where he came from." 1869 MS., p. 141.

[Page 93] ¹ Four lines are here crossed out. They read: "[He] was President of the State Bank of Indiana, and President of the Madison and Indianapolis Rail Road during its palmiest days His history is in part the history of his adopted state."

² "Among those who, it is recollected, dealt out the O' be joyful to their thirsty customers in Vevay, within the recollection of the writer may be mentioned. Frederick and Otis Waldo, who kept their shop at the corner of ferry and Market Streets, for several years, when they commenced keeping dry goods, the latter was the father of O. S. and F. J. Waldo, and the former was their grand father.

"Edward Patton who kept, whiskey, cider and wine, to sell by the small, in a log house, opposite to the residence of J. L. Thiebaud on Market Street, and on the lot on which O. S. Waldo's residence stands.

"Daniel Debetaz who held forth on a house which stood on Main Street where Charles Thiebaud's residence, and the National Bank are situated. He remained there for some years, and finally removed to New Castle Ky.

"Israel R. Whitehead had an establishment on the lot where Mathias Madary now resides, he also had a bakery, which was attended to in the mechanical department by Mr. Madary for a few years, when Mr. Madary bought the house and lot and set up for himself and carried on a thriving business, in the bakery and retailing liquors. An anecdote worthy of relating took place about this time. A law had been enacted by the Legislature of Indiana requiring the boards doing county business to procure and keep in the office of the Clerk of the County a Standard of weights and measures, these had been procured, and placed in possession of Edward Patton who was then clerk of the County, one day the Clerk visited some of the shops and places where liquors were sold at retail, not by the drink, but by the gill, half pint &c, calling in at Mr. Madarys, the clerk informed him that he had called to try his weights and measures, and as the glasses on the counter and Shelves were third pints, instead of half pints Mr. Madary called on his wife to bring him the 'big tumblers'. It is useless to say any thing further of this matter, than, that is [it] was a joke gotten up by the Clerk for his own sport.

"Later years brought upon the stage as retailers of spirituous liquors, as a beverage, William Shaw and Zadig Rous who were in their day the most popular caterers, to the appetites of their numerous customers, who could be counted by hundreds, in arranging mint Juleps, Tom and Jerry, Irish and Italian punch, &c. during their continuing in that business they were very successful and made considerable money and eventually abandoned that business, which was carried on at the corner of Ferry and Main Streets, where J. C. Wells store in [is] kept, but in a different building, and entered into the Dry goods & grocery business.

"Percy Rous also was engaged in the retail liquor trade in this place, and from appearances did a tolerably fair business, but did not continue at it for any considerable length of time.

"Many others have been engaged in the retail liquor trade in Vevay who have left long since and who did not make much of a mark in the business; Some of our most prominent business men, have at some time during their lives been engaged in the business.

"There is perhaps no business, on which the opinion of many persons, has, undergone, so radical a change as the business of retailing Spirituous liquors; many who were engaged in it and secured quite a competency of this worlds goods, and thought it a laudable business, and respected those engaged in it, as men of good moral character, and good citizens now hold the opinion that no man of good moral character would engage in the 'iniquitous' business." 1869 MS., pp. 123-25.

"And thus at a general election on the first Monday in August, when several officers were to be elected, and several aspirants for each office, there might have been seen on the counters from ten to fifteen bottles filled with whiskey, with the name of a candidate on each bottle; and as the voting proceeded through the day, those who were watching, the interests of their favorite candidates, would step into the grocery to see how the whiskey of their favorites, was being drank. If the bottle of the friend was full, enqu[i]ry would be made of the bar-keeper how many times he had filled that bottle. It it had been filled oftener than the bottle of his favorites opponent, he went away with a light heart, assured that his favorite's friends were in the ascendency and thus the whiskey bottle was regarded as the thermometer of the state of the public mind, in relation to the success or defeat of the candidates. 1869 MS., pp. 143-44.

[Page 95] [1] "To give the reader some idea of, the privileges, for mail facilities we enjoy at present, over the citizens of this county in 1818 the following editorial is copied from a number of the *Indiana Register* published in Vevay January 27, 1818 by John F. Dufour Editor.—'Three weeks have elapsed since we have re-'ceived any news from Corydon, the seat of Government of our 'own state, owing no doubt, to the unpardonable negligence of 'mail contractors.'

"On the 1st of January 1818 Mr Frederick L. Thiebaud being at Georgetown Ky on business had the misfortune to have the mare which he rode taken away from him, and on his return to Vevay he caused the following notice to be published in the *Indiana Register.*

" 'Notice'.

" 'The person who, on the evening of the 1st inst. before a public 'house in Georgetown, Ky. took a dark bay mare, with a saddle 'and bridle, and left in her stead a bay horse, about 4 or 5 years 'old, with saddle and bridle, is informed that he may get his horse, 'by returning said mare to the subscriber living three miles below, 'Vevay Indiana, who did not discover the exchange until the next 'morning, being on his way home.'

" 'FRED'K L. THIEBAUD'

" 'The editor of the *Georgetown Patriot* will insert the above 'three times, and forward his account to the Post Master at Vevay 'who will pay for the same.'

"Whether Mr Thiebaud ever effected an exchange by which he obtained his mare again is not known to the writer." *Ibid.*, p. 117.

[2] For a short sketch of Smith's life, see William Wesley Woollen, *Biographical and Historical Sketches of Early Indiana,* 196 ff. (Indianapolis, 1883).

[3] The name of this Switzerland County town was changed about 1846 or 1847. In the United States *Official Register* for 1847, it is listed as "Florence (Late New York)." [Ed.]

[Page 100] [1] Wilson H. Gray served only until October 26, 1841. His term was completed by Abner Clarkson. United States, *Official Register,* 1843, p. 530*. Frederick L. Courvoissier served from 1861 until 1863, when Frederick J. Waldo's appointment took effect. *Ibid.*, 1863, p. 373.

² Beginning with "J. C. Long," this list has been amended to read: "J. C. Long from 1869 untill 1877. Alfred Shaw from 1877 until the present and was lately appointed by the President and confirmed by the Senate."

[Page 101] ¹ The phrase "It is true," apparently refers to an account of the Lochry massacre and the later development of the country, which immediately preceded this sentence in the original draft of the manuscript. An account of the massacre now appears on pages 2 to 5.

² "Truman Richards a young lawyer from the State of New York an estimable young man, who was writing for John F. Dufour in the Clerks office fell a victim, to the dreadful scourge, his estate was administered on by Dr William Stephenson, a brother in law of Judge Stephen C. Stevens; the interest in the estate was sold by the heirs who resided in New York, to Jonathan Hawkins the father of Ainsworth Hawkins, and Mrs Rosetta Ransom, by this Sale of the estate by the heirs, there is nothing to be seen standing in the Grave yard to mark where his remains were deposited save perhaps a rough lime stone, with the letter R roughly cut on it; this ought not to be thus, for Mr Richards was truly a worthy and estimable young man and his remains deserve a better memorial, but as he died in a strange land among strangers, far away from, home, and friends, it cannot be expected to be otherwise.

"It may be proper here to state, that instead of there being but two lawyers or attornies at law buried in the Vevay Cemet[e]ry there are certainly known to be four, Truman Richards, James M. Kyle, Aurelius W. Dumont and Robert Drummond the three latter of whom many of your readers, especially in Switzerland County will doubtless recollect." 1869 MS., p. 123.

For a further account of the fever, see *ante*, 62.

[Page 109] ¹ "The Lieutenant Colonel, did not cut quite such a fantastic figure on parade as his superior in command, and they two frequently differed as to the manner in which certain evolutions should be performed, which on more than one occasion was the cause of a regular battle between the two field officers, in the evening after the Regiment was dismissed, in which the claret imbibed, caused the 'claret' to flow freely from the wounds received; and these differences of opinion not only caused these two *heroes* to shed their blood in these battles, but caused the Grand Jurors, and the Judges, and officers of the courts to spend some of their time in vindicating the civil law, for violations of its wholesome provisions, as the records of the courts about that time will make plain." 1869 MS., pp. 79-80.

# NOTES

[Page 110] ¹ See *ante*, 55-57 and notes.

[Page 113] ¹ "Is the present...proprietor," has been changed to "has sold the establishment to P. T. Hartford and ———— Dalmazzo."

[Page 114] ¹ "Is now...business," has been amended to read, "was a Justice of the peace and engaged in the Real estate and Insurance agency business, and died two years since."

² "Is" has been changed to "was."

³ "Has," at the beginning of the sentence, has been changed to "Had," and at the end of the sentence, the following words have been added: "died two or three years ago."

⁴ "Is at present...county," has been amended to read: "was engaged in business at Markland in this county, at present in the wharf boat business with Wesley McHenry."

[Page 115] ¹ The following words have been added: "and is at this time in Florida cultivating oranges."

² This sentence has been amended to read: "John H. Wright was engaged in the publication of the *Independent* at Carrol[l]ton Ky."

[Page 120] ¹ The phrase "and are yet both living" has been crossed out, and the following sentence inserted at the end of the paragraph: "Frederick L. Grisard died in January 1881 leaving his widow a competency, to serve her during her life."

² An account of the Red River Colony by Augustus L. Chetlain appeared in *Harper's New Monthly Magazine*, December, 1878 (59:47-55). Mr. Chetlain also wrote a pamphlet, *The Red River Colony* (Chicago, 1893), which included a letter from Zelie Simon Grisard (pp. 29-34). Perret Dufour's account follows this letter for the most part, though there are occasional discrepancies in matter of detail.

[Page 125] ¹ The following names have been crossed out: William Cotton, Jr., Elijah Dickason, Lewis W. Beal, William Roberts and Daniel Ramseyer.

[Page 131] ¹ *Revised Laws of Indiana*, 1824, pp. 86 ff.

² *Laws of Indiana*, 1825-26, pp. 84-85.

[Page 132] ¹ See *ante*, 95, note 3.

² The law was approved February 8, 1836. *Laws of Indiana* (local) 1835-36, p. 68.

[Page 133]   ¹ *Revised Laws of Indiana*, 1831, pp. 129 ff.

[Page 134]   ¹ *Laws of Indiana*, 1840-41, pp. 3 ff.

[Page 139]   ¹ "And is at this time...county," has been amended to read: "at the October ele[c]tion 1878 Robert T. F. Abbott was elected for four years—and is a candidate for reelection at the election in November 1882."

[Page 141]   ¹ The following incomplete statement has been added: "At the October election 1876 Americus Benedict was elected for 2 years and in 1878."

[Page 142]   ¹ *Laws of Indiana*, 1840-41, pp. 10 ff.

² "Is at present...office," has been amended to read: "at the October election 1878 was re-elected for fo[u]r years. Philip C. Holland is the Democratic and Richard Moore the Republican candidate, at the November election 1882."

[Page 145]   ¹ *Laws of Indiana*, 1828-29, pp. 33 ff.   See also Monks, L. J., *Courts and Lawyers of Indiana*, 3:1026 ff.

² See also *ante*, 55-56 and index.

[Page 146]   ¹ *Revised Statutes of Indiana*, 1852, vol. 2:16 ff.

[Page 147]   ¹ *Laws of Indiana*, 1873, p. 96.

[Page 148]   ¹ Alexander A. Meek was president judge from January 2, 1819, until February 2, 1819. John W. Spencer was appointed August 9, 1858, and served until October 26, 1858. Monks, *Courts and Lawyers*, 3:1030.

[Page 155]   ¹ *Laws of Indiana* (local) 1838-39, p. 38.   *Ibid.*, 1840-41, pp. 27 ff.

[Page 157]   ¹ "Stephen C. Stevens was elected Speaker, over David H. Maxwell by a vote of 23 to 20.

"At the August election of 1824 three members of Congress were elected to represent the State in the 19th Congress."   1869 MS., p. 158.

[Page 158]   ¹ See *ante*, 174.

[Page 160]   ¹ *Laws of Indiana*, 1853, pp. 29 ff.

² United States, *Statutes at Large*, 3:289.

# NOTES

[Page 161]   ¹ This parenthesis should stand immediately after "Randolph."

² Dufour gives the vote for Test as 3,522 and for Caswell, as 1,459. 1869 MS., p. 159.

[Page 163]   ¹ "In concluding the address the committee in relation to the great New York Canal which was at that time unfinished 'We have fellow citizens, this cheering answer—2,398 boats arrived at Utica—119,142 barrels flour,—15,164 barrels salt—5,675 barrels provisions—8,594 barrels pot and pearl ashes—59 barrels kelp—125,793 bushels wheat, 67,917 Barrels western lime 175 M. lathe, 2,690 M. shingles 14,762 cedar posts, 20,032 square feet of timber—1,364,147 feet boards 601,911 Oak staves—229,857 gallons whiskey' and many other articles. 'Who has been the projector and effector of all this'? DeWitt Clinton 'the man whose 'excellence and practical worth we hope you will equally appreciate 'with us, leave no fair and honorable means unemployed to promote 'his election.'

"This address was signed by James Welsh chairman and John Dumont Secretary." *Ibid.*, p. 160.

[Page 167]   ¹ "She was used by the Whig and Democratic parties, on occasions of party meetings, and on other occasions, in which both parties, as citizens of the town were alike interested.

"On occasions of Celebrating the 4th of July, in which Whigs and Democrats alike participated 'Old Betz' was called into requisition to fire salutes. On several occasions, when the Cin. & Lou. mail line Company, placed a new boat in the Mail line, our citizens without respect to party would have 'Old Betz' hawled to the river bank on the day such new Boat was first to pass our town, and as the Boat neared the landing 'Old Betz' would growl fiercely and loudly.

"After an election was over and the result known, whether favorable to the Whig or Democrat side 'Old Betz' would [be] brought out to proclaim victory to the victorious party, and on many occasions Democratic men would assist in manning the Gun to fire at a Whig victory and vice versa; but since the evil days of Know Nothingism, no such harmonious action has occurred, but on the contrary, the defeated party in one instance at least, took 'Old Betz' at the dead hour of night and near Vevay Island, buried her beneath the water and mud where she remained for about one and a half or two years, before being recovered.

"About the time of the commencement of the War the Carriage of 'Old Betz becoming unfit for use the Corporation trustees, caused her to be remounted, at a cost of nearly or quite two hundred dollars—, and during the continuance of the war, was manned by a company of the old citizens of the town whose ages were mostly fifty years, and some over that age, but the age of the first members being such as to cause the name of 'Old Specks' to be given to the Company.

"Sometime after the war and on an occasion of rejoicing over a Republican Victory in an election, 'Old Betz' was seen travelling through the Streets of Vevay accompanied by members of the Republican party, with a banner bearing the inscription 'A Terror to Rebels' since which time no trace of 'Old Betz' can be had, some supposing that as she had accomplished her destiny, she has been committed to her grave, the whereabouts of which it is said no one knows." 1869 MS., pp. 150-151.

[Page 170] ¹ In the reapportionment of 1833, Switzerland County was placed in the fourth district. In the next apportionment, 1842, it was returned to the third district, and remained there until 1872, when it was again placed in the fourth district. Indiana, *Legislative Manual*, 1899 and 1900, pp. 464 ff.

[Page 171] ¹ James H. Lane represented the fourth district in the session of 1853-55. Indiana, *Year Book*, 1917, p. 867.

² William M. Dunn represented the third district from 1859 until 1863, and Jeremiah M. Wilson the fourth district in the session of 1873-75. *Ibid.*, 867-68.

³ Samuel Merrill was not in the senate, but in the house of representatives during 1820-21. William Cotton represented Switzerland, Jefferson, Ripley and Jennings from 1819 until 1821, and Switzerland and Ripley during the session of 1821-22.

[Page 172] ¹ The following sentence has been inserted here: "From 1878 to 1882 Levin J. Woollen has been the Senator."

² See *ante*, 171, note 3.

[Page 173] ¹ "A period of...Philander S. Sage," has been amended to read: "a period of Fifty years only three are known to be living, and Philander S. Sage—Benjamin L. Robinson and Alexander C. Downey."

[Page 174] ¹ See *ante*, 158-59.

[Page 175] ¹ No evidence has since been found to establish this fact.

[Page 177] ¹ This treatise was published at the *Indiana Register* office, Vevay, in 1824, as a small paper-bound volume con-

## NOTES

taining eighty-eight close-set pages. Jesse Holman's letter is reproduced inside the title page.

[Page 181] ¹ "About the year 1821 or 22 the exact period not now recollected". 1869 MS., p. 105.

[Page 184] ¹ A blank was left at this point in the manuscript for the insertion of the sons' names.

[Page 185] ¹ The following sentence has been inserted here: "John L. Armington had some disagreement with his wife, obtained a bogus Divorce, married again, he was indicted for bigamy found guilty and sentenced to the penetentiary."

[Page 188] ¹ The following sentence has been inserted here: "For the last few years George W Murphy, Manford, Weaver and now Martin are the only persons who have worked at the business."

[Page 194] ¹ Switzerland County.

² "About...stands," has been changed to read, "on the lot on which the National Hotel stands."

[Page 198] ¹ There were twenty-seven farmers in the house of representatives.

[Page 199] ¹ *Revised Laws of Indiana*, 1824, pp. 188 ff.

[Page 208] ¹ See map, *Indiana Historical Collections*, 12:457.

[Page 209] ¹ *Laws of Indiana*, 1829-30, pp. 111 ff.

[Page 221] ¹ A document showing the manner of acquiring property and title.

[Page 223] ¹ The signature is in the form of a paraph, or flourish of the pen peculiar to a given individual.

# INDEX

# Index

Abbott, Robert T. F., clerk of circuit court, 402.
Adams, John Quincy, 161; elected president, 165-66.
Adkins, Martin, constable, 59.
Adkinson, Francis, judge, court of common pleas, 146.
Allain, ———, dealings with John James Dufour, 241.
Allegheny Mountains, 8, 12.
Allegheny River, 10.
Allen, John, publishes *Indiana Register*, 56, 111; publishes Salem *Annotator*, 56, 111, 113, 376.
Allensville (Indiana), 65, 192, 194; laid out, 144.
Allensville, Center Square, and Vevay Turnpike, 190, 191.
Amboy (New Jersey), John James Dufour at, 323.
Anderson, Catharine (Mrs. Isaac Naylor), attends Vevay school, 356.
Anderson, Lieutenant Isaac, describes Indian massacre, 2-5; journal, 351.
Anderson, John, 74.
Anderson, William, county commissioner, 134.
Anderson, ———, 289.
Andrews, John, land entry, 36.
Antwerp (Holland), John James Dufour at, 18, 335.
Archer, William, 26, 38, 105, 106.
Armington, Dr. Charles L., 185.
Armington, John L., sketch of, 184-85; bogus divorce, 405.

Armington, Dr. William, sketch of, 184.
Armstrong, David, lays out addition to Vevay, 144.
Armstrong, Irvin, publishes *Vevay Democrat*, 57, 113, 376.
Armstrong, John, sheriff, 137.
Armstrong, Margaret, 381.
Armstrong, Thomas, 80, 365, 381, 387; county recorder, 141; political affiliations, 162, 164; state representative, 173, 174; tavern keeper, 48, 371; statement on condition of Vevay branch bank, 388.
Armstrong, Mrs. Thomas, 372.
Armstrong, Walter, associate judge, 148.
Armstrong, Lieutenant William, killed at City of Mexico, 113.
Arnold's Creek, 95.
Ash, George, early settler, 53; ferry, 49.
Aurora (Indiana), 2, 114, 351; wants Lake Michigan-Ohio road terminus, 208.
Ausset, ———, dealings with John James Dufour, 341.
Auxerre (France), John James Dufour at, 339.
Averil, Philo, 366; lays out Mount Sterling, 144; tavern keeper, 48, 371.
Azores Islands, 247.

Bachman, ———, 75.
Backus, Marvin, 393.
Baird, William J., publishes

Vevay *Reveille and News*,
112-13; and *Reveille*, 57.
Bakes, John, 23, 103, 105, 206;
operates mill, 110.
Bakes, Lewis C., 123.
Bakes, Robert, 52, 373; carding
machine, 38, 196, 364; mill,
105, 196, 364.
Baldwin, Jonas, 387; tavern
keeper, 48, 372.
Baltimore (Maryland), 321;
John James Dufour visits,
249; vines purchased at, xiv,
10.
Banks: Vevay, 381, 387-88;
Vincennes, 78, 79, 381, 384,
388; Madison, 384; Lawrence-
burgh, 384.
Banta, Henry, county commis-
sioner, 130; collector of rev-
enue, 156; sheriff, 135-36.
Banta, Henry D., 67; Baptist
preacher, 66, 68.
Banta, John W., 185.
Banta, ———, tanner, 102, 194.
Baptist Church, *see* Churches.
Bard, ———, dealings with
John James Dufour, 319.
Barnes, Francis, 204.
Bashop, Anderson, dealings with
John James Dufour, 299.
Battle of Tippecanoe, 358.
Baum, Martin, land entry, 36.
Beagle, Reverend T. Warren,
Baptist minister, 68.
Beal, John A., candidate for
state senate, 158-59, 174.
Beal, Lewis W., 122, 124, 125,
401; county commissioner,
134.
Beal, Samuel, sketch of, 178;
county supervisor, 131; lays
out addition to Mount Ster-
ling, 144.
Bear Creek, 208.

Bebee (Beebee), David, trial,
52, 367-68, 373.
Bebus, ———, 122.
Beelens, ———, dealings with
John James Dufour, 295.
Beguin, ———, dealings with
John James Dufour, 267.
Bell, John, presidential candi-
date, 169.
Bell, ———, dealings with John
James Dufour, 315.
Bellamy, Flavius J., state sen-
ator, 172.
Bellons, Andrew, 124.
Belrichard, ———, Vevay shoe-
maker, 75.
Benedict, Americus, county
treasurer, 402.
Bennet, George, tax lister, 60.
Bennington (Indiana), road,
190.
Bentley, Joseph, 49, 387.
Berdez, ———, dealings with
John James Dufour, 345.
Berkshire, John G., 147.
Berne (Switzerland), 225, 235,
237, 239, 241.
Berne, Canton of (Switzer-
land), 8, 28, 116, 117.
Berryman, Thomas, 113; pub-
lishes *Indiana Register*, 56,
111; sketch of, 111.
Bethel (Indiana), 67.
Bethlehem (Indiana), 75.
Bettens (Betens), J. Philip, Sr.,
23, 31, 315, 325, 366; arrives
at First Vineyard, xv, 11, 12;
allotted lands, 17, 20, 231, 233,
307; signs vineyard covenant,
21; moves to New Switzer-
land, 353; in militia, 395;
death, 362.
Bettens, Mrs. Philip, death, 362.
Bettens, Philip, Jr., county commissioner, 133, 134.

## INDEX

Bicknell, George A., judge, 148.
Bienvenu, ———, dealings with John James Dufour, 271.
Big Bone Creek, 69.
Bigelow, J., 72; letter to John Francis Dufour about canal company, 380, 381, 382-83.
Birdstown (Kentucky), John James Dufour at, 277.
Bishop, George B., Presbyterian minister, 65.
Blach, Julius, 106.
Blackford, Isaac, 80; report on financial condition of state, 390.
Blake, Thomas H., candidate for Congress, 162.
Blanc, Daniel Dufour, see Dufour, Daniel.
Bland, F. D., Baptist minister, 68.
Blaney, ———, Vevay shoemaker, 193.
Blankenship, Lewis, 32.
Blankenship, Lieutenant William, 32.
Bledsoe, Elizabeth, 50.
Bledsoe, Isaac, 50.
Blunk, David H., hay dealer, 205.
Boerner, Charles G., Vevay silversmith, 186.
Boerner, Frederick A., Vevay silversmith, 186.
Bolens, James, 75; marriage, 385; robbed, 385-86.
Bonne (Holland), John James Dufour at, 18.
Bonner, Francis, builds mill, 88.
Bonner, Francis, 396; grandson of Francis Bonner, 88.
Bonner, Robert, 88, 396.
Boon, Ratliff, candidate for Congress, 162.
Booth, Reverend L. R., 65.

Borallay, (Boralley, Boralay), Jean Daniel, 345.
Borallay, Marie (Mrs. Jean Daniel Borallay), 345.
Borallay, Peter, Sr., 227, 229, 305; arrives at First Vineyard, xv, 11; death, 362.
Borallay, Peter, Jr., arrives at First Vineyard, xv; death, 362.
Bordeaux (France), 285, 325, 327.
Bornard (Bornaud), Andrew, in militia, 108, 395.
Bosseau, John, 83, 393, 394.
Bosseau, Joseph, 83, 393, 394.
Boyland, Nicholas, 124.
Boyle, James, 176.
Boyle, Margaret (Mrs. James Boyle), 176.
Brachman, Henry, 31.
Brachman, Mrs. Henry, 31.
Bracken (Braken), ———, dealings with John James Dufour, 297, 305.
Bradley, William, 372, 381; associate judge, 148; state representative, 172; tavern keeper, 179-80.
Brand, ———, Baptist minister, 68.
Brandenburg, William, 157.
Brant, Indian chief, 5.
Braun, ———, Vevay shoemaker, 193.
Bray, Daniel, 59, 123, 393.
Breckenridge, John C., presidential candidate, 169.
Breda (Holland), John James Dufour at, 18, 333, 335.
Briants Creek, see Bryant's Creek.
Brielle (Holland), John James Dufour at, 331.
Brig *Sally*, brings John James

Dufour to America, xiii, 8, 245.
Bristow, Isaac W., joint publisher of *Reveille and News*, 112-13.
Bristow, James F., 35.
Broadhead, Colonel, 5.
Brookville (Indiana), 95, 99.
Brown, Amos A., 366; early settler, 48; trustee of school sections, 53, 374; county supervisor, 131; justice of peace, 132.
Brown, Ignatius, 379.
Brown, James, 122, 123, 124, 125, 190; sketch of, 98.
Brown, James, teaches Vevay school, 195, 356.
Brown, John, senator from Kentucky, 9, 289, 352.
Brown, John, 122, 124; sketch of, 98.
Brown, Johnson, 123; sketch of, 86; county supervisor, 131.
Brown, Joseph, Sr., 86, 123, 164.
Brown, Joseph, Jr., 123, 125.
Brown, Ralph, 86.
Brown, Samuel, 86, 123, 125.
Brown, Samuel R., describes Swiss vineyards, xviii.
Brown, William, 122, 124.
Browning, ———, Vevay harness maker, 193.
Brussels (Belgium), John James Dufour at, 335.
Bryant's Creek, 2, 42.
Buchanan (Buchannon), James, 114; presidential candidate, 169.
Buchannon, John, land entry, 36.
Buchannon's Station, blockhouse at, 32.
Buchetee, J. F., teaches school, 69-70; author of "Empire of Bacchus," 70-71, 380.

Burchfield, Robert, 381; joint publisher of *Indiana Register*, 55, 110.
Burlington (New Jersey), John James Dufour at, 323.
Burns, Edward, state representative, 173.
Burton, Allen, 122, 124.
Butler, Samuel, 30-31, 35, 46.
Butler, Mrs., 46, 370.
Butler County (Ohio), 2.
Cain, David, state representative, 173.
Cain, Joshua, 53.
Cain, ———, 88.
Caldwell, Colonel, 5.
Caldwell, ———, 97-98.
Call, Jacob, candidate for Congress, 162.
Cambrai (France), John James Dufour at, 335.
Campbell, Charles, 48, 52.
Campbell, James, adds to town of New York, 144.
Campbell, John, 367, 374.
Campbell, William, 44, 52, 373, 374; early settler, 48; county commissioner, 130; petitions formation of new township, 132; state representative, 172.
Canton de Leman, *see* Leman, Canton de.
Canton de Vaud, *see* Vaud, Canton de.
Cape Girardeau (Missouri), 265, 269.
*Captain Beacon*, steamboat on Wabash River, 82.
Carnine family, early settlers, 73.
Carpenter, William, admitted to practise law, 379.
Carrell, John, dealings with John James Dufour, 253.

INDEX 413

Carrollton (Kentucky), 24, 104, 144, 401. *See also* Port William.
Cart, ———, dealings with John James Dufour, 227.
Carter, James S., 140.
Carter, Scott, judge, court of common pleas, 146, 147.
Cartwright, Peter, early Indiana minister, 379.
Cass, Lewis, presidential candidate, 169.
Caswell, Daniel J., admitted to practise law, 379; candidate for Congress, 161, 403.
Center Square (Indiana), laid out, 145; county seat contest, 158, 160; road, 190.
Chamberlin, Isaac, favors change of county seat, 157.
Chamberlin, William B., state representative, 172, 173, 174; tax lister, 202.
Chambers, Samuel, state senator, 181.
Chambers, William, 32.
Chapman, Joseph W., president judge, circuit court, 147.
Chatelard (Switzerland), Vevay settlers from commune of, xiii, 7.
Chaudet, ———, Vevay shoemaker, 193.
Chetlain, Augustus L., writings on Red River colony, 401.
Child, ———, joint publisher of *Weekly Messenger*, 56, 111, 376.
Chillicothe (Ohio), 6.
Chittenden, William, 127.
*Christian Herald*, (Mount Sterling), 178.
Churches:
  Baptist, 35, 66-68; controversies, 120-21; early ministers, 63, 65, 66, 120, 195, 212-13, 355, 360.
  Seventh Day Baptists, 74.
  Methodist, 62, 66, 154, 379; camp meetings, 69, 207-8; early ministers, 46, 63, 66; quarterly meetings, 206-7.
  Presbyterian, vii, 62, 379; Cincinnati Presbytery, 64; Oxford Presbytery, 64; early ministers, 63, 64-65, 178, 210, 392; in Pleasant Township, 73; in Vevay, 63-64, 65, 211.
  Universalist, 69.
Cincinnati (Ohio), 2, 17, 25, 36, 79, 83, 168, 273, 277, 279, 303; reception for Lafayette, 84, 108; trading point for Swiss settlers, 23, 24, 25, 30, 102; road to Vincennes, 209.
*Cincinnati Gazette*, 66.
Circuit courts, first term, 365; cases tried, 368-69; rules for procedure, 366-67.
Citti, John, 122, 124.
Clark, Bazilla, 98, 387; establishes nail factory, 50, 373.
Clark, George Rogers, expedition, 2-5.
Clark, Lewis A., 66.
Clark, Orange, 67.
Clark, Walter, 52, 373.
Clark, ———, Baptist preacher, 66-67.
Clark County (Indiana), 75; representation, 161.
Clarkson, Abner, vii, 63, 69, 82, 87; associate judge, 60, 148; Clinton supporter, 163; justice of peace, 74, 127; postmaster of Vevay, 100, 399; resident of Madison, 66; Vevay druggist and merchant, 76-77, 187.
Clarkson, Mrs. Abner, 63.

414  INDIANA HISTORICAL COLLECTIONS

Clarkson, Eliza M. (Mrs. Perret Dufour), vii.
Clarkson, Dr. Samuel W., Vevay druggist, 187; physician, 81, 392-93.
Clay, Henry, 55, 164; presidential candidate, 161, 162, 165, 166, 168; friendship with Swiss colonists, 128-29; opinion on slavery, 375.
Clay, James B., 129.
Clay, ———, dealings with John James Dufour, 319, 321.
Claypool, Solomon, judge, 148.
Cler, John D., 176.
Cler, Madeline (Mrs. John D. Cler), 176.
Cleveland (Kentucky), 291.
Cline, Abraham, in militia, 32, 360.
Cline, Adam, 52, 373.
Clinton, Dewitt, presidential candidate, 162, 163, 403.
Coen, Thomas, 45.
Coggshell, George, 366, 381; director Vevay Literary Society, 46, 370.
Cole, Benjamin, 393.
Cole, Clarissa (Mrs. Daniel Cole), 176.
Cole, Daniel, 46, 176.
Cole, James, 35, 192, 355.
Cole, James W., Vevay harness maker, 193.
Cole, Rebecca (Mrs. Enos Littlefield), attends Seminary of Vevay, 355.
Cole, Thomas, T., 46; Vevay cabinet maker, 191.
Cole, Mrs. ———, 46.
Connorsville (Connersville, Indiana), 95.
Cook, Larkin, 59, 60.
Cooper, William, tavern keeper, 48, 371.

Copenhagen (Denmark), 285.
Cord's Ferry, John James Dufour arrives near, 289.
Corydon (Indiana), 56, 91, 399; meeting of constitutional convention at, 58; seat of government removed from, 391.
Cotton, Henry, 124, 381; lays out addition to Mount Sterling, 144.
Cotton, James M., 122; state representative, 173.
Cotton, John F., 103, 122, 124, 125.
Cotton, Reverend John R., Baptist minister, 67, 68.
Cotton, Nathaniel, 366, 393; Clay supporter, 162.
Cotton, Ralph, Sr., 98, 382, 393; coroner, 38, 39, 46; associate judge, 60, 148; sheriff, 135; state representative, 172, 199, 200; tax lister, 46.
Cotton, Ralph, Jr., 52, 75, 373.
Cotton, Ralph B., collector of revenue, 156; sheriff, 136.
Cotton, Robert, 52, 98, 373, 393; constable, 44.
Cotton, William, Sr., 39, 40, 44, 72, 86, 151, 380; early settler, 7, 23; land entry, 37; associate judge, 38, 42, 50, 51, 58, 148, 207, 209, 365, 367; constitutional convention delegate, 58; builds mill, 104; in state legislature, 171, 172, 404.
Cotton, William, Jr., 122, 124, 125, 401.
Cotton Township (Switzerland County), 104, 108, 115; organized, 59-60, 377; attached to Ohio County, 158-59; Baptist Church organized, 121; county supervisor for, 131;

# INDEX 415

justices of peace, 131, 132; votes for president, 165.
Coudere, ———, 327.
Couk, ———, dealings with John James Dufour, 267.
Courts, 145-49; imprisonment for debt, 374-75. *See also* Switzerland County.
Courvoissier (Courvoisier), Augustine, 67.
Courvoissier, Benoit, 67, 75.
Courvoissier, Frederick L., county treasurer, 75-76, 140; postmaster of Vevay, 100, 399.
Covington, Samuel F., state representative, 173.
Covington (Kentucky), 75, 174.
Cowan, Donald, 74.
Cracraft, Major, 3.
Craig, George, 49, 154; early settler, 37, 53; justice of peace, 44; tax lister, 45-46; election inspector, 59; state senator, 94, 171; county commissioner, 130; death, 102.
Craig, Stuman, 53.
Craig Township (Switzerland County), 76, 108, 115, 120, 133; organized, 59-60, 377; county supervisor, 131; justices of peace, 86, 132; religious revival, 68; squirrel hunt, 123, 125.
Cranbury (New Jersey), John James Dufour at, 323.
Cravens, James H., judge, 148; congressman from Indiana, 171.
Crawford, William H., presidential candidate, 164, 166.
Crawfordsville (Indiana), 356.
Cross Plains (Indiana), 121, 208.
Culbertson, James, 74.
Culbertson, John, 74.

Culbertson, Samuel, 74.
Culbertson, William, 74; state senator, 172.
Cullen, William A., judge, 148.
Cumberland River, 83.
Cunningham, William H., county commissioner, 134.
Cushing, Courtland, president judge, circuit court, 147.

Dallarde, Pierre Le Roi, fraudulent sale of lands, 223-25.
Dallas, George M., candidate for vice-president, 168.
Dalmazzo, Mrs. Elizabeth (Mrs. Joseph Dalmazzo), 46.
Dalmazzo, F. J., buys *Vevay Democrat*, 376, 401.
Dalmazzo, James, 49, 382; imprisoned for debt, 127.
Dalmazzo, Joseph, 46, 372.
Dalmazzo, Lucy, 67.
Dana, Edwin, xviii.
Danglade, John L., 17, 128, 194; Vevay cabinet maker, 191.
Danville (Kentucky), John James Dufour at, 277.
David, ———, settles at Hunt's Creek, 7.
Davis, Hannah, 65.
Davis, Samuel, 45.
Day, Rawleigh, 52, 373; colonel of militia, 109, 400; issues temporary currency, 78, 387.
Daybook of John James Dufour, 235-347.
Dayton, Jonathan, 179.
Dearborn County (Indiana), organization, 6-7, 351; delinquent taxes, 57, 178-79; representation, 161; tax receipt, 22.
Debetaz, Daniel, sells liquor, 397.
Debts, imprisonment for, 126-28.

Decatur (Indiana), 179.
Decatur County (Indiana), 120.
Delany, Thomas, 194.
Demans, ———, 106.
Demaree, Daniel, 73; in militia, 32, 360.
Demaree, Peter, 73, 366; lays out Allensville, 144.
Deming (Demming), John T., 52, 373.
Democratic Central Committee, publishes *Village Times*, 56.
Deserens, Frederick, 22; joins Swiss colony, 16-17, 18; in militia, 395, 396.
Deserens, Moése, suicide, 213-14.
Detraz, Abraham, 74.
Detraz, Benjamin, 74; in militia, 395, 396.
Detraz, Daniel, blacksmith, 386.
Detraz, Francis, 74.
Detraz, John, 74, 362; manufactures liquors, 205; in militia, 395, 396.
Detraz, Mrs. John (née Bettens), death, 362.
Detraz, Louis, 74.
Detraz, Mrs. Lucy, 154-55, 195; frightened by Indians, 101.
Detraz and Tandy, Vevay milliners, 358.
Detroit (Michigan), 5.
Dickason, Elijah, 122, 125, 208, 401.
Dickason, Griffith, 367; land entry, 37; settles on Indian Creek, 7, 23, 85; builds water mill, 104.
Dickason, John, 150.
Dicky, John M., aids in reorganization of P r e s b y t e r i a n Church, 65.
Dijon (France), John James Dufour at, 18, 339.

Dill, James, lawyer, 58; commissioner to locate county seat, 365.
Divorce, 175-76, 368, 405.
Doan, John F., 48; county treasurer, 140.
Dobbins, Robert B., preaches in Vevay, 64.
Dodd, Hazelett E., state representative, 173, 174.
Doge, Mrs., dealings with John James Dufour, 345.
Dôle (France), John James Dufour at, 339.
Don, ———, dealings with John James Dufour, 271.
Donahoe (Donahue), Patrick, land entry, 36; lays out Montgomery, 144.
Dort (Holland), John James Dufour at, 333.
Douglas (Douglass), Stephen A., presidential candidate, 169.
Douglass, John, newspaper ventures, 56, 110, 113.
Dow, Lorenzo, preaches in Vevay, 155.
Dow, Robert, 317.
Downey, Alexander C., president judge, circuit court, 147; state senator, 172, 404.
Downey, Captain James, 108.
Drake, Benjamin, early settler, 7, 47; proposed donation for county seat, 42, 43; proprietor of New York, 95, 144.
Drake, Robert, early settler, 7, 47; marriage, 95.
Droz, *see* Humbert, Zelim.
Drummond, Robert, lawyer, 400; judge, probate court, 146.
Dubardeau, ———, dealings with John James Dufour, 263.
Ducret, ———, 345.

# INDEX 417

Dufour, Adam, 221.
Dufour, Aime (Amie), birth, 7; comes to New Switzerland, 20, 49, 362, 373; receives share of property 231, 233; settles in Louisiana, 362.
Dufour, Antoinette (Mrs. Jean Daniel Morerod), 49, 219, 373; birth, 7; sails for America, 11; arrives at First Vineyard, xv; moves to New Switzerland, 17, 20; marriage, 12; receives share of property, 229, 231, 233; death, 362.
Dufour, Daniel, ancestor of Daniel Dufour, 221.
Dufour, Daniel, 53, 82, 227, 305, 315, 325, 347, 381, 387; birth, 7; sails for America, 11; arrives at First Vineyard, xv; wishes to leave family, 307; removes to Indiana, xvii; share in vineyard association, 17, 20, 21, 229, 231, 233; clears lands, 353; offers land for county seat, 42, 365; director Vevay Literary Society, 46-47, 370; holds religious services, 63, 68-69, 379; directs bank subscriptions, 79; lays out Vevay, 144; presides at Jackson meeting, 163; partnership with Whitemore and Barnes, 204; daughter, 31; death, 362; Dufour-Blanc explained, 352.
Dufour, Mrs. Daniel, death, 362.
Dufour, Daniel Vincent, 362; receives share of lands, 17, 20, 307; donates lot to Presbyterian Church, 64; lays out addition to Vevay, 144; captain of militia, 395, 396.

Dufour, Etienne Pierre André, 221.
Dufour, Frances E. (Mrs. Daniel Dufour), xv, 11.
Dufour, Hevila, 100.
Dufour, Jean Jaques, Sr., 7, 303, 305; commits children to care of eldest son, 219, 363; bids departing colonists farewell, xiv, 11; recognition of common rights in Noville and Rennar, 221-23; division of property among children, 229-31; account from eldest son, 225-33.
Dufour, Jean Jaques, Jr., see Dufour, John James.
Dufour, Jean Jaques Rodolph, recognition of rights in Noville and Rennar, 221-23.
Dufour, Jean Pierre, 341.
Dufour, Jeanne Marie (Jeane, Jane Maria, Mrs. John Francis Siebenthal), 219, 317; birth, 7; sails for America, 11; arrives at First Vineyard, xv; receives share of property, 17, 20, 229, 231, 233; marriage, 17; death, 362.
Dufour, John David, 101, 219; birth, 7; sails for America, 11; abandons First Vineyard, 15; share in vineyard association, 17, 20, 231, 233; clears land for Hiram Ogle, 85; death, 362.
Dufour, John Francis (Jean Francois), xviii, 32, 49, 82, 96-97, 103, 106, 174, 182, 187, 219, 311, 317, 319, 354, 400; birth, 7; sails for America, 11; arrives at First Vineyard, xv; wishes to leave family, 307; removes to Indiana

418    INDIANA HISTORICAL COLLECTIONS

xvii, 15-16, 25-26; carries wine to President, 19, 229, 315; takes land in New Switzerland, 17, 20, 21, 22-23, 229-31, 233, 353; describes New Switzerland in 1810, pp. 28-30; lays out Vevay, 34-35, 144; builds house in Vevay, 38, 105; Vevay postmaster, 26-27, 100; lobbies for organization of county, 35; offers site for county seat, 41-42, 43, 365; donates lots for schools, 370; holds county offices, 33, 38, 39, 40, 53, 58, 137, 141, 365, 374; secures books for Vevay Literary Society, 46, 370; editor *Indiana Register*, 55-56, 110, 399; deeds lot to Baptist Church, 67-68; agent of canal company, 72, 380, 381, 382-83; issues temporary currency, 78, 387; president Vevay Branch Bank, 79-80, 388; associate judge, 115, 148; judge, probate and common pleas courts, 146; Fourth of July orator, 152; state representative, 172; friendship with Henry Clay, 128, 375; children, vii, 26, 100; death, 148, 362.

Dufour, Mrs. John Francis, 363.
Dufour, John James, Sr., *see* Dufour, Jean Jaques.
Dufour, John James, Jr., 148, 382; birth, 7; voyage to America, xiii, 8; plan for American vineyards, vii, 12-13, 15; connection with Kentucky Vineyard Association, xiii-xiv, 8-11, 13-15, 289-93, 295, 299, 303-11, 315, 317; joined by family, xiv-xv, 12, 219, 363; buys land for Swiss colonists, 17, 19-21, 28, 231, 303; petitions Congress for extended land credit, xvii, 16, 21; visits Europe, xvii, 15, 18, 323-47; renders account to father, 225-33; land entry, 37; introduces Swiss artillery company to Lafayette, 84, 395; Fourth of July orator, 151; manufactures liquors, 204-5; day book of travels and expenses, 235-47; child, 64; death, 361.

Dufour, Marcellina, 100.
Dufour, Oliver, state representative, 173, 174.
Dufour, Perret, 58, 100, 401; sketch of, vii; brought to New Switzerland, 26; justice of the peace, 93; Vevay postmaster, 100; candidate for state legislature, 159, 173, 174; state representative, 173; smokes peace pipe with Indians, 101; druggist, 187; lays out addition to Vevay, 144; writings, vii-viii, xviii; introduction to history of county, 351-52.
Dufour, Mrs. Perret, vii.
Dufour, Pierre David, 221.
Dufour, Polly (Mrs. John Francis Dufour), 26, 100, 105-6, 353.
Dufour, Susanne Margarette (Mrs. Elisha Golay), 219; birth, 7; sails for America, 11; share in New Switzerland lands, 17, 20, 231, 233; marriage, 17; death, 362.
Dufour, Vincent, host to John James, in Paris, 241, 339.
Dufour, Keen and Company, publish *Indiana Register*, 115, 375.

## INDEX

Dugan, James, 124; constable, 59; mail carrier, 100; owns horse mill, 104.
Duhlmire, ———, 106.
Dumont, Abraham B., 381; county recorder, 141.
Dumont, Aurelius W., county auditor, 142; lawyer, 400.
Dumont, C. T., 50.
Dumont, John, 58, 94, 98, 115, 356; settles in Vevay, 35; inspector of elections, 44; justice of the peace, 45; coroner, 46; admitted *ex gratia* as attorney, 379; president Vevay Literary Society, 46, 370; Clinton supporter, 403; in state legislature, 171, 172; candidate for governor, 171.
Dumont, John J., 50.
Dumont, Mrs. Julia L., 192; teaches Vevay school, 195-96, 355.
Dumont, Richard, marriage, 50.
Duncan, Alexander, 178.
Duncan, R e v e r e n d James, treatise on slavery, 177; Presbyterian minister, 178.
Dunham, Cyrus L., representative in Congress, 171.
Dunn, George H., admitted to practise law, 379; representative in Congress, 171.
Dunn, Isaac, commissioner to locate county seat, 365.
Dunn, William M., congressman from Indiana, 404.
Dunn, Colonel William McKee, 360.
Dunn, Williamson, in militia, 32, 360.
Duplan, Mrs. (née Bettens), 362.
Durbin, Hosier J., Methodist minister, 66; state representative, 173.
Dutch settlement, in Pleasant Township, 73.
Dutoit, Eugene, 123.

Early settlers, 7, 23, 34 ff, 47 ff, 53, 73-77, 85, 98-99, 103, 115-16, 183 ff.
East Enterprise (Indiana), 114, 121, 144; road, 190.
Edger, Alexander, 65.
Edwards, Eden, county commissioner, 133.
Edwards, James, 32.
Eggleston, Joseph C., candidate for state senator, 111-12; state representative, 173; s t a t e senator, 171; backs Whig *Statesman*, 376.
Eggleston, Miles C., admitted to practise law, 58, 379; president judge, circuit court, 60, 121, 147.
Egypt Bottom (Indiana), 42, 201.
Elam, John, justice of peace, 131.
Elections, 58-60, 91-94, 129 ff, 157-75.
*Eliza*, steamboat on Ohio River, 82, 119.
Elson, ———, 122.
Emerson (Emmerson), Frank, judge, 148.
"Empire of Bacchus," ode to Swiss, 70-71.
English, Isabel, indictment, 373-74.
Erin (Indiana), laid out, 144.
Estrée St. Denis (France), John James Dufour at, 337.
Evans, Thomas, 98, 104.
Everden, Ira, 122, 124.

## 420  INDIANA HISTORICAL COLLECTIONS

Evertson, Jacob R., 83.
Ewing, James S., 200.

Fairview (Indiana), 115, 144.
Fallis, Samuel, 382; county treasurer, 139; tavern keeper, 48, 372.
Fanning, James G., 113; publishes *Spirit of the Times*, 57, 112.
Farley, Joseph F., 51, 58; admitted to practise law, 368.
Farmers and Mechanics, Bank (Madison), 384.
Fenton, John, 367; land entry, 37.
Fidds, William, 32.
Fillmore, Millard, presidential candidate, 169.
First Vineyard (Kentucky), vii, 17, 18, 25, 100, 151, 219, 225, 229, 305; organization, xiii-xiv, 8-11, 291-93, 295, 299; arrival of Swiss colonists, xv, 12, 303; development, 12-15, 18-19, 311, 315, 317; separation of family partnership, 229-31; 307-9; failure, xvi-xvii, 14-16.
Fisher, Elwood, 111; state representative, 173.
Flint, Timothy, xviii.
Florence (Indiana), 17, 42, 44, 113, 184; incorporation, 132-33; laid out, 144; change of name, 95, 132, 144, 399.
Flotron, Francis L., Vevay silversmith, 186.
Flynn, William, county commissioner, 134.
Forbes, Dr., 81.
Fort Harrison, 33.
Fort McHenry, 3.
Fort Recovery, 36.
Fort Snelling, 118, 119.

Fort Wayne (Indiana), canal to Vincennes proposed, 95.
Fowler, ———, carpenter, 313.
Fox, Captain John, 108.
Frankfort (Kentucky), 9, 86, 277, 289, 291; road from New Switzerland, 30.
Franklin County (Indiana), representation, 161.
Frazier (Fraser), ———, dealings with John James Dufour, 297, 299.
Free Masons, 62.
Frelinghuysen, Frederick T., 168.
Fremont, John C., presidential candidate, 169.
French, James G., 64.
French, Nathaniel, admitted *ex gratia* as attorney, 379.
French, William, 64.
Frenchtown (New Jersey), John James Dufour at, 321.
Fry, Philip, 367; arraigned for contempt of court, 368.
Furgeson, James S., county commissioner, 134.

Gaines, Reverend Ludwell G., 64.
Gallatin, Albert, vice-presidential candidate, 164.
Gallatin County (Kentucky), 120.
Gard, William, county commissioner, 130; favors change of county seat, 157; state representative, 172.
Garrard County (Kentucky), 103, 362.
Gary, Charles A., county commissioner, 134, 135.
Gazley, Aribert, county supervisor, 132; justice of peace, 132.

# INDEX 421

*General Green*, steamboat on Ohio River, 82.
Georgetown (Kentucky), 100.
*Georgetown Patriot* (Kentucky), 399.
Gerard, Jonathan A., 124.
Gerard, Nathaniel, 123, 393.
Gerard, William, lays out addition to Jacksonville, 144.
Germantown (Pennsylvania), 113.
Gex, E., 381.
Gex, Louis, 311, 313, 366; joins Swiss colony, 16, 18, 231, 307; improves land, 22; sells land, 115; host to Henry Clay, 128; manufactures liquor, 128-29; Gex-Oboussier explained, 352-53.
Gex, Lucien, 49, 129, 381; builds house in Vevay, 50; county commissioner, 130; issues temporary currency, 78, 387; teaches school, 30.
Gex, Victoir Helvetia (Mrs. Justus Vairin), 115.
Ghent (Kentucky), 90, 129.
Gibb, James, 183.
Gibbons, John, 149; county supervisor, 132; justice of peace, 132.
Gibbs, William J., county commissioner, 135.
Gibson, John, secretary Indiana Territory, 38, 39, 40.
Gibson County (Indiana), representation, 161.
Gilbert, Amos, 361, 373.
Gilbert, Nancy, 65.
Gill, John, 88; county auditor, 142, 402.
Gilliland, Alexander, admitted to practise law, 379.
Gilliland, John, 44, 137, 367, 380; agent canal company, 72; connection with Vevay Branch Bank, 79, 80, 388.
Gilliland, Thomas, 367; county commissioner, 130.
Giroud, ———, dealings with John James Dufour, 239.
Glenn, Hugh, 74, 79-80.
Glenn, James, 74, 79-80.
Golay, Clarissa (Mrs. William Armington), 184.
Golay, Constant, 155, 362.
Golay, Mrs. Constant (née Morerod), 89, 155.
Golay, David, settles in New Switzerland, 17, 18; enlists in militia, 33.
Golay, Elisha, 34, 38, 44, 96, 184, 311, 325; associate judge, 146, 148; county agent, 45, 53; justice of peace, 115, 116; lobbies for organization of Switzerland County, 35; marriage, 17; militia captain, 31-32, 358-60; representative in territorial legislature, 174, 363-64; death, 362.
Golay, Lawrence W., Vevay druggist, 187.
Golay, Lewis, 32, 33, 89; in militia, 360.
Golay, Lewis F., 123.
Golay, Seldon T., 360.
Goldsmith, ———, Vevay minister, 379.
Goose Creek, 311.
Gordon, Lawrence W., county auditor, 142.
Gouffond (Goufond, Goufon), dealings with John James Dufour, 227, 287, 301, 303, 305, 307.
Graham, Reverend John, Baptist preacher, 63, 66, 68.
Graham, William, state senator, 181.

## 422  INDIANA HISTORICAL COLLECTIONS

Grammer, Charles, 167, 204.
Grand Masonic Hall Lottery, 384.
Granger, Gideon, postmaster general, 27.
Grant, Ulysses S., presidential candidate, 169-70.
Grant's Creek, 2, 6, 35, 96.
Grass, Daniel, state senator, 181.
Gravesend (England), John James Dufour at, 331.
Gray, John, state senator, 181.
Gray, John W., sheriff, 136.
Gray, Mary Ann, 65.
Gray, Wilson H., 113; newspaper ventures, 56, 111, 112, 376; postmaster of Vevay, 100, 399.
Great Miami River, 4, 143.
Greentown (Kentucky), John James Dufour at, 277.
Gregory, James, state senator, 181.
Gregory, William H., state representative, 173.
Greeley, Horace, presidential candidate, 170.
Green, Bunn, 124.
Green, Martin R., favors relocation of county seat, 158; lays out addition to Patriot, 144; operates bark works, 77; state senator, 158, 159, 171, 172, 173, 174.
Green, ———, 118.
Greensburg (Indiana), 185.
Griffith, Francis M., county treasurer, 141.
Griffith, Joshua D., 188; county treasurer, 140.
Grisard, Frederick L., Sr., county treasurer, 140; in militia, 395, 396; marriage, 120; Vevay blacksmith, 75, 76, 89, 187-88, 385; death, 401.
Grisard, Frederick L., Jr., 75, 120; blacksmith, 187-88.
Grisard, James S., 120.
Grisard, Rodolph F., 75, 97, 120, 193, 195, 356.
Grisard, Zelie Simon, 117-20, 401.
Gullion, John, land entry, 37.
Gullion, Robert, 48, 366.
Gwathmey, Samuel, manager canal lottery, 381; appoints collector for canal company moneys, 384.

Hagan, Wilford, 126.
Haines, Dr. Joshua, 91.
Hale, Peter H., newspaper editor, 57, 112, 114.
Hall, Gabriel, manufactures liquor, 205.
Hall, John, 32, 205.
Hall, William, 23, 205, 353; county treasurer, 140.
Hall, Squire, 32.
Hamburg (Germany), 285.
Hamilton, Edward P., 372.
Hamilton, Elizabeth, 65.
Hamilton, James, Vevay hatter, 372.
Hamilton, John, 372.
Hamilton, J., 381; sheriff, 22.
Hamilton, William, 372.
Hamilton (Ohio), 55, 110.
Hammond, Lot, 59.
Hammond, Reverend Rezin, Methodist minister, 66, 379.
Handy, Henry S., editor of *Annotator*, 376.
Hannas, Henry, 98, 366; sketch of, 103-4.
Hannas, William, sketch of, 103-4.

## INDEX

Hannegan, Edward A., senator from Indiana, 205.
Harcoat, William, 367.
Hardinsburg (Indiana), 179.
Hare, Elizabeth, 182.
Harmon family, early settlers, 73.
Harper, John, blacksmith, 188.
Harper, Peter, 99, 122, 124.
Harper, William, 99.
Harrington, Henry W., congressman from Indiana, 171.
Harris, Daniel K., Allensville tanner, 194.
Harris, Jacob R., county commissioner, 134.
Harris, Peter, 366; lays out Jacksonville, 144, 371; tavern keeper, 371.
Harrison, Christopher, manager canal lottery, 381.
Harrison, Eli, state senator, 181.
Harrison, William Henry, presidential candidate, 166-68; issues proclamation for erection of Dearborn County, 351; calls militia against Indians, 358-59.
Harrison (Indiana), 179.
Harrison County (Indiana), representation, 161.
Hart and Brown, dealings with John James Dufour, 309.
Hartford, P. J. (P. T.), buys *Vevay Democrat*, 376, 401.
Harvey, Pruit, collector of revenue, 156; county supervisor, 132; justice of peace, 132.
Harryman, George W., state representative, 173.
Harwood, James, postmaster of Vevay, 100.
Haselrig, James, sells land to vineyard company, 9, 291.

Haskell, Reverend E. C., Presbyterian minister, 65.
Haskell, Thomas A., 76.
Hastie, Charles, 375.
Hastie, George, 375.
Hastie, James, early settler, 375.
Hastie, John, 375.
Hastie, William, 375.
Hastings, Charles O., 96.
Hatch, Cyrus, 87.
Hatch, Henry, Vevay blacksmith, 188, 386.
Hathorn, George W., 38.
Havre (France), John James Dufour at, 8, 243, 247.
Hawkins, Ainsworth, 400.
Hawkins, Jonathan, 400.
Haycock, Daniel, candidate for legislature, 91, 393, 397.
Hayden, John J., judge, court of common pleas, 146; state representative, 173.
Heady, Stilwell, 206, 207, 366; land entry, 37.
Heady, Thomas, 122.
Heath, Charles, clerk, circuit court, 138.
Helvetia (Switzerland), 7.
Hemphill, Peter, constable, 127.
Henderson, Charles, imprisoned for debt, 127; militia captain, 108; Vevay cabinet maker, 191.
Hendricks, William, admitted to practise law, 366, 378-79; offices held by, 51, 52, 180, 368.
Henny, ———, deals with John James Dufour, 237.
Henry, David, 73; county commissioner, 133, 134; state senator, 171, 173, 206.
Henry (Indiana), 178.
Herr, Benjamin, dealings with John James Dufour, 259.

Herrick, Bela, county commissioner, 134; lays out addition to Patriot, 144.
Herrick, Horace B., county recorder, 141.
Herrick, James, 144.
Hettich, ———, dealings with John James Dufour, 343.
Hewitt, Samuel, 184.
Hickman's Creek, xiii, 9.
Hicks, James, 32.
Higby, Henry P., Presbyterian minister, 65.
*Highland Laddie*, steamboat on Ohio River, 82, 83.
Hilderbrand, Benjamin, 106.
Hill, John, buys lot in Vevay, 34.
Hill, Mrs. Josephine (née Morerod), 155.
Hill, Ralph, congressman from Indiana, 171.
Hillis, Lieutenant Colonel David, orders militia against Indians, 359-60; state representative, 360; lieutenant governor, 360.
Hogan, Lewis, 21.
Holland, Philip C., 402.
Holland, William G., state representative, 173.
Holliday, Fernandez C., 379.
Holman, Jesse L., commissioner to locate county seat, 41-44, 365; president judge, circuit court, 51, 147, 368; judge, supreme court of Indiana, 51, 177, 178, 377; recommends slavery treatise, 405.
Holman, William S., congressman from Indiana, 41, 171.
Holton, Alexander, admitted to practise law, 51, 368, 379; teaches Vevay school, 354-55.
Hopkins, John, land entry, 36.

Hopkins, Thomas, land entry, 36, 37.
Horton, Charles S., 113, 114; publishes *Ohio Valley Gazette*, 57, 112.
Hotchkiss, George A., 102.
Hotchkiss, Luther M., 102; county commissioner, 135.
Hotchkiss, Dr., Vevay physician, 81, 102.
Houze, Andrew, 104.
Hovey, Reverend A. C., Presbyterian minister, 65.
Howard, Samuel, candidate for state senate, 206; state representative, 173.
Howard, Samuel W., sheriff, 136.
Howard, Tighlman A., 206.
Howe, Sylvanus, 149.
Howe, William, county commissioner, 134, 142.
Huff, William T., 48, 367.
Huffman, Thomas, 361.
Hughes, James, congressman from Indiana, 171.
Hull, Hezekiah B., attorney, 51, 58, 378; prosecuting attorney, 60.
Humbert, Zelim, Humbert-Droz explained, 352.
Hummer, James, Presbyterian minister, 65.
Humphrey, Arthur, county commissioner, 134.
Humphrey, James B., 127.
Hunter, Morton C., congressman from Indiana, 171.
Hunter, Patrick, 3.
Hunt's Creek, boundary of New Switzerland, xvii, 16; early settlers on, 7, 23.
Huston, William W., attends Seminary of Vevay, 355.

# INDEX 425

Imiel family, 183.
Independent (Carrollton, Kentucky), 401.
Indian Creek, see Venoge Creek.
Indiana, conditions in 1765, p. 1; in 1876, p. 6; early representation, 161; constitutional conventions, 55, 58, 170; convention voted down, 391; constitutions, 58, 160-61, 172; electoral district, 161-62; state treasury, 391-92;
legislature: adopts Bank of Vincennes, as state bank, 78; changes law on property executions, 199; charters Jeffersonville - Ohio Canal Company, 71; authorizes canal lottery, 72; measures advocated, 94-95; state representatives, 91, 172-74, 199, 200; senators, 171-72, 174, 181;
militia, 31-33, 108-10, 358-60; railroads first mentioned, 94-95; representatives from, 51, 161-62, 171; senators from, 51, 99.
Indiana Journal (Indianapolis), 56, 110.
Indiana Palladium (Lawrenceburgh), 57, 112.
Indiana Register (Vevay), notices appearing in, 177, 178, 179, 197, 198, 200, 354-55, 357; publication of, 55-56, 57-58, 110, 375, 376, 399; editor publishes treatise on slavery, 404-5.
Indiana Register and Vevay and Ghent Advertizer, 110.
Indiana Reveille, see Vevay Reveille.
Indiana Statesman, 56-57, 112, 376.

Indiana Territory, formed, 6; commissions to Switzerland County officers, 38-40; delegate to Congress elected, 55; execution on debtors' property, 126; governor of, 33; legislature: charters Bank of Vincennes, 78; incorporates Vevay Literary Society, 47; organizes Switzerland County, 35, 38; grants wolf bounty, 47.
Indianapolis (Indiana), 91, 113; becomes seat of government, 391.
Indianapolis Journal, 113.
Indians, 25, 118, 119, 361; boundary, 36; cede lands to United States, 36; hostilities, 2-5, 24, 31, 33, 100-1, 109, 358; suggest route for Lake Michigan-Ohio Road, 209; origin of term Indian Summer, 202-3.
Isenschmid, Kinkelin, and Roupp, 235, 239, 241.

Jack, Samuel, county supervisor, 132; justice of peace, 131, 132; state representative, 172.
Jackson, Andrew, 162; presidential candidate, 163-66.
Jackson, Ibzan, 66.
Jackson, Mordecai, 63, 66.
Jackson County (Indiana), organization, 161.
Jackson Township, see York Township.
Jacksonville (Indiana), 47, 109, 111, 157, 192, 208; laid out, 144, 371.
Jagers, Joseph, Vevay blacksmith, 188, 386.
Jagers, Mrs., 85.
James, Pinkney, admitted to practise of law, 51, 367.

Jefferson, Thomas, 19.
Jefferson County (Indiana), organization, 6-7, 35, 351; blockhouse built in, 32; county business, 33, 126-27; justice of peace, 126, 127; representation, 161; road, 30; militia, 358-59.
Jefferson Township (Switzerland County), 53, 92; organization and officers, 44, 59-60, 98, 131, 132, 178, 369, 377-78; militia, 108; votes for president, 165.
Jeffersonville (Indiana), land district, 36, 37, 99-100; penitentiary, 113, 145.
Jeffersonville and Ohio Canal Company, 71-73, 357; incorporated, 380; lottery tickets, 381-84; dissolution, 384.
Jemmapes (Jemappes, Belgium), John James Dufour at, 335.
Jenckes, John, state senator, 181.
Jennings, Jonathan, 375; offices held by, 55, 161-62; visits Vevay, 149.
Jessamine County (Kentucky), First Vineyard located at, vii.
Johannoz, Colomb (Johannot, Colombe), dealings with John James Dufour, 331, 341.
Johnson, Gabriel, 364-65.
Johnson, John M., 34, 52, 373.
Johnson, Lewis, state senator, 181.
Johnson, William, 48.
Johnston, Andrew, 100.
Johnston, Isaac M., admitted *ex gratia* as attorney, 379.
Johnston, Larkin, sheriff, 136.
Johnston, ———, Vevay shoemaker, 193.

Jones, Charles T., clerk, circuit court, 138; state representative, 173, 174.
Jones, Elizabeth, 47.
Jones, James, Methodist minister, 66.
Jones, John J., 81.
Jones, Joshua, 35.
Jones, Lewis, 44, 47; land entry, 36.
Jones, Stephen C., in militia, 395, 396.
Jones, William H., in militia, 395, 396.
Jourdan, ———, dealings with John James Dufour, 301, 305.

Kains, Joshua, 366.
Kaskaskia (Illinois), John James Dufour visits, 8, 261.
Keen, William C., 137, 357, 381, 384; sketch of, 113, 145; buys cotton gin, 89; Clay supporter, 162; justice of peace, 131, 181; newspaper ventures, 55-56, 110, 111, 200, 369, 376; state representative, 172; brigadier general of militia, 394.
Keeney, Harris, sheriff, 136.
Keeney, William J., 183-84.
Keith, William, 33, 122, 124; sheriff, 135.
Kelley, ———, Vevay shoemaker, 193.
Kelso, Daniel, 174; state representative, 172-73; state senator, 171, 206.
Kelso, William H. H., county recorder, 141.
Kent, Josephus B., publishes newspaper, 376.
Kentucky, 2, 97, 289-93; slavery agitation, 120. *See also* First Vineyard.

## INDEX

*Kentucky Reporter* (Lexington), 45.
Kentucky River, 83; lands on, purchased by Swiss, 9, 291.
Kentucky Vineyard Society, *see* First Vineyard.
Kern, Edward, 193.
Kern, Jacob, Sr., 122.
Kern, Jacob, Jr., 124.
Kern, Joseph, Vevay harness maker, 193.
Kessler, George, Vevay harness maker, 193; in militia, 395, 396.
Kessler, Victor, Vevay harness maker, 193.
Kidder, Reuben, attorney, 51, 58, 368.
Kilgore, John, 48.
King, John M., county auditor, 31, 142; county offices, 134; postmaster of Vevay, 100, 358.
King, Mrs. John M. (née Dufour), 31.
King, ———, tailor, dealings with John James Dufour, 291.
Kinkelin and Roupp, 225.
Kinsman, Isaac B., Jackson supporter, 163-64; Vevay school teacher and writer, 196, 356-57.
Kirby, James, in keel-boat business, 83-84; loses steamboat, 69.
Kirby, James D., Jackson supporter, 164.
Kirtley, Lydia, 67.
Knox, George G., sketch of, 86-87; Clay supporter, 162; county treasurer, 87, 140; erects carding machine, 197; militia captain, 108; Vevay cabinet maker, 86, 191; offer regarding county seat, 365.
Knox, George P., 86.

Knox, James, 86.
Knox, Robert A., 76, 86, 197, 386.
Knox County (Indiana), representation, 161.
Krutz, Charles F., 44, 132, 382, 387; river trader, 373.
Krutz, William G., 44.
Kyle, George H., associate judge, 148; county treasurer, 140.
Kyle, James M., lawyer, 400.
Kyle, Mrs. Tabitha O. (née Craig), 44.

La Chapelle, Anthoine, dealings with John James Dufour, 263.
Lafayette, Marie Joseph, Marquis de, reception at Cincinnati, 84, 108, 394, 395-96.
Lake County (Indiana), 65.
Lake Michigan, road to Ohio River, 208-9.
*La Liberté*, ship bound for Bordeaux, 285.
Lamb, Hugh H., 204.
Lamb, Robert N., county auditor, 142; judge, court of common pleas, 146; state representative, 173.
Lamme, Jessee, buys Vevay lots, 34.
Lancaster (Pennsylvania), John James Dufour visits, 249.
Land, George, justice of peace, 133.
Lands, entries, 36-37; first deed recorded for Switzerland County, 50-51; frauds, 116 ff; sold for taxes in Dearborn County, 178-79; Swiss settlements, 16-17, 19 ff; Vevay lots sold, 34-35.
Lane, Amos, attorney, 51, 58, 366, 377; congressman from

## 428   INDIANA HISTORICAL COLLECTIONS

Indiana, 51, 171; receives land as fee, 361.
Lane, James H., congressman from Indiana, 171, 404.
Lanham, R. J., postmaster of Vevay, 100.
Lansdale (Lonsdale), Francis, 144, 393.
La Prairie, 265.
Larwill, ———, dealings with John James Dufour, 283.
Lattimore, Samuel, 32.
Laughery, Archabald,. see Lochry.
Laughery Creek, 2-5, 33, 104, 351.
Laughridge, William, 32.
Lausanne (Switzerland), Swiss colonists leave, xiv, 8; John James Dufour visits, 341.
Lawrence, John, attorney, 51, 58, 367, 378; congressional candidate, 55.
Lawrence, William, lays out Center Square, 145.
Lawrenceburgh (Indiana), 179, 384; road to Port William, 30; wants Lake Michigan-Ohio road terminus, 208.
Laycock, ———, confused with Haycock, 91.
Leap, Dudley, 205.
Leavy, ———, dealings with John James Dufour, 299.
Le Clerc, Mrs. Julia (née Morerod), 48, 90, 155, 188.
Le Clerc, Peter, 75, 187.
Lee, David, 189-90.
Lee, Eliza B. (Mrs. John L. Armington), 185.
Lee, James, sketch of, 88.
Leesburg (Virginia), 114.
Legaux, ———, vines purchased from, xiv, 10, 14, 295.

Le Grix, Madame, 247.
Leman, Canton de (Switzerland), 7.
Lentz, Nicholas, 367.
Lentz, ———, 237.
Lester, ———, 122.
Levi, Abraham, 81.
Lewis, William, preaches in Vevay, 64.
Lexington (Kentucky), 10, 46, 100, 128, 277, 279, 289, 291, 299; Fourth of July barbecue at, xv, 12; vineyard association organized at, xiii, 9, 13-14; Dufours arrive at, 303.
*Liberty Hall*, 45.
Lincoln, Abraham, 114; presidential candidate, 169.
Lindley, Captain Francis S., 108; Vevay tanner, 46, 194.
Lion, Joseph, dealings with John James Dufour, 299.
Little, Henry, Presbyterian minister, 65.
Littlefield, Enos, 355; county commissioner, 133.
Littlefield, Harvey, county commissioner, 134, 135.
Livings, Daniel L., collector of revenue, 156.
Livings, Theodore, 156.
Lochry, Colonel Archabald, killed on Indian excursion, 2-5, 400; monument to, 351.
Lock, Peter, 33, 361, 367.
Log Lick (Indiana), 64; county seat contest, 160.
Log Lick Creek, 17, 313; blockhouse on, 150.
London (England), John James Dufour at, 329, 331.
Long, James C., postmaster of Vevay, 100, 400.
Long, ———, 74.

Long Run, 86, 123; Baptist Church, 67; mills on, 105, 364; Scotch settlers, 74, 83.
Lorimier, ———, dealings with John James Dufour, 269.
Lostutter, Peter, 47.
Loudon, Daniel W., lays out Bennington, 144.
Louis, ———, dealings with John James Dufour, 301.
Louisville (Kentucky), 3, 25, 275; market for Vevay produce, 102.
Lunger, Isaac, 179.
Luster, Benjamin, 102, 183.
Lutz, Moses, 123.

McAfee, Robert Breckenridge, 129.
McCallum, Duncan, 74, 83.
McCallum, John, 74.
McCallum, Niel, 74.
McClellan, James B. (George B.), presidential candidate, 169.
McClure, James, associate judge, 38, 42, 47, 51, 58, 148, 365, 378.
McClure, John, 366.
McCorcles, early settlers, 48.
McCorkle, Robert, 157.
McCormick, David, 49, 86, 387; tavern keeper, 48, 372.
McCormick, John, 54, 375.
McCormick, Mrs. John, 54, 375.
McCray, William, admitted *ex gratia* as attorney, 379.
McCreary, Hugh, early settler, 48; marriage, 50.
McCreary, Mrs. Hugh, 50.
McCullough, William, Jackson supporter, 163, 164.
McCutchen (McCutcheon), Dr. Joseph, 81, 393.
McFall, Joseph, 366.

McFall, ———, 104.
McGruder, Norman B., 367.
McHenry, Joseph, 121; county supervisor, 132; justice of peace, 131, 132.
McHenry, Wesley, in wharfboat business, 401.
McIlvain, William, buys Vevay lot, 34.
McIntire, Edward, ferry of, 49; lays out Erin, 144; miller, 104.
McIntire, Thomas, 122.
McKay, Abisha, 53, 123, 366.
McKay, James, 53; land entry, 37; arraigned for contempt of court, 368.
McKay, Robert, 52, 53, 373; buys land, 50-51; has corn husking, 85-86.
McKenzie, Mordecai, 67.
McMakin, Henry, collector of revenue, 156; sheriff, 136.
McMakin, Jonathan, 99, 189.
McMakin, Julius, 23.
McMillen, Amity, 65.
McNutt, Colin, county commissioner, 133.
Madary, Mathias, 397.
Maddox, D. T., attorney, 51.
Madison, Channing, 78.
Madison, Joab, buys Vevay lot, 34.
Madison (Indiana), 64, 88, 111, 114, 193, 384; county business transacted at, 33, 35, 50, 361; justice of peace, 74; preaching at, 66; road from Jefferson County, 30; terminus of Lake Michigan-Ohio Road, 208-9.
Madison Township (Jefferson County), 127.
Magues, Samuel, dealings with John James Dufour, 259.

Magues, Thomas, dealings with John James Dufour, 259.
Maguire, ———, 7, 23.
Mails, 24-25, 26, 99-100, 399.
Makensies, early settlers, 74.
Malcomson, William, blacksmith, 386.
Malcomson family, early settlers, 74.
Malin, Ira N., clerk of circuit court, 138; county treasurer, 140; county recorder, 141; Vevay harness maker, 193.
Malin, Jacob, 381, 385.
Malin, Joseph, 175, 381; associate judge, 148; county treasurer, 139; lays out addition to New York (Florence), 144; sheriff, 136; Vevay harness maker, 76-77, 193, 386-87.
Manford, ———, Vevay blacksmith, 405.
Manville, Mrs., Vevay tailoress, 192.
Marechal, ———, dealings with John James Dufour, 257, 261, 289.
Marietta (Ohio), 8, 12, 257, 281, 303.
Markland (Indiana), 114, 401.
Martin, Dr., 91.
Mary's, John James Dufour boards at, 283, 287.
Massacre of Pigeon Roost, 358.
Maxwell, David H., state representative, 402.
May, Captain, promotes land scheme, 116 ff.
Mayfield, Mrs. (née Borallay), 362.
Mayor, ———, dealings with John James Dufour, 345.
Mead, William, sheriff, 136.
Mecbean, ———, dealings with John James Dufour, 299, 301.

Meek, Alexander A., 368; commissioner to locate county seat, 41-44, 365; lawyer, 41, 58, 377; president judge, probate court, 402.
Meek, John, justice of peace, 126.
Melcher, John, 106, 180, 196.
Menard, ———, 257; dealings with John James Dufour, 259, 261, 263, 265, 267, 269, 271, 273.
Menard, Mrs., 263.
Mendenhall, Ira, 381; county treasurer, 139, 140; county recorder, 141.
Mendenhall, John, 98; imprisoned for debt, 127.
Mendenhall, Dr. John, 81, 87, 392; county commissioner, 130.
Mendenhall, Martha B., 65.
Mendenhall, Miles, 124, 125; Vevay harness maker, 193.
Mennesier, ———, boards John James Dufour at Cincinnati, 277.
Mennet, Francis E., 16, 22, 28, 152, 203.
Mennet, Samuel, 152; joins Swiss colony, 16; marriage, 17-18; improves land, 22; manufactures liquor, 203.
Mennet, Mrs. Samuel, 18.
Menola, John B., 90.
Mentelle, Charles, 21.
Mentelle, W., 21.
Merrill, Samuel, 381; sketch of, 91-93; admitted to bar, 58, 91, 379; contractor for building jail, 78; member Vevay Literary Society, 73; state representative, 91, 171, 172, 404; state treasurer, 93, 200; Sunday school superintend-

## INDEX

ent, 63; opposed in election, 396-97; president Madison and Indianapolis railroad, 397; president state bank, 397.
Miami Reserve, 209.
Miami River, 2.
Mikesell, Jacob, buys Vevay lot, 34.
Mikesell, Peter, buys Vevay lot, 34.
Militia, see Indiana, militia.
Millen, Eliza, divorce case, 368.
Millen, George, divorce case, 368.
Miller, Abraham, 33, 92-93.
Miller, David, 364.
Miller, John, Jackson supporter, 164.
Miller, William, 33.
Millersburg (Kentucky), 279, 297.
Mills, John, 367.
Milroy, Samuel, state senator, 181.
Mississippi River, barges and keel boats, 83.
Mitchel, Captain William C., 108.
Mitchell, Captain, of brig *Sally*, 245.
Mix, Lyman W., 124; county commissioner, 133; lays out addition to Mount Sterling, 144.
Mix, Nathaniel, 122, 124.
*Monitor* (Vevay), 56, 111.
Monroe, Osborn, 32.
Monroe County (Indiana), 362.
Mons (France), John James Dufour at, 335.
Montgomery, Isaac, state senator, 181.
Montgomery (Indiana), 144.

Montieth, William J., Presbyterian minister, 65.
Montreux (Switzerland), John James Dufour at, 18, 221, 233, 341.
Moore, Harbin H., visits Vevay, 149.
Moore, Richard, 402.
Moorefield (Indiana), 86, 103; laid out, 144.
Moors, Thomas, 287.
Moreau, Francis, dealings with John James Dufour, 261.
Moreillon, Madame, dealings with John James Dufour, 345.
Morerod, Amie, 35, 155; schooling, 196.
Morerod, Dr. Eugene R., 154.
Morerod, Frederick, in militia, 395.
Morerod, Henriette L., marriages, 154; second child born in Swiss colony, 31, 154.
Morerod, Jean Daniel, 23, 82, 89, 101, 208, 325, 353, 354, 358, 381; sails for America, 11; arrives at First Vineyard, xv; marriage, 12; assigned lands, 17, 20, 229, 231, 233, 307; moves to New Switzerland, 353; signs covenant, 21; in Cincinnati, 24; daughter, 31; manufactures liquor, 34, 204; raises cotton, 88; befriends strangers, 119-20; death, 362; curious will, 153-54.
Morerod, Mrs. Jean Daniel, see Dufour, Antoinette.
Morerod, John R., 362; county treasurer, 140, 155; marriage, 154; sheriff, 136, 155.
Morerod, Louisa (Mrs. Constant Golay), 89, 155.

## 432  INDIANA HISTORICAL COLLECTIONS

Morerod, Rodolph, in militia, 395, 396.
Mormons, 184.
Morral, John, preaches in Vevay, 64.
Morris, Gouverneur, 223.
Morris, Captain Patterson (Moris, Paterson), of brig *Young Edward*, 18, 327.
Morris, Thomas, 67.
Morrison, ———, dealings with John James Dufour, 271.
Morton family, early settlers, 74.
Mosbyer, Peter, 32.
Moss, Zela, 367.
Mount Pleasant (Kentucky), Baptist Church, 67.
Mount Sterling (Indiana), 75, 185, 192, 204, 360; county seat contest, 160; post office established, 178; squirrel hunts, 122-25.
Mounts, Caleb, 149; county commissioner, 58, 130, 377; early settler, 47; justice of peace, 44, 131.
Mounts, Thomas, 366.
Munfort, Peter, preaches in Vevay, 64.
Munson, Lewis, 65.
Munson, Rebecca, 65.
Muret, Dr. Benjamin, early physician, 54, 375.
Muret, Dr. Charles, 375; sketch of, 54; first physician in Swiss colony, 54, 80.
Muret, John Louis, 54, 375.
Muret, Julius, 54, 375.
Muret, Mary (Mrs. John McCormick), 54, 375.
Murphy, George W., Vevay blacksmith, 405.
Murphy, Mrs. Jane, marriages, 115.

Murphy, Jesse, 115, 356; acquitted of murder charge, 98.
Muscle Shoals, trade with Vevay, 83.
Muskingum River, 5, 83.

Nancaron (Nancarron), ———, dealings with John James Dufour, 291, 301.
Nashville (Tennessee), 83, 114.
Naylor, Isaac, 356.
Naylor, Mrs. Isaac, *see* Anderson, Catharine.
Neal, John, 48.
Nelson, Alexander, 124.
Nelson, John, 366.
Nelson, Reuben W., admitted to practise law, 378.
Netherland, Joseph H., 104; clerk, circuit court, 139.
Neville (Switzerland), 116, 117.
New, Jeptha D., judge, circuit court, 148; representative from Indiana, 171.
New Hanover (Indiana), 179.
New Harmony (Indiana), loan to state, 200.
Newkirk, Barnabas, 122.
New Lawrenceburg (Indiana), 179.
New Liberty (Kentucky), 91.
New Madrid (Indiana), earthquake shocks, 32.
New Orleans, 116; market for Vevay produce, 77, 83, 96.
*News, The* (Vevay), published by Charles Scott, 376.
Newspapers, 55-58, 110-15, 375-76, 401.
New Switzerland (Indiana), 69, 351-52; Swiss settlers arrive at, xvii, 16, 17, 18, 22-23, 25-26, 49, 82, 353; conditions in 1810, pp. 28 ff; cotton raised, 88; Fourth of July celebra-

## INDEX 433

tions, 151 ff; first child born in, 31; first physician, 54; first wine, xviii; Indians feared, 31, 33, 358; mills in, 30; post office established, 27; roads, 30; schools, 30-31. *See also*, Switzerland County, Vevay, Dufour, John James, etc.

Newton, Asa, 95; subscription to road company, 190.

Newton, Mrs. ———, oldest resident of Switzerland County in 1876, p. 95.

New Washington (Indiana), 65.

New York (Indiana), name changed, 399.

New York (New York), 325; vines purchased at, xiv, 9-10; John James Dufour at, 285, 293, 323.

New York Canal, 403.

Nichols, Edward, attorney, 51.

Nicollier (Nicolier, ———), dealings with John James Dufour, 343, 345.

Nihell, Lawrence, 381; directs bank subscriptions, 79; inspector of elections, 59; juror, 98; sinks salt well, 96.

Nighswonger, Peter, 33.

Nighswonger, Solomon, 367.

Nighswonger, Mrs., first person buried in Vevay, 46, 370.

Noble, Charles, 44.

Noble, James, attorney, 51, 379; president judge, circuit court, 51, 147, 368; prosecuting attorney, 52, 366, 367, 368; senator from Indiana, 51, 99.

Noble, Joseph, 387; buys Vevay lots, 34; constable, 44; juror, 98; tax lister, 60.

Noble, Lewis, 44.

Noble, Oliver, 44.

Nollnaguel, ———, dealings with John James Dufour, 285.

Norfolk (Virginia), Swiss colonists arrive at, xv, 12.

Norrisez, Charles, 12, 353.

Norrisez, Mary, 65.

Norrisez, Victor, 213.

Norrisez, William, 17, 65; sketch of, 185-86, 362.

Norrisez, Mrs., 16, 128.

North, Benjamin, state representative, 173.

North, James, state representative, 173.

Norton, Dr., 81.

Noville and Rennar (Switzerland), Dufour's common rights in, recognized, 221-23.

Obersteg, Joseph James, of Boltigue, 227, 249.

Oboussier (Obousier), Louis Gex, *see* Gex, Louis.

Oboussier, Luke, 52, 373; settles in New Switzerland, 16, 18, 22; sergeant in militia, 32, 360.

Ogule, ———, dealings with John James Dufour, 257, 259.

Ogle, Achillis, 85.

Ogle, Eli T., county treasurer, 140.

Ogle, Hiram, Sr., 85, 103; builds county jail, 45, 86; mail carrier, 100.

Ogle, Hiram, Jr., 85.

Ohio County (Indiana), part of Dearborn County, 6-7; boundary, 351.

Ohio River, 8, 101; Swiss buy lands on, 15, 17, 37; canal project, 71-73; transportation on, 82-83; road to Lake Michigan from, 208-9.

## 434 INDIANA HISTORICAL COLLECTIONS

*Ohio Valley Gazette* (Vevay), 57, 112.
"Old Betz" (Old Betts), 84, 167-68, 403-4.
Olean (Indiana), 91; road to, 208.
Olmstead, John S., 102.
Orange County (Indiana), organization, 161.
Ormsby, Oliver, land entry, 36; clerk, circuit court, 138.
Ormsby, Mrs., 50.
Ortubise, ———, dealings with John James Dufour, 267.
Osserlee, ———, Cincinnati blacksmith, 76.
Ouabash River, *see* Wabash River.

Pache, ———, dealings with John James Dufour, 343.
Paris (France), visited by John James Dufour, 8, 18, 237, 239, 241, 243, 337, 339.
Paris (Kentucky), 297.
Parker, ———, 301, 305.
Parkinson, Abraham, 123, 214.
Pate, William T., state representative, 173; owns Patriot distillery, 205.
Patriot (Indiana), 35; distillery, 205; formerly called Troy, 144; laid out, 144.
Patterson, John, 34.
Patton, Edward, 127, 382, 397; sells printing establishment, 56, 111; clerk of church meeting, 64; takes cargoes to New Orleans, 77; clerk, circuit court, 137-38; president county commissioners, 131; secretary of Jackson meeting, 163; marriage, 154; rescues girl from well, 182.

Patton, George C., Vevay postmaster, 100.
Patton, Morgan, elder in Presbyterian church, 64.
Patton, Major William M., county commissioner, 134; clerk, circuit court, 138; county auditor, 142.
Paul, John, state senator, 171.
Pavy, Absolem, missionary among Indians, 120.
Pavy, James, 213.
Pavy, Reverend John, Baptist minister, 120, 212-13.
Pavy, Samuel H., 120, 213.
Paxton, Thomas, 52, 373.
Paxton, William, Vevay silversmith and watch maker, 185.
Payen, ———, dealings with John James Dufour, 319.
Payen-boisneuf, J., tricked in land sale, 223-25.
Peabody, Hiram, 183.
Peacock, ———, partner of Wrenshall, 283.
Peak, Nathan, teaches school, 30.
Peak, Samuel, 124; border ranger, 33.
Peck, Robert, Vevay cabinet maker, 191.
Peelman, Joseph, 31, 195, 370; Vevay cabinet maker, 191.
Peira, ———, dealings with John James Dufour, 261.
Peirson, Williams, *see* Pierson, Williams.
Penwell, David, 98.
Perkins, Garret, 382; collector of revenue, 156; Vevay blacksmith, 188.
Pernet, David Emmanuel, 75, 385, 386.
Pernet, John, 75, 386.

## INDEX 435

Pernet, Susan S. (Mrs. Augustus Vairin), 116.
Peronne (France), John James Dufour at, 335.
Perret, F., dealings with John James Dufour, 327, 331, 341.
Perry County (Indiana), representation, 161.
Peters, Captain Henry, 108.
Petty, Ezekiel, 47.
Petty, Joshua, 47; justice of peace, 210.
Philadelphia (Pennsylvania), 8, 227; vineyard association at, xiii, 13; vines purchased at, xiv, 10; John James Dufour at, 251, 255, 257, 273, 285, 287, 293, 295, 301, 321.
Philips, Matilda (Mrs. Richard Dumont), 50.
Philips, William, land entry, 36.
Pickett (Picket), Benjamin, Sr., 124, 125, 183.
Pickett, Benjamin, Jr., 23, 360.
Pickett, James, 122, 124; private in militia, 32, 360; border ranger, 33; mistakes wolves for dogs, 47.
Pickett, Heathcoat, 95, 360; early settler, 7, 23; hunting experiences, 47, 182-83; pilots flatboats to New Orleans, 96.
Pierce, Franklin, 113, 169.
Pierson, Williams, 374; early settler, 47; inspector of elections, 44, 59.
Pigeon Roost, Massacre of, 358.
Pirous, ———, dealings with John James Dufour, 267.
Pittsburgh (Pennsylvania), 8, 9, 12, 83, 229, 255, 257, 271, 273, 281, 287, 295, 297, 305.
Plasants, John, dealings with John James Dufour, 253.

Pleasant Grove and Indian Creek road, 190-91.
Pleasant Township (Switzerland County), 95, 131; Dutch settlement, 73; Scotch settlement, 73-74; deaths from cholera, 102; militia, 108; squirrel hunt, 123; addition to, 130.
Pleasants, George E., 372; county supervisor, 132.
Pleasants, James K., 69, 387.
Pleasants, Samuel E., 30, 69, 362, 387.
*Ploughboy*, steamboat on Ohio River, 82.
Plum (Plumb) Creek, 15, 22, 28, 89, 95, 102, 107, 361, 363, 375.
Plymouth (England), John James Dufour at, 18, 327.
Polk, James K., 168-69.
Pontarlier (France), John James Dufour at, 341.
Population, of Vevay, 28, 101; of Switzerland County, 33, 35, 60.
Port William (Kentucky), 26, 27, 30, 85, 353. *See also* Carrollton.
Porter, Samuel, state representative, 173, 174.
Posey, Thomas, 365; appoints Switzerland County officers, 33, 38-40, 135, 137, 141.
Posey Township (Switzerland County), 53, 165, 201, 202, 210, 374; formation, 44, 59-60, 369, 377; officers, 44, 59-60, 131, 132; attached to Ohio County, 158-59; representation, 161.
Post Vincennes (Indiana), 311. *See also* Vincennes.

## 436  INDIANA HISTORICAL COLLECTIONS

Powell, William H., state senator, 172.
Prat, Joseph, dealings with John James Dufour, 263.
Presbyterian Church, see Churches.
Prewit, "Aunt Polly," 207.
Price, William, 67; sheriff, 136.
Priestly, William, 70, 380.
Prince, William, election to Congress, 162.
Printer's Retreat (Indiana), 87, 111, 113, 145, 376.
Pritchet, Noah, 85-86.
Probasco, George W., 122, 124.
Produce, 62-63, 73, 188-89, 197.
Protsman, Charles, 44.
Protsman, John, 104.
Protsman, Samuel, 104.
Protsman, Mrs. Samuel, 369.
Protsman, William, 30, 44, 104.
Protsman, Mrs. William, 369.
Pugh, Joseph, county offices, 59, 131.

Quercus Grove (Indiana), 77, 121, 144.

Railroads, 94-95, 397.
Ramsey, Thomas, 150.
Ramseyer, Daniel, 123, 125, 401; county commissioner, 134, 142.
Ramseyer, Philip, 123.
Randall, Richard, publishes *Monitor*, 56, 111; rivalry with Keen, 376; removes to Vernon, 111, 113.
Ransom, Mrs. Rosetta, 400.
Rariden (Raridon), James, state senator, 181.
Ray, James B., admitted to practise law, 379; candidate for Congress, 161; state senator, 181.

Rayl, John, 367; early settler, 7, 23.
Rayl, Thomas, border ranger, 33.
Rayles, Mrs., frightened by Indians, 361.
Raymond (Raimont, Raimond), Abraham, in militia, 395, 396.
Raymond, Francis L., 176.
Raymond, Frederick Louis, 49, 325; joins Swiss colony, 16, 18, 22, 307.
Raymond, Orlando, letter to John Francis Dufour about canal lottery, 383.
Raymond family, 231, 360.
Rector, ———, carpenter, 313, 315.
Red Bank, 311.
Red River colony, 117-20, 401.
Reed, John, 126.
Reeder, Jonathan, 49, 387.
Reiner, ———, dealings with John James Dufour, 263.
*Reveille and News*, see *Vevay Reveille*.
Reynolds and Company, Cincinnati printers, 79.
Richard, Father, 265, 271.
Richards, Isaac, 123, 393.
Richards, Truman, 382; prosecuting attorney, 379; death, 400.
Richie, Viletta, 374.
Ried, A. S., Presbyterian minister, 65.
Riley, F. S., Baptist minister, 68.
Ringo, James, mail carrier, 100.
Ripley County (Indiana), 91, 208; Baptist Church organized, 121; part of Ross Township added to, 6, 91, 130; senator from, 94.

## INDEX 437

Rising Sun (Indiana), 91, 114, 159, 178, 207, 395.
*Rising Sun Recorder*, 114.
Roberts, Hezekiah, 123.
Roberts, John, 126.
Roberts, Redding, 123.
Roberts, William, 123, 125, 401.
Robinson, Benjamin L., lays out addition to New York, 144; state senator, 172, 404.
Robinson, John L., congressman from Indiana, 171.
Robinson, ———, tanner, 194.
Rochat, William, blacksmith, 386.
Rohl, ———, dealings with John James Dufour, 263.
Rolling Fork (Kentucky), John James Dufour at, 277.
Romeril, John, 74.
Romeril, Philip, 74.
Rosebrough, Robert, lays out addition to Mount Sterling, 144.
Rosenbrough, Moses K., state senator, 172.
Ross, William, 59; county commissioner, 130.
Ross Township (Switzerland County), organization, 59-60, 377; part attached to Pleasant Township, 130; part attached to Ripley County, 6, 91, 130; road, 208.
Rossier, ———, dealings with John James Dufour, 285, 313, 325, 327.
Rotterdam (Holland), John James Dufour at, 18, 331, 333.
Roulet, Madame, 325.
Rous, Alfred, clerk, circuit court, 138.
Rous, James, 104, 366; settles in Vevay, 38; county commissioner, 58, 130, 377; librarian of Vevay Literary Society, 46; operates horse mill, 105, 364; teaches school, 31, 195, 355; witnesses whipping, 81.
Rous, Lucien, first male child born in Vevay, 38.
Rous, Percy, 31, 38, 81, 195, 355, 398; sheriff, 136.
Rous, William, clerk, circuit court, 138.
Rous, Zadig, 31, 38, 81, 82, 123, 125, 195, 355, 398.
Routein, Michael, 176.
Roux, Jean, 309, 313, 317.
Royal Arch Masons, 80.
Roye (France), John James Dufour at, 335.
Ruggles, William H., Vevay silversmith, 186.
Rush County (Indiana), first newspaper printed in, 115.
Russell House, 31, 104, 355, 378.
Ruter, Martin, Methodist minister, 66.
Rutherford, Joseph, 360.
Rutherford, Stephen, 32, 360.

Sage, Philander S., state senator, 172, 404.
St. Louis (Missouri), xiii, 8, 9, 83, 119, 265, 267, 269.
Saint Vincennes, *see* Vincennes.
Sales de Montreux (Switzerland), 219, 235.
Saline River, 311.
Salins (France), John James Dufour at, 339.
Sample, Adoat, 367.
Sanders, Ab., 393.
Sanders, John, 393.
Sanders, Lewis (Louis), 229; manufacturer and merchant, 393.

Sanders, Samuel, 100; proprietor of Ghent, 90.
Sandos, ———, repairs watches for John James Dufour, 255.
Saugrin, ———, dealings with John James Dufour, 291, 299, 307.
Schenck, Benjamin F., 114; publishes newspaper, 57, 112; death, 401.
Schenck, John James Philip, 115, 204, 386; sketch of, 76; county commissioner, 133, 134.
Schenck, Ulysses P., 66, 114, 152, 353, 386; sketch of, 76; Vevay druggist, 187.
Schenck and Sons, 196.
Schroeder, John T., county recorder, 141.
Schroeder, Lewis, 361.
Schwartz, John, judge pro tem., court of common pleas, 147.
Scotch settlers, 73-74.
Scott, Charles C., newspaper ventures, 57, 112, 114, 376.
Scott, David, county commissioner, 134, 135.
Scott, James, judge, state supreme court, 377; president board of directors, Jeffersonville and Ohio Canal Company, 72.
Scott, Dr. John, attends Seminary of Vevay, 355.
Scott, John, Vevay tailor, 35, 192.
Scott, Rufus, 382; Vevay blacksmith, 188.
Scott, Walter, 104.
Scott, William, digs well for John James Dufour, 354.
Scott and Edward, dealings with John James Dufour, 297, 299.

Scoville, Linus, favors change of county seat, 157; state representative, 172.
Scudder, William, county commissioner, 133.
Searcy, Elizabeth, 59.
Searcy, William, 98.
Sebastian, Reverend Alexander, 149; forms separate Baptist church, 120-21.
Second Vineyard, Dufour family removes to, vii; extended credit on land entries, xvii; successful beginning, xviii. *See also* New Switzerland and Vevay.
Selkirk, Lord, 116.
Seminary of Vevay, description, 355.
Senegal, ———, dealings with John James Dufour, 261.
Senlis (France), John James Dufour at, 337.
Seymour, Horatio, presidential candidate, 169.
Shannon, Captain, 3.
Shaw, Alfred, Vevay postmaster, 400.
Shaw, William, sells liquors, 398.
Sheets, Francis G., lays out addition to Vevay, 144.
Sheets, John, lays out addition to Vevay, 144.
Sheldon, David, 122.
Shippingport (Kentucky), 76, 119.
Sholts, Frederick, state senator, 181.
Short, Jacob, commissioner to locate county seat, 365.
Short, Joseph, commissioner to locate county seat, 41-44.
Shuff, Enoch, 156.

Shull, David, county commissioner, 134.
Shull, Jacob, county commissioner, 134, 142.
Shupe, John, 393.
Siebenthal, de, Benjamin F., 86, 105, 395.
Siebenthal, de, Francis Louis, sails for America, 11; arrives at First Vineyard, xv; assigned lands, 20; signs covenant, 21; Vevay blacksmith, 187; death, 362.
Siebenthal, de, John Francis, 174, 213, 315, 381, 387; sails for America, 11; arrives at First Vineyard, xv; assigned lands, 17, 20, 231, 233, 307; marriage, 17; signs covenant, 21; imprisoned for debt, 127-28; collector of revenue, 156, 179; sheriff, 38, 58, 81, 135, 179, 366; Clay supporter, 162; death, 362.
Siebenthal, de, Mrs. John Francis, see Dufour, Jeanne Marie.
Siebenthal, de, John Louis, Vevay tanner, 194.
Siebenthal, de, Lemuel, blacksmith, 386.
Simmons (Sinimons), Benjamin L., 114; county commissioner, 135; publishes *Indiana Palladium*, 57, 112; in wharfboat business, 401.
Simon, John J., Swiss colonist, 117-20.
Simon, Zelie C. (Mrs. Frederick L. Grisard), 117-20.
Sisson, Daniel, 188.
Sisson, Zenas, 122, 124.
Six Nations, 1, 351.
Slaughter, James B., state senator, 181.

Slavery, agitation, 55, 120; treatise written on, 177.
Slawson, Simeon, Clinton supporter, 163.
Smith, Benjamin F., Vevay shoemaker, 193.
Smith, Mrs. Bettie Dufour, presents Dufour manuscripts to Indiana State Library, viii, xviii.
Smith, John, county commissioner, 131; justice of peace, 131.
Smith, Oliver H., 399; sketch of, 95; congressman from Indiana, 171.
Smith, "Rarified," sketch of, 77.
Smith, Samuel, digs well for John Francis Dufour, 354.
Smith, Thomas, congressman from Indiana, 171; state senator, 171.
Smith, William, 367.
Smithson, Joshua, cards and gins cotton, 88-89, 197; Vevay cabinet maker, 88, 191; sells mill, 376.
Smock, Jeremiah, buys Vevay lot, 34.
Snelling, Colonel Josiah, 118.
Snodgrass, ———, 275.
Soapville (Indiana), 144.
Sonnette, ———, dealings with John James Dufour, 269.
Soulard, ———, dealings with John James Dufour, 267, 269.
Sparks, Elijah, president judge, circuit court, 51, 147, 365, 367.
Spencer, John W., president judge, probate court, 402; state representative, 173.
*Spirit of the Times* (Vevay), 57, 112.

Springfield (Kentucky), John James Dufour at, 277.
Stall, Dr. Edward, 81; Vevay physician, 392.
Stanley, Isaac, 49, 387; county commissioner, 58, 130, 377.
Stapp, Milton, state senator, 181.
Starr, Abner K., buys Vevay lots, 34.
Steele, Mrs. Jane, Vevay school teacher, 356. *See also* Mrs. Jane Murphy.
Stein, M. D. A., Presbyterian minister, 65.
Stephenson, Dr. William, 81, 400.
Stepleton, John, 33, 108, 122, 124.
Stevens, Edward M., Vevay druggist, 187.
Stevens, Isaac, newspaper ventures, 56, 57, 111, 112; Vevay druggist, 113, 187, 376.
Stevens, Mrs. Jane (née Lee), 88.
Stevens, Stephen C., 45, 400; attorney, 51, 58, 368, 377; judge, supreme court of Indiana, 51; prosecuting attorney, 58-59, 60; state representative, 157, 172, 199, 200, 402; state senator, 171; statement about state treasury, 197-99; wife, 88.
Stewart, Andrew, county commissioner, 133, 134.
Stewart (Stuart), James A., 367; early settler, 7; holds land in Swiss colony, 17, 229, 231, 307; dealings with John James Dufour, 313, 315.
Stewart, Stephen H., state representative, 173.
Stewart, Colonel William J.,
123; county commissioner, 134, 135; justice of peace, 131.
Stickler, Jacob, 122.
Stickler, John, 124.
Storm, Peter, 32.
Stow, Jonah, 122.
Stow, Shilometh, sketch of, 87.
Stow, Solomon, sketch of, 87.
Stow, Uzial H., sketch of, 87-88.
Strange, Reverend John, Methodist minister, 66.
Subletts Ferry (Kentucky), 83.
Sulgrove, Berry R., 379.
Sullivan, Mrs. Huldah (née Walden), 99.
Sullivan, Jeremiah, attorney, 51; candidate for Congress, 161-62; judge, supreme court of Indiana, 51.
Swan, James, fraudulent sale of lands, 223-25.
Sweet, William W., 379.
Swiss Artillery Company, 84, 108, 154, 167-68.
Swiss colonists, leave Switzerland, xiv, 11; arrive at First Vineyard, xv; remove to Second Vineyard, xvi-xvii; buy Indiana lands, xvii, 16; covenant of association, 19-21; credit extended for land payment, 28; guard against Indians, 31; improve lands, 22 ff, 26, 29-30; send wine to President, 315; meet for religious services, 68-69. *See also* New Switzerland, Switzerland County, and Vevay.
Switzerland, form of government changed, 352; colonists sail for America, xiv, 11.
Switzerland County (Indiana), xiii, 1, 374, 378; area by townships, 142-43; Baptist churches organized, 120-21;

## INDEX 441

blockhouses, 150-51; branch bank, 79-80;
county officers: agents, 45, 53; auditors, 31, 134, 142; attorneys, 51, 58, 91; board of county commissioners, 133-35; board of justices, 202; board of supervisors, 131-33; clerks, 58; collectors of revenue, 155-56, 179; commissioners, 58, 59, 129-31, 133-35; coroners, 38, 39, 46, 58; first elections, 160; justices of peace, 131-32; presiding judges, circuit court, 147-48, 371; probate judges, 145; prosecuting attorneys, 52, 58-59, 60, 366; recorders, 48, 141-42; sheriffs, 38, 58, 81, 135-37, 179, 366; surveyors, 38, 44, 111; tax listers, 45-46, 59-60; treasurers, 75-76, 87, 139-41;
county organization: 7, 35; attached to Dearborn County, 6; attached to Jefferson County, 6, 33, 35; divided into townships, 44, 59; location of county seat, 40-44, 365; legislation regulating transaction of county business, 130 ff; named by John Francis Dufour, 38; officers appointed by territorial governor, 38 ff; officers elected after organization of state, 58; part of Ross Township transferred to Ripley County, 130; proposition to unite with Ohio County, 159; surveyed, 36;
courts: 40-45, 47, 51-53, 378; bill on crime and punishment, 180-81; circuit court, 50, 52, 81-82, 97-98, 121, 130; terms and officers of circuit court, 38-40, 58-60, 137-39; probate court, 145; common pleas, 146-49;
representation: 161, 363-64; electoral district, 161, 170, 171, 172; congressional representatives, 51, 171; state representatives, 172-74, 199, 404; state senators, 51, 94, 171-72, 206, 404;
taxes: 388-91; delinquent, 57; levy in 1816, pp. 48-49; increase from 1824 to 1875, pp. 201-2; listers of property, 45-46, 59-60; receipt, 22;
deaths from cholera, 102; earthquake, 32; first flatboat, 96; first hay barn, 87; first land deed, 50; first marriage license, 50; first Methodist minister, 46; hunting, 24, 89-90, 121-26, 182-83; Indian massacre, 2; land entries, 36-37; mills, 103-5; newspapers, 55-58, 110-15, 368-69; physicians, 54, 80-81, 185; political affiliations, 162-70; population, 33, 35, 60; rivalry between sections, 156-60; roads, 189, 378; settlers endure privations, 25 (*see also* early settlers); towns laid out, 144-45; votes against constitutional convention, 170.
*Switzerland County News*, 80.

Tague (Teague), George, 157, 164.
Tague, John, in militia, 32, 360.
Tague, Joseph, 360.

Tague, Merrit W., justice of peace, 114, 401; publishes *Weekly News*, 57, 112.
Tait, John, Jr., state representative, 158, 159, 173, 174.
Tandy, George, 75, 103.
Tandy, Mrs. Harriet, *see* Henriette L. Morerod.
Tandy, John, builds county courthouse, 45.
Tandy, John F., marriage, 154.
Tapp, Newton H., 157; associate judge, 146, 148; bailiff, 59; constable, 59.
Tarkington, Joseph, Methodist minister, 66.
Taylor, Thomas, 32.
Taylor, Zachary, elected president, 169.
Tennessee River, 83.
Test, John, attorney, 51, 366, 379; congressman from Indiana, 51, 161, 171, 403; president judge, circuit court, 58, 147; prosecuting attorney, 52.
Texas, myth about annexation, 205-6.
The Hague (Holland), John James Dufour at, 333.
Thiebaud, Caroline E., 67.
Thiebaud, Charles, Vevay shoemaker, 193.
Thiebaud, Charles O., 75, 372, 397; Vevay druggist, 187; in militia, 395.
Thiebaud, Frederick L., 67; robbed, 399.
Thiebaud, Henriette, 67.
Thiebaud (Thibaut), John Louis, 35, 48, 68, 325, 397; sketch of family, 75-76; Vevay druggist, 187.
Thiebaud, Justin, 68, 75.
Thomas, Booth, 32.
Thomas, ———, preaches in Vevay, 64.
Thompson, Dr. Jacob W., 88.
Thompson, John H., state senator, 181.
Thompson, J., preaches in Vevay, 64.
Thompson, Thomas, land entry, 37.
Thornton, Henry P., admitted to practise law, 379.
Thrall, Friend, 122, 124.
Thruston (Thurston), Buckner, letter to John Francis Dufour, 26-27; senator from Kentucky, 321, 353.
Tift, ———, 89.
Tiller, ———, dealings with John James Dufour, 249.
Tilly, William, 75.
Tinker, Stephen R., 192.
Tinker, Mrs. Stephen R., tailoress, 192.
Tippecanoe, Battle of, 358.
Titus, James H., county recorder, 141.
Todd, Henry, 193.
Todd, James, Vevay harness maker, 193.
Todd, Lieutenant Colonel Paxton W., in militia, 109, 400.
Torrence, James, 185.
Transportation, 8-9, 10, 12, 19, 24-25, 25-26, 35, 63, 69, 71-73, 77, 82-84, 94-95, 96, 104, 189-191, 373, 375, 393-94.
Trotter, Robert M., 42, 44, 299, 364; director Vevay Literary Society, 46, 370; justice of peace, 50; tavern keeper, 372.
Troy (Indiana), *see* Patriot.
Truesdell (Treusdel), James, 48.
Truesdell, Job, 48, 52, 374.

# INDEX 443

Tull, Joshua, 32.
Turner, George, trader, 51; purchases reserved land, 364.
Turner, John, 51.
Turner, Robert, 51.
Tyler, John, elected vice president, 168.

Underwood, Colby, 127.
United States Congress, acts on behalf of Swiss settlers, 15, 16, 18, 19, 28, 231, 303; reserves land sections, 364.
Ungler, Mrs. ———, 396.
Upper Blue Lick, 311.

Vairin, Augustus, Sr., 115, 116.
Vairin, Mrs. Augustus, Sr., 116.
Vairin, Augustus, Jr., 116.
Vairin, John Peter, 115.
Vairin, Julius, 115, 116.
Vairin, Justus, 115, 116; in militia, 395, 396.
Vairin, Mrs. Justus (née Gex), 115.
Vairin, V., 388.
Vanbriggle, Peter, 105-6, 123.
Van Buren, Martin, presidential candidate, 166-67; pardons William C. Keen, 113, 145.
Vandever family, early settlers, 73.
Vandoren family, early settlers, 47.
Vandusen, Abram, constable, 59.
Vaud, Canton de (Switzerland), xiii, 28.
Vawter, Achillis, 32.
Vawter, Beverly, 32.
Vawter, Major John, commissions Captain Golay to convene militia company, 358-59; United States marshal for Indiana, 360; early minister, 360.

Vawter, ———, preaches in Vevay, 63.
Velocipede, The, steamboat on Ohio River, 82.
Venoge Creek (Indian Creek), 2, 26, 30, 49, 82, 102; Baptist Church on, 67; boundary of New Switzerland, xvii, 15; deer hunting on, 89; early settlers on, 7, 22, 23, 75, 85, 103, 104, 192, 206, 207; formerly called Indian Creek, 28; road, 190; valuable timber on, 107.
Vernon (Indiana), 111, 113.
Versailles (Indiana), 33.
Vesta, steamboat, 69.
Vevay (Indiana), viii, xiii, 17, 21, 91; bakers, 207; blacksmiths, 75, 76, 187-88; cabinet makers, 86-88, 191; druggists, 186-87; hatters, 372; justices of peace, 45, 113, 114, 115, 116, 181; physicians, 392-93; postmasters, vii, 26-28, 100, 114; saddlers, 76-77, 193; shoemaking, 75, 77, 192-93; silversmiths, 185, 186; straw hat manufacturers, 23, 30; tailoring, 35, 77, 191-92; tanners, 46, 193-94; buildings and trades, 47, 60, 62, 75-77, 114; branch bank, 78-80, 387-88; carding machines, 38, 88, 364; celebrations of July Fourth, 151-53; celebration of McDonough's victory, 155, 371; cemetery, 400; churches, 63-69; cotton gin, 88; development, 15, 33, 34-35, 38, 47, 50, 144, 353-54; made county seat, 41-44; county seat contest, 157-60, 365; early schools, 194-96, 354-57; first steam engine, 89; in 1820, pp.

60-62; jails, 45, 53, 78, 126-28, 369; law against profanity, 181; mails, 30, 100, 111, 399; mills, 88, 104, 376; nail factory, 50; newspapers, 55-58, 110-15, 375-76; opposition to incorporation, 175; population, 28, 62, 101, 384-85; roads, 208-9; seminary, 195, 370-71; squirrel hunt, 124; taverns, 48, 90-91, 371; temporary currency, 77-78, 387; wine, 382; Literary Society, 46-47, 73, 370.
*Vevay Democrat*, vii, viii, 57, 113, 376.
*Vevay Enterprise*, vii.
Vevay Island, 23, 85, 167, 183, 209, 364.
Vevay, Mount Sterling, and Versailles turnpike, 208.
*Vevay Reveille*, vii, 57, 89, 112, 376.
*Vevay Times*, 80.
Vevey (Switzerland), John James Dufour at, 341.
Vevey (Switzerland), district in Canton de Vaud, xiii, 7, 235.
*Village Times* (Vevay), 56, 111, 376.
Villard, ———, boards John James Dufour, 319, 321.
Vincendiere family, land fraud, 225.
Vincennes (Indiana), canal to Fort Wayne proposed, 95; Indians troublesome, 24; seat of government of Indiana Territory, 6; steamboats, 82. *See also*, Banks.
*Vine-Dresser's Guide, The American*, xiii, 352.
Vineyard, Nicholas, 174.
Vineyards, *see* First Vineyard.
Violet, Edward, 33, 360, 361.

Voris, Cornelius A., 73.
Vuichoud, Judge, 347.

Wabash River, proposal for canal along, 95; steamboats on, 82.
Wade, Elisha, early settler, 47; lays out town of Troy, 144.
Wade, George, bailiff, 59; constable, early settler, 47; tax lister, 60.
Walden, Henry, 99.
Walden, Nathan, sketch of, 99-100.
Walden, Solomon, 194, 203.
Waldo, Ann, 65.
Waldo, Frederick, tavern keeper, 397.
Waldo, Frederick J., 207, 356, 397; bailiff, 59; constable, 59; coroner, 58; newspaper ventures, 57, 112, 114, 376; offices held by, 114; postmaster of Vevay, 100, 399.
Waldo, Horatio, 65.
Waldo, Mehetabel, 65.
Waldo, Otis, tavern keeper, 397; baker, 207.
Waldo, Otis S., 31, 114, 207, 356, 397; newspaper ventures, 57, 112.
Waldo, Sylvanus, Vevay school teacher, 31, 356.
Walker, Charles E., 64.
Walker (Waker), David, 9, 64, 289.
Walker, John K., 149.
Wallace, Robert, agent to collect canal company moneys, 384.
Wallick family, early settlers, 48.
Walter, ———, dealings with John James Dufour, 343.
Warden, Jesse, 33, 123.

## INDEX

Warley, Sl., dealings with John James Dufour, 265.
Warrick County (Indiana), representation, 161.
Warsaw (Kentucky), 56, 111; formerly Fredericksburg, 120, 212.
Warthman, Mrs., 287, 293.
Washington (D. C.), 10, 19, 315, 319-21.
Washington (Kentucky), 9.
Washington County (Indiana), representation, 161.
Wason, Reverend Hiram, Presbyterian minister, 65, 210-11; teaches Vevay school, 210.
Wason, Mrs. Hiram, teaches Vevay school, 210-11.
Watches, sold by John James Dufour, 247, 255, 257, 261, 267, 275.
Watts, John, president judge, circuit court, 60, 147.
Watts, Johnson, 60.
Watts, Thomas, 139.
Wayne County (Indiana), representation, 161.
Weaver, John, county commissioner, 134.
Weaver, ———, Vevay blacksmith, 405.
Weber, ———, dealings with John James Dufour, 319.
Webster, H., 72.
*Weekly Messenger* (Vevay), 56, 111.
*Weekly News*, see *Vevay Reveille*.
Welch, Augustus, county commissioner, 135; county treasurer, 141; state representative, 173.
Wells, Jacob C., 57, 112, 387, 398.
Wells, Walter H., 57, 112.

Welsh, George W., Vevay druggist, 186, 392.
Welsh, Hester, 63.
Welsh (Welch), Dr. James, 81, 107-8, 199; Presbyterian minister, 63-64, 392; Vevay druggist, 186, 392; Clinton supporter, 403.
Welsh, Joseph S., Vevay druggist, 186.
*Western Annotator* (Salem), 56, 111, 113, 376.
*Western Eagle* (Lexington), 45.
*Western Sun* (Vincennes), 368.
Whalon, Reverend Thomas, Presbyterian minister, 65.
Wheeling (West Virginia), 9, 289.
Whitcher, Stephen, Jr., Clay supporter, 162.
White, John P., county recorder, 141.
White, Rebecca (Mrs. Hugh McCreary), 50.
White, William, 48; active against Indians, 150-51; inspector of elections, 132; land entry, 37.
White, ———, 33.
Whitehead, Israel R., 64, 381, 397; clerk, circuit court, 137; Clinton supporter, 163; collector of revenue, 156; sheriff, 81, 135.
Whitehead, Mrs. Rachael, 185.
Whitemore, Nathan M., 204.
Whitson, Thomas, 32.
Wibel, ———, sells share in vineyard company, 315.
Wick, William W., 356; president judge, circuit court, 148.
Wickham, William D. M., prints first paper in Rush County, 115; proposes to publish gazetteer of Indiana, 177.

Wickham, ———, 115.
Wiles, Thomas, justice of peace, 131.
Wiley, Reverend Allen, Methodist minister, 46, 63, 66; tax lister, 46.
Wiley, Lemuel, county commissioner, 135.
Wilkill, Davis, 127.
Williams, Hugh T., state representative, 173.
Willis, John, 214.
Wilmington (Delaware), John James Dufour arrives at, 247.
Wilmington (Indiana), 179.
Wilson, Benjamin, 189.
Wilson, James, 127; inspector of elections, 59.
Wilson, Jeremiah M., congressman from Indiana, 404.
Wilson, Reverend John, Baptist minister, 67, 68, 195, 355; teaches Vevay school, 195.
Wilson, John, 382; associate judge, 110, 148; manufactures liquors, 110, 204.
Wilson, Reverend Joshua L., Presbyterian minister, 64, 392.
Wilson, Maria, divorce case, 368.
Wilson, William, divorce case, 368.
Winteroad, David, 393.
Wolf, ———, marriage, 392.
Wood, Enoch G., Methodist minister, 66.

Woods, John, state senator, 172.
Woods, Richard, 98.
Woollen, Levin J., state senator, 404.
Woollen, William Wesley, 399.
Works, Lewis F., county recorder, 141.
Worstell, Mathew, sheriff, 136.
Wrenshall, ———, dealings with John James Dufour, 283, 287, 295, 297.
Wright, John, tax lister, 60.
Wright, John H., 115; publishes *Vevay Democrat*, 113; publishes *Independent* at Carrollton, 401.
Wright, John W., state representative, 173, 174.
Wright, Mary, 115.
Wright, Sarah (Mrs. Justus Vairin), 115.
Wright, Thomas D. (T.), 401; newspaper ventures, 57, 113, 114; state representative, 158, 173.
Wright, ———, tanner, 194.

Yates, Richard, early life in Indiana, 213.
Yaux, Judge, 239.
York Township (Switzerland County), 132, 355.
*Young Edward*, brig carrying John James Dufour to Europe, 18, 325-27.

Zanesville (Ohio), 83.